MONASTERIES AND LANDSCAPE IN NORTH EAST ENGLAND

The medieval colonisation of the
North York Moors

Rievaulx Abbey : a frontier zone in the twelfth century
(Committee for Aerial Photography, Cambridge University)

MONASTERIES AND LANDSCAPE IN NORTH EAST ENGLAND

The medieval colonisation of the North York Moors

BRYAN WAITES

MULTUM IN PARVO PRESS
Oakham, Rutland

© Bryan Waites 1997

ISBN 0 9524544 3 2

All rights reserved. No part of this publication may be reproduced, stored in a retrieval system, or transmitted, in any form or by any means, electronic, mechanical, photocopying, recording or otherwise without the permission of the publishers.

Published by
MULTUM IN PARVO PRESS
6 Chater Road
Oakham
Rutland LE15 6RY
England

Monasteries and Landscape in North East England has been published in a Limited Edition of which this is

Number
361

Printed in England by Warwick Printing Company Limited
Theatre Street, Warwick CV34 4DR

Contents

List of Illustrations & Abbreviations vi
Preface ix
Acknowledgments x
Introduction 1

PART ONE : THE LANDSCAPE 5
   Chapter 1 North East Yorkshire 6
   Chapter 2 The Domesday Landscape 13

PART TWO : SETTLEMENT 27
   Chapter 3 Monastic Settlement 28
   Chapter 4 The Monastic Grange 45

PART THREE : LAND USE 71
   Chapter 5 Medieval Assessments and Agricultural Prosperity 72
   Chapter 6 Arable Farming: The Moorlands 86
                                                 The Coastal Plateau 90
                                                 The Vale of Pickering 96
                                                 The Yorkshire Wolds 102
                                                 The Vale of York & Cleveland 111
   Chapter 7 Pastoral Farming: Introduction 117
                                                 On the Duchy of Lancaster Pickering Estate 125
                                               A Yorkshire Farmer in the Memoranda Rolls 135
                                               On the Monastic Estates 138
   Chapter 8 Medieval Industries: Ironworking 147
                                                 The Salt Industry 156
                                                 Other Industries 158

PART FOUR : THE ECONOMIC LANDSCAPE 161
   Chapter 9 Medieval Ports and Trade 163
   Chapter 10 Medieval Fairs and Markets 176
   Chapter 11 Monasteries and the Wool Trade 183

Conclusion 197
Bibliography 201
Index 207

ILLUSTRATIONS

Frontispiece:		Rievaulx Abbey: a frontier zone in the twelfth century	ii
Introduction:		Byland Abbey c 1840	2
		Kirkham Priory c 1840	3
Chapter 1	1.1	North East Yorkshire	7
	1.2	Regions	8
	1.3	Moorland View	9
	1.4	Hambleton Hills and the Vale of York	11
	1.5	Wapentakes	12
Chapter 2	2.1	Topographical Names: Marsh	13
	2.2	Topographical Names: Woodland	14
	2.3	Domesday Settlements	15
	2.4	Uninhabited Vills	19
	2.5	Domesday Woodland	21
	2.6	Domesday Meadow	23
	2.7	Waste in 1086	24
Chapter 3	3.1	Religious Houses	29
	3.2	Whitby Abbey c 1840	32
	3.3	Whitby Abbey : Lands and Churches	34
	3.4	Guisborough Priory c 1840	36
	3.5	Guisborough Priory : Lands and Churches	37
	3.6	Rievaulx Abbey c 1840	38
	3.7	Rievaulx Abbey : Lands	39
Chapter 4	4.1	Monastic Granges	45
	4.2	Granges on the Limestone Slopes	50
	4.3	Granges in Bilsdale	52
	4.4	Bilsdale	60
	4.5	Contributions to the Fifteenth of 1301	62
	4.6	Granges and the Salt Industry	66
Chapter 5	5.1	Assessments in 1292, 1318, 1342	75
Chapter 6	6.1	Arable Land on the Estates of Malton Priory in 1254	104
	6.2	Location Map : Speeton and Burton Fleming	106
	6.3	Lake Gormire and the Vale of York	112

vi

Chapter 7	7.1	Location Map : the Duchy of Lancaster Estate	124
	7.2	Monastic Sheep Pasture	137
	7.3	Rievaulx Abbey 1956	145
Chapter 8	8.1	Location Map	147
	8.2	Forges and Iron Working	149
	8.3	Monastic Lands and Medieval Slag Heaps in Eskdale	151
	8.4	Rosedale	154
Chapter 9	9.1	The Position of Scarborough	162
	9.2	Scarborough c 1560	168
	9.3	Origin of Merchants Trading with Whitby and Scarborough	170
	9.4	Port Hinterlands : Yarm and Scarborough	174
Chapter 10	10.1	Medieval Fairs and Markets	176
Chapter 11	11.1	Places Where Wool was Purchased Against the Statute	184
	11.2	Origin of Merchants Buying Wool Against the Statute	187
	11.3	Transport of Corn and Wool	190
Conclusion		The 'Canals' of Rievaulx Abbey	198

Please note that tables have not been listed.

ABBREVIATIONS USED IN THE TEXT

AJ	Archaeological Journal		Inq	Inquisitions
BC	Bridlington Chartulary		MA	Monasticon Anglicanum
BM	British Library		NI	Nonarum Inquisitiones
CCR	Calendar of Close Rolls		NRRS	North Riding Record Series
CChR	Calendar of Charter Rolls		PRO	Public Record Office
CIPM	Calendar of Inquisitions Post Mortem		RC	Rievaulx Chartulary
CIMisc	Calendar of Inquisitions Miscell.		RotH	Rotuli Hundredorum
CBM	Chapters of the Black Monks		TS	Thoresby Society
CPR	Calendar of Patent Rolls		VCH	Victoria County History
DReg	Diocesan Registry, York		VE	Valor Ecclesiasticus
EcHR	Economic History Review		WC	Whitby Chartulary
EHR	English Historical Review		YAJ	Yorkshire Archaeological Journal
EPNS	English Place Name Society			
EYC	Early Yorkshire Charters		YAS	Yorkshire Archaeological Society Record Series
GC	Guisborough Chartulary			

This book is dedicated to the cherished memory
of my dear grandson Ryan Benjamin Coates
Loved and Remembered Always

Preface

When we see the bright lights of Whitby, Scarborough and Bridlington and the carefully managed North York Moors National Park, surrounded by civilised, neatly cultivated lowland like the Vales of York and Pickering, it is hard to think of this area as a wilderness.

Yet, for centuries, this was a frontier zone waiting to be colonised. Early settlers, especially in the fifth and sixth centuries, began to extend the farming frontier from the outside inwards, but the real process started with the well-organised, strongly motivated monastic settlers in the early 1100s.

Throughout Europe, in the twelfth and thirteenth centuries, monastic farmers reclaimed marsh, cleared woodland and penetrated highland. From the North York Moors to the eastern marchlands of Germany the agricultural frontier moved forward and the face of the landscape was changed.

The devastation left after the Harrying of the North by William the Conqueror in 1069 presented the monastic farmers with a great opportunity also. Within fifty years of this date the great colonisation had begun. To-day, we are the inheritors of this landscape revolution.

I have been trying to work out this story for over forty years. I started with a great love of the North East which is my homeland. I had a passion to discover the landscape legacy left to us and which we can decipher to-day. How did it all happen?

I began as a postgraduate student at the Institute of Historical Research, London, under the supervision of Professors H C Darby and J Goronwy Edwards. I have continued my research and writing on this topic but with decreasing intensity as I have lived some distance away.

Over the years I have published many articles on the theme and one reason for this book is the frequent requests to put it all together so that the whole story can be read in one place. Additionally, I have been expecting others to enter the fray and produce a definitive work on the monastic impact on the area. Despite the scholarly attention of Messrs Platt, Donkin, Hodgson and others the comprehensive account has not yet been delivered.

Consequently, I have endeavoured to fill the gap. I hope there are not too many creaking joints; certainly the references are largely antediluvian but they still retain their authenticity. This is a limited edition of 500 copies since the topic is so specialised. Yet my dearest hope is that although the subject is academic it will be read by others who want to know the story, for North East England was not unique: all over Britain and Europe, in all kinds of regions, monasteries and monks were engaged in a landscape revolution lasting for at least two hundred years between 1100 and 1300.

Bryan Waites
Oakham, Rutland
Ascension Day, 1997

Acknowledgements

The author and publishers are pleased to acknowledge the use of articles written by the author which have appeared in the following publications: Yorkshire Archaeological Journal; Geography; Mariner's Mirror; Borthwick Papers No. 32; Ryedale Historian; Yorkshire History Quarterly; Scarborough & District Archaeological Society Transactions.

Figures 1.3, 1.4. 4.4, 6.3, 7.3 and 8.4 are by courtesy of the *Yorkshire Post*. A & C Black kindly gave permission to reproduce the cover illustration which is from Gordon Home's *Yorkshire*, Adam & Charles Black, 1908. The frontispiece was provided by D. R. Wilson Esq., Curator in Aerial Photography, University of Cambridge Committee for Aerial Photography. Figure 9.2 is from the Scarborough & District Archaeological Society Transactions and the Department of Air Photography, Air Ministry, provided the final illustration in the Conclusion.

Figures 2.3, 2.4, 2.5, 2.6 and 2.7 are reproduced by permission of the Cambridge University Press from the *Domesday Geography of Northern England* by H. C. Darby & I. S. Maxwell, 1962. The drawings of monastic houses in the Introduction and Figures 3.2, 3.4 and 3.6 are by William Richardson in *Monastic Ruins of Yorkshire* by Revd. Edward Churton, 1843.

Introduction

Perhaps no comparable area of England was as intensively settled by great monastic houses as the north-east. It included monasteries which represented most Orders: Whitby Abbey, as the second most important Benedictine house in Yorkshire, still retained much of the prestige of the older Saxon foundation of St Hilda; Guisborough, Newburgh and Bridlington Priory, together with Kirkham Priory were, even at the Dissolution, foremost among Augustinian houses in England.[1] Rievaulx and Byland, in numbers, wealth and influence, were among the leading Cistercian monasteries. Rievaulx, especially, held a spiritual leadership directly derived from Citeaux and Clairvaux which was amplified by the saintliness and influence of Ailred, one of its early abbots. Malton Priory, too, was one of the wealthiest of the few Gilbertine houses in the country.[2] Besides the major houses, however, were a number of smaller priories and abbeys which provided a background and a contrast.

Though the north-east contained Whitby Abbey, refounded as early as 1087, it was most notably a centre for monasteries of the New Orders. Guisborough (1119), Bridlington (1113-14) and Rievaulx (1131) were among the earliest of their respective Orders to be founded in England.

But despite this, little has been written about the north-east or its monasteries. The distribution of monastic lands, their growth, the policies of the houses and their influence in the area have never been fully or comprehensively examined. Even local writers have been few, and were antiquaries rather than historians. Besides, much of their work was written during the 19th century.

Canon Atkinson, the greatest of them all, published his *Memorials of Old Whitby* in 1894 and *Forty Years in a Moorland Parish* shortly after. Ord's *History of Cleveland* was completed in the middle of the 19th century whilst George Young had published his *History of Whitby* even earlier, in 1817.

Subsequent works have been few and largely based on Atkinson. Though they knew and loved their countryside, such antiquaries confined their attention to limited, even obscure topics. Their opinions often bore little relation to documentary evidence. This neglect of the north-east has been, unfortunately, typical of geographers also. The first *Land Utilisation Report* of the 1930s edited by Dudley Stamp remains a major source, although in more recent times the publications of the North York Moors National Park and visitor guides have treated the area in general terms.

Such neglect may be due to the scattered and imperfect nature of the evidence relating to the north-east, and in particular to the monasteries. Certainly a great deal of vital material has been lost, and it would be very hard indeed to make a study of one single house on present evidence. That is why this book is chiefly concerned with the three

---

[1.] e.g. the net income of Bridlington was £547 and of Guisborough £628, in 1535. Knowles describes both as among "the largest houses of the Order." *Medieval Religious Houses* (1953) p.142.
[2.] Mount Grace Priory, licensed in 1398, was a leading Carthusian Monastery. More of a hermitage, it had a short life of 140 years.

Byland Abbey c1840

major houses in the area: Whitby, Rievaulx and Guisborough. These have been chosen as the centre of this study and wherever possible supplemented by discussion about the other monasteries in the area.

Similarly, the availability of evidence, has largely determined the period of study, that is from the 12th to the 14th century – from the foundation of the monasteries to their high point of development. This period is not treated as a rigid, immovable division however. Wherever necessary, reference has been made to earlier or later times. The outstanding examples of this are the use made of the *Domesday Survey* (1086) and the *Valor Ecclesiasticus* (1535).

Fortunately, the chartularies of most of the monasteries have been preserved and are either in manuscript or published. These provided a basis for the study of the impact of the monasteries on the area. In fact, they are the chief source 'form which much of our knowledge of post-Conqueror Yorkshire must be recovered', as T. A. M. Bishop wrote in his classic paper 'Monastic Granges in Yorkshire', *English Historical Review*, April 1936.[1]

They are a relatively untouched source for the north-east. Luckily, there are many other sources also, which often indirectly, help in providing evidence and these will become apparent later as the study unfolds.

[1.] T. A. M. Bishop "Monastic Granges in Yorkshire" *E.H.R.* (April 1936). Especially valuable because they contain "unintentional" evidence … "we prick up our ears far more eagerly when we are permitted to overhear what was never intended to be said … Despite our inevitable subordination to the past we have freed ourselves at least to the extent that, eternally condemned to know only by means of its 'tracks' we are nevertheless successful in knowing far more of the past than the past itself had thought good to tell us …" Marc Bloch, *The Historian's Craft* (1954). pp. 63-64.

There is, then, ample opportunity to examine the influence of the monasteries on the development of the area. But what is meant by 'development'?

First, it might be advisable to establish what is meant by the 'north-east'. For the purpose of this study it comprises the wapentakes of East and West Langbaurgh; Allertonshire; Birdforth; Ryedale; Pickering Lythe; Whitbystrand; Buckrose and part of Dickering (see Fig. 1.5). Defined in these terms, the area has also a physical distinctiveness. The sea is the eastern boundary; the River Tees the northern; the Yorkshire Wolds the southern, and the Vale of York is the western limit.

By the 'development' of this area is meant its evolution in terms of settlement, land use and economy. Particular attention is given to the evolution of the historic landscape and the impact that the monasteries had upon it, much of which can be deciphered to-day.

The main aims are to set the scene for the monastic entry into the north-east in the twelfth century; to describe the distribution, growth and character of their settlements; to examine the regional pattern of wealth and prosperity and within that the secular and monastic agricultural and industrial activities. This is followed by a consideration of economic development such as growth and character of ports, markets and trade. Finally, an assessment is made of the monastic contribution to the development of the area and the impact on the landscape. What did it consist of? Was it permanent? Did different religious orders contribute in different ways? Was the monastic impact greater than the secular?

Kirkham Priory c1840

Two themes must be remembered throughout: the development of the area and its landscape plus the contribution of the monasteries to both. Above all the area is the pivot of this study.

There is a strong sense of the past still lingering on the windswept hills and lifeless valleys of the Wolds, which penetrates the tree-clad dales and haunts the lonely heather moors. It is a persuasive magic. The traces of the pre-historic lake-dwellers of Star Carr and the worshippers of the Eye-Goddess on Folkton Brow; the Roman road striking boldly into the moors and then suddenly disappearing; the solitary sombre crosses which every now and then break the dreary moorland skyline; the melancholy ruin of an abbey – all these distil that sense of the past which seems so ever-present. The countryside around, created and nurtured by many centuries of toil; influenced by many diverse circumstances, which have left their imprint – holds many secrets. Often they lie unsuspected. Perhaps the rediscovery of its medieval development may reveal some of them. At least it should tell something of that intimate harmony between Man and his Landscape.

PART ONE : THE LANDSCAPE

'The land is the most certain of our documents'
J. R. Green

> 1 North East Yorkshire
>
> 2 The Domesday Landscape

1. NORTH EAST YORKSHIRE

"But if we attend to the Eastern Division", wrote William Marshall, "we shall find collected, within comprehensive limits, almost every description of country which is interesting in rural affairs. A rich, well cultivated plain; a group of almost barren mountains inviting objects of improvement; a fertile vale, various in soil and cultivation; with a tract of chalky downs, terminating in a rich marshland fenny country: including grassland of every class, and arable land of almost every description. It is the island in miniature"[1]. The North East is indeed a region of contrasts: its central core of highland, which reaches a height of over 1500′ in the north-west, is in itself a variety composed of dale and barren moor; peat-bog and fertile limestone soils. But besides this, there is the contrast between the highland and the lowland which surrounds it. To the north and west a great scarp – "an abrupt and broken precipice"[2] – marks the sudden change from the North Yorks Moors to the flat Cleveland Plain and the Vale of York. To the south, the contrast is less striking: the "moorlands dip gently southward to the Vale of Pickering; on whose verge rise abruptly a range of thin soiled limestone heights; which, in a similar manner shelve gently into the Vale; forming its northern margin.[3]

Because such contrasts are well-marked the North-East can be readily divided into regions. This has been done under the following headings, with the main purpose of providing a clear insight into the physiography of each region, and thus of the area as a whole. (See 1.2).

The Wolds
The Wolds are an outcrop of chalk extending in a crescent from Flamborough Head, where they reach the sea, to Ferriby on the Humber estuary. They present a high scarp-face to the north-west which ranges in height from about 800′ at Garrowby Hill to about 400′ elsewhere. South-eastwards the Wolds dip gently beneath the plain of Holderness. The present study is concerned with the northern part of the Wolds only. Here the hills are at their highest, the average elevation being between 400′ and 500′. The soil is thin and the chalk never far from the surface. The characteristic topography is one of the deeply-cut dry valleys, separated by well rounded hillsides. The relief is rarely sharp or precipitous but rather billowy and smooth swells which one writer aptly compared to "Biscayan waves half pacified".[4] One large valley, with an intermittent stream in it, extends almost the entire length of the Wolds from west to east. This was and is the main area of settlement on the Wolds, and during the time of the Anglo-

---

[1] *The Rural Economy of Yorkshire* (1788) I.p.10.
[2] *ibid* I.p.6.
[3] *ibid* pp.6-7
[4] *ibid* p.8.

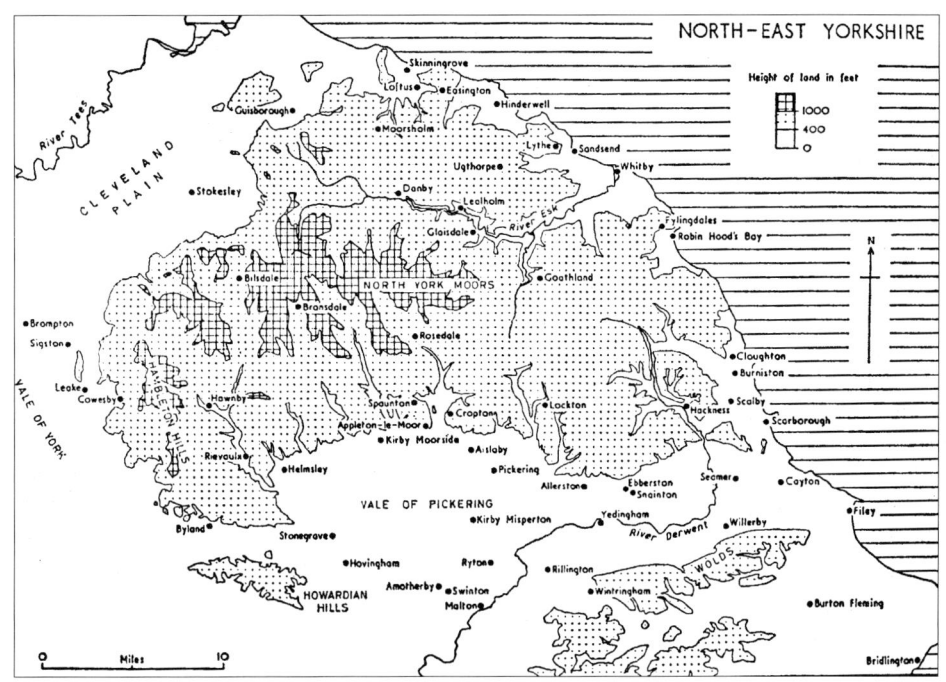

Figure 1.1 North East Yorkshire

Saxon and Scandinavian invasions appears to have been an important means of penetrating inland.[1]

The Vale of Pickering

The Vale is, "a basin, formed by eminences on every side, save one narrow outlet of the waters collected within its area, and upon the adjacent hills…"[2] The scarp of the Wolds forms its southern boundary together with the Howardian Hills. To the north is the great bastion of the North York Moors. The Vale is perfectly flat – due to its once having been a glacial lake – and has several significant differences in the soils composing it.[3]

The major difference is between the central parts and the margins of the Vale. The former consists mainly of warp and alluvial soils which towards the eastern end become inferior because of the difficulty of drainage. In consequence the areas which are not marsh or carrland are usually heavy peaty soils. In contrast the margins of the Vale consist

---

1. This is particularly evident from the place names of the valley. Scandinavian endings are many e.g. Butterwick, Boythorpe, Weaverthorpe, Helperthorpe, Caythorpe. Settlement of the East Riding seems to have had a nucleus in the Bridlington Kilham area from which movement spread in three main directions.
    i) along the northern scarp foot of the Wolds
    ii) along the great Wold Valley
    iii) along the lower dip slope of the Wolds in a south-west direction.
2. W. Marshall, *op. cit.* I, p.7.
3. This is not the place to expand about the fascinating glacial history of the North-East. If any further information is required P. F. Kendall's great work "A System of Glacier Lakes in the Cleveland Hills" in *Q. J. Geological Society*, August (1902) Vol.58, Part 3 should be consulted.

of a sound deep loam, which on the south is a raised bench of chalky-gravel soils, providing an area of great fertility and concentrated settlement.[1] The fact that these soils are raised from the level of the Vale by about 30' has been a crucial factor in their value. At Pickering and in the Seamer district patches of gravel soils, also above the general level of the Vale, have provided attractive sites to settlers, away from the marshy land of the central vale and yet near enough to exploit it. The Hertford and Derwent rivers flow through the middle of the Vale and leave it through the Malton-Kirkham gorge. On their journey they collect a large number of rivers and becks which issue mainly from the high moorland to the north, hardly any from the chalk Wolds.

North York Moors

The northern boundary of the Vale of Pickering is marked by a range of hills which, because of their flat-topped appearance have been named the Tabular Hills.[2] These are composed of grit-stones and limestones mostly grouped under the term Corallian. The

Figure 1.2 Regions

---

[1] "The soils at the foot of the north margin consist of an hazle loam upon a clay bottom, or a deep warp or silt upon gravel and clay ... these are soils of extraordinary fertility." J. Tuke, *General View of the Agriculture of the North Riding of Yorkshire*, (1794), pp.15-16. Some very interesting soil profiles for the district are given in *Water Supply of the East Riding of Yorkshire*, C. Fox Strangeways, London, (1906).

[2] The term 'Tabular Hills' is used to describe the area in the handbook *Regional Geology of the North Riding* issued by the Geological Survey.

PART 1 : THE LANDSCAPE

Figure 1.3 Moorland View

Hambleton Hills mark the western limit and here a height of over 1200′ is reached. But the height declines eastwards. The Tabular Hills have a north facing scarp which overlooks a narrow, but clearly defined vale of Oxford clay extending from west to east (Sometimes called the Vale of Lastingham – about a mile wide). The highest point of the scarp is over 1000′ but southward this slopes down to the Vale of Pickering. Because many moorland streams cut through the Tabular Hills, forming deeply-incised valleys, they have been severed into blocks, which from the map resemble flat-irons.

The Tabular Hills and Lastingham Vale are, then, the southern part of the moors. North of them the High Moors comprise the most dominant and characteristic part of the region. Reaching from the great Stokesley-Broughton embayment across to the coast at Robin Hood's Bay, the Cleveland anticline is the highest west of Newtondale. In this region it comprises two main masses which are separated by a narrow belt of lower land – Westerdale Moor. On either side of this the land exceeds 1400′ and is composed of infertile Jurassic sandstones.[1] This highland is the major watershed of the whole North Yorks Moors. Since it performs this function its appearance is correspondingly altered. It has been extensively cut into by the streams flowing from it. In the south, Rosedale, Farndale, Bransdale and Bilsdale; in the north, Glaisdale, Danby Dale, Westerdale and Fryupdale have cut deeply into the moorland and left as interfluves the typical Riggs or ridges which themselves often rise over 1000′ and reach out like fingers. The characteristic view of the moorlands is not one of jagged and broken mountain sides but rather of flat uninterrupted horizons. (see 1.3)

---

[1] "The immediate subsoil is generally sand; which in some places is formed into a pan or crust resembling rusty half-decayed iron rather than an earthy substance; being almost as impervious by water as an iron vessel". Marshall, *op. cit.* II, p.276.

The valleys or dales within the moorland are extremely important. As will be shown later much of the colonisation and exploitation of the High Moors originated from them. Eskdale and its southern tributaries are the most penetrating of the valley systems, but the southerly trending dales such as Rosedale and Farndale extend far into the moors also. All the dales consist of heavy clayland[1]; in Eskdale Boulder Clays and elsewhere Liassic clays. These soils are of varying fertility, but in such a barren moorland area even partially fertile soils become enhanced in value. The dales vary in shape though generally "the bottoms are mostly narrow, seldom more than 200 yards."[2] In Tuke's day "The cultivated dales situate amongst the moors are pretty extensive, some of them containing from five to ten thousand acres; and Eskdale, and Bilsdale much more ... the land is generally cultivated from half a mile to a mile up the hills though the surface is in many places irregular."[3]

The Coastal Plateau

The North Yorks Moors are flanked on their eastern, coastal side by boulder clay deposits which form, north of the Peak, a plateau area, and south of the Peak an area of plain. The plateau stretches north-west from Hawsker and varies from 1 mile to more than 4 miles in width. The relief is almost everywhere over 200′ rising to 600′ at the junction between the boulder clay and the moorland. A series of coastal denes have dissected the plateau, sometimes across the whole of its width (e.g. Roxby Beck, Kilton Beck, Sandsend Beck). Though not large, these valleys are deeply cut and consequently have acted as an impediment to movement northwards along the plateau.

The coastal boulder clay between Cloughton and Scarborough is almost entirely below 200′ and has the characteristics of an undulating plain. Glacial sands and gravels make noticeable features near to the moor edge (e.g. in Sea Cut Valley and in Harwood Dale). The region is a small one being no more than 6 miles from north to south. It has affinities with the area south of Scarborough which, in fact, may be regarded as a continuation of the plain.

The coastal denes and the Peak have tended to isolate settlement to certain sections along the coast such as the Cloughton-Burniston area, Robin Hood's Bay, Eskdale and Loftus.

The soil varies greatly in fertility: it is "in some vallies west of Whitby, a deep rich loam"[4] but elsewhere it may be a brownish clay, a clayey loam or a lightish soil upon alum shale. The greatest drawback to any form of cultivation throughout this region is its situation exposed to the full force of easterly winds; and its liability, during early summer, to sea fogs, when crops inland are able to enjoy the full benefit of the sunshine.

Teesmouth

This region could have been grouped with the Vale of York and the Cleveland Plain which it resembles in many of its features. However, it seems that it possesses enough distinctive characteristics of its own to be treated separately. In its historical development it showed similar peculiarities, as will be seen later. The region is one of extremely low relief,

---

[1]. "In the vallies, particularly towards their heads, are peat bogs of several feet deep buried in which, trees of great size have sometimes been found." *ibid*, p.277
[2]. J. Tuke, *op.cit.* p.17.
[3]. *ibid.*
[4]. *ibid,* pp.11-12.

especially in the Coatham marshes, and the numerous becks flowing into the Tees estuary make some of the land ill-drained. The soils vary from alluvium near the river to fertile boulder clays, with clayey loam, and a fine red sandy soil derived from glacial or post glacial gravels. Blown sand is a feature along the coast in the neighbourhood of Coatham.

The Vale of York and the Cleveland Plain

This region lies west of the great scarp of the North York Moors. Its general flatness is a sharp contrast to the abrupt scarp – "at the top a barren heath; at the foot the Vale of York and the fertile plains of Cleveland"[1] (1.4). But it is not one homogeneous region: below the scarp a broad bench of boulder clay and gravels extends the length of the Vale. In the central Vale, from the Tees south to Northallerton and Thirsk the bench is replaced with much lower land through which the rivers Wiske and Swale run. Here, although boulder clay predominates it is less well drained and is mixed with alluvium and gravels. The latter are often the areas chosen for village sites since they stand slightly above the general level.

The clay soils are heavy except in places like the Cleveland embayment (i.e. around Stokesley) where "particularly in the neighbourhood of Kildale is a good deal of deep rich loam."[2] This is the case in many places near to the moors. The region as a whole is one of noted fertility. It was, for instance the most important area in Yorkshire during the 18th century for the production of wheat: "Wheat is the staple produce of Cleveland", wrote Tuke, "No other district in the Riding, or perhaps in the north of England produces as much in proportion to its size, or of as good a quality…"[3]

Figure 1.4 Hambleton Hills and the Vale of York

---

[1] W. Marshall, *op.cit.* p.6.
[2] J. Tuke, *op. cit.* p.12.
[3] *ibid*, p.35.

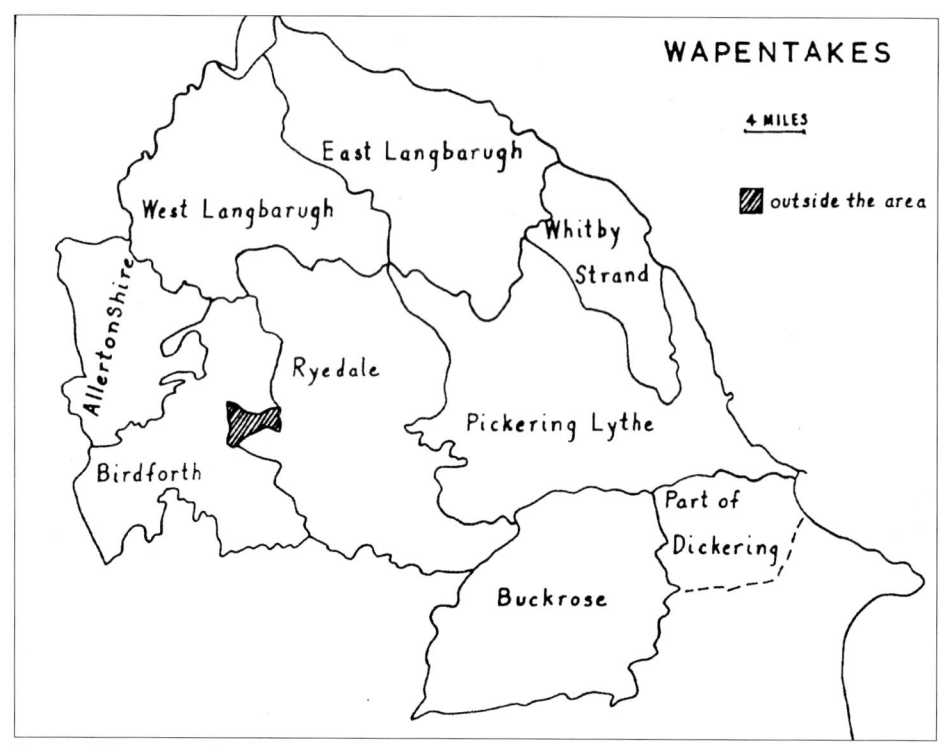

Figure 1.5 Wapentakes

The importance of this regional division will become more obvious as the study progresses. It is essential to have such a framework in mind because much can be built upon it. A region is by no means solely the product of physical factors: it grows and develops through history so that it acquires a particular ethos of its own which makes it distinctive. This process, which the present study aims to unfold, can be most clearly followed if the fundamental physical regions can be remembered. Several themes keep persistently recurring too: the distinction between highland and lowland is an important one. The effects of this will be shown to be manifold; the very shape of the wapentakes, for example, varied between highland and lowland; the type and density of settlement was influenced by it. Other themes, such as the significance of the boulder clay and moorland boundary; the continuing influence of the fertile gravel soils of the Vales of Pickering and York; and the importance of valleys within the Moors and Wolds – all these are some of the persistent themes which illuminate the development of the North-East.

2. THE DOMESDAY LANDSCAPE

"On the shore where Time casts up its stray wreckage", said Professor Trevelyan, "we gather corks and broken planks, whence much indeed may be argued and more guessed; but what the great ship was that has gone down into the deep, that we shall never see."[1] Rarely can the historical present be recovered as it once existed, and the possibility of recapturing some of its elements must inevitably vary from century to century, as the chance survival of records varies. It is all the more impressive, then to find in Domesday Book an incomparable source of information which, with all its limitations, provides a picture of the landscape impossible to obtain so comprehensively at any other time during the Middle Ages. Its value is emphasised in the context of this study because the landscape and conditions it portrays were the framework and basis of later developments in the North-East.

But Domesday Book for Yorkshire contains many special difficulties not found elsewhere. These mainly result from the extensive devastations carried out by the Conqueror in 1069 which left the county a wilderness. "For nine years at least no attempt was made at tilling the ground;" wrote Simeon of Durham, "between York and Durham every town stood uninhabited; their streets became lurking places for robbers and wild beasts."[2] Almost 200 places are recorded as wholly or partially waste in the North-East alone in 1086. Only 52

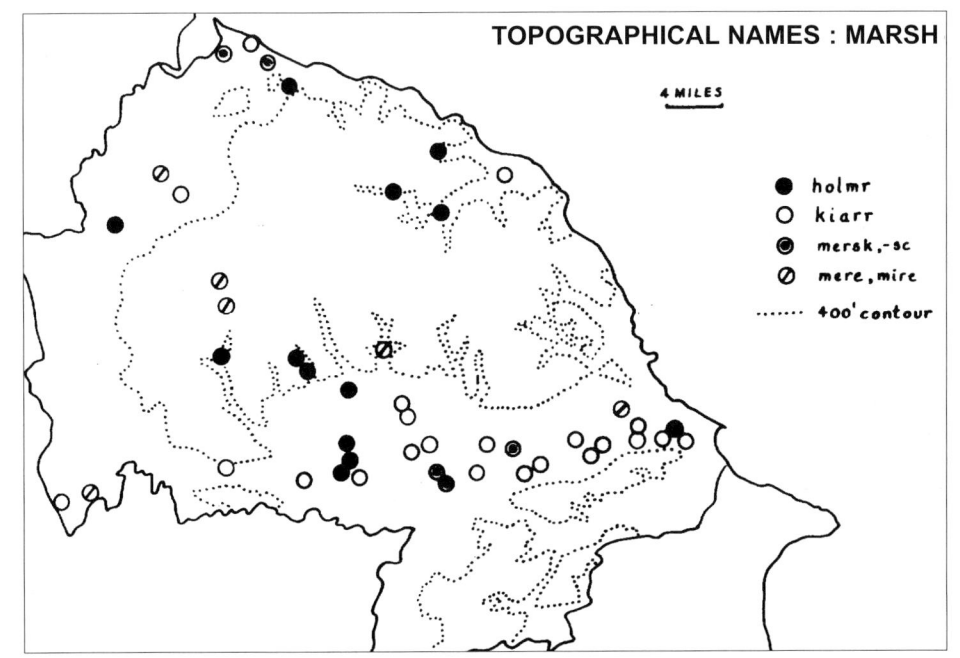

Figure 2.1 Topographical Names: Marsh

---

[1] Inaugural lecture at Cambridge in 1927.
[2] *Historia Regum* (Rolls Series.75) Vol.II, p.188.

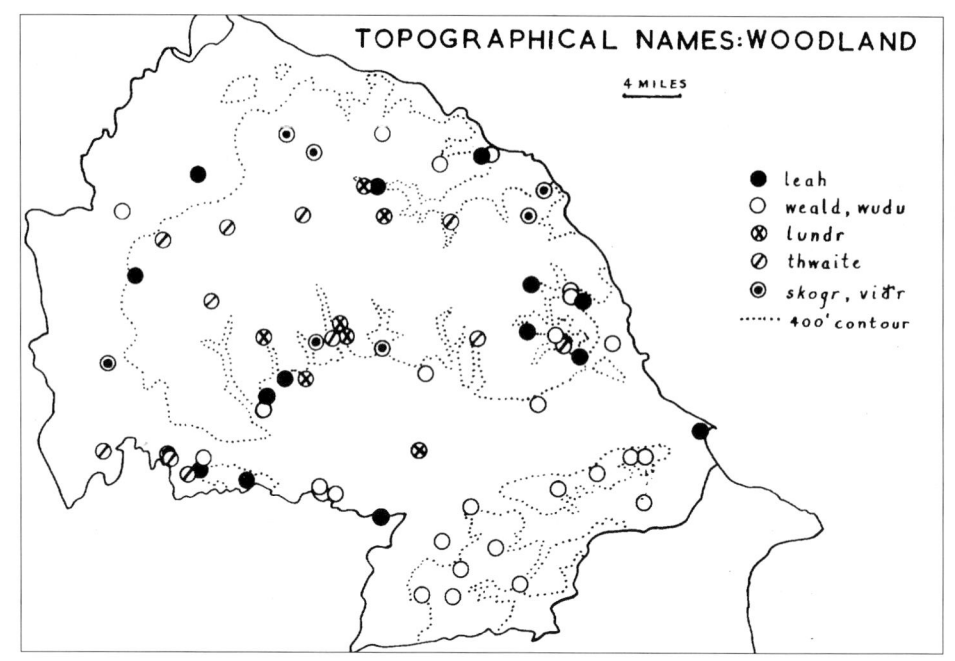

Figure 2.2 Topographical Names: Woodland

places waste are recorded for the whole of Lincolnshire and none at all for Norfolk, Suffolk, Essex and Cambridgeshire (2.7).[1]

Nor was this state of affairs temporary. William of Malmesbury wrote that, "Even a generation later the passing traveller beheld with sorrow the ruins of famous towns, with their lofty towers rising above forsaken dwellings, the fields lying untilled and tenantless, the rivers flowing idly through the wilderness."[2] But the Survey, itself, taken seventeen years after the devastation provides adequate testimony to its lasting effects.

Such an extent of waste really turns the map of Domesday settlement (2.3) into a picture of conditions before 1069, while Figures 2.4, 2.7 showing the uninhabited vills and waste, portray the scene in 1086. The contrast is striking: but Figure 2.3 gives some idea of settlement under normal conditions. In fact, the difficulty is to work out what Yorkshire was like in normal, pre-devastation times. References to T.R.E. are so few in the Survey that little can be discovered about the regional variations in prosperity which undoubtedly existed before 1069.

Besides these major difficulties the Yorkshire entries in Domesday Book are very limited in scope and give only a minimum amount of information. This might be due to the difficulty the Conqueror's clerks had in collecting their information "in respect of ploughland and habitations, and of men both bond and free, both those who dwelt in cottages and those who had their homes and share in fields, and in respect of ploughs and

---

[1] See H. C. Darby *The Domesday Geography of Eastern England*. (1952)
[2] *De Gestis Regum Anglorum* (Rolls Series.90) Vol.II, pp.306-309

horses and other animals, and in respect finally, of the services and payments due from all men in the whole land."[1] If parts of the county were largely waste and uninhabited who were the clerks to interrogate? The Survey makes little or no mention of pasture, marsh, fisheries or salt-pans (contrast with the Eastern Counties); woodland is quoted in linear dimensions without any other helpful indications such as the number of swine pasturing there (as in Norfolk, Suffolk, Essex and Sussex for example); and no details of livestock are given. Information about two, three or more places is frequently combined into one statement. Thus Guisborough, Middleton and Hutton are described together. Such linked entries add difficulties to the mapping of the information, especially when they occur so often.[2] However Figures 2.5, 2.6 show vills with meadow or woodland in linked entries, but this must be remembered when the maps are interpreted. Despite these hazards the Domesday Survey remains of unique value.

The Distribution of Settlement

The pattern of Domesday settlement in the North-East is similar to present day settlement. If Figure 2.3 could be examined in detail, however, it would show that many Domesday places do not exist as villages to-day. Some of them are represented by farm houses, e.g. Stilton, Grif and Dalby. Others have left no trace at all e.g. Chigogmares, Odulfmersc and Maxudesmares. Occasionally others can be identified only in the field, e.g. Argam.

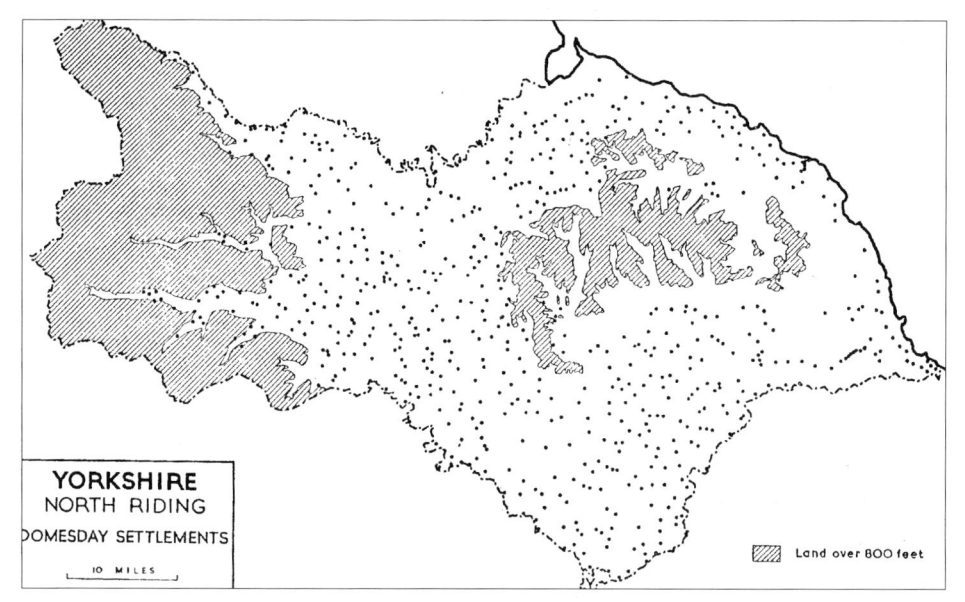

Figure 2.3 Domesday Settlements

---

[1] Written by Robert Losinga, Bishop of Hereford given in W. H. Stevenson "A Contemporary Description of the Domesday Survey" *E.H.R.* (1907), xxii, p.74.
[2] See the section on Domesday mapping in H. C. Darby *op. cit.* pp. 13-21.

Conversely, certain settlements have grown up apparently after the eleventh century and are unrecorded in the Survey. Thus Bilsdale, first mentioned about 1155 in the Rievaulx Chartulary, is one of these later settlements.

The most striking feature of Domesday settlement is that it was marginal to the main moorland mass which is shown as a blank area in Figure 2.3, comparable to the other sparsely settled region of the North Riding – the Pennines. This distribution was to be a persistent trait in the settlement geography of the North-East. The settlement, almost entirely lowland, was disposed in five main groups which reflected the physical circumstances in a striking manner.

The first group lay roughly between Whitby and Skelton, along the coast within four miles of the sea. The boulder clay plateau overlying moorland sandstones and grits, and deeply entrenched by coastal denes, provided a suitable background for the settlement. Despite its bleakness and height it was certainly a more amenable environment than surrounding areas. Although the region was important in the later Middle Ages for salt-working and fisheries there is no indication from Domesday Book that these were then practiced. The concentration of vills was close, especially so around Whitby. It seems that the wide mouth of Eskdale, also largely boulder clay soils with some alluvial deposits, was more sheltered than the coast to the northward. The religious associations of Whitby, its traditional function as an administrative centre, and the proximity of the Eskdale route through the moors no doubt contributed to the agglomeration of settlements here.[1] Newholm, Dunsley, Stakesby, Scourby, Prestby, Sneton, Ugglebarnby, Brecca and Baldby were all within three miles of each other and Whitby.

Settlements elsewhere along the coastal plateau were distributed in two main lines: one followed close to the coastline; the other extended along or near to the 600′ contour which marks the junction between the moorland and clayland. The coastal denes often influenced the settlement pattern.

An interesting off-shoot of the coastal group of settlements was in Eskdale. Here several villages were sited far into the moors. Such settlement was uncommon in the 11th century and it was not until about a century later that a comparable penetration of the moorland was made. This was in Ryedale and Bilsdale and was undertaken by the monasteries.

The second group of settlements was in the Cleveland area. Here again, heavy boulder clay soils often diversified by gravel deposits flanks the moors to the north-west and is raised up as a north-south trending platform along the foot of the moorland escarpment. Two lines of settlement were especially prominent: one followed along the foot of the moorland scarp from Guisborough to Kildale and then to Faceby; the other was north-west of this, nearer to the River Tees and stretched from Marske to Normanby through Stainton towards Hilton and Crathorne. Between the two lines of villages, in the

---

[1] "...the Whitby Thingwala tells us ... that Whitby, under the occupation and rule of the Danes was, out of all Cleveland, by far the most important and most frequented town, as being the seat of all their principal civil and religious procedures and observances" J. C. Atkinson in *Whitby Chartulary* (Surtees Soc.) Introduction XXIII.
(Thingwala: "undoubtedly ... the moatstead of a very strong Scand. colony in Eskdale" *Place Names of the North Riding*, p.128)

neighbourhood of the Cleveland embayment lay a concentration of villages, some sited on soils derived from glacial gravels, e.g. Seamer, Great and Little Ayton, Stokesley; others followed the course of the River Leven, e.g. Hutton Rudby, Rudby, Skutterskelf. The avoidance of the Teesmouth lowland comes out clearly from Figure 2.3. From Thornaby to the mouth of the Tees settlements avoided the river plain and the map shows a blank area for about two miles south of the Tees. Upstream from Thornaby, however, settlement followed closely along the river bank.

The third group, lying in the Vale of York, might be regarded as a continuation of the settlements of the Cleveland Plain, just mentioned. However, there was a distinct "gap" between the settlements of the two areas, which extends from Whorlton north-west to the River Tees. Settlement seems to have been absent from this district. This "gap" separates the settlements of the Cleveland Plain and the Vale of York into different groups. However, the general conditions are similar in both. A line of villages continued along the scarp zone of the moorland at just over 400'. This stretched from Ingleby southwards to the Coxwold gap. Most of these villages were sited on the narrow shelf of glacial gravel which follows the scarp e.g. Thimbleby, Over Silton, Nether Silton, Kepwick, Kirby Knowle, Boltby. A second line of villages followed along the edge of the boulder clay platform as far as Thirsk. Finally, the River Wiske was marked by a series of villages along its course, with a concentration especially around Northallerton.

The fourth group of settlements was the largest. It comprised the Vale of Pickering and nearby areas. The greatest concentration of settlement was in the western half of the Vale. Here, the large number of rivers passing through acted as natural drainage channels and made the district more suitable for settlement than the central and eastern parts of the Vale. Besides, "islands" or hillocks stood out above the level of the western Vale and provided very favourable sites for villages, e.g. Kirby Misperton, Normanby, which the eastern Vale lacked. But Figure 2.6 shows that the valuable meadowland here was also a primary consideration. The absence of settlement from the eastern Vale contrasts sharply with the concentration of the western. Although Figure 2.3 shows some settlements in the Pickering Marshes it was limited to about half a dozen sites: further eastwards for a distance of ten miles there was a complete absence of settlements. This was along the course of the River Derwent and two miles north of the river. Place-name evidence shows that in Pre-Domesday times this region had been largely marshland (2.1). Apparently little reclamation had been attempted, and even by 1086 its emptiness suggest that little improvement had been made. The scene was set for the monastic entrance into this marshland just over sixty years later.

Both northern and southern margins of the Vale were clearly demarcated by lines of villages. Indeed, on the north, an unbroken series stretched from Helmsley to Pickering and Seamer, outlining the junction between the limestone and clayland.[1] The pattern of parish boundaries was typical in such circumstances.[2] They included stretches of high

---

[1] "It may be stated as a general principle that human establishments preferably select lines of contact between different geological formations." Vidal de la Blache, *Principles of Human Geography*, p285.
[2] In fact, this was as classical a region of strip-parishes as the Lincoln Edge or the Wealden Downland.

moorland, limestone and carrland e.g. Middleton, Pickering. Two particular concentrations of villages occurred around Pickering and between Brompton and Seamer. These were located on patches of glacial gravels which provided dry sites and fertile soils.

A line of villages, equally prominent, extended along the foot of the Howardian Hills from Hovingham to Malton and continued (although the map does not show this because the villages were in the East Riding) along the scarp-foot of the Wolds to Muston. Although the appearance of these villages resembled those on the northern margins of the Vale their physical setting was different. They too marked a junction, between the chalk Wolds and Vale clayland, but their actual sites were on the narrow and very fertile bench of post glacial sands and gravels which lies immediately below the north-facing chalk escarpment. The broadening of the chalky-gravel bench together with the proximity of the routeway through the Malton gap and the meadowlands of the Derwent, induced a multiplication of villages near to Malton. Beyond Malton the bench narrows but still provided the sites for a continuing series of villages, e.g. Swinton, Appleton le Street, Amotherby.

Outside the immediate area of the Vale, in the Low Moors, a coherent pattern of settlement was equally evident. Settlement extended along the top of the Corallian limestone escarpment which faced northwards e.g. Carlton, Fadmoor, Gillamoor, Spaunton, Cropton, Newton, Lockton. Besides the advantage of the fertile limestone soils of the dip slope, by 1086 partially cleared of woodland, the narrow vale of clayland at the foot of the scarp offered similar facilities to those of the villages in the Vale of Pickering (plus a spring line). These settlements appear as a distinctive line on Figure 2.3 but the deeper dissection of the limestone hills east of Newtondale caused the line of villages to end abruptly and it is not until the valley system around Hackness is reached that comparable settlement resumed.[1]

The fifth group of settlements comprised the villages to the north and south of Scarborough. These were all situated on clayland, very near to the coast. There was a remarkable concentration between Scarborough and Filey; many of the villages there have subsequently disappeared. Scagethorpe, Etersthorpe and Rodesthorpe disappeared without trace, and Deepdale became a grange of Byland Abbey. The site was suitable because the undulating clayland stood above the marshy peaty alluvium of the Derwent and Hertford rivers.

The Distribution of Uninhabited Vills in 1086

Figure 2.4 presents the realities of settlement as they existed at the time of the Survey. The differences between 1068 and 1086 are striking. The Vale of York and Cleveland have the greatest number of uninhabited vills but the Coastal Plateau, north of Robin Hood's Bay, shows almost as many. In fact, in this comparatively small area between Robin Hood's Bay and Skelton there are only ten inhabited vills; thirty four vills are uninhabited. This contrasts rather sharply with the coast south of Robin Hood's Bay. Here the number of uninhabited vills is small, in fact between Staintondale and Filey only three vills were uninhabited while

---

[1] Settlement on the northern Wolds at Domesday was situated almost entirely within the valley of the Gypsey Race.

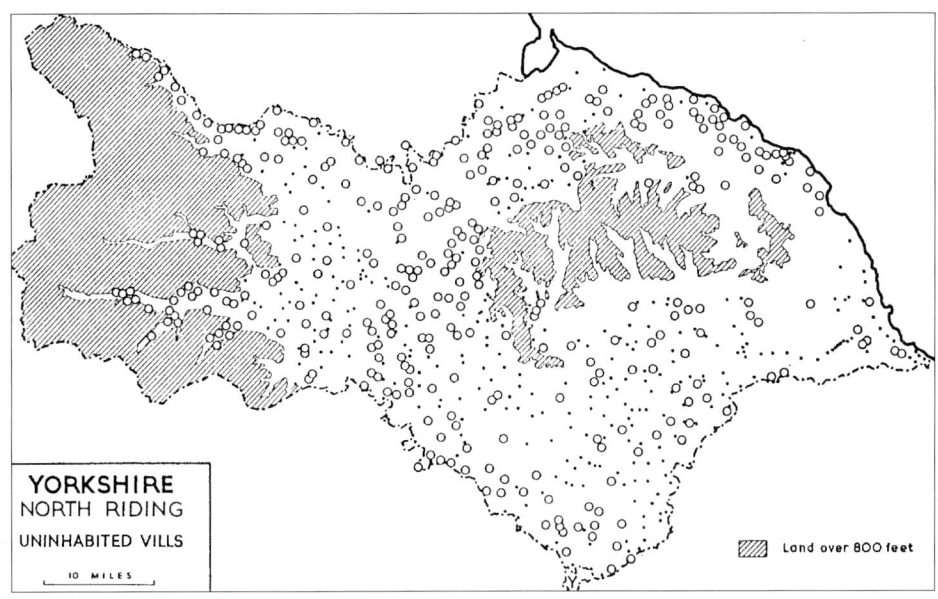

Figure 2.4 Uninhabited Vills

fourteen were inhabited. Obviously this district had suffered less severely from the devastation. Similarly the Vale of Pickering seems to have been more fortunate than either the Vale of York or the Cleveland Plain. Both the Vale of Pickering and the Coxwold area have considerably fewer uninhabited vills. Only about one-third of the villages of the Vale are uninhabited. It is significant, too, that the line of settlements along the northern margin still stood out as inhabited villages. From Wykeham to Helmsley, on the coastal plain near Filey, and in most of the western half of the Vale inhabited vills predominated. In fact, the rather surprising feature is that many of the uninhabited vills of this area were in the Low Moors and Ryedale – places which in theory might be expected to be safe from devastation because of their inaccessibility. Similarly Eskdale, also well hidden in the moors, yet had only two of its six villages inhabited in 1086.

It seems clear that the Vale of Pickering was making a quicker recovery than other districts. Such a recovery of the land might have been delayed longer in moorland areas which were marginal. That could be one explanation of the unexpected number of uninhabited vills in such areas in 1086. Besides, it is possible that many villages farming inhospitable moorland migrated to the more fertile lowlands shortly after the devastation and began to farm recently wasted lands, then tenantless. This could account for the uninhabited vills evident in the moorland in 1086. Re-settlement of the moorland vills might have occurred later. Of course, all this is surmise: but the problem is an interesting one especially since the route taken by the Conqueror in his devastation of the North seems never to have reached certain places which, even so, are uninhabited in 1086. The effects of the devastation were clearly felt in areas which had not actually felt the passage of his armies.

The population of the inhabited vills was generally low. Northallerton with 66 and Coxwold with 54 persons were the largest – both in the Vale of York. Other vills in the same area had very low totals however, usually about ten persons or below. Cleveland and the Vale of Pickering had slightly higher numbers. In the former, the villages stretching south-west of Marske had about twenty persons each. In the latter two clearly defined groups were evident; at the eastern and western ends of the Vale. In both, it was the villages situated along the north and south margins which had the largest populations e.g. Kirby Moorside, Welburn, Pickering, Leidthorpe. But even here the average was fairly low. Welburn with 21 and Leidthorpe with 31 were the largest.[1] The eastern group was situated mainly on the sands and gravels to the south of Forge Valley. It was significant that this district was one of the few in the North-East to show any rise in value at Domesday.

The actual meaning of such values is doubtful because it is not understood what they comprise or how directly they are related to the land. Even so, it is likely that where values increased, or at least did not fall between T.R.E. and 1086, they reflected areas resiliant enough to withstand the adverse conditions of 11th century Yorkshire. Such resiliance might have derived, in no small degree, from the peculiarly advantageous siting of most of these vills. Of the twenty-three recorded vills in the North-East showing an increase or remaining at the same value between 1066 and 1086 thirteen were in or near to the Vale of Pickering.

The distribution of plough teams in the Vale of Pickering emphasises its importance, although the figures are often not as high as might be expected from the size of the population. Leidthorpe, for example, though having a population of 31 has only one plough recorded.[2] In general, a comparison between the distribution of plough teams and population shows that while the Vale of Pickering was perhaps the most important single region in the North-East in terms of relative prosperity in 1086, the Cleveland Plain and the Vale of York retained more plough teams (and thus presumably more arable land in use) than the great extent of waste and large number of uninhabited vills in the areas would suggest. The large extent of meadowland available in the Vale of Pickering might have given the region just that little extra predominance, for while arable holdings would suffer considerably from the devastation, meadowland would remain an unaffected source of prosperity, more quickly returned to use after any possible lapse.

The Distribution of Woodland

Woodland is given lineally in leagues and furlongs in nearly every recorded instance. Four main groups of woodland are evident. The largest area of woodland seems to have been immediately north and south of Whitby, in the mouth of Eskdale. However, Eskdale itself shows up very clearly as an elongated extent of woodland projecting far into the High Moor (as far up the dale as Danby). Except for this incursion, the moors show no signs of woodland in 1086 and must, indeed, have appeared much as they are today – covered in

---

[1] *Liber Censualis vocati Domesday Book*. Ed. by A. Farley (1783) Vol.I, p.314.
[2] *loc. cit.*

PART 1 : THE LANDSCAPE

YORKSHIRE
NORTH RIDING
DOMESDAY WOODLAND

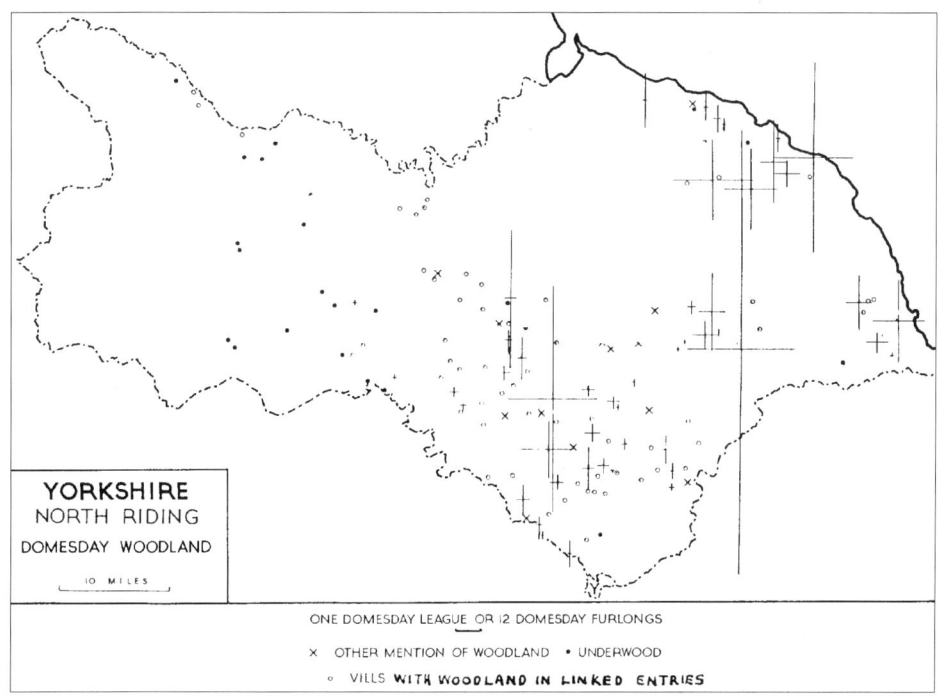

10 MILES

ONE DOMESDAY LEAGUE OR 12 DOMESDAY FURLONGS
× OTHER MENTION OF WOODLAND • UNDERWOOD
○ VILLS WITH WOODLAND IN LINKED ENTRIES

Figure 2.5 Domesday Woodland

ling and bracken with peat bogs here and there but nothing to obstruct the flat, unbroken skylines.

Further south, still along the coast, was the well-wooded district around Scarborough. Like the Coastal Plateau this was an area of heavy boulder clays which was very suitable for tree growth. The Hackness valleys appear heavily wooded while at Falsgrave a fairly extensive area 3 leagues by 2 leagues is recorded as woodland. This no doubt included Scalby Hay on the heavy clayland north of Falsgrave, which continued to be an important woodland well into the later Middle Ages.

Some of the most extensive woodland was to be found just north of the Vale of Pickering. This was associated with the limestone dip slope from Helmsley to Pickering and not with the central Vale. Indeed, the emptiness of the central Vale is a remarkable feature of Figure 2.5. Except perhaps south of Pickering this area seems to have been marshland, with little or no woodland. The most dominant area of woodland was the Forest of Pickering, said to extend to 16 leagues by 4 leagues. Whether, in fact, this represented actual woodland is not easy to determine. It seems likely that the southern part of the forest was more probably marshland than woodland.

The extent to which clearing of the woodland from the limestone slopes had reached by Domesday is an interesting question. Saxon clearance seems to have begun chiefly from the Helmsley and Pockley direction (as the names suggest), but how thick and extensive the tree cover was, and how far they progressed in its clearance remains uncertain. Figure 2.5 suggests that by 1086 a good deal of woodland still remained in this district. It is highly likely, however, that this was in the deep valleys which cut through the limestone rather than on the intervening dip slopes. It is interesting to compare the present-day land use in the area, which shows that the valleys are still the main areas of woodland.

The Vale of York was extensively wooded especially between Northallerton and York. In fact, the Forest of Galtres occupied a dominant place in this woodland, showing a partiality for the heavy boulder clay soils like much of the other woodland so far discussed. The Coxwold-Gilling gap seems to have been extensively wooded, especially near Coxwold itself. Around, and south-east of Northallerton, but well clear of the River Wiske there appears to have been another well wooded area. Much of the woodland here, at such places as Kirby Knowle, Sutton-under-Whitestone Cliff and Thirlby might have been mainly on the scarp face of the Hambleton Hills, or in the valleys which broke into it.

The absence of woodland from the High Moor and the marshy central Vale of Pickering was to be expected. It is significant that not one area of woodland is recorded for the northern Wolds. But the surprising feature is really the absence of recorded woodland in Cleveland. The marshy alluvial flats around Teesmouth would not encourage tree growth but why is the area to the south-west devoid of woodland? Surely the scarp face of the Cleveland Hills at least would have been wooded. It is largely so to-day. Two explanations are possible: the area might have been almost entirely cleared by 1086, it had been after all, a closely settled region; or, the records might be incomplete for the region. The latter reason may be a strong possibility. Since most of the vilages in the area were waste and many were uninhabited statistics of woodland might have been unobtainable by the Commissioners.

The Distribution of Meadowland[1]

All the entries for the North-East refer to meadow; no pasture is recorded. Except for Pickering and Hunmanby which are expressed in leagues, all the meadowland is given in Domesday acres.

The lowland areas predominate as meadowland, especially where they were traversed by a large number of rivers. The moors and the Tees valley had little or no meadowland recorded. The northern Wolds (not shown on the maps), except for Hunmanby showed no meadow – strange, perhaps in view of the large scale pasture farming there by the monasteries, no more than a hundred years later. The answer may lie in the distinction between meadow and pasture; the former implied land bordering a stream liable to flood, and producing hay; the latter denoted land available all year round for feeding cattle and sheep. It is unlikely that meadow would be found on the waterless Wolds or even in the moors. Both areas would have figured prominently in any survey of pastureland, it seems, had it been taken.

---

[1]. "Meadow and pasture were important elements in village economy in an age when root crops and artificial feeding stuffs were not available, and when the winter-feed of the village animals depended largely upon hay from the meadows." H. C. Darby, *op. cit.* p60.

PART 1 : THE LANDSCAPE

The Coastal Plateau between the River Esk and Teesmouth showed a fairly general distribution of meadow, although individual amounts are not high. Along the coast to the south there is a notable absence of meadow; so, in Eskdale none is recorded although later medieval inquisitions indicate that there was valuable meadowland in the dale.[1]

The Vale of York had fewer areas of meadowland than might be expected, although the number of vills with meadow in linked entries here, as in the Vale of Pickering is high. There seems to be a small concentration near to the River Wiske around and south of Northallerton.

The Vale of Pickering, in particular the western part, had the heaviest concentration as well as the largest amounts of meadow. This was to be expected in an area where so many tributary streams joined the Rye and Derwent. It was here that the monastic farmers from Malton Priory and Rievaulx Abbey were to bring many of their flocks. The peripheral villages again predominated with the largest amounts of meadow. Slingsby had 20 acres, Kirby Moorside 29 acres, and Welburn 40 acres. Although such amounts were among the largest recorded in the whole North-East they compare very poorly with many other places in Domesday Book. On the chalky boulder clay country of Lincolnshire, for example, amounts from 200 to 400 acres were frequent.[2]

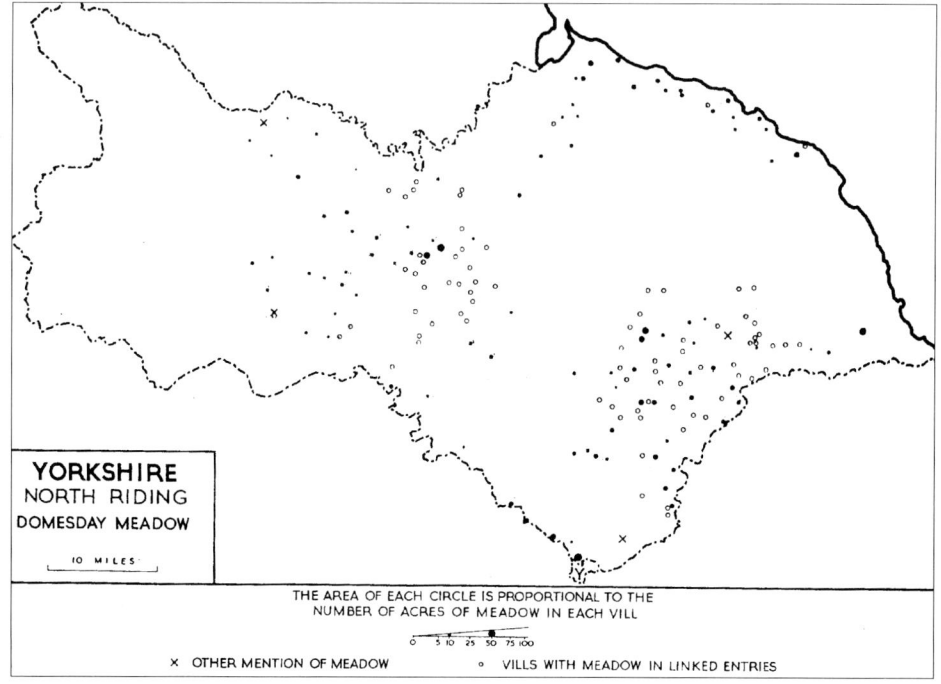

Figure 2.6 Domesday Meadow

[1.] An inquisition taken in 1335 describes "divers parcels of meadow next to the Esk river containing 60 acres and worth £3" at Lealholm. The same document gives details of meadowland elsewhere in Eskdale and its tributary valleys; in Danby there were at least 460 acres of meadow. P.R.O. C135/44/6.
[2.] See H. C. Darby, *op. cit.* pp.60-64.

The Distribution of Waste

The great extent of waste is a remarkable feature of the Yorkshire Domesday. Such waste was presumably not the waste of moor, marsh, and so on, but refers to a lapse of former land utilisation. Figure 2.7 distinguishes between wholly waste, partially waste and no mention of waste.

No settled area was unaffected, although some were much more severely wasted than others. Along the coast, north-west of Whitby, the majority of vills were wholly waste. In fact, from Robin Hood's Bay to Skelton 23 vills were wholly waste, 6 partially waste, and only 14 with no mention of waste. In nearby Eskdale, too, 3 vills were wholly waste, 1 partially waste and the remaining two show no mention of waste. The Vale of York had been similarly affected, especially near the centre of the Vale. In 1086 many of the vills in the neighbourhood of Northallerton and Topcliffe were still completely waste. Recovery of the land seems to have been slow here as it was in the Pennine dales. Like Eskdale, most of the Pennine dales and particularly Teesdale appear clearly on Figure 2.7 as areas in which the vills were completely waste in 1086. This is one of the most striking features of the map: it shows, first how complete the devastation had been, and second how slow such areas of marginal agriculture were to recover (almost every vill in these areas was uninhabited in 1086. But the Pennine dales seem to have been more severely hit than the Moorland dales of the North-East. Many of the vills in the Vale of Lastingham, have no mention of waste so that presumably they had made a fairly quick recovery.

Both the Cleveland Plain and the Vale of Pickering contrast sharply with other regions

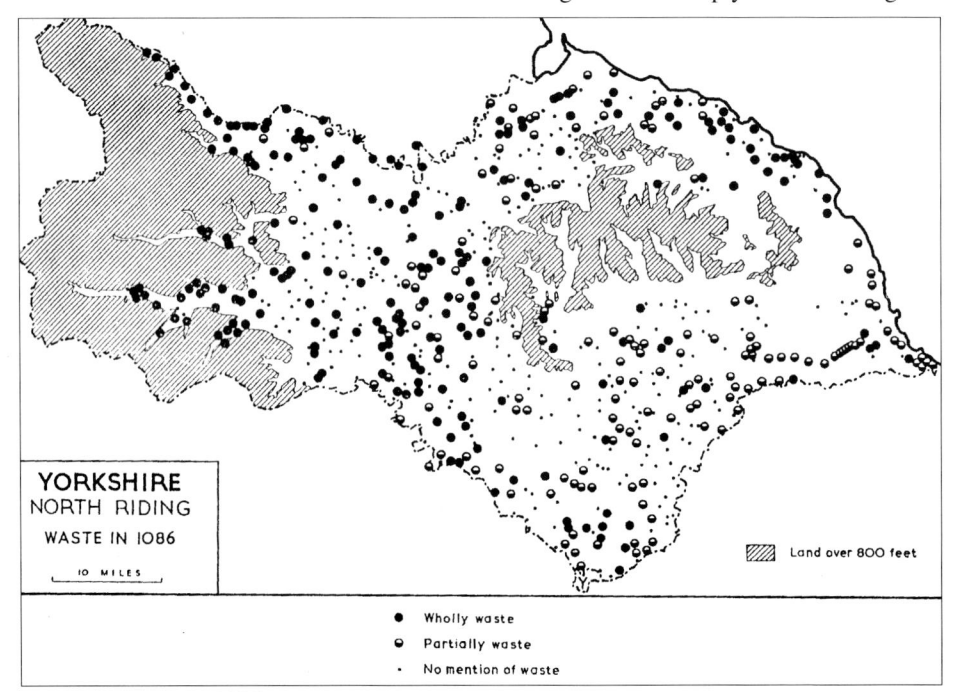

Figure 2.7 Waste in 1086

in respect of the degree of wasting evident in 1086. The former has only 17 vills wholly waste, 17 partially waste and 38 with no mention of waste. Some of the vills not mentioned as having waste were uninhabited, but most of them had inhabitants (especially evident in the Cleveland embayment where inhabited vills without evidence of waste are most numerous). The line of settlements nearest to the River Tees appears to have been most severely affected; at least such settlements show more complete wasting in 1086 than elsewhere in the Cleveland region. This is to be expected since Ordericus Vitalis describes in his history how the Conqueror set forth from York on a special journey of destruction to Teesmouth "Learning that a fresh band of marauders was lurking in a corner of the country defended on all sides by either sea or marsh ... the indefatigable King pursued his desperate foes to the river Tees, through such difficult roads that he was obliged sometimes to dismount and march on foot."[1] He remained fifteen days in this district.

The Conqueror's return from the Tees was by way of Helmsley. Oderic eloquently describes the difficulties of this moorland march. The King made his way "amid the cold and ice of winter ... through hills and vallies where the snow often lay while neighbouring districts were rejoicing in the bloom of spring."[2] Once, William and six of his horsemen lost their way and had to spend the night ignorant about the location of the main army.[3] The choice of this difficult route is hard to explain; although in a direct line from the Tees to York it crossed the highest and most inhospitable moorland. But the Conqueror might have been intending to visit the Vale of Pickering to continue his devastation there, if so his route seems explicable.

Certainly the Vale of Pickering and nearby areas show evidence of wasting. As in Cleveland, however, so here the number of wholly waste vills in 1086 is limited. In the whole Vale and its neighbourhood there are only 15 completely waste vills. Half of the remaining settlements are partially waste and have no mention of waste. The concentration of waste vills in Ryedale and near Helmsley seems to substantiate the chronicler Oderic when he describes the Conqueror's routeway southwards from the Tees as lying in this direction. It seems clear that the Vale of Pickering had made a quicker recovery than most other regions, after the devastations. The majority of the vills were inhabited in 1086 and though many of them were partially waste (note especially the vills along the northern margin of the Vale) only a few were completely so.

Conclusion

The landscape portrayed by the Domesday Survey offered a great opportunity for settlement, especially by the monasteries. Large areas still remained unreclaimed: parts of the land which had been recovered and tilled before 1069 had reverted to waste through the depopulation of the district. The moors themselves were not settled and scarcely used; a large part of the Vale of Pickering was marshland, often at best providing occasional pasturage; extensive areas of woodland yet remained to be cleared, especially along the

---

[1] *Historia Ecclesiastica.* (Soc. de l'Histoire de France 1840). Vol.II, pp.196-197.
[2] *ibid.* pp.197-198.
[3] *loc. cit.*

clayland of the coast and in the Vale of York. The opportunity for an expansion and reconstruction of settlement was almost unlimited. Even by 1086 much of the settled area had not recovered from the devastatation of 1069. The way was open for a new era in settlement, and it is one of the most significant facts in history that the rise of the new Orders of monasticism should follow so closely upon the devastation of Yorkshire. For it was no more than fifty years later that the Augustinians established themselves at Guisborough.

Undeniably, the monasteries were to the forefront in the resettlement of the area. The coincidence between places waste in 1086 and later monastic granges is so notable that it seems such sites were just what the monks wanted. A benefactor would be more willing to part with the waste lands he owned if he had not the resources to utilise them himself. For their part, the monasteries, especially the Cistercian, welcomed donations which they could use, unimpeded by feudal restrictions, where a completely fresh start was possible.

Many instances occur of whole vills wholly or partially waste in 1086 becoming monastic granges. This happened at Griff, Stilton, Deepdale, and Loftmarshes for example. Elsewhere granges were established alongside restored vills (e.g. Great Broughton, Wintringham). How much of this restoration was brought about by the monasteries will, perhaps, never be known. It is certain, however, that the large extent of waste in the North-East must have been the most important single factor determining the site and proliferation of lay donations to the monasteries. In this respect, it is worthwhile to compare the maps showing Domesday waste and monastic settlement. Looking at the North-East as a whole it is plain that monastic lands and granges were most highly concentrated in just three areas which had a large amount of waste in 1086. Thus Guisborough Priory's lands were concentrated in Cleveland and the Coastal Plateau; Whitby Abbey's also along the coast.

A more subtle influence on monastic settlement was the relative importance of one region to another within the North-East. The Domesday maps studied show that even in 1086 a regional hierarchy was evident. The predominance of the Vale of Pickering was well marked – it was the most closely settled; potentially and actually the wealthiest region, which had recovered more rapidly from the devastation than any others. Later developments emphasised the already apparent regional patterns of 1086. The settlement of the monasteries in the North-East was the most fundamental factor in this: but the disposal and character of such settlement is the subject of the next chapter.

PART TWO : SETTLEMENT

'I find no terror in the hard mountain steeps, nor in the rough rocks nor in the hollow places of the valleys, for in these days the mountains distil sweetness and the hills flow with milk and honey, the valleys are covered over with corn, honey is sucked out of the rock and oil out of the flinty stone, and among the cliffs and mountains are the flocks of the sheep of Christ ...'

St. Bernard

3 Monastic Settlement

4 The Monastic Grange

3 MONASTIC SETTLEMENT

"They are all things for all work," said Walter Map of the Cistercians, "and so the whole earth is full of their possessions."[1] If the latter statement is exaggerated in fact at least it is accurate in sentiment. The rapid growth of monastic lands, especially during the middle and late twelfth century, due mainly to the advent of the new orders, must have seemed the most remarkable phenomenon of the times to laymen. Their world, at least, was being filled out with "an exceedingly great people ... spread in many establishments".[2] In particular, the North-East of Yorkshire was very intensively settled by the monasteries – predominantly those belonging to the new orders. A glance at the maps showing the lands of Whitby Abbey, Guisborough Priory, and Rievaulx Abbey is enough to show how widespread their possessions were.[3]

But such expansion was hardly accidental. Neither did it rely solely on the superstitous fear of damnation which prompted the generosity of lay donors, nor their desire for the prestige which went with the foundation of a monastery.[4] Rather, it was the industry and efficiency of the monasteries themselves which "obtained from a rich man a valueless and despised plot ... by much feigning of innocence and long importunity, putting in God at every other word. The wood was cut down, stubbed up and levelled into a plain, bushes gave place to barley, willows to wheat, withies to vines; and it may be that in order to give them full time for these operations their prayers had to be somewhat shortened ..."[5]

Coupled with this innate necessity to work in response to the demands of the Order, was the notable advantage that a religious corporation had over a lay owner. Both its aims and accomplishments were potentially and actually higher. Besides, the popularity of the new orders at first had attracted a wide and varied following who were able to enlist as lay brethren in monastic service and by doing so increase the possessions of the monasteries. Byland Abbey, for instance, was compelled to move from Hood where it had been established for four years because the site was not big enough for all the new converts, "–Locus de Hode nimis arctus fuit ab abbaciam construendam et quod alium provideret in situm aptiorien ad monachos suos qui in possessionibus et personis cotide multiplicabantur Siquidem veterani et emoriti milites de curia et familia dicti domini Rogeri (Roger de Mowbray, founder) conversi fuerunt ad eos et de bonis temporalibus secum attulerunt non modica quibus suffragantibus constructa fuit una grangia apud

---

[1] *De Nugis Curialium.* English Translation in Cymmrodorion Society R.S. No. IX (1923), p.46.
[2] *Ibid.*, p.55.
[3] The maps have been compiled from the chartularies of the monasteries concerned, as well as several other sources such as the Registers of the Archbishops of York (partly published by the Surtees Society; partly in MS at the Diocesan Registry, York). They show the maximum picture of monastic settlement.
[4] The fear of damnation must not be underestimated however. "He who chooseth purgatory knoweth not what he asketh", said St. Augustine, "for to dwell there but the twinkling of an eye is more grievous torment than any that St. Laurence suffered on his gridiron" quoted by G. Coulton, *Five Centuries of Religion*, Vol.I, p.75.
    "Satan covers a gloomy earth with his sombre wings ... According to popular belief, current towards the end of the fourteenth century, no one had entered Paradise since the beginning of the great Western schism". J. Huizinga *The Waning of the Middle Ages,* p.21.
    The stories of Bede and Roger of Wendover were a stronger admonition against treating damnation recklessly.
[5] Walter Map, *op. cit.,* pp.40-41.

Wildon."[1] These new converts after their entry soon spread abroad throughout the province "quod illa nova habitatio de nobilibus viris et personis generosis erat mirabiliter infra breve suffulta, unde devotio omnium audientium inclinavit ad dictum locum."[2] So the expansion of monastic settlement began: it was to be a factor of supreme importance in many areas. There can, however, have been few areas where it was so concentrated and integrated into the scene as in the North-East.

The whole perimeter of the moorland was studded with monastic houses, large and small, old and new, some in already settled areas, others outside. Along the coast were Whitby, Handale and Grosmont; inland, south of the Tees river, was Guisborough, while southwards again the Vale of Pickering contained Rievaulx, Malton, Yedingham, Wykeham and Keldholme, with Byland, Newburgh and Bridlington nor far away. Within the moorlands several smaller houses had been founded – Basedale, Rosedale, and Arden.

Three maps have been drawn which show the possessions of Whitby, Guisborough and Rievaulx at their greatest extent. The sources used were mainly the monastic chartularies, but many other varied documents were used, for example, the registers of the Archbishops of York (in particular for details of appropriated churches), lay subsides, Dissolution

Figure 3.1 Religious Houses

---

[1] *Monasticon Anglicanum* V, p.350f.
[2] *Monasticon Anglicanum* V, p.350f.

Accounts, and so on. But before the distribution of the monastic estates can be discussed a word must be said about their growth.

Few additions were made to monastic lands after 1279, when the statute of Mortmain forbade alienation of property to monasteries without licence. But long before this the monastic estates in the North-East had generally become stabilized, and remained so until the Dissolution in the middle sixteenth century. The pattern of monastic development in this area, however, was slightly different from that of more southerly monasteries such as Ely, Crowland, and Christ Church Canterbury.

After the foundation, sometimes a very large grant as at Guisborough and Whitby, or a very niggardly one as at Rievaulx, the accumulation of lands and rights was rapid – alarmingly so.[1] At Rievaulx, for example, the greater part of the lands were acquired and a large number of granges established by the end of the twelfth century. Even by 1170 the monks had acquired all Bilsdale, Pickering Marshes, parts of Farndale and Bransdale, the vills of Griff, Tileston, Stainton, Welburn, Hoveton, and the lands in Hunmanby, Crosby, Morton, Welbury, Allerston, Heslerton, Folkton, Willerby, Reighton … .[2] Some donors had apparently not bargained for such a rapid increase in monastic possessions. It came as a shock to find that the monks were not "all that was simple and submissive; no greed, no self-interest..."[3] The result was that men like Roger de Mowbray, Robert de Stutville, Everard de Ros and other great lords (formerly great donors and founders) began, unsuccessfully, to evict the monks from certain lands – but monastic expansion continued.[4]

Whitby and Guisborough had been more fortunate than Rievaulx in their lavish foundation grant, which provided an excellent basis for subsequent acquisition of land. Guisborough's greatest period of expansion after the foundation (c.1119) was chiefly from the late twelfth century until the middle thirteenth century, and lands were still being acquired by licence in the fourteenth century.[5] Malton Priory had a similar period of expansion which reached a peak during William of Ancaster's rule (c.1234-56). Whitby Abbey, too, after a preliminary burst of activity at, and immediately after, its foundation lapsed in this activity but resumed again during the early thirteenth century, especially during the abbacy of Roger de Scarburgh – "Never did the Abbey make so illustrious a figure as when governed by Roger, nor ever after his death in 1244 did it add to its riches and power'.[6]

---

[1] All the territory of Guisborough viz. 20 carucates etc., all the vill of Kirkleatham and part of Coatham and much more given to Guisborough Priory in the Foundation grant q.v Chartulary pp.1-5 (Surtees Vol. 86).
 In contrast Rievaulx received 4 carucates in Griff and 5 carucates in Stilton. Bilsdale seems to have been included in a later confirmation charter. q.v. Chartulary pp.16-21. (Surtees Vol. 83).
[2] *Rievaulx Chartulary*, pp.260-263. List of early acquisitions.
[3] Walter Map *op. cit.*, pp.41-42.
[4] Papal command to Archbishop of York and Bishop of Durham that they stop the injust evictions from the land to which the monks of Rievaulx have been subjected by the parishioners of the two clerics and to see to it that their land is no longer exposed to such deprivations (between 1154-81) *Rievaulx Ch.*, p.189.
 Bull against such as lay violent hands on … "monachos vel conversos ipsius Monasterii …" *Ibid.*, p.193.
 Pope Alexander III directs that amends be made to the Convent for grave acts of spoilation by great men e.g. Robert de Stutville has seized "…nemus de Hovetun et navalia ejusdem villa…". Roger de Mowbray, Everard de Ros and others must restore what they have stolen. *Ibid.*, pp.194-195.
[5] e.g. at Thornaby in 1342 2 tofts and 1 bovate. Guisborough Chart. No. 914 B, 914 C.
[6] Lionel Charlton *History of Whitby and Whitby Abbey* (York 1779) Note also, "The eighth abbot of Whitby was Roger de Scarborough who is said to have spent some of his younger years in the cell at Middlesburgh. In this time the abbey received a great accession of territory and wealth and was then at the zenith of its grandeur". G. Young *History of Whitby* (1817), p.265.

Part Two : Settlement

The North-Eastern monasteries were, then, well set to participate to the full in the period of economic expansion which marked the thirteenth century.[1] Unfortunately, when this period was at its height in the latter part of the century, a series of individual and collective disasters combined to deny these monasteries a full share in it. While Crowland Abbey was flourishing in the 'high farming' years (1276-1322), and Christ Church Canterbury guided by the economic wisdom of Henry of Eastry, was more prosperous than ever before, Whitby, Rievaulx and Guisborough were on the verge of collapse.[2]

The great murrain had been so severe in the district that Rievaulx had to be taken into the King's custody because it was "in a state of decay" (1276).[3] Only twelve years later the great accumulation of debts, mainly to Italian merchants, resulted in similar action because the abbey was unable to pay.[4] About the same time Guisborough Priory was destroyed by a great fire (1289),[5] and the great monastery which in 1276 had goods temporal and spiritual worth 2,000 marks was compelled to petition the Archbishop for permission to sell corrodies, appropriate churches, and let out its churches.[6] But besides individual catastrophes the effect of the Scottish raids during the late 13th century and early 14th centuries was another devastating burden.[7] At Whitby, for example, the abbot had to send away for corn and victuals since those of the abbey had been destroyed by the frequent inroads of the Scots.[8] Even as late as 1328 the Archbishop appointed some "trusty men to survey the benefices ... that have been destroyed by the Scots" and to cause them to be newly taxed.[9] The Scots penetrated the Vale of Pickering in 1322, sacking Rievaulx Abbey on their way, and reaching as far south as Hull.

Thus the main monasteries of the area suffered a decline while others elsewhere reached their high point. Recovery was delayed, and when the monasteries were again

---

[1] Professor Postan is chiefly responsible for postulating the theory of expansion of economic activity in England before 1300 and after c.1450, and a contraction beginning about 1300-1320 – in "The Chronology of Labour Services" *Trans. Royal Hist. Society* 4th series pp.169-93 (1937) and "Some Economic Evidence of Declining Population in the Latter Middle Ages" *Economic History Review* 2nd Series II, pp.221-46. (1950), etc.

[2] "The years 1306-24 were the 'high farming' period par excellence ... the decline of demesne farming ... began in the third decade of the 14th cent. and gathered increasing momentum as the century advanced". R. A. L. Smith *Canterbury Cathedral Priory* (1943), pp.144f. Eastry's re-organisation began in 1288. Compare F. M. Page *Estates of Crowland Abbey*.

[3] C.P.R., p.152.

[4] C.P.R. (1288), p.294. Debts to Italian merchants between 1279-1303, given in P.R.O. E159/60-65. Rievaulx compelled to borrow £250 from General Chapter in 1291 R.C., p.376.

[5] Note on this and later fire in a Missal of Guisborough Priory in B.M. Add. MS. 35285 folios 168-173. Fuller description in Chartulary II, pp.353-57. Details in Walter Hemingboro's Chronicle. See also *Registrum Palatinum Dunelmense* (Rolls Series 62), p.57.

[6] Appeal to appropriate churches (1290) G. C. II, p.354; to let churches e.g. Kirkburn; they sold corrodies in 1321, 1323, 1327, 1351. Newly taxed in 1328.

[7] "CXXVIII villae combustae et devastatae ... per scotos" in the N.R. and 12 in the E.R. besides damage to Hedon, Ravenser and Hull. See P.R.O. E359/14/ collection of 1322 for tax concessions made to lay men in villages damaged by the Scots. Inquisitions of this period reflect the disturbance to farming activities.

[8] C.P.R. (1316), p.389.

[9] C.C.R. (1328), p.280. Whitby Abbey appealed for assistance from the Archbishop 7th Oct. 1333 to receive alms through the diocese for one year. J. C. Atkinson *Memorials of Old Whitby*, p.131. The monks were allowed by Papal Mandate "to appropriate the church of Semere value 80 marks to the A. and C. of Whitby who suffer from the Barreness of the Soil, and the Incursions of The Scots". *Reg. Papal Letters II* (1305-42).

The writs and returns relating to the new tax of benefices unable to pay the tenth of 1318 show that Guisborough, Newburgh, and Malton petitioned to be newly taxed due to frequent Scottish devastations of their property. Clerical Subsidy P.R.O. E 179/67/9. Also gives new tax on each of Whitby's benefices (m.8), tax on various churches in the Riding (m.19) and possible new tax on temporalities (m.13) – Kirkham £60, Newburgh £20, Malton 120 marks.

able to resume something resembling their old power, the economic climate had changed. The great era of demesne farming had been replaced by large scale leasing and a contraction replaced the expansion of economic activity.

DISTRIBUTION OF MONASTIC LANDS

1. *Whitby Abbey*

The lands of Whitby Abbey were mainly confined to the coastal district of the North-East, to which the high moorland provided a formidable barrier. Formidable, at least, in the monk's own opinion: "dictum suum monasterium in littore maris situm crebris inimicorum insultibus undique expositum necnon propter longa et periculosa viarum discriminina et hominibus et jumentis per terram de difficili accessione …"[1]

The lands themselves were disposed in four main groups: the greatest concentration was in the vicinity of the abbey and in particular on the lowland Boulder Clay soils which comprise the mouth of Eskdale. Just south of this another smaller pocket of Boulder Clay provided the site for lands in the Fyling-Stoupe region. The abbey had been granted most of these nearby vills by William de Perci in his foundation grant.[2] The subsequent policy of the abbey seemed directed toward increasing their possessions in this area. Abbot William (early twelfth century), for instance, bought Hawsker, Normanby, north and south Fyling from Tancred the Fleming, and it was here that many of the purchases and exchanges of land negotiated by Abbot Roger de Scarburgh occurred.[3] Roger Burrigan,

Figure 3.2 Whitby Abbey c.1840

---

[1] Petition for the appropriation of Hutton Buschel Church (1453) *Reg. W.R. Booth* folio 224 York.
[2] W.C. Volume I, pp.3f.
[3] *Loc. cit.*

for example, sold all his land in Fyling to Abbot Roger "pro quatuor marcis argenti, quas mihi dedit in magna necessitate mea", and Richard de Filynge granted all his pastures of Bothem in Hawsker "pro quinque marcis argenti, quas michi dederunt in necessitate mea".[1] The phrase recurs regularly. Despite the heavy building programme at the abbey, it seemed that Abbot Roger still found money enough to extend and consolidate abbey lands.[2] This speaks well for the richness of the abbey and for the importance of the area close by. In fact the establishment of at least six granges within this small area emphasises its importance in the abbey economy.[3]

The second group of lands was as distinctive as the first and its physical setting was similar. The great Boulder Clay plateau which fringed the coastline from Teesmouth to Eskdale came to an abrupt end just south of Whitby. Here, a great finger of moorland reached irresistibly to the coast and occupied the five miles of coastline between Robin Hood's Bay and Hayburn Wyke. South of this moorland the Boulder Clay continued as an area of low relief from Cloughton to Flamborough Head. The second group of Whitby lands were situated on or near to this Boulder Clay zone, and so were clearly separated from the abbey lands in the Whitby district.

The lands were closely concentrated, as they were about Whitby; they were similarly located on clayland; the proximity of the port of Scarborough paralleled that of Whitby in the first group. But, topographically, the Hackness region was much more diversified. While the mouth of Eskdale was mainly a broad, uninterrupted lowland, the Hackness region comprised several valleys which thrust deeply into the moor edge carrying alluvium and Boulder Clay with them. It was in such valleys that the lands of the second group were mainly found. Everley, Hackness, Broxa and Dales followed the Derwent valley, and Harwood, Kesebeck and Gaitla were in Harwoodale.

Although these lands were separated from the abbey by twelve miles of difficult country, it seemed to be the monk's policy to develop them as carefully as they were doing in the Whitby estates. Indeed, it seemed that both groups were developed in a specialised way, so that they were supplementary to each other – the Whitby group being mainly concerned with arable production and the Hackness with cattle farming. However, consolidation and expansion of lands in the area is evident enough, especially in the early thirteenth century. For example, Isode de Angotby resigned all her lands in Hackness to the abbey for three marks; William fitz Thomas Cocus granted land here "pro quadam summa pecuniae quam michi dederunt in magna necessitate mea" and sold his toft in Silphow on the same terms.[4] The large number of quitclaims secured by the abbey in Suffield suggest similar expansion.[5] The abbey's recourse to frequent litigation over property was a sure sign that it held particular ambitions in the district. Abbot Roger, for instance, had his rights in 100 acres at Hackness recognised by the justices in 1227 after it had been disputed by a layman.[6] Later, in 1260, Abbot William

---
[1] *Ibid.* No. 181. He sold other land here to the Abbot too. No. 160. Pasture in Hawsker – W.C. vol. 2. No. 492.
[2] For extensive building during the early 13th century see Ministry of Works Pamphlet *Whitby Abbey* and Atkinson, *op. cit.*
[3] The granges were: Whitby lathes, Lathegarth, Fyling, Hawsker, Stakesby, Eskdale, Normanby, Lairpool.
[4] W.C. No. 501, No. 502, No. 500.
[5] W.C. No. 511.
[6] W.C. II, p.668.

gave 50 marks to have his rights in Everley, which John de Greddynges had disputed in the King's Court.[1]

The third group of abbey lands were along the northern margin of the Vale of Pickering, together with the lands in Fordon, Wold Newton and Butterwick on the Wolds. Althouth the former district was so prosperous, with a concentration of population and a high degree of fertility, the monks seemed disinclined to make great efforts here as they had done in the two previous areas. The distance from the abbey and the generally small donations they had in these villages no doubt encouraged this. Also, they had entered the sphere of other monasteries (Bridlington, Malton, Rievaulx, Byland, Wykeham, Yedingham) and the opportunities for expansion would be less, especially if other houses were attempting the same policy. Looked at in this way it becomes clear why large scale leasing of abbey lands was characteristic of the Vale area, even from early times and even in the period when the abbey was expanding so much elsewhere. Abbot Roger, for example, leased 5 bovates in Irton for ever, 8 bovates in Cayton to Rievaulx Abbey and 3 in the same place to William fitz Durand.[2] He leased a carucate in Butterwick, in 1227, in order to secure his rights in Hackness – it meant no more than a bargaining counter to him. Later, in 1246, the abbey sold part of its lands in Wykeham and Ruston and allowed others

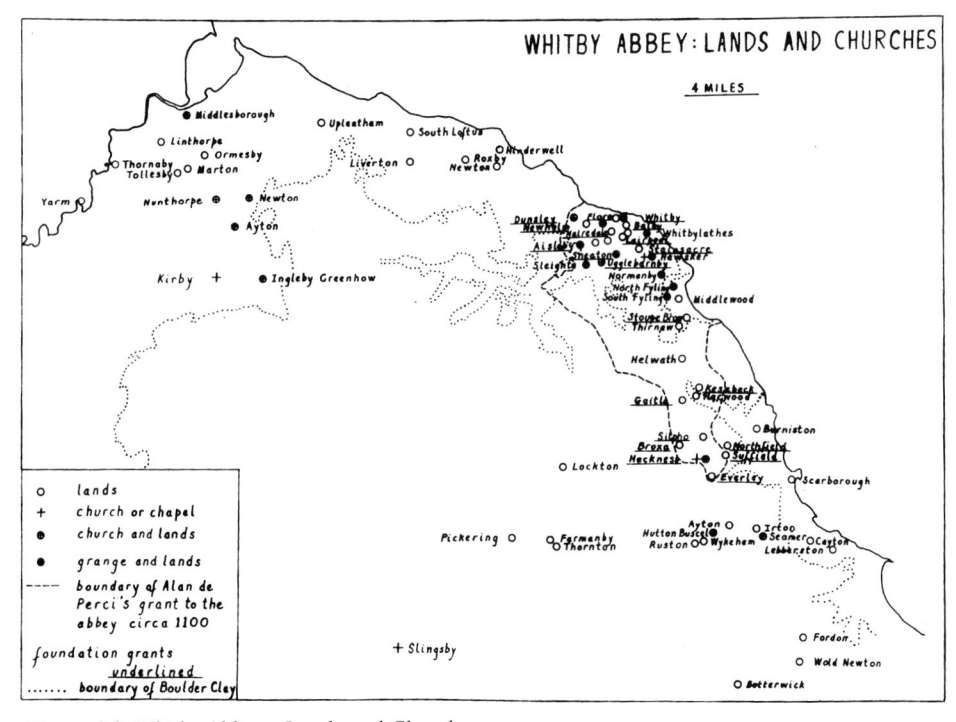

Figure 3.3 Whitby Abbey : Lands and Churches

---

[1] W.C. No. 516.
[2] W.C. No. 541. No. 84.

to be granted to the nunnery of Wykeham.[1] The rest were disposed of in leases. The abbey, then, had apparently no wish to retain this group of lands under its direct control, but it is likely that the income derived from sales and leases in the area was used to finance expansion elsewhere.

There was one notable exception to this however. This was at Seamer where the abbey held little land but had the tithes of the parish, and of Irton, Osgodby, Cayton, Killerby and Deepdale which were included in Seamer church.[2] These were so lucrative that the abbey took particular interest, at least in this part of their Valeland property. Since Seamer was fairly near to the Hackness estates, the two could be utilized jointly. Seamer, including rich meadowland, marshland, very fertile gravel-soils and moorland in its parish, was an especially rich area in which the value of tithes was high and their composition varied (i.e. tithe on crops, lambs, wool, pigs ....) £101/13/14 derived from them in 1366, for instance, more even than from Whitby itself (£98/14/9) and much greater than the next most profitable, Hackness (£60/1/10).[3] This provides a useful reminder that the wealth of a monastery must not always be judged by the extent of its territories alone.

The fourth group of lands belonging to Whitby Abbey were in Cleveland. They were scattered fairly evenly, and generally the lands owned were of small amounts. However, the lands at Middlesbrough, which included parts of Newham and Aresum were an exception. The abbey had established a cell at Middlesbrough with its own prior and its own separate accounts. It had a good deal of independence which was especially well marked in the fourteenth century. Its value at this period, £30, indicates, too, its importance.[4] The church and the tithes belonged to the abbey and there was ample land for expansion in the alluvial flats bordering the Tees river. It seemed, from all such factors, that this spot was the most important part of the monastery's possessions in the Cleveland group – emphasised because the Middlesbrough cell most probably administered the scattered lands of the abbey in nearby Linthorp, Ormesby and Marton. But apart from this one instance there is no evidence to show that the abbey's Cleveland possessions were regarded as being as valuable and worth development as those in the Whitby and Hackness areas.

2. *Guisborough Priory*

Little needs to be said about the distribution of Guisborough lands because it was quite simple and clear. With the exception of Sinnington, Heslerton, Sherburn and Thirsk the Priory's lands were crowded together in the vills of the Cleveland plain and along the

---

[1] W.C. No. 521, No. 522.
[2] Appropriated 1323. Reasons: the monastery "quod in loco vastato et sterili situm est, per hostiles scottorum aggressus, qui villas et oppida, bonaque mobilia ejusdem Mon'ii feritate barbarica pluries devastavunt, necnon per communem morinam animalium .... " W.C., p. 485.
[3] In Abbey Accounts in *Chapters of the English Black Monks* (1215-1540) pp. 63-68 Edited by W. A. Pantin (Camden Series, Vol. III, 1937).
[4] *Loc. cit.* N.B. Value at Dissolution given as £25-17-5 (*Supression of Yorkshire Monasteries*, p. 24) which was more than many of the smaller religious houses of the area at that time e.g. Grosmont £12-2-8, Basedale £20-1-4, Handale £13-19-0, Yedingham £21-16-6.
Middlesbrough-Newham was a great area of arable farming on the abbey estates q.v. Dissolution Accounts.

coast – a crescent stretching from Welbury in the south-west to Ugthorpe in the southeast. Almost all the lands were situated on the Boulder Clay or gravel soils which comprise the Cleveland lowland, or on the alluvium which occupies the Tees Valley.

But there was one very important area which did not fall into this category: that was Upper Eskdale. The foundation charter of Robert de Brus had given the Canons a large area, mainly moorland. The development of this previously deserted area encouraged them to extend their lands further southwards into Eskdale. The valuable pastureland and iron deposits were attractions. Settlement which began in the Commondale area (Wayworth, Skelderskew, etc.) soon spread into Baysdale and Kildale Moor. The

Figure 3.4 Guisborough Priory c.1840

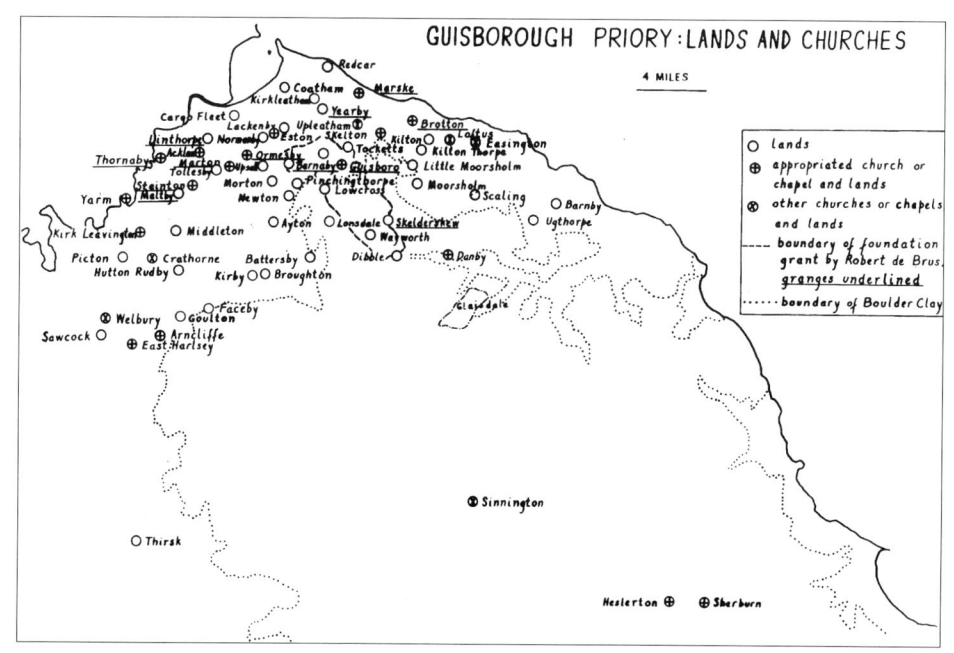

Figure 3.5 Guisborough Priory : Lands and Churches

foundation grant of Danby church had also given them an early footing in Eskdale. By the middle of the thirteenth century they were established in the heart of the moorland at Glaisdale, where they had obtained a considerable land grant.[1]

3. *Rievaulx Abbey*

The lands of this abbey extended over a much wider area than those of either Guisborough or Whitby.[2] But although many were located along the western margin of the moors and in Cleveland the vast majority lay in the Vale of Pickering. Six groups can be isolated, and in each the Cistercians were very active during the twelfth and thirteenth centuries.

The most northerly group was along the river Tees. The abbey had lands both at the mouth (Redcar, Normanby) and at the sources of the river (in Upper Teesdale e.g. Middleton – outside the North-East). Between these extremities the abbey held lands at intervals along the course of the river – at Newsham, Worsall, Angram, Yarm, Thornaby and Stainsby. The importance of the Tees as a navigable waterway and an artery of trade enhanced the value

---

[1] By 1301 Guisborough's settlement of Upper Eskdale had reached extensive proportions. This, together with their lands and pastures in middle Eskdale e.g. Danby, Glaisdale, Waytlandside etc. made their influence great and variable in the dale.

[2] As early as 1191 the General Chapter tried to check further purchases of landed property because, "the Order has the reputation of never ceasing to add field to field, and the love of worldly goods has become a scandal". G. Coulton *op. cit.*, Vol. I, p. 379.
"While the Cistercian hungered for Christ and strove to eat their bread in the sweat of their brow, the spiritual value of *pietas* gave rise to worldly virtue of economic *providentia*; by piety they had become rich and they were now in danger of the sin of *avaritia*". Giraldus Cambrensis.

Figure 3.6 Rievaulx Abbey c.1840

of such lands. In particular, they were well sited in relation to Yarm, the principal port and crossing point of the Tees in the middle ages. The river was an important and much used fishery, too, and at its mouth a great salt panning industry had developed (Cowpen – Coatham) which stressed the attractiveness and possibilities of the area close by. The abbey made active use of these advantages and consequently the Tees valley estates had a particular and important contribution to make to the abbey economy as a whole.

In fact, Rievaulx held a very great interest in the Tees fisheries along almost the whole lower course of the river – an interest which attached a large measure of control, occasionally monopoly, to itself. The monks, for instance, had the entire fishery of Newsham and no one else was to fish there but them; sometime between 1170-80 they received confirmation of Stainsby fishery and about the same time they acquired the fisheries of Worsall and Normanby.[1] Since several granges were established in these places at a very early date (e.g. Newsham, Normanby, Angram) it was evident that the abbey intended to make full use of the resources so near to their lands, despite the distance from the mother house.

The second group of lands was further south and followed the Boulder Clay and gravel soils which fringed the moors to the west, from Greenhow to Boltby. The abbey possessions in this area were often considerable, especially in those places where granges had been established (e.g. Broughton, Morton).[2]

The third group was in Bilsdale and Ryedale a north-south trending valley penetrating deeply into the moors. The abbey itself was situated at the southern end of the valley.

---

[1] R.C. pp. 66-67, 221, 69-71, 216-17, 266. e.g. "... totam pischariam de Neuhusum ... ita quod nullus alius pischabitur in eadem aqua, nec se intromittet in alique de eadem pischaria, quantum aqua mea durat ..."
[2] e.g. at least 4 carucates in Gt. Broughton in 1299 each worth 40/- a year. *Inq.*, Y.A.S. III, p. 117.

PART TWO : SETTLEMENT

Walter de Espec had granted all Bilsdale to the monks as a later supplement to his somewhat small foundation grant. It was not long before they had established themselves along the whole of its length of ten miles. They had a remarkable concentration of granges in the valley and owned all the vill of Stainton and the manors of Great and Little Raysdale. Extensive pasture rights, especially near Raysdale, emphasised the importance of the valley, which was also a principal routeway between the Vale of Pickering and Cleveland.

But, the greatest concentration of lands was in the Vale of Pickering. Here three main groups were evident. The first and largest was in the western half of the Vale. The fertile limestone slopes of the Tabular Hills together with the extremely valuable meadow of the clay Vale provided very favourable conditions. Griff, Newlathes, Stiltons, Skiplam, and Welburn were situated on the limestone and were developed as predominantly arable granges which had the additional advantage of pasture land for working plough teams close by in such places as Rook Barugh, Waterholmes and Sunley.

The second concentration of lands was entirely in the central part of the Vale, in Pickering Marshes. The monks devoted much time to the reclamation and development of this area, once almost uninhabited marshland. They began early, soon after the King granted the area to them in 1158. After obtaining a large number of quitclaims from everybody with the least claim or right in the waste, they began to exploit it by the grange system. By 1301 it contained several of the abbey's most prosperous granges.[1]

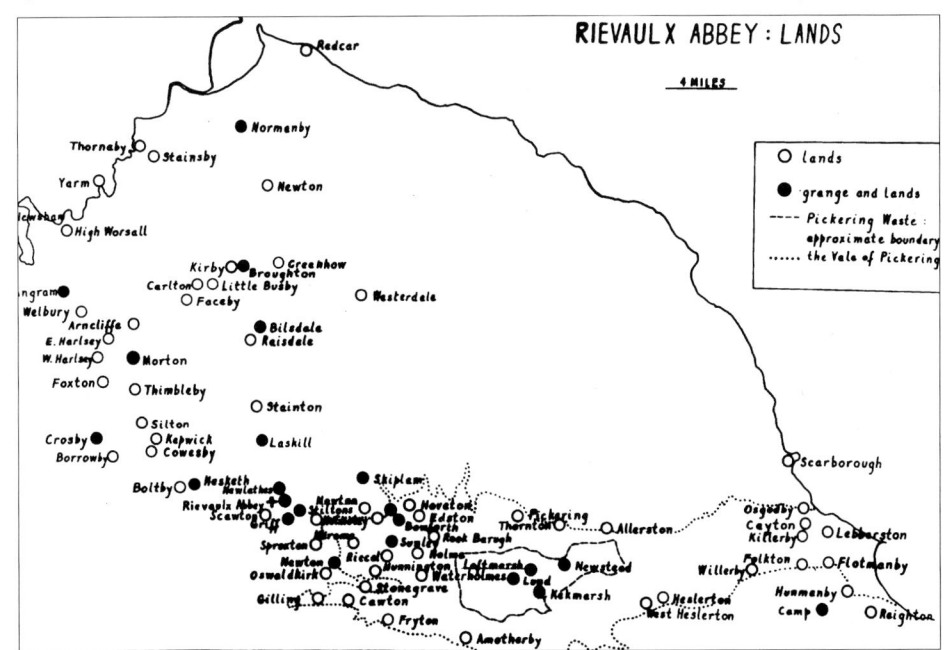

Figure 3.7 Rievaulx Abbey : Lands

---

[1] Loftmarsh contributed 25/0¾ to the 1/15 subsidy, Kekmarsh 38/7¾, Lund 15/6¼, Newhouse 16/0½. N.B. also 'cote' development.

The remaining group was at the extreme eastern end of the Vale, near the coast. Here the abbey owned lands which were situated in very different kinds of country, such as in the marshland of Folkton, Killerby and Cayton and the chalkland of Hunmanby and Camp. The nearness of the port of Scarborough was important to this group.[1] Although only one grange is known to have existed in this area it is likely that there was at least another, since the abbey was a considerable distance away and the extent of the lands owned in this district was quite large.[2]

4. *Other Monasteries*
Such was the distribution of the lands of the three main monasteries in the North-East. But to complete the picture brief mention must be made of the lands of Bridlington Priory, Byland Abbey and Malton Priory in this area.[3]

The larger part of Bridlington's lands lay outside the North-East, being mainly in Holderness. The Priory did, however, hold land in Scalby, north of Scarborough, and along the northern edge of the Wolds, for instance, in Burton Fleming, Ganton, Willerby, Hunmanby, and at Filey.

Byland had a few possessions in the Vale of Pickering (e.g. Deepdale grange) and more along the crest of the limestone Hambleton Hills (e.g. Murton grange, Byland grange and Sneilsworth). But the majority of its lands and granges were located immediately to the west and south-west of the abbey on the Boulder Clays and gravels at the entrance to the Coxwold gap. (e.g. Sutton Under Whitestone Cliff, Bagby, Kilburn, and the granges of Wildon, Osgodby, Estcambe, Westcambe, Balke, Mederby, Oldstead, Thorpe, Angrom and Baska.)

Malton Priory was established more firmly in the Vale of Pickering. Indeed, the greater part of its lands and granges were either here or on the Wolds. The neighbourhood of the Priory itself was the chief location of many lands especially in the vills which lay on the gravel bench on the southern margin of the Vale (e.g. Slingsby, Amotherby, Appleton-le-Street, Broughton, Swinton, Rillington, West Heslerton, Wintringham, Thorpe Basset). Others were situated above, on the chalk Wolds (e.g. Linton, Mowthorpe, Duggleby). On the northern side of the Vale were a series of holdings in Ebberston, Snainton, Thornton, Farmanby, Kingthorpe, Lockton, Newton, Sawden, Sinnington and Aislaby, while in the central Vale the Gilbertines were established at Kirby Misperton, South Holme and

---

[1] The burgesses of Scarborough despoiled the granges of Rievaulx of 78 qts. corn. *Hundred Rolls*, Vol. I, p. 131. N.B. that Burton Fleming, a grange of Bridlington Priory on the Wolds sold much of its corn etc. in Scarborough in the 14th century. York Diocesan Registry R.H. 60. Account of Bro. John Russel (1355-6).

[2] The known grange was Camp(dale) near Hunmanby. It had been one of the earliest of Rievaulx' granges. R.C. pp. 115-116. The possible granges were at Allerston and Cayton.

[3] Obtained from several sources, mainly:
  Abstract of the Bridlington Chart. Edited by W. T. Lancaster (1915)
    Malton Chartulary B.M. Cotton MS Claudius D XI
    Byland Chartulary B.M. Egerton MS 2823.
  Ministers Accounts at the Dissolution:
    Bridlington   P.R.O. S.C. 6/Hen. VIII /4430
    Malton   P.R.O. S.C. 6/Hen. VIII/4618
    Byland   P.R.O. S.C. 6/Hen. VIII/4550
    1301 Lay Subsidy, etc.

Edston. Their lands were not as scattered as those of Rievaulx and Whitby but were almost entirely within or around the basin-shaped Vale of Pickering, the furthest not more than twelve miles from the Priory.

Can any general conclusions be drawn about the character and significance of the distribution of monastic lands? Several facts immediately arrest the attention. Without exception the greatest concentration of lands and granges was always round the House. This is especially evident at Whitby and Rievaulx – both representative of Orders with very distinctive economic organisations. This distinction in itself would suggest that the reasons for such a distribution are unlikely to be economic, although later the tendency of the monks to expand and develop land nearest to the House at the expense of more distant lands had a strict economic relevance. Rather, the explanation seems to lie in the nature of the original foundation grants. These generally donated not only lands usually near the House (as at Whitby Abbey: Sourby, Brecca, Balby, Flore, Stakesby, Ruswarp, etc.) but an area, sometimes very large, as at Guisborough, with the House as its centre. Since the monastery was given extensive legal as well as property rights within such an area it was natural that subsequent expansion would be concentrated hereabouts.[1] The interesting fact is that irrespective of the physical conditions, which varied around each House, the same phenomenon resulted and became emphasised when the granges were later established. For instance, the concentration round Rievaulx Abbey is as well marked as that round Guisborough Priory and yet while the latter had a comparatively level lowland as its site, the former found itself in a narrow valley frowned upon by high limestone cliffs with scarcely room to construct an abbey let alone a concentration of lands.[2]

The second significant fact about the distribution maps is that when closely compared it is at once evident that the possessions of each house were generally confined to certain different areas. Whitby Abbey, for example, held the majority of its lands along the coastline. Guisborough's lands were almost exclusively found in Cleveland, while those of Rievaulx were mainly located in the western half of the Vale of Pickering, in Bilsdale and west of the Hambleton Hills.

The distribution of lands overlap only in two main areas: Cleveland and the Vale of Pickering. In the former, lands of Rievaulx, Byland, Guisborough, Fountains, Newburgh and Whitby coincided, while in the Vale, Malton, Rievaulx, Whitby, Byland, Newburgh and Bridlington had lands. It is interesting to notice that of all the regions within the North-East it was always these two – Cleveland and the Vale of Pickering – which drew to themselves the greatest economic activity, prosperity and population.[3]

Though the term, "spheres of influence", had not been invented it is evident that it was in operation here in medieval North-East Yorkshire especially in the great period of monastic expansion in the twelfth century. It was, too, a very conscious process, which geographical conditions, among other things, encouraged. Thus, the moorland, occupying

---

[1] "Concedo etiam eis in eadem villa burgagium, et feriam ad festum S. Hyldae, cum socha et sach, et tol et them, et infangentheof... " similar privileges elsewhere. Grant of Henry II W.C.I, pp. 147-149.
[2] In fact, the abbey had to be orientated north-south instead of the usual east-west because of the narrowness of the terrace between the river and the valley side.
[3] This is also clear from Domesday evidence and the Lay Subsidy of 1301.

the centre of the North-East, acted as the greatest stimulus to the development of spheres by holding the monasteries apart. The general agreement made between Rievaulx and Byland between 1154-67 illustrated the idea of monastic spheres very well.[1] In it the boundaries between their lands were guaranteed and particular reference made to grange boundaries. Limits of pasture rights were defined, and the right of Byland to hold and acquire lands in the eastern part of the Vale of Pickering was allowed by Rievaulx. It is obvious from this latter clause that both Houses regarded the eastern Vale as being pre-eminently Rievaulx's sphere. The final clause had a very twentieth century ring about it; it provided an arbitration device to be used in case of further controversy.

A similar, though more restricted agreement between Rievaulx and Fountain's Abbey defined the limits of their granges in Normanby.[2] The possession of the church and tithes of a particular vill seemed to have been the deciding factor in excluding one House to the advantage of another. At Willerby, for instance, Rievaulx disposed of certain land there to Bridlington who owned the church, and apparently made no further efforts to expand in this area – despite the fact that Rievaulx had licence to acquire land and pasture in the parish by gift or purchase (1170-84).[3]

It is significant that Rievaulx gave up its direct interest in Normanby as it had done in Willerby – both places where other Houses had granges. This leasing of property occurred not long after the lands had been acquired there. Thus, Rievaulx's land and pasture in Willerby was given them in 1152; the grant was confirmed in 1172, but only three years later the monks leased their property to the canons of Bridlington. At Normanby, they leased "omnes terras et pasturas cum piscaria et aqua de Taisa …" to Walter, parson of Eston, a nearby village. This occurred sometime between 1192 and 1199. It is interesting to note that the increment from the lease was to be used to buy land and pasture nearer to the abbey, "… per commune consilium tam monachorum quam Conversorum nostrorum empsimus in territorio de Sproxton … quinquaginta acras terrae arabilis, et pasturam ad centum oves et ad boves (48) in majorem fructum et utilitatem Domus nostrae".

It seems that where granges belonging to different Houses were sited very close together either special agreements had to be made (e.g. at Normanby, Hesketh and Old Byland) or one House had to abandon its interests in the area. Both Willerby and Normanby were a long way from Rievaulx Abbey and this, together with non-possession of the church, made relinquishment understandable. Generally, however, although one village was often the site of several different monastic holdings (e.g. this was very usual in the villages of the Vale of Pickering) it was very rare for there to be more than one

---

[1] R.C., pp. 176f.
   "…Porro domus quam aedificaverunt fratres Bellelandae apud Depedalam remanebit eis quiete, cum omnibus quae habent vel adquirere poterunt in his villis – scil. in Grisethorp, Hwallisgrava, Semara, Iretun et in Etun … de quibus nichil habebunt nisi per voluntatem monachorum Rievallensium …" (pp. 178). In Hotun etiam … constitutum est nichilominus ut de inceps Abbas vel aliquis frater unius Domus locum ad aedificandum non recipiat nisi prius alterius Domus Abbati et Cellerario fuerit ostensum ut communi consideratione ad pacem utriusque Domus fieri possit".

[2] R.C. pp. 175-176.
   " – quod grangia fratrum de Fontibus in Clivelanda stabit imperpetuum: similiter et grangia fratrum de Rievalle in eadem terra stabit in perpetuum, ita quod Rievallenses non transibunt versus fratres de Fontibus, nisi cum assensu illorum, nec fratres de Fontibus transibunt versus fratres de Rievalle, nisi cum assensu illorum …".

[3] E.Y.C. II, pp. 501-2. Rievaulx granted $10^{1}/_{2}$ acres of land with other tenements and pasture for 300 sheep, to Bridlington (1175) Rievaulx acquired the land, etc. in 1152.

grange to a village. Many Houses had granges in the same parishes, thus Malton had Kirby grange and Rievaulx had Lund grange both in Kirby Misperton parish, but more than a mile apart. In fact, the Cistercian Statutes had enacted that granges should be no nearer than a specific distance, and laymen were not to erect similar establishments within that distance. Even so, a glance at the maps will soon show that concentration of granges was very usual, especially in valuable agricultural areas. Out of over one hundred monastic granges in the North-East, however, less than perhaps half a dozen were sited in the same village (e.g. Normanby, Bilsdale (?), Ebberston). It will be shown below that several factors influenced the site of monastic granges.

A third point which arises from the distribution of the monastic lands is that they were situated predominantly on lowland. This might imply that arable cultivation would be the basis of monastic farming activity. But the common background which the moors gave to most of the monasteries must not be forgotten. Looking at the maps it can be seen that, regarding their setting in the region as a whole, the monasteries were each favoured in particular ways: Guisborough was well placed in relation to the River Tees, a very important routeway; Whitby Abbey, though shut in by the high moors, had its coastline; Rievaulx, Byland and Malton, though far from the sea, lay close to the main crossing point of east-west, north-south routes (i.e. Vale of Pickering, Vale of York).

Finally, something must be said about the types of settlement made by the monasteries. Briefly, they fell into two groups: lands in, and lands outside settled areas. The former comprised land in a vill, that is strips in the open field, or on the outskirts of a vill. In the North-East ownership of strips seems to have predominated (e.g. Guisborough Priory at Ormesby and Guisborough; Malton Priory in Broughton and Amotherby).[1] But settlement outside a vill was frequent among the Cistercians. Rievaulx, for instance, had 8 acres of "outland" in Givendale on the northern outskirts of Allerston. The suggestion made by Mr. Bishop that monasteries were mainly interested in strip land because of the waste it entitled them to outside the vill, may have relevance to this particular type of settlement.[2]

The monasteries sometimes colonised previously unsettled areas (e.g. Guisborough in Upper Eskdale and Glaisdale; Rievaulx in Bilsdale and Pickering Marshes) and occasionally settled on the sites of vills which had disappeared or, in the case of the Cistercians, had been destroyed. Rievaulx Abbey had such settlements at Griff, Skiplam and Stilton.

The distribution of such sites must, of course, have been determined mainly by the donor. But what determined him? It is likely that the large extent of waste in 1086 and after largely influenced the donor in making his decision. The coincidence between waste and monastic settlement at any rate suggests this.[3] But though early donors laid the basis of the monastic settlement it was not long before the monasteries developed their own policy which resulted in a selection from among their lands of those which they most

---

[1] Despite Professor Knowles's statement that, "the grange as a unit of agriculture stood outside the normal open-field strip cultivation" (*Religious Orders* I, p. 65) it is evident that many of the North-East granges originated from such strips. And, that even when largely consolidated, the grange lands might still lie in the open field, though not subject to the same feudal demands as village strip land was. How far did this contribute to the break-up of open field agriculture?
[2] T. A. M. Bishop "Assarting and the Growth of the Open Field" *Ec. H.R.* 6 (1935).
[3] The coincidence between granges and areas formerly waste was quite remarkable.

wanted to develop, consolidate and extend. Such a policy had purchase and exchange of lands as its main instruments. The grange system was its principal result. It is precisely because the granges rather than the lands of the monastery alone show this evidence of policy and selection that they are a better guide to the real factors which influenced monastic settlement. How important were physical factors? Were they more or less important than economic factors such as routes, markets, salt pans, fisheries? If not, what conditions were considered when a grange was established? How was this unique form of settlement brought about, and what was its contribution to the medieval settlement pattern of the North-East?

PART TWO : SETTLEMENT

4 THE MONASTIC GRANGE

1. *The Monastic Grange*

The Oxford English Dictionary defines the grange as "an outlying farmhouse with barns, etc., belonging to a religious establishment, or a feudal lord, where crops and tithes in kind were stored"[1] T. A. M. Bishop goes further when he says, "The term *grangia* strictly means a granary, and is naturally extended to the land from which produce was derived; we may think of the grange for the present, as a large and – so the derivation of the word suggests – predominantly arable farm"[2] Both definitions are unsatisfactory. The first fails to emphasise the grange as an active instrument of economic policy and farming; the second over emphasises the arable cultivation of the grange. The monastic grange was not a passive storehouse but an active instrument in the exploitation of the land; and although there was an arable basis to all granges their functions varied with their situations, so that in one place the grange might be an arable farm, elsewhere a unit based on pastoral or industrial activities.

In the North-East, where the monastic grange was so well developed and so much part of the scene, its many sided character can be clearly seen. Before discussing the distribution of the granges and their effect upon the general settlement pattern something must be said about the differences between granges in the area. Such

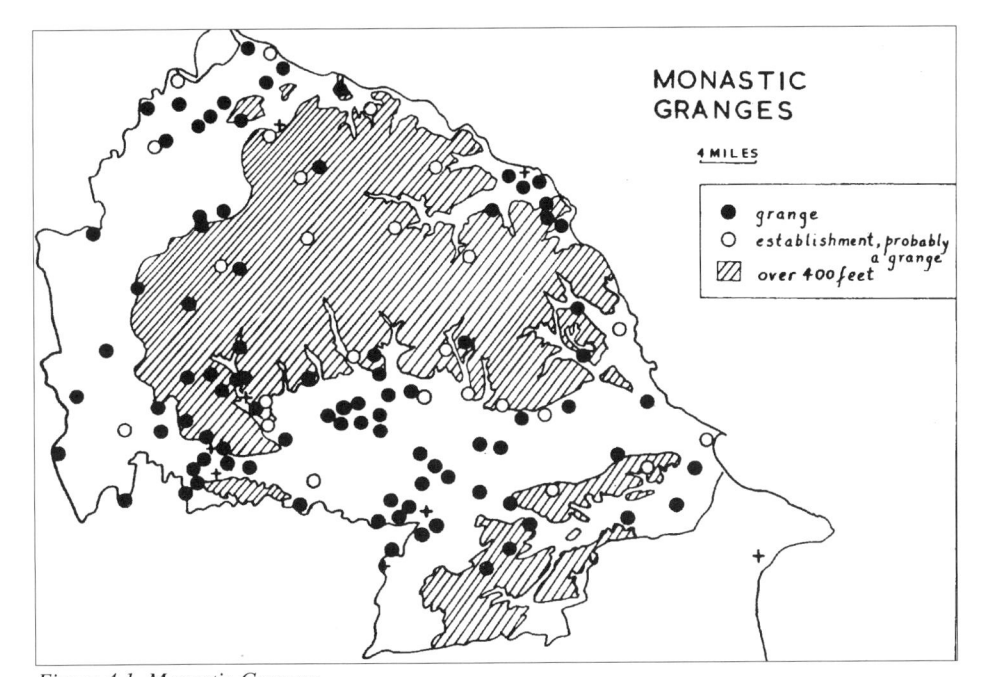

Figure 4.1 Monastic Granges

---

[1] 1901 Edition. Volume iv, p. 353.
[2] T. A. M. Bishop "Monastic Granges in Yorkshire", *E.H.R.* April 1936.

differences varied according to several factors, for instance, the particular religious order involved, the diversity of lands on a monastic estate, and the function of the grange.

Though never rigidly specialising the grange was always biased towards a particular function. The granges of Byland, Guisborough and Rievaulx in the Tees Mouth area were predominantly occupied with fisheries and salt-panning. In contrast, the moorland granges were almost wholly concerned with sheep farming, as in Westerdale, or with cattle farming as in Bilsdale and Upper Eskdale. In Glaisdale, the Guisborough canons were engaged in mining iron ore, so that another type of grange evolved.

The size, structure and staffing of granges emphasised such differences and, indeed, largely derived from them. At Westerdale on the moors, for instance, Rievaulx had only two bovates of land attached to its grange but the amount of pastureland was very extensive. Griff grange, on the other hand, contained 490 acres of arable and sent its plough beasts to Sproxton Cote, a mile to the south, for pasture.[1] The actual site of the grange, as well as the function, helped to determine its size. The monks of Rievaulx had a free hand within Pickering waste, Hesketh waste, Crosby marsh and Killerby marsh and could, within broad limits, make the granges as big as they wished. It was the speed of their reclamation in such areas which determined the actual size of the grange, though no doubt they had ideas on the ideal size for a holding to be most easily worked. The canons of Guisborough had fewer areas where expansion was so easy. Their granges were mostly sited in, or near to vills (e.g. Marton, Ormesby, Marske). However, in Glaisdale and Upper Eskdale they had large land grants which allowed them more freedom in the expansion of grange land.

Function, situation, size of original donation and opportunities for consolidation of scattered strips or unlimited expansion had all a decisive influence on the structure of the monastic grange. Such factors caused the variations between granges. But so too did the different religious orders concerned. The part played by the Cistercians in the development of the grange system was substantial, but it has been over emphasised at the expense of other orders. The grange was not the sole prerogative of the Cistercians, although it achieves its clearest expression on their lands. The Benedictines of Whitby Abbey, for instance, frequently refer to their granges (after 1301) and it is clear that they worked a system something similar to the Cistercians.[2] But since the organisation of the order was different, their granges had differences.

The monks at Fyling, Hackness, Hawsker granges had to provide for storage of tithes extracted, and a larger complement of servants was employed to deal with the large scale rent collecting and organisation of works due from abbey tenants.[3] The Benedictine *grangia* seemed to be a blend between the Cistercian grange, a manor house, and a cell. Certainly the numerous household officials and the semi-independent status of such

---

[1] R.C., p. 67, pp. 312f., pp. 43-44. "*Praeterea concessi eis communem pasturam animalibus suis quibus colunt terram suam in Grif in silva de Scaltuna a Brochesheved usque ad divisas inter Scaltunam et Sproxtunam… .*"
[2] Referred to as granges in 1301 subsidy (Y.A.S. 21 [1897] ed. W. Brown), and Abbey accounts of 1394.
[3] See for example the abbey accounts in 1366 (in *Chapters of the Black Monks*, ed. W. A. Pantin, vol. iii (Camden Series vol. liv, 1937) and 1394-96 (in W.C. ii. pp. 553-625).

grangia caused them to be more elaborately developed than the Cistercian grange, which sometimes was a simple wooden lodge with a staff of three.[1]

The strong system of centralisation which the New Orders had developed was absent from the Benedictines, at least on the Whitby Abbey granges. At Hackness and Middlesbrough, for example, there is plenty of evidence to show how independent they were of the abbey. Peter de Hertlipool, for instance, collected the goods of the monastery at Middlesbrough for his own use, when he was bursar. Thomas de Hawkesgarth, monk at the same place, rebelled against the abbot and refused to obey his orders (14th century). He put the goods of the abbey to his own use and with other accomplices took the common seal of the monastery and used it to obtain 300 florins. Finally, he arrived at the abbey and stirred up the prior and half of the convent against the abbot, and then had the effrontery to complain to the Archbishop against the abbot's dictatorial powers.[2] Such was the autonomy of the Whitby granges, establishments which Geraldus Cambrensis deplored and vigorously attacked in his writings.[3]

Cistercian Statutes and Gilbertine Rules did not allow such autocratic powers to develop in their granges. Frequent reports had to be made by the Granger to his abbey and at Malton the Prior supervised all business dealings very strictly.[4] The New Order granges were in much closer contact with their abbey, on the Cistercian granges, for instance, the lay brother in charge had to report to the abbey each night, except on the most distant granges (e.g. Newsham, Normanby, Broughton, Camp …).[5]

The staffing of the granges varied too. Those of Rievaulx and Byland had lay brethren to work them. If the suspiciously high number of 640 monks and *conversi* at Rievaulx in Ailred's time is correct it would go far to explaining the rapid expansion of the house in the middle twelfth century.[6] As at Byland the lay response was immediate and almost excessive: " … those who were restless in the world to whom no house of religion gave entrance, came to Rievaulx, the mother of mercy, and found the gates open and entered by them freely … on feast days you might see the church crowded with brethren like bees in a hive unable to move forward because of the multitude clustered together, and compacted into one angelic body …"[7] Large numbers would be recruited, too, from the evicted villagers in such places as Welburn and Hoveton. Here Roger de Mowbray gave his villeins the right to go or stay as they pleased, when he gave the vills to Rievaulx. No doubt many stayed to work the grange land.[8] But on the pastoral granges the staff required was smaller. At Westerdale, for example, one lay brother was in charge of two servants. The same number operated the horse farm at Middleton-in-Teesdale.

---

[1] e.g. Rievaulx's holdings in
　A. Westerdale: lodge 15′ × 15′. Brother and two servants in charge
　B. Teesdale: house, 10 perches × 20′ and 5 acres of land. Brother and two servants in charge of horses there. R.C. p. 157.
[2] This autonomy comes out very well, from the enquiry into the affairs of the abbey in 1366, see C.B.M., pp. 63-68.
[3] *Speculum Ecclesiae* (Rolls Series) iv, p. 102, 114. On wealth and luxury of Benedictines *Itinerarium Kambriae* vi, p. 41.
[4] See Gilbertine Rules in *Monasticon Anglicanum* vi, part 2, pp.v-lix.
[5] *Institution es capituli generalis* in *Nomast. Cist.* (1892)
[6] Walter Daniel says that Ailred (1147-67) " … doubled all things in it – monks, conversi, laymen, farms, lands, and every kind of equipment…. Hence it was that the father left behind him at Rievaulx, when he returned to Christ, one hundred and forty monks and five hundred conversi and laymen". *Vita Ailredi* (Nelson's Medieval Classics, London, 1950), p. 38.
[7] *Loc. cit.*
[8] Not always the case. Examples of displaced peasantry in Revesby . (Lincs.) and Old Byland. See below, p. 64-65.

At Malton and Guisborough granges hired workers were more important, although lay brethren were also employed. In addition, many grants of homage and service of villeins by their lords showed that both priories had large numbers of workers actually attached to them in the same way as the feudal lord had his villeins. Appendix I shows the numbers of hired workers on Malton granges in 1244. The numbers are often quite large, especially at Swinton, Rillington and the Priory itself. At Mowthorpe the yearly total was high, while had the Wintringham figures been given they would probably have exceeded all the rest, since arable farming was so much more important on this Wold grange (11 ploughs). A distinct connection existed between workers and tofts. It seems that the canons at Malton and Guisborough made it their business to acquire tofts to house their workers, for in such cases no land is attached to the toft. Often the canons of Malton may have caused houses to be built for their workers. Several entries in their chartulary relate to new tofts, variously described as built on, or not yet built on. These are most numerous in the vills where the numbers of hired workers was largest, as might be expected (see appendix). Thus it appears that, whatever the religious order involved, the establishment of a grange at a particular place eventually brought about the entire reorientation of that place and its people so that they were compelled to adjust themselves to the conditions and demands which the grange imposed.

The staff of the Whitby Abbey granges was generally larger and contained a more elaborate hierarchy of servants than was usual elsewhere. This organisation on a household basis may have contributed to the development of independence, already stressed.

It was especially well marked at Hackness. No doubt the frequent visits of the abbot, especially in the 14th century, necessitated a larger staff. It was a usual thing for the abbot and monks to visit the granges "*pro solaciis suis*".[1] Indeed they exceeded themselves in zeal, it seems, in the early part of the 14th century, for both the visitations of 1320 and 1366[2] accused them of taking seculars and hunting dogs with them when they made their frequent visits. The Bailiff or Reeve was the Benedictine equivalent of the New Order Granger, and yet, in fact, his tasks being so various made him much more. He had to superintend rent collection and tithe gathering, and see that the villeins' services were fulfilled or their commutation paid, among many other duties. His expenses were often high. At Seamer, for instance, where tithe collection was his main job, they amounted to more than £13 in six months (1394-95); at Ayton and Ingleby the amount was £7. 6. 4. for the same period.[3]

It has been essential to establish the real meaning of the monastic grange in the North-East and to show in what ways it varied. The monastic grange was, basically, a farm established under many varying conditions and directed towards varying ends. But it was always an active exploiter of the area in which it found itself, whether in an arable, pastoral, industrial or administrative capacity. It was differently composed according to the different orders establishing it, but with all, in the North-East, it was a principal, widespread and effective instrument of economic policy.

---

[1] Whitby Abbey accounts *op. cit.* Financial Statement (1366), *op. cit.*
[2] W.C. ii. No. 600.
[3] W.C. ii. pp. 616-620.

2. Distribution of Monastic Granges

There has been a tendency in the past to regard the northern monasteries of England like a hermit crab, buried away in a moorland shell, happily getting rich on the vast proceeds of sheep farming; isolated alike from laymen and lowland. Such a conception is false. Though the monasteries played a vital role in the colonisation of uninhabited areas, their main efforts and activities were in already settled regions. Despite the larger part of the North-East being occupied by rugged moorland, often more than 1000 ft. high, monastic granges were concentrated mainly in the lowland. In particular, the western half of the Vale of Pickering, and the Cleveland Plain attracted the greater proportion. The granges established within the moorlands were more limited in number, but because of that, perhaps, their significance was enhanced. Such granges were created in the sheltered dales, for instance, Bilsdale and upper Eskdale.

Generally, the distribution of granges followed the pattern of lay settlement though by no means always identical with it. For example, although the Vale of Pickering was a concentrated area of lay settlement the monastic granges here were often well away from the villages-in Pickering Waste or on the limestone slopes of the Tabular Hills (Loftmarsh, Kekmarsh, Lund, Newplace, Griff, Stiltons, Skiplam).[1] Invariably the granges were sited in extremely good – often the best – geographical conditions. That is to say, when their sites are studied as they existed in medieval times it is evident that consciously or unconsciously the monks selected the most favourable sites in terms of accessibility to the mother house, to markets or ports or routes; of soil fertility, relief, proximity to meadow, pasture, and so on. A few examples may make this close adaptation to environment more evident.

The fertile limestone soils of the gently sloping Tabular Hills were particularly attractive to monastic granges. Fig. 4.2 shows, for instance, that five of Rievaulx's principal granges were sited on them – Newlathes, Griff, Stiltons, Skiplam, and Sproxton. These granges were all situated close to the valleys which cut through the limestone dip slope at regular intervals. Griff and Sproxton were near Ryedale, for example; Stiltons and Newlathes close by Etton Gill, and Skiplam on the edge of Kirkdale. Two of Byland's granges – Murton and Old Byland grange were similarly sited on the limestone to the west of Ryedale. Several granges of St. Mary's, York (Benedictine) emphasised, too, the value of a limestone site, although their granges, unlike those of Rievaulx and Byland, were in or near to already existing vills of Spaunton and Appleton le Moor.

The advantages were clear: the soils were potentially fertile and former use by laymen had been limited. In fact, as Domesday suggests parts of the area might have still required clearance of woodland.[2] Such conditions especially suited Rievaulx Abbey:- the extent of lay settlement was at a minimum; the opportunities for large scale expansion were there; the abbey itself was easily accessible being no more than half a dozen miles from the most

---

[1] For pattern of lay settlement use Domesday maps and the map of the 1301 subsidy. Compare these with the three maps of monastic lands and the map showing monastic granges. Observe overlap in Cleveland and Vale of Pickering.

[2] e.g. in Walter Espec's charter to the abbey frequent mention is made of the hays of Griff and Stiltons. The grant of Gundreda de Mowbray in Skiplam had made provision for assarting by the monks " ... *ad colendum et sartandum et utendum in omnibus sicut suis propriis*". R.C., p. 31.

easterly grange of Skiplam. Further, the original land grants in this area were favourable to expansion and development. The monks had "...*terram de Grif, ubi sunt quatuor carrucatae, et terram de Thillestona, ubi sunt quinque carrucatae, cum omnibus appenticiis et rebus eisdem terris pertinentibus, in boscho et plano et pastura et pratis et aquis ...*", and a much wider area, comprising much of the limestone slope between the Rye and Etton Gill. This was granted by Walter Espec at the foundation (1131).[1] The monks had a larger area given to them at Skiplam by Gundreda de Mowbray (1138-43). This allowed for expansion since the grant included Farndale Head and Bransdale-about 18 square miles of dale pastureland.[2]

It must not be imagined that the monks were beginning colonisation in an area entirely unused. Although the extent of settlement and cultivation was small it had existed. Griff and Stiltons, for example, were vills before 1069 but in 1086 were waste. Presumably the monk's grant here was of land which had gone out of cultivation. Their task would be one of re-establishment rather than colonisation of new land. It was a decided advantage to have such a tried starting point. At Skiplam, too, although the greater part of the area had never been settled or tilled, there is evidence to show that the monks began their efforts from land already or recently cultivated. Gundreda's grant, for instance, included "*de culta terra*", as well as a grant "... *ubi culta terra deficit versus aquilonem*".[3] Of course, the subsequent work of the monks in all these places did result in a very great extension of the cultivated area. But it is worthwhile to point out that the Cistercians-so called solitaries-did in fact owe something to previous lay efforts. In fact, it was largely the success or failure of lay farmers in a particular area which helped the monks to see the potentialities it offered them.

GRANGES ON THE LIMESTONE SLOPES

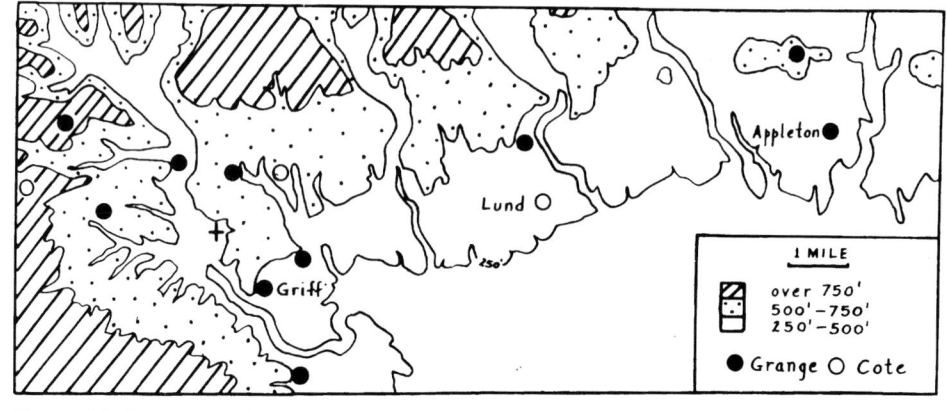

Figure 4.2 Granges on the Limestone Slopes

---

[1] R.C., pp. 16-21.
[2] *Ibid.*, pp. 30-31.
[3] *Loc. cit.*

But, to continue the advantages of granges sited on the limestone. The dip slope had a well-trodden routeway at its foot which joined together the line of villages east and west of Pickering. The granges had easy access to two types of pasture- moorland and valeland. Skiplam, for instance, had extensive pasture in the moorland dales only a few miles north. There was the rough pasture (*saltum*) of Farndale Head and common pasture in Farndale and Bransdale. It had, too, the meadow of the clayland at its disposal. This was even nearer, being no more than 3 miles to the south. The plough teams from Skiplam could easily pasture at Welburn, where the monks had common pasture rights, or at Rook Barugh, Muscoates, and several other places, just as the animals from Griff went to Newton grange for pasture.[1] The limestone hills had then a great deal to recommend them to the observant eyes of the monks.

So, too, had other areas: in Bilsdale, as Figure 4.3 clearly shows, a series of granges and subsidiary animal houses (cotes) were set up.[2] Here again conditions were extremely favourable. The abbey and its granges were easily accessible to one another along what was the principal routeway from the Vale of Pickering into Cleveland. As well as facilitating internal administration on the estates, this accessibility was useful to the Italian wool merchants inspecting flocks, or collecting wool. Rievaulx owned the larger part of Bilsdale which had been given to them by Walter Espec. Other monastic activity was at a minimum here and lay settlement was only just beginning to establish itself in the moorland dales.[3] The dale itself, not entirely cleared of woodland, provided a region of splendid water meadows, while around it the moors gave summer pastures (e.g. Cold Moor, Raisdale). The iron working in the dale provided another stimulus and another variation in the economic structure of the Bilsdale granges.[4]

A final example of the close adaptation which monastic granges showed to geographical conditions can be quoted from the Malton Priory granges. The adherence of these granges to the narrow gravel bench which lies along the southern margin of the Vale of Pickering was remarkable. Wintringham, Rillington, Sutton, Swinton, Amotherby, and Broughton granges were all located on it either at the foot of the chalk scarp or the base of the limestone slope of the Howardian Hills along the spring line. The only roadway in the southern Vale ran along the bench, linking together a string of prosperous villages and, most important, to the granges, it converged on Malton Priory. This was important because of the extreme centralisation which persisted in Gilbertine monasteries: the Prior had to check all business dealings the granges might make and, "The whole of the wool of any Gilbertine house was ordered ... to be collected from the various granges and brought together at the abbey without any separation of the wool or of any fleeces or woolfells".[5] Accessibility was a particularly significant feature in New Order monasteries whose centralisation contrasted with the devolution practised on most Black Monk estates.

---

1   Common pasture for demesne pigs of Newton and Griff and for 15 beasts to sustain their works of Griff R.C., p. 293.
2   Map constructed from information given in 1301 Lay Subsidy, Rievaulx and Byland Chartularies.
3   Kirkham Priory had goods etc., temporal property in Bilsdale, which in 1301 contributed 48/3 to the 1/15 Subsidy.
4   Dissolution Accounts show that in 1538 much of Ryedale and Bilsdale was covered in woodland.
5   Gilbertine Rules in *Monasticon Ang.*

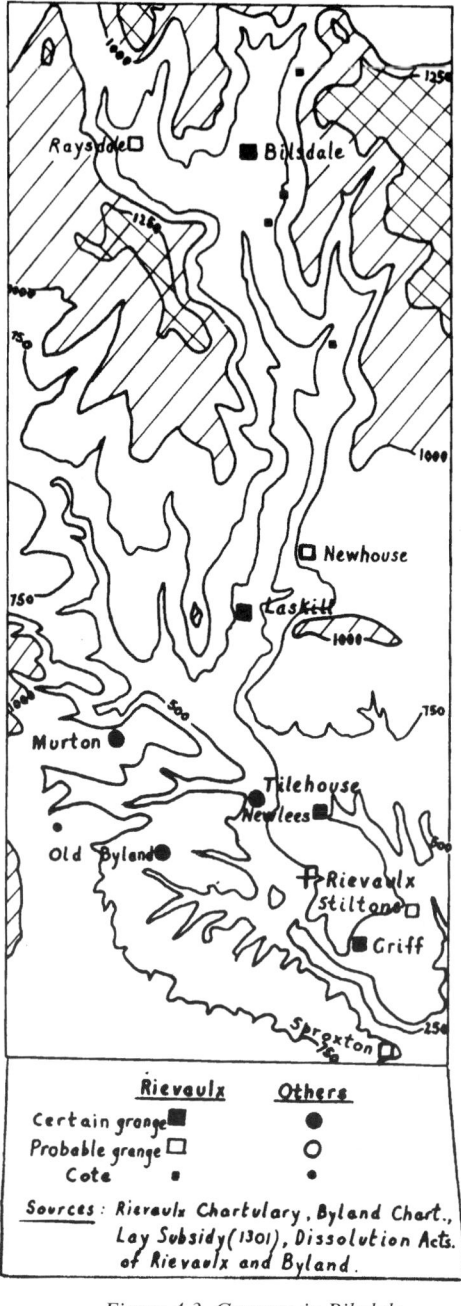

Figure 4.3 Granges in Bilsdale

Malton Priory and its granges were a supreme example of this. The east-west route along the scarp foot converged on the Malton gap which, in turn, led directly into the Vale of York and to York itself; the River Derwent, navigable below Malton was an additional route, used for example to transport wool to Hull: over the Wolds lay the wool road from Malton to Wansford and thence by river to Hull; and not least was access to Pickering, north of Malton, by one of the few bridges crossing the Rye. Such advantages, together with the natural fertility of their site, placed the granges in an unsurpassed position. The nearness of Wold pasture and Valeland meadow added to it.

No mention can be made of the Malton granges which clustered round the Wold wool route; of the Guisborough granges in the East Riding which were similarly situated round the southern extremity of the wool route and the navigable head-waters of the River Hull; or of the Guisborough granges in Glaisdale and Teesmouth-in the former near the iron deposits and fast flowing becks, in the latter grouped relevantly to the areas of salt panning. They and others too, were all significantly adapted to special circumstances, each in its way notable. Notable because such adaptations resulted in particular economic responses – the predominance of arable granges on the limestone and sandy gravel, for instance; the stress given to animal husbandry in the dale granges. But how far did the monasteries consider such factors as accessibility, fertility, and site when they wished to establish a grange? What other factors were considered? Were they relatively more important than the geographical?

3. *Grange Establishment*

Indeed, several other factors were of the utmost consequence to those monasteries which founded their granges among settled communities. The first was quite obviously the nature and extent of the original land grant in a particular place. Rievaulx was granted all the vills of Stainton, Hoveton, Welburn, and apparently the same at Griff and Stiltons. It was natural that any idea of grange establishment would focus on such places where the extent of property owned was large and the freedom for development greatest. Guisborough similarly had all Kirkleatham (9 carucates) given to them by Robert de Brus in his foundation grant, and Whitby, too, had many entire vills donated to them, many of which later had granges there e.g. Fyling, Hawsker, Stakesby, Hackness.[1]

The location of such donations, then, partly influenced the selection of a grange site. But much more important was the possession of the church and tithes of a place. This was important mainly to the Canons and Black Monks rather than the Cistercians, although even they were anxious to secure tithe rights over certain properties, anxious enough to pay for the right. They paid 2 marks to the church of Leake for Crosby tithes, for example, and contributed a yearly sum to Scawton church for the tithes of Scawton and Oswaldhenges.[2] It is noticeable that most of these rights were acquired very early-tithes of Griff and Stiltons were in the Foundation Grant (1131), those of Scawton before 1154, and Crosby tithes about 1153.

---

[1] G.C. i., pp.1-5. W.C. i, p.2f.
[2] R.C., p.27: p.167.

T. A. M. Bishop has mentioned how the possession of tithes and impropriated churches could be "the chief factor in deciding where they (the canons) should acquire temporal property".[1] How could this be? The process is quite clear: those religious who found themselves in possession of the tithes of vills would need agents or officials on the spot to superintend tithe-collection. They would also require a storehouse for corn, hay, wood, wool, and so on, which constituted the tithe.[2] As the products of the tithe increased the canons would want to sell the surplus, which they did not need for themselves. This was most easily accomplished on the spot, especially in those places some distance from the Priory where cartage was a burden. So it was that what began as a granary acquired the wider role of a disposal point. Where the monastery also held extensive lands in the same vill it was a natural process for the administrative functions to be conducted from the same place, so that what originated as a granary or barn became elaborated to accommodate monastic officials and to conduct the monastery's business in that particular area. As monastic lands increased and became more consolidated by a distinct and often a vigorous policy they were worked by the canons dwelling on the spot-the granary had become a grange.

The granges of Whitby Abbey and Guisborough Priory appear to have evolved along these lines.[3] An attempt has been made in Appendix 2 to show the places where both monasteries possessed church and tithes and where granges were established. The correspondence is almost complete. Whitby Abbey owned church/chapel and tithes in all places where granges were established. The canons had appropriated churches and tithes in at least seven of the vills where they had granges.[4] But one important question must be answered before it can be stated that tithe ownership played a vital part in grange establishment. Which came first, the possession of church and tithe or the grange? Obviously, if the grange preceded the tithe then the theory is wrong. Fortunately, the dates when the churches and tithes were acquired is known precisely for Whitby and Guisborough. In both cases the foundation grants include the gifts. William de Percy donated Whitby Church and its many associate chapels as well as the two churches of Hackness, to the abbey, about 1087. Robert de Brus donated the churches of Marske, Kirkburn, Skelton, Danby, Uppleatham, Stainton, Levington, Hert, and Stranton to the canons in 1119, and in the same document confirmed the donation of Ormesby, Marton and Acklam churches made by his men. Clearly, the possession of the churches preceded the establishment of the granges, and the evolution already mentioned probably occurred.

The process no doubt gained great stimulus when the Cistercians came into the North-East and began to establish their granges-often with great rapidity, in contrast to the slower evolution of Benedictine granges. But did the Cistercians owe anything to the

---

[1] *op. cit.*, p.205.
[2] Tithes were sometimes paid in church, Addy, *Church and Manor* (1913), p. 196. This might have contributed to the strong connection between Grange site and church land on the Guisborough estates (see below).
[3] Malton Priory not so, except perhaps at Wintringham.
[4] NB. Hamilton Thomson says "This close connexion of parish churches with Augustinian priories was due to the ideal entertained at an earlier date, of establishing such houses as centres from which parochial ministrations could be supplied to the parish churches of the neighbourhood", *Register of Archbishop Greenfield* (Surtees Society 151, 153), volume iii, Introduction xlii.

Benedictines in this respect? The monks of Whitby had presumably been developing their grange system with a fifty year start over the Cistercians. It may be that the monks of Rievaulx discovered a functioning grange system in the North-East when they arrived in 1131-not, perhaps, as systematic or coherent as their own was to be, but even so in active existence.

But important as the possession of the church was in this way, it had other advantages which favoured the establishment of a grange. The grant of a church almost always included a grant of associated land-sometimes quite considerable. One carucate was given with Ormesby church, for example.[1] Such land was usually the nucleus of the monastic possessions in the vill because it had been the first donation they had there. Consequently, many granges when established were built on this land. On the Guisborough estates for instance, at Ormesby "*Mansio nostra sita est super terram Ecclesiae, et pertinet*"; at Thornaby – "*ad terram Ecclesiae, in qua Grangia nostra sita fuit*"; at Stainton – "*Grangia nostra et aedificamenta sita sunt in parte tofti terrae Ecclesiae*"; and again in Kirkburn " ... *habemus mansum nostrum cum grangia situm in terra Ecclesiae, cum toftis quae spectant ad* 4 *bov. terrae in Suthbrune, quae sunt dos Ecclesiae...*"[2] This correspondence between grange site and church land on the Guisborough Priory estates is remarkable. What was its cause? Undoubtedly the church land being the primary donation would become the nucleus for further expansion in the vill. It was suitable for this because it often was not scattered in strips but was one compact unit.[3] This offered an excellent basis for monastic farming, whose main object, if it was to be economical and successful, was to work land which was compact. Strip farming might have been all right for the ordinary villager who provided for his own sustenance and no more, but for the highly populated monastery something more efficient was required. That is why the canons' policy was to "concentrate monastic demesnes in certain vills, to consolidate them within those vills in certain places in the fields and eventually to enclose them and hold them in severality".[4] Now, in beginning such a policy the principal object would be to acquire land already consolidated and then to extend this where possible. The church land seemed to fall into this category.

The key thought in the canons' minds was this: are the possibilities of consolidating our scattered lands in this vill good? Shall we be able to consolidate and expand quickly and effectively given this start? Certainly the ways open to them were many and various. Besides straightforward donation of lands, consolidation could be achieved by exchange or purchase of land, by loaning money in return for land or by paying off mortgage due on land usually held by the Jews. All these methods can be seen working on the estates of most of the North-Eastern monasteries as a means to the end – the consolidation and expansion of monastic demesne. Malton Priory, for example, acquired large grants in Little Edston and Levisham (where they had established granges) by paying off debts

---

[1] G.C. No's 477, 478
[2] Priory Rent Roll (late 13th century) G.C. ii, pp. 412-450.
[3] Due, perhaps, to the fact that a continuity of possession was maintained on church land: "although a rector should die the church however does not fall from his seysine of anything, of which the rector died seysed in the name of his church". Bracton. *De Legibus Angliae* iii, p. 521. Rolls Series 70.
[4] Bishop, *op. cit.*, p. 202.

which Ralph de Bolebeck and William Redburn owed the Jews. In this way the canons acquired 6 bovates in Edston and in Levisham pasture for 130 animals, sites for sheep folds and an animal house as well as 32 acres of cultivated land.[1]

The clearest policy of consolidation by purchase and exchange of land was seen on the Malton and Guisborough estates. At Ormesby, Barnaby and Yearby-the three largest and richest granges of Guisborough Priory-consolidation was still a very active policy in the middle thirteenth century. Phrases such as "next to the canons' land", "next to the yard of their grange", "at the rear of their grange", "all my land extending from the canons' grange to . . ." recur persistently. The policy is difficult to illustrate because it was apparently very painstaking and lands acquired were often small parcels, but acquisitions from Peter de Ormesby provided a typical example.[2] He gave "all my land called Tunge next to the canons' land at Neudic. All my land called Halfarige, lying between the canons' land and land of Walter de Percy. All my land in Sandwath (etc.) near the two bovates which I previously gave them to the west." He later continued "granting" adjacent lands – "1 bovate at the south of the 2 bovates above, 1 acre near Sandwath, 2 acres near Walter de Percy's land, 1 acre in Peselandes lying between the lands of the canons, 2 acres in Langelandes near that which I previously gave them, $1/2$ acre at Scortesandes and 3 roods at Hueflat, all near land which I previously gave them" ...[3] The canons acquired land nearby from many others too. For example, Roger, chaplain of Ormesby, quitclaimed all his rights in Peselandes; Robert de Ormesby gave his lands here, Ralph de Cleveland gave 1 acre here, his brother Henry all his land in Peselandes, and so on.[4] Consolidation was a definite and planned process but apparently very slow.

Apparent donations of land were often in effect purchases by the Priory. And laymen may indeed have made quite a business out of such transactions. Alexander de Pugeys, for example, a native of Guisborough town obtained land from his fellow townsmen by purchase or exchange and then passed it over to the Priory:

"All my land of Elnetro which I bought from William de Lyum.

2 acres $1^{1}/_{2}$ roods which I bought from Ymana Bigot.

2 acres 1 rood which I bought from Nicholas Fitz Richard.

3 roods bought from Eustace fitz Eustace in Adthewaldes.

3 roods 1 acre given to me by Simon Prior in exchange for land in Langecroft ..."[5]

It seemed that Alexander may well have been an agent for the Priory, buying land for them.[6] It is a little too much to expect him to donate all this land which had cost him a great deal of money to acquire.

---

[1] Malton Chartulary B.M. Cotton MS Claudius D XI folios 113-115 and 116-118.
[2] I have an idea that if the open field system could be worked out for some of these places, particularly Guisborough and Ormesby,from later materials such as 17th and 18th century Terriers and later Tithe Maps, then a great deal of this consolidation policy could be visually portrayed. Certainly the chartularies give much information about field names, etc. Whether later evidence could be tied up with them remains unknown
[3] G.C. Nos. 489, 490, 494, 495, 497 etc.
[4] G.C. Nos. 542, 527, 520 etc.
[5] Ibid., No. 107. See also Nos. 23, 24, 33, 98, 111, 134 for real nature of his transactions.
[6] One complaint made against the canons after Wickwane's Visitation in 1280 was directed at " . . . Agents who rapidly became enriched by managing their (the canons') manors /who/ were to be removed at once' . Introduction to volume ii G.C. p. xv.

On the Whitby estates, too, a similar process of consolidation was well marked, especially during Abbot Roger's time. It was mainly in two areas that the abbey consolidated its lands-near to Middlesbrough and in those vills near to the abbey itself.

Despite Mr. Bishop's statement that "Granges were created very rapidly" ... it seems that, at least on the Guisborough granges the process was more gradual.[1] The grange itself might be set up quickly but its essence – a compact amount of land – was not so speedily acquired. But the monasteries possessed the continuity of administration and the financial power to follow through a land consolidation policy no matter how long it took. Sometimes it could be accomplished quickly: Malton Priory, for example, spent over £500 on land purchases between 1244-57 and at least 135 bovates, according to the Chartulary, were acquired during William de Ancaster's reign (c.1234-1256).[2] In one year alone over £162 was spent (1251). Fortunately the nature and success of this policy can be estimated from some details of Priory lands collected for the Norwich Taxation in 1254.[3] This shows that the vast sums of money had not been spent haphazardly: a great deal of consolidation had been achieved on the estates where granges were located. At Swinton grange, for example, out of 26^1/$_2$ bovates owned by the priory in the vill 8 lay together in the mill culture and 10 together in another culture. The remaining 8 bovates lay elsewhere in two parcels of 4. At Sutton grange all 16 bovates lay together and only 2^1/$_2$ acres were elsewhere. At Rillington grange 21 out of 22 bovates lay together. At Hutton grange 9 bovates were together and 1 bovate lay scattered in acres.[4] Invariably those places where granges were located in 1254 showed a high degree of consolidation of lands.

"Several of the largest granges of Malton Priory were not in existence in the period 1244-57",[5] but appear by 1301. Why is this? Why, for instance, was Amotherby a grange by 1301 but not in 1257? Is it because consolidation of lands here had not gone far enough? The evidence of the Norwich Taxation suggests this to be the reason. The Priory held very scattered lands in the vill in 1254 – 3 bovates in West Field, 8 bovates in East Field, ^{1}/$_2$ bovate variously distributed, and 14^1/$_2$ acres in many places – 1 acre on Anger, 1 acre abutting on Estfeldcroft, 1^1/$_2$ roods by Lyngmor, 2 acres in sellions on the west part of the vill.[6] This is a great contrast to those places which were granges in 1254. Amotherby and Broughton seemed to be in the latter stages of consolidation. The fulfilment of the process would have occurred within at most twenty years. Until then the lands there would be administered and worked from some nearby grange, perhaps Sutton.[7]

The degree of consolidation of lands emerges as a principal factor in the establishment and growth of a monastic grange. It was, as indicated, associated with the acquisition of church land. But, it may be argued, is this over-exaggerated as a factor? Can you show us

---

[1] Bishop *op. cit.*, p. 200.
[2] Malton Chartulary B.M. Cotton MS Claudius D XI folio 2.
[3] *Ibid.* folio 279f.
[4] *Loc. cit.*
[5] Bishop *op. cit.*, p. 198. Many of them were being gradually created.
[6] B.M. Cotton MS Claudius D XI fo. 279f.
[7] Several Guisborough and Whitby granges administered nearby lands, i.e. the Granger was responsible for rent collection and payments in kind. A Rent Roll (*c.* late 13th century) for Guisborough, and the Whitby Accounts (late 14th century) make this plain.

a picture of the process completed so that we can assess how far it went? Is there a comprehensive body of evidence that would show this?

Indeed there is, but it has the disadvantage of being sixteenth century evidence. It is the Dissolution Ministers Accounts (1538-41) for the various monasteries of the North-East. Many details of monastic lands and granges are given, and it is possible to estimate how much land a monastery owned in a particular place and very often (though not invariably) to see what proportion of this land was actually grange land. Although this gives a picture for the middle sixteenth century it will in fact give a picture of many centuries earlier too, because after the middle of the thirteenth century monastic lands changed very little.[1] Therefore, despite the evidence being late it is immensely valuable. Especially since the maximum degree of consolidation of monastic lands can be gauged from it. On this basis a table has been constructed which will be found in Appendix 3.

It is evident at once, from the table, that the degree of consolidation was generally high- in some cases complete; in very few only was it low. The Guisborough granges in the East Riding were very highly consolidated; at Bernalby (Barnaby) and North Cote the grange land comprised the whole land owned. This was so at Welham, Sinnington, Hutton, Griff and Newlathes (Malton and Rievaulx granges) Ormesby and Rillington granges provide a difficulty. On both the grange land was only a third of the whole and yet both had been the most prosperous and among the largest of all monastic granges in the North-East. Consolidation would have been expected to have been complete on such granges. What is the explanation? That is a difficult question which cannot be answered satisfactorily. However several tentative suggestions can be made. One is that land consolidation had a limit, which perhaps varied from place to place. Such a limit might have been imposed by the canons themselves or by the territorial organisation of the vills in which their grange was situated. The former suggestion is most likely, and Appendix 3 supports the view that the canons had, perhaps, an optimum size for their granges. For example, it is clear from Appendix 3 that much grange land varied between 10 and 14 bovates. In fact 10 out of 26 places quoted were between these limits, and 3 were only just outside. The monastic property not actually associated with the grange was probably given over to the housing and sustenance of the many villeins who worked for the canons.

Three main factors have been suggested as being of primary importance in the selection of sites for monastic granges. The first was the size of the initial grant in a particular place. The second was the possession of the church and tithes. The third was the extent to which these lands were consolidated into a whole, and the possibility there was of further extension and consolidation. Where all three factors coincided in a favourable way for the canons they would establish their grange.

Occasionally, ownership of the manor of the vill in which the grange was sited seemed to be an important additional advantage. Guisborough, for instance, was willing to pay 380 marks to Ivo de Seton for his manor of Castle Eden "*et omnes nativos meos de eadem villa cum tota sequela ...*" (mid 12th century).[2] Later, in 1199, the canons received the

---

[1] e.g. at Rillington, Malton Priory had about 32 bovates at the end of the 13th century. In 1540 it had 33 bovates; at Welham there were 12 bovates in 1254 and 1540; Kirby 18 bovates late 13th century and the same in 1540 etc,
[2] G.C. No. 1162, 1163. No. 686C. Eden is in Co. Durham.

chapel and tithes of Eden. Malton Priory, too, was willing to spend as much as 220 marks for Swinton manor (1275), where they had a grange. But obviously the possession of the manor was not a vital consideration to be made before a grange could be established. Most monasteries, for example, did not possess the manor where they had a grange-out of 18 Malton granges at only Yarpesthorpe and Swinton was the manor owned, and of 11 Guisborough granges, the only manor held was at Thornaby-on-Tees. The coincidence between manor and grange on the Whitby estates is greater, but not invariable: by 1394 the monks held the manors of Stakesby, Fyling, Hawsker, Normanby and Eskdale, all places where they had granges.[1] On the other hand, Rievaulx Abbey possessed only Foxton and Raisdale manors and only the latter place had a grange there.[2]

To have been a vital consideration in grange establishment, possession of the manor, like possession of church and tithes, would have been made early. But, except in an odd instance, (Castle Eden) most of the manors mentioned were acquired very much later than the grange was established. Swinton grange, for example, was set up between 1234-44 but the manor was not purchased until 1275; Yarpesthorpe grange had been created between 1178-1220 but the manor was not acquired until 1294.[3] Other manors were acquired even later (Thornaby 1311-12; Hawsker 1298).[4] Though not then a factor in the selection of grange sites the possession of the manor could stimulate the growth of a grange. The advantages were great as this grant of Hawsker manor to Whitby shows – "*cum omnibus quae ibi habui vel habere potui, in d'nicis et servitiis, villenagiis et cotagiis, cum homagiis et servitiis lib. hominum, villanis et eorum sequelis, et tenementis, redditibus et releviis, wardis et omn. eschaetis quae inde accidere potuerunt, et cum omn. boscis, planis, pratis, pasturis, moris, mariscis, turbariis, aquis, vivariis, piscariis, viis, semitis et omn. aliis rebus, in quibusc unque locis, ad praed. maner ...... pertin*[5] Such advantages would contribute to the growth already made by land consolidation-in fact, could, perhaps, facilitate it.

The accumulation of common pasture rights, right of way, enclosure, dyking, and so on, might have been more influential in the selection of grange sites. In fact, on granges which were to be devoted mainly to sheep or cattle farming pasture rights were a primary consideration (e.g. Kirby Misperton, Edston, Ryton granges). Although arable granges would require access to pastureland this would be more important to pastoral granges in which movement of animals, sometimes over great distances, was an economic necessity. Most grants of common pasture to the monasteries were made early. Rievaulx had common in Welburn (1138-43); Wombleton (1145-52); Farndale (pre 1155), for example, and sometimes the privilege was purchased e.g. Arden-Hesketh (pre 1159 1½ marks), Morton (1158-60 1 mark) ...[6] Some specific grants of sheep pasture were very large, e.g. Folkton- Hunmanby area 1500; Sproxton 800; Arncliffe-Morton 1000 and undoubtedly induced the monasteries to set up their granges nearby.

---

[1] W.C. Accounts, pp. 553-625.
[2] R.C., pp. 249, 226.
[3] Details about Yarpesthorpe manor in Malton Chartulary fo. 73-74.
[4] G.C. No. 233; W.C. 401, 476, 477.
[5] W.C. No. 476.
[6] R.C.. pp. 31, 36, 30. 33. 53

Such privileges were frequently purchased by Rievaulx and Malton. Oliver Busci, for example, granted all his meadow in Stiltons to the monks, with free access for their men, animals and carts *"pro quandam summa pecuniae, quam recepi ab eisdem in necessitate mea"*. Walter Engleram received fifteen marks silver, a gold ring and 2/- as well as an annual rent of 12d for allowing the monks to pasture 600 sheep in Arncliffe (1160-70). Robert de Sproxton charged the monks 3/- a year for pasture through all the woods and moors of Sproxton.[1] The accumulation of pasture and meadow is especially well marked in the valeland granges of Malton and Rievaulx. These, together with the right to enclose and dyke were very important, especially the latter because it largely controlled the rate of expansion and this in turn was a consideration in grange siting. The accumulation of such privileges, especially of pasture, may have been the counterpart of land consolidation on arable granges. It was certainly as important a factor to pastoral granges as a compact body of lands was to arable granges.

Geographical conditions, it will be seen, did not appear to play more than a secondary part in the selection of grange sites (at least as far as the black monks and canons were concerned). Of course fertility and accessibility were basic demands, but the intricate web of feudal economy was an even more fundamental condition. That is why donation grants, possession of churches and possibilities of land consolidation were of primary importance. It was not so much a question of where the monastery wanted to establish a grange as where it could establish a grange. Of course, the geographical environment profoundly influenced the subsequent economic development of a grange, even though its effect on selection of a site was limited.

Figure 4.4 Bilsdale : Looking North up the Dale from the surrounding moors. The Dale still gives the appearance of being well wooded, as it was in medieval times. Bilsdale was the site of many monastic granges.

---

[1] R.C.. pp. 234, 55. 79

One reservation about the effects of geography on grange establishment must be made. Where large tracts of sparsely settled lands were owned by a monastery, geographical factors played a more influential role. There was then more freedom of choice, because land consolidation for example, was unnecessary. The Cistercians held the greater amount of this kind of land – their land in Pickering Waste, for instance, which covered a large part of the central Vale allowed them unlimited expansion within wide boundaries. At least four granges were established within the area. Their sites were strictly controlled by the availability of firm land within the marsh and the planned direction reclamation was to take. Similarly in Bilsdale the grange sites were all predominantly influenced by geographical factors. In Glaisdale, too, where Guisborough worked iron ore during the thirteenth century the siting of the grange and lodges was directly related to the exploitation of the mineral. The canons had a wide grant and could build anywhere within its limits. Such factors as proximity of wood for charcoal, iron stone, running water and pasture for pack horses were primary considerations.[1] Thus where monastic granges were established in uninhabited regions geographical factors were of considerable influence on the sites chosen.

4. *Contribution to Settlement*

Domesday Book, whatever its disadvantages for Yorkshire, does give a clear indication of settlement before the great devastation of 1069, and shows the extent of wasting by 1086. If this settlement pattern could be compared to settlement, say a century later, the extent of recovery could be seen. But is there any comparable source at a later date which is so comprehensive? There are certainly several documents which can give an excellent picture of settlement in the fourteenth century. The Poll Tax of 1377 is useful, especially for its details about town populations, but the North Riding section of it has been less well preserved than the West Riding.[2] A series of Lay Subsidies beginning in 1297 and recurring in 1301, 1327, 1334 hold out more hope.[3] Unfortunately that of 1297 is complete for the East Riding only, and those of 1327 and 1334 while being comprehensive are rather late for the purpose and so is Nomina Villarum (1316).[4] Besides, none of these give full details of the temporal possessions of the monasteries (This is the disadvantage of Kirkby's Inquest (c.1284) which is otherwise very valuable.[5] It does not record, for example, the settlements that Rievaulx and Guisborough had outside the settled areas.) There remains the Lay Subsidy of 1301. It is certainly comprehensive enough for the North Riding because in spite of its title it covers the possessions of the monasteries and so includes granges and lands which they had inside and outside settled areas.[6] The Subsidy has several uses too: it gives a clear picture of monastic and lay settlement in 1301; it shows which areas were the most prosperous because it indicates 1/15 of the value of moveable goods (i.e. cattle, corn, etc); and

---

[1] There is no indication that streams were used for motive power in the iron working here, but it seems a distinct possibility.
[2] P.R.O. E. 359/8 B.C.
[3] All these are published in either the Yorkshire Archaeological Society Record Series or North Riding Record Series.
[4] Kirkby's Inquest and Nomina Villarum published together with –
[5] Knight Fees in vol. 49. Surtees Society.
[6] For meaning of tax on moveables in Subsidies see J. E. Willard *E.H.R.* vols. 28 (p.517), 29 (p.317), 30 (p.69).

because it lists the lay contributors for each vill it affords some idea of the distribution of population in 1301. The most interesting deduction it allows, however, is the relative importance of monastic settlement in the area, and the extent to which settlement had expanded or contracted since Domesday.

For these reasons the Subsidy of 1301 has been plotted on Figure 4.5 and will be used to assess the relative importance of lay and monastic settlement in the North-East. Although 1301 is a considerable time after the Domesday records its choice has several advantages in addition to those already mentioned. Monastic lands had by 1301 become stabilised; the monasteries were near a climax in their development;[1] Their settlements outside inhabited regions had reached maximum; they still retained the bulk of the grange land in their own hands – the leasing which was to become so marked in the middle and later fourteenth century had not yet set in. Lay settlement and prosperity, too, was at a maximum which preceded a series of drastic crises later to strike down the North-East.

A comparison of settlements in 1086 and 1301, introduces an immediate, but not unexpected, contrast. In 1086 the greater part of the settled area (with notable exceptions, e.g. Seamer) had been waste; in 1301 these places had largely been re-established so that

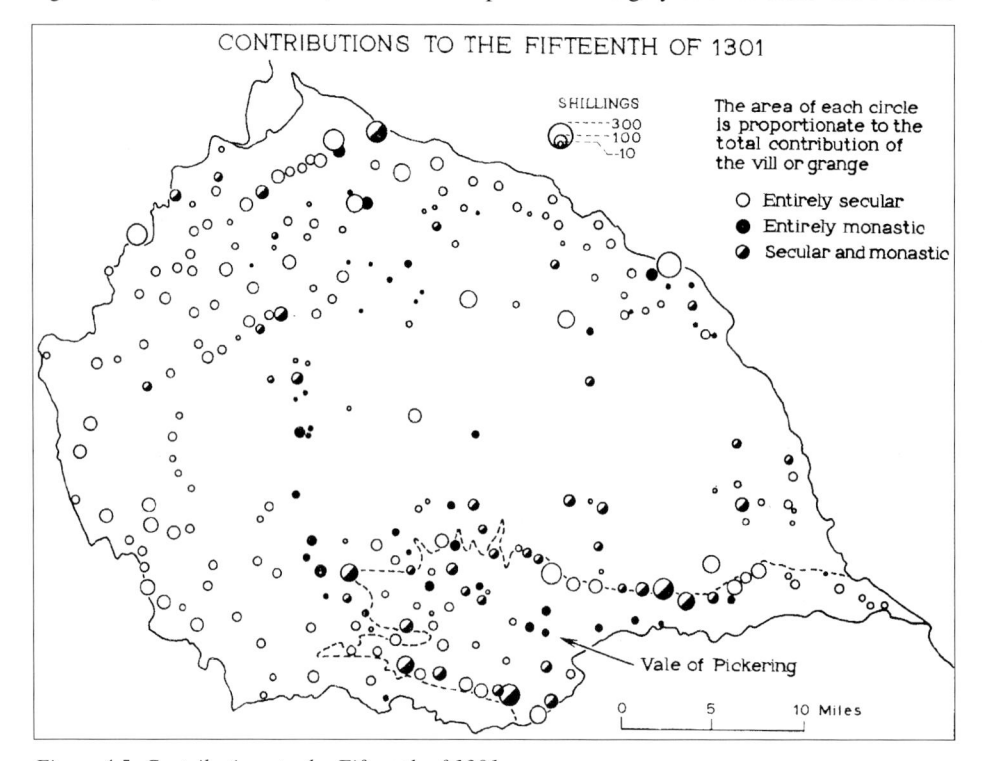

Figure 4.5 Contributions to the Fifteenth of 1301

---

[1] They had, as already mentioned, suffered some serious set backs in the last two decades of the 13th century, but it was subsequent to 1301 that the greatest crisis came, due to the increase in Scottish raiding and the general economic decline.

the picture reproduced a good deal of the pre-devastation pattern of settlement in the North-East. The centres of population and prosperity were in two main areas: Cleveland and the Vale of Pickering. This again, reproduced a good deal of what Domesday has suggested in terms of such relative values. Then, as in 1301, the Vale and Cleveland had predominated; then, as in 1301, the clearly defined lines of villages on the north and south margins of the Vale were evidently of the most significance. But in 1301 the emphasis was multiplied many times. The whole settlement was clearly rejuvenated and although the degree of continuity preserved was remarkable its development in terms of settlement, population and wealth had been considerably strengthened.

A closer inspection of the maps suggests that some vital changes had occurred by 1301. These comprised an extension of the settled area. Those areas colonised since Domesday were mainly of two kinds: in the marshy valelands and in the moorland dales. In the latter, Bilsdale, Farndale, Bransdale and Eskdale were mainly concerned. In the former the Vale of Pickering especially in its central part was affected, but settlement on the limestone dip slope to the north had also increased (e.g. Skiplam, Carlton).

One outstanding fact is evident-that the monastic share in the expansion of settlement after 1086 was very great indeed. In Bilsdale, for example, Byland and Rievaulx between them had settled almost the whole of the valley by 1301 while lay settlement was confined to a few vills in the north of the valley (e.g. Raisdale, Broad Fields, Bilsdale)-and these were largely dominated by Rievaulx.[1] In Eskdale, too, a whole series of new settlements had been established by Guisborough Priory at Skelderskew, Wayworth, Dibble Bridge, Glaisdale ... Rosedale was entirely a monastic settlement although the iron stone in the dale was to attract lay settlers there by the mid-fourteenth century.[2] Bransdale and Farndale had apparently been colonised by laymen-although even here Rievaulx had twelfth century pasture rights which presumably led to some form of small settlement. At any rate, by 1282 lay settlement here was considerable. There were, for instance, 90 natives in Farndale and 54 natives and bondmen in Bransdale.[3] Along the north-east fringe of the moors at Stanghow, Scaling, Sandsend .... and in certain spots deeper in the moors (e.g. Hartoft) laymen had played a major part in the expansion of settlement.

Significant as the monastic colonisation of uninhabited areas was it must be remembered that their greatest contribution was to the development of the already settled areas. Their granges were often inside vills or on the outskirts of them. In the North-East the monastic contribution to the revival of settlement after 1069 was great. The great extent of waste presented them with an unsurpassed economic opportunity. If so much waste had not existed it is quite possible that the donations to the monasteries would have been less; that the chance to secure and enlarge a foothold would have been decreased. For the Cistercians in particular it gave a perfect start which can hardly be equalled

---

[1] e.g. Rievaulx held the manors of Great and Little Raisdale after 1260. They had their grange of Bilsdale, at or near the lay settlement. At the Dissolution the Abbey had many tenants in Bilsdale cum Raisdale who paid a total of £90-6-2 in rents. P.R.O. E315/401.

[2] Lay iron works were probably established before the fourteenth century, but it was not until the fourteenth century that mineral exploitation became widespread.

[3] *Yorkshire Inquisitions*, Y.A.S. i. 249. In 1276 there were 141 acres of land in cultures in Bransdale. (Inq. P.M. YAS i. 167). By 1353 there was one water mill at Bransdale, two at Farndale and a fulling mill. Extents. P.R.O. C 135/118 and C 135/97.

anywhere, except perhaps in the eastern marchland of Germany in the 12th century.[1] The coincidence between granges and places formerly waste is adequate testimony that the monasteries took full advantage of their opportunity.

The monasteries sometimes took from the settlement pattern as well as giving to it. The Cistercians caused a contraction of settlement in certain areas because when they obtained the grant of a whole vill they occasionally reduced it to a grange (*"redigere in grangiam"*) so that it disappeared – "How gratefully do they enter upon the lands that are given them," said Walter Map describing the Cistercians, " ... caring not so much how they get them as long as they may keep them. And because their rule does not allow them to govern parishioners they proceed to raze villages and churches, turn out parishioners, destroy the altars of God, not scrupling to sow crops or cast down and level everything before the ploughshare, so that if you looked on a place that you knew previously you could say, 'and grass grows now where Troy town stood' ... they make a solitude that they may be solitaries .... Every other invader has some pity and spares something.... These take every precaution that there should be no return .... an invasion of that Order (and that alone) leaves absolutely nothing .... Those upon whom comes an invasion of Cistercians may be sure that they are doomed to everlasting exile. In other cases part of the population are deported for definite reasons".[2] Though dramatised and exaggerated Walter Map's account was basically true.[3] The Meaux Chronicle provides several examples, and in the North-East both Byland and Rievaulx reduced several vills.[4]

A twelfth century incident shows Abbot Roger of Byland establishing a grange in the vill of Byland. He assigned part of the vill for the villagers and took the rest of it for his grange:

"Cum vero dictus abbas R. et monachi ejus dictam villam Bellelandae habuissent, decreverunt illam in grangiam unam redigere. Haec illis cogitantibus assignaverunt quandam partem terrae ejusdem villae hominibus ibi manentibus scilicet apud Stute Kelde, ubi dicti homines de novo inceperunt unam villulam et ibi manserunt per plures annos, eidem nomen primum impotentes, et sic eadem villa redacta est in grangiam".[5]

Rievaulx was involved in similar schemes about this time. In fact, perhaps the best evidence for a village desertion due to the Cistercians is associated with this house and its daughter foundation of Revesby in Lincolnshire. In 1142 William de Roumara, Earl of

---

[1] Cistercian colonisation: use of conversi with monks as directors at St. Peter in the Black Forest (1093) and Pegan on the White Elster in the land of the Sorbs (1101); differences between English and Continental clearance; monastic settlement of high ground in Germany etc. See *Cambridge Economic History* vol. i., pp. 74-79. Also R. Dickinson, *Germany* (Methuen Geography Series).

[2] Walter Map. *op. cit.*, pp. 49-50.

[3] Compare Archbishop Peckham in 1284 protesting against a new Cistercian foundation because, "they are the hardest neighbours that prelates and parsons can have. Wheresoever they set their foot, they destroy villages, take away tithes and detract from the authority of the bishops." *Registrum Epp. J. Peckham* (Rolls Series) ii, p. 726. Similar sentiment to Walter Map's but over a century later. The Cistercians, it seems, carried their policy on into the late 13th century and it was not confined to their hey-day during the 12th century.

[4] Where the vill of Meaux was sited "there is now our grange which is called North Grange". In 1175 Fountains removed the inhabitants of Thorpe Underwood in order to convert it into a "productive grange" (Dugdale), *Monasticon Ang.* v., p. 305.

Lay villagers often resented this policy and took reprisals against it. During Richard I's reign, for example, Abbot Lambert of Kirkstall made Accrington into an abbey grange but the infuriated inhabitants set fire to it and murdered some of the lay brothers who were in charge. *M.A.* v., p. 531 Compare this to the despoiling of Rievaulx's property about the same time.

[5] "*Incipit Fundatio Domus Bellelandae edita à Philippo Abbate tertio Domus praedictae ...* " in *Mon. Angl.* v., p. 351a.

Lincoln, gave all his lands in Revesby, Thoresby and Sythersby to the Abbot of Rievaulx for the foundation of a Cistercian abbey.[1] The charter recording the gift offered the displaced peasantry the alternative of fresh land elsewhere on his estates or freedom to "go and dwell where they will". Only three men accepted his offer; thirty-one left his land and went elsewhere. If this was typical the monks could not expect much labour from the villages they controlled. Perhaps they could expect a great deal of resentment. Subsequently two of the villages disappeared, and only Revesby is left today.

But this was not an isolated incident in Rievaulx's early history. Several examples occur in the North-East. Roger de Mowbray granted all the vill of Welburn to Rievaulx in 1154 and in an interesting supplement he added, "*Sciatis quod omnes rusticos meos de Wellebrunna concedo Abbati de Rievalle quietos, et ipsis do omnem libertatem eundi et remanendi quocunque voluerint, et ubi locum invenerint, absque omni calumpnia imposterium de me et haeredibus meis ....*"[2] From that time the vill disappeared. It is not recorded in either Kirkby's Inquest or the 1301 subsidy, although the grange of Welburn is frequently mentioned. However, resettlement must have occurred sometime after the fourteenth century because there is a present day village of Welburn. It seems certain that here too was an instance of "*redigere in grangiam*".

The monks were granted the vills of Hoveton and Stainton and all Griff and Stiltons[3] – but no more is heard of them as vills afterwards. Neither Kirkby's Inquest, the 1301 subsidy nor the Nomina Villarum had any reference to them as vills. Griff and Stiltons were granges but whether Hoveton and Stainton were remains a mystery. All the men of Hoveton were granted with the vill for which the monks were to pay 2 marks a year.[4] The abbey might have bought some of them out in this case. For example they paid Peter de Hoveton 20 silver marks and 1 horse for five bovates of land here, and gave his wife 2 cows, 10 sheep, 10 lambs (1161-80).[5] Perhaps a dowery to set up elsewhere in business? They also gave 6 silver marks and a cow to Sunnive, wife of Lambert de Hoveton, for 1 bovate and 2 assarts (1160-74) and rented 2 bovates from the Hospitallers of Whitby for 3/- a year. (1147-57).[6] There is little doubt that the monks were quick to consolidate an initial advantage, such as they were given by the donation of a whole vill. It would be most valuable and interesting if the preliminary negotiations between abbots and donors could be discovered because the facts seem to suggest that some degree of pressure may have been exerted by the abbots. Whether this really was so cannot be determined on the present evidence. The results, such as the logical acquisition of lands over a short period of time, suggest that the monasteries "pursued an active policy, not merely in disposing of land acquired but also in acquiring it. Granges were not the result of casual benefaction."[7]

---

[1] Facsimiles of *Early Charters from Northamptonshire Collections*. Edited by F. M. Stenton (1930), pp. 1-7.
[2] R.C., p. 36, he also granted the tithes of Welburn to Rievaulx but excepted the church and its 6 bovates, (p. 113). Roger de Mowbray was said to have given 8 carucates here (p. 263).
[3] R.C., pp. 16f., 38, 41-4 carucates in Griff; 5 carucates in Stiltons; Roger de Mowbray said to have given 4 carucates in Hoveton. (p. 263). Monks had tithes of Griff, Stiltons, Hoveton. (p. 113).
[4] " .... *cum omnibus etiam hominibus in eadem villa manentibus*". R.C., p. 169.
[5] R.C., p. 169
[6] *Ibid.*, p. 174.
[7] Such a policy has been shown to be evident in land consolidation. Quotation from Bishop *op. cit.*, p. 201.

The grange then was the spearhead of the monastic blitzkrieg – the impact was just as startling; the results just as overpowering. It contributed to the settlement of areas previously uninhabited, often unused. Even more important it was the first of a new type of settlement in the area. The grange was a dispersed form, perfectly adapted to the development of areas such as the North-East Moorlands, where nucleated settlements were almost non-existent (N.B. extreme nucleation in Valeland areas in contrast). In fact, the value of the monastic grange site is emphasised today by the many isolated farmhouses that are on the same spots.[1] The grange began a traditional form of settlement in the North-East which was well adapted to the exploitation of the area. But the grange influenced settled areas too. Mainly by inducing a revival of previously devastated villages and creating a rejuvenated economy. Previous patterns of settlement were renewed and emphasised; sometimes vills were destroyed.[2] The monasteries derived a great deal from lay endeavours

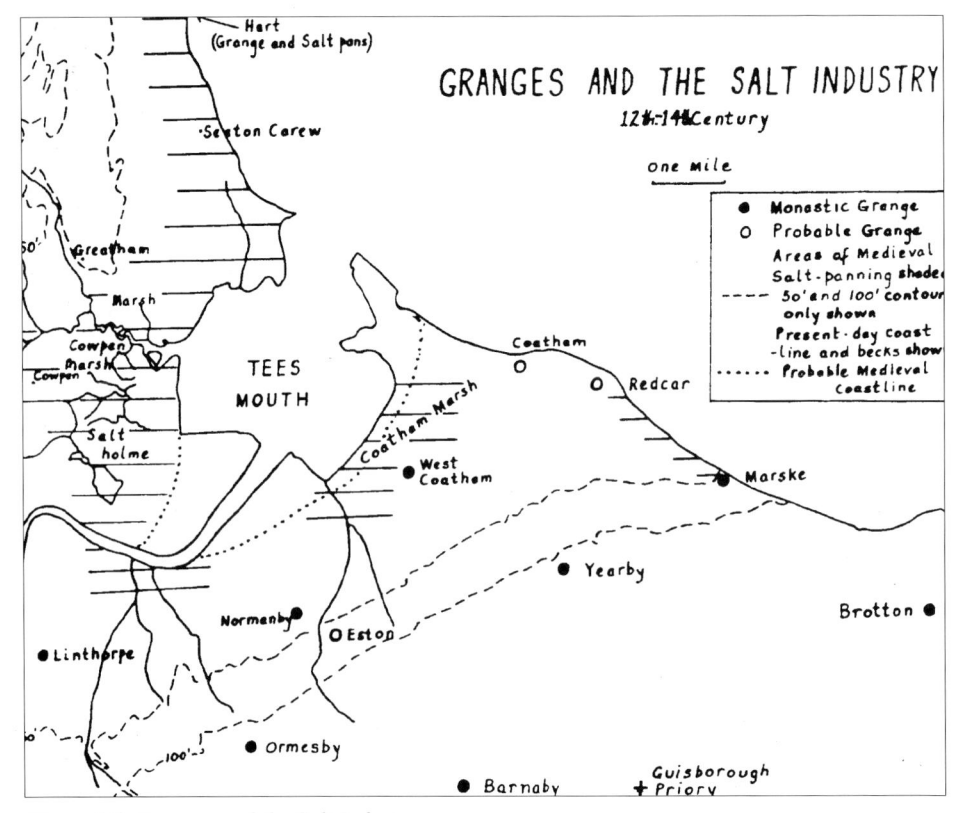

Figure 4.6 Granges and the Salt Industry

---

[1] e.g. Griff farm, Stiltons farm, Skiplam farm.
[2] N.B. a reversal of this policy, though rare, it is often overlooked, e.g. the Fountains grange of Bradley was converted into a vill about 1363 and let to secular persons. *Y.A.J.* 29, p. 101; C. T. Clay.

but the extent to which they, in turn, stimulated lay efforts in agriculture and settlement cannot be accurately assessed because it was so large and so pervasive.

But the grange was not only influential in the settlement of the North-East; it played a distinctive part in all aspects of the area's development. In doing so it emphasised the intimate harmony which existed between Man and his Landscape.

APPENDIX 1

Some Details of Malton Granges in 1244

Place	Ploughs	Hired Workers	Tofts	Annual Expense Workers	Total Grange Expense	Location
ABBEY	3	16	19	57/10	148/10	Old Malton
WINTRINGHAM	11	n.g.	50	176/10	404/2	Gravel Bench
MOWTHORPE	7	19 (17)		70/–	119/3	Wolds
SWINTON	7	29	10	97/4	211/8	Gravel Bench
RILLINGTON	4	17	18*	57/6	163/2	Gravel Bench
KIRBY	2	9 (8)	11	28/5	40/5	Mid-Vale
SUTTON	4	11(12)	3	36/2	69/2	Gravel Bench
HUTTON	2	9(8)	13•	29/11½	52/4	Malton Gap
EBBERSTON	3	11(10)	3	30/8	60/10	Limestone
DUNDALE	1	6 (6)	n.g.	19/10	33/6	Moors
RYTON	1	n.g.	n.g.	15/–	39/–	Mid-Vale
SINNINGTON	2	9	12	20/1	55/8	Vale

Source: B.M. Cott. MS. Claudius D XI folios 267-71; 273-74.

Notes:
(1) All places are granges.
(2) Figures in brackets refer to numbers of workers during term of St. Martin. Unbracketed figures in same column give numbers during Pentecost term.
(3) *includes "new tofts".
(4) n.g. not given.

APPENDIX 2
Granges and the Possession of Churches

1. **Guisborough Priory Granges**   **Church Granted**
    - Marton — Foundation (1119)
    - Ormesby — Foundation (1119)
    - Thornaby — Chapel (pre 1309)
    - Yearby — tithes of Kirkleatham (1119)
    - Marske — Foundation (1119)
    - Brotton — Chapel (pre 1309)
    - Maltby — tithes (included with Stainton)
    - Stainton — Foundation (1119)
    - ?Eston — Chapel (pre 1309)
    - Kirkburn — Foundation (1119)
    - ?Hart — Foundation (1119)
    - New Grange (Guisborough par.) — Foundation (1119)

2. **Whitby Abbey Granges**   **Church Granted**
    - Stakesby
    - Eskdale
    - Fyling
    - Normanby
    - Hawsker
    - Whitbylathes
    - Lathgarth
    - Lairpool

    All included in the Foundation Grant of William de Perci (late 11th century) with the Church of B. Mary, Whitby (associated chapels at Fyling, Hawsker, Sneton, Ugglebarnby, Dunsley, Aislaby)

    - Hackness — Both churches here at the Foundation.
    - Harwood — With Hackness?
    - Newsham — Probably under the patronage of St. Hilda's church, Middlesbrough, which the abbey was granted, *c.* 1120.

? doubtful granges

Sources: Chartularies and Archbishops Registers.

APPENDIX 3

AMOUNT OF LAND ATTACHED TO GRANGES AND THE PERCENTAGE THIS WAS OF THE ENTIRE MONASTIC HOLDING
(from the Ministers' Accounts 1538-41)

Place	Grange Land (in bovates)	Entire Property	Grange Land to Whole	Distance of Grange from House in Miles
i GUISBOROUGH PRIORY				
Ormesby	12$^1/_2$	37$^1/_2$	33%	5
Thornaby	16	31+	51%	12
Ayresome	12	12+	100%	8
Loftus	13	45	29%	7
Bernalby	38$^1/_2$ (347 acres)	?	Prob. 100%	4
North Cote	(395 acres)	(395 acres)	100%	*c.* 1$^1/_2$
Mersk	14	30$^1/_2$	46%	5
Southburn	13	13	100%	East Riding
Bottleburn	17	17	100%	East Riding
Bainton	4	5	80%	East Riding
Rotsea	7	8	87%	East Riding
Lund	7	7	100%	East Riding
ii MALTON PRIORY				
Sutton-Norton	5	8+	62%	1$^1/_2$
Wellom	12	12	100%	1$^1/_2$
Carre Cote	2+	6+	33%	6
Sinnington	6	6	100%	8
Aislaby	7	9	78%	9
Swinton	11 (& 60 ac.)	26 (&60 ac.)	42%	3
Hutton	9	9+	100%	4
Rillington	11	33	33%	4
Thorpe	11	15	73%	4
Duggleby cum Mowthorpe	5	9+	56%	6
Kirby Misperton	10	18	56%	4$^1/_2$
Aymonderby	4	12	33%	3
iii RIEVAULX ABBEY				
Griff	(490 ac.)	Same	100%	1
New Lathes	(374 ac.)	Same	100%	1

Source: Ministers Accounts for Guisborough Priory P.R.O. S.C.6/Hen VIII/4636
for Malton Priory P.R.O. S.C.6/Hen VIII/4618
for Rievaulx Abbey Surtees Society, Vol. 83.

Notes: The information is not available for all the granges of the various orders. This is the reason for the short Rievaulx list and the absence of reference to Byland and Whitby. In such cases the amount of land actually attached to the grange is not given.

PART THREE : LAND USE

'A people expresses itself through its landscape'
F. Ratzel

5 Medieval Assessments & Agricultural Prosperity

6 Arable Farming

7 Pastoral Farming

8 Medieval Industries

5 MEDIEVAL ASSESSMENTS AND AGRICULTURAL PROSPERITY

'The English landscape itself, to those who know how to read it aright, is the richest historical record we possess', wrote Dr. Hoskins.[1] But 'to read it aright' calls for skill and knowledge which needs to be attached to documentary sources wherever possible. 'To write the history of the English landscape requires a combination of documentary research and of fieldwork, of laborious scrambling on foot wherever the trail may lead.'[2]

The Domesday Survey has, perhaps of all the documentary sources, most to recommend it as an instrument for re-creating the 'historical present'; for portraying the landscape of the eleventh century. Unfortunately, so far as Yorkshire is concerned it gives little information about the normal distribution of agricultural prosperity. The reason for this is not difficult to find: the results of the great devastation of 1069 were still very evident in 1086. The recovery of the land had not proceeded far, and certainly the return to normal agricultural production was delayed and, in 1086, not evident. Even so, it is possible to see from the Survey that certain regions within the northeast were clearly of greater significance than others.[3] Cleveland and the Vale of Pickering, for instance, showed the elements of that preponderance which was to become so marked later in the middle ages. But what was their place in the distribution of agricultural wealth under normal conditions? Was it as great as in other spheres of economic activity? What documents will help to solve this important problem?

It is not until the late thirteenth century that any major document can be produced which is comprehensive enough to indicate the distribution of agricultural prosperity in the northeast. Between the eleventh and thirteenth centuries many scattered sources such as monastic registers, feet of fines, and inquisitions throw light on the question, but they cannot stand alone- their information is too local and diverse to give the complete picture required. However, later assessments, made for the purpose of levying clerical and lay subsidies are more helpful.[4] They were usually based either partially or wholly on the agricultural produce of the parish, vill or manor. In the case of the Ninth taken in 1342 on corn, wool and lambs, the basis was entirely agricultural and the unit was the parish.[5] Such assessments can be of great value for indicating where agricultural prosperity was greatest, where it was at a minimum, which regions were richest and which soils the most influential in agricultural production. The information which such assessments provide lays the foundations, too, for a more detailed study of arable and pasture farming in the area.

The fifty years between 1292 and 1342 contained four major assessments, which,

---

[1] W. G. Hoskins, *The Making of the English Landscape*, 1956, Introduction.
[2] Ibid.
[3] I. S. Maxwell, *The Domesday Geography of Northern England*, Cambridge 1962.
[4] E. M. Yates has used the Pope Nicholas Valor and the Nonarum Inquisitiones to illustrate the historical geography of Northwest Sussex in 'Medieval Assessments in North-West Sussex', *Trans. Institute of British Geographers*, 20 (1954), pp. 75-92. See also his thesis for M.Sc. (GEOG.) 1953, University of London Library.
[5] A. R. H. Baker, 'Evidence in the Nonarum Inquisitions of Contracting Arable Lands in England during the early Fourteenth Century', *Economic History Review*, 2nd Ser. xix (1966), pp. 518-532.

though imperfectly preserved, at least give an insight into relative agricultural prosperity within northeast Yorkshire during this time. The relevant assessments are the Valor of Pope Nicholas IV (1292); the Lay Subsidy of 1301; the 'New Tax' or Reassessment of the North (1318); and the Nonarum Inquisitiones (1342).[1] All are sufficiently detailed, reasonably comprehensive and close together in time. Moreover, they occur at a critical period in medieval agricultural history when the High Farming of the thirteenth century was being replaced by recession and, in some areas, threatened collapse of former agricultural prosperity.

The purpose and working of these assessments will be explained under their appropriate headings but first something should be said about how they will be used. The details of the 1292 and 1318 Valors have been set down in Appendix I and the benefices upon which the valor was made have been arranged in their geographical regions. This has been done to try to obtain a clear picture of the relative prosperity of these regions. The acreage of each region has been calculated and the value per acre of the assessments worked out for each region in 1292 and 1318. By comparing these figures an idea of the relative regional prosperity can be adduced since, as will be shown later, the value of the benefice is a reliable indicator of the prosperity of the parish in which it is situated.

The Inquisition for the Ninth is too long to arrange similarly but an extract has been included in Appendix II to show the character of information given.

Four maps illustrate the assessments of 1292, 1301, 1318 and 1342 (Figs 4.5, 5.1). Unlike the information in the appendices which was arranged regionally, the maps have been drawn to show the assessments arranged in terms of wapentake divisions. Again pence per acre figures are quoted. It is hoped that a combination of both methods will contribute to a clear picture of prosperity in the northeast as a whole.

THE VALOR OF POPE NICHOLAS (1292)
1. *Purpose*
The Pope was entitled to take the First Fruits and Tenths of all ecclesiastical benefices. Sometimes he allowed the King to extract the tenth, usually for specific purposes, such as a proposed Crusade. Thus Pope Innocent IV granted it to Henry III for three years in 1253, which resulted in the Norwich Taxation of the following year. 'In the year 1288 Pope Nicholas the Fourth granted the tenths to King Edward the First for six years towards defraying the expense of an expedition to the Holy Land: and that they might be collected to their full value, a Taxation by the King's precept was begun in that year (1288) and furnished as to the Province of Canterbury in 1291 and as to that of York in the following year.'[2]

The Valor of Pope Nicholas, then, consisted of the assessment made for the purpose of levying the tenth on clerical incomes. These incomes were derived largely from the agricultural produce of the parish by way of tithes. The relationship between the Valor and the agricultural production of the parish was partly obscure, since clerical income also included such non-agricultural items as oblations and mortuary fees, but this does not

---

[1] *Taxatio Ecclesiastica Angliae et Walliae auctoritate P. Nicholai IV,* Record Commission, 1802; *Nonarum Inquisitiones,* Record Commission, 1807; *Yorkshire Lay Subsidy* (1301) ed. W. Brown, Yorkshire Archaeological Society Record Series, xxi (1897). The Lay Subsidies of 1297, 1327 and 1334 are of restricted value.

[2] *Taxatio Ecc. Angliae et Walliae auctoritate P. Nicholai IV,* Introduction.

materially affect the picture of relative prosperity since the amounts were usually small from non-agricultural items.[1]

Three reservations must be made about the Valor. Benefices not exceeding six marks were exempt from the tax if the rector held no other living and unless they were appropriated to a religious house. Templars, Hospitallers and poor nunneries were exempt.[2]

Fortunately neither of these are important drawbacks. There was a more significant reservation however. Many benefices in the north did not pay on the basis of the 1292 Valor since the devastations of the Scottish armies at the turn of the thirteenth century had made them incapable of paying. They were consequently reassessed in 1318 and contributed on the basis of this, not the 1292 Valor. The significance of this is dealt with later. The non-payment of the 1292 tax by no means invalidates its use as an indicator of agricultural prosperity in 1292. It was an accurate assessment of conditions at that time, even though conditions quickly deteriorated.

Thus, although certain reservations must be remembered, the Valor of 1292 remains a useful indicator of relative agricultural prosperity.

2. *Agricultural Prosperity in 1292*

Appendix I shows that the Pickering Vale region had the highest value per acre. The other regions were as follows:–

Region	pence per acre
Pickering Vale	1.71
Teesmouth	1.12
Pickering Vale/Moors	0.97
York Vale	0.84
York Vale/Moors	0.62
Coastal Plateau	0.39
Moorlands	0.34

The parishes of Pickering Vale were almost entirely situated in lowland but some of them, such as Barton, Hovingham and Appleton, extended over the limestone soils fringing the Howardian Hills. The high assessment of this region is rather surprising since much of Pickering Vale consisted of marshland and intractable peaty soils. Its prosperity undoubtedly derived from the parishes which fringed the central vale, and though including some marshy land, were mainly composed of gravel or limestone soils. Thus Hoveringham (800*s*), Appleton (1033*s*) and Stonegrave (667*s*) fell into this category. The diversity and fertility of land included in such parishes was probably the main reason for their high assessments. On the other hand, the parishes of the central vale were more

---

[1] Several items which might at first sight appear non-agricultural elements of a clerical income were, in fact, quite closely related to the agricultural realities of the parish, Glebe land and church demesne, for example, had much of their profits derived from their agricultural production. Within the scope of small tithes, too, fell the profits from such items as honey, flax, cider, cheese, etc.
[2] R, Graham, 'The Taxation of Pope Nicholas IV' in *English Ecclesiastical Studies*, 1929, chapter xi.

PART THREE : LAND USE

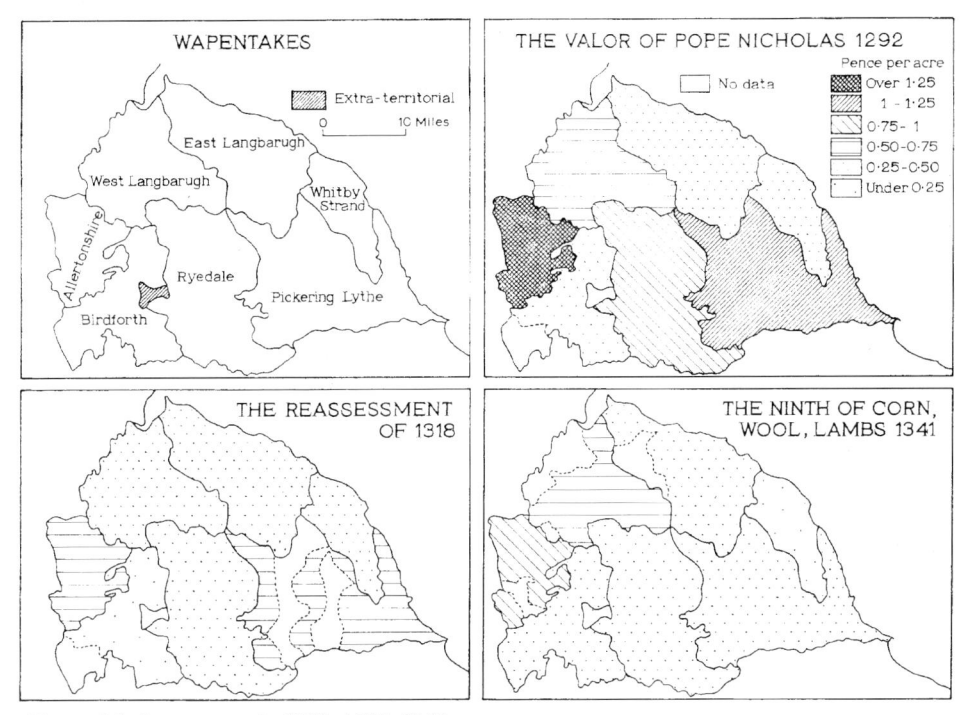

Figure 5.1 Assessments in 1292, 1318, 1341

homogeneous, being entirely clayland, and this as well as the marshland in them accounted for lower assessments. Thus Edston was only 133*s* and Normanby 267*s*. In exceptional cases, such as Salton and Kirby Misperton, higher assessments probably resulted from monastic interest in the parishes. Salton, for instance, was a Prebend of St. Peter's, York, and both Rievaulx and Malton Priory had granges in Kirby Misperton parish.

Teesmouth, though a small region, came second to Pickering Vale, again emphasising the prosperity of lowland areas. In contrast the parishes of the moorland and coastal plateau regions were characterised by low assessments per acre. This was largely due to the infertility of the soils and the consequent dependence on sheep farming. A few parishes had high individual assessments; Hackness and Lastingham, for example, were 667*s* and 600*s* respectively. This might have been due to the stimulus given to agricultural production in the parishes by the monasteries. Whitby Abbey had important cattle farms and arable holdings in Hackness,[1] and Lastingham included the granges of St. Mary's, York, at Spaunton and Appleton within its boundaries. In addition, half of Rosedale was also within its area – this was a principal pasture ground for the sheep of Rosedale Abbey. Whitby and Lythe parishes in the Coastal Plateau region were situated partly in the mouth of Eskdale where the soil was a deep rich loam, the altitude less than it was elsewhere on

---

[1] E.g., the vaccary of Kesebeck; the 'Bohus' of Harwood, valued at £11.3.6 in 1301; 'instauro de Hakenesse' worth £34.1.0.

the plateau, and the shelter more complete. Arable farming was thus of more importance and monastic participation in it was great (Whitby Abbey had most of its granges in the parishes).

Although the strip parishes of the Pickering Vale/Moor region had often as much as three-quarters of their area barren moorland the region as a whole was rated highly at 0.97d per acre. The Moor was barren of arable cultivation but certainly not useless. Its value as sheep range was immense. A large part of the income of the benefices in the region came from such a source.[1] For the rest, the fertile limestone soils of the Corallian, and the valuable water meadows fringing the River Derwent, contributed to this income. The open fields were situated at the junction between the limestone and clayland, often extending over both.[2] This was the main area of arable production in each parish. It was undoubtedly the many-sided economy possible in such parishes which contributed to their high position in terms of agricultural prosperity.

The York Vale region, on the other hand, was probably that in which arable cultivation was emphasised and pastoral activities were less important.[3] As might be expected of a lowland area of mainly fertile, though heavy, clay soils, the region had the high value per acre of 0.84d. The parishes with the highest individual assessments were those of the central Vale, near to the River Wiske. Thus Northallerton was 1467s, Kirby Wiske 1200s, and Thirsk 733s. These parishes were situated on the gravel and alluvial soils of the mid-Vale. As in the Teesmouth region, so here, the highest assessments appear to be in those parishes which contain a good deal of fertile alluvium within their boundaries. Kirkleatham (1600s) is the best example of this from the Teesmouth region.

An interesting and very important change occurs as the eastern margin of the York Vale region is approached. Parishes situated entirely in the lowland Vale give place to parishes situated partly on lowland and partly on moorland. The assessments of 1292 reflect this change and show that, as the York Vale/Moor region is reached, lower assessments are recorded. The value per acre of the region was only 0.62d as compared to 0.84d for the Vale, indicating a general decrease in prosperity between the regions. The parishes of the York Vale/Moor region contained much moor and woodland. Several, for instance, had the scarp face of the Cleveland or Hambleton Hills running through them. This was very heavily wooded in medieval times as, indeed, it is today. Consequently parishes like Kildale, Cowesby, Ingleby, Whorlton, Arncliffe and Felixkirk had rather low assessments. Stokesley, Osmotherley and Leake had higher assessments (1067, 560, 1067 shillings respectively) but much of these parishes was lowland. Stokesley, for instance, was situated entirely in the Cleveland Plain, and had only a detached part of the parish on Westerdale Moor.

How far does the arrangement of the Valor by wapentakes confirm the regional pattern

---

[1] The wool tithe at Brompton was worth 200s and at Middleton 267s. The *Nonarum Inquisitiones* emphasises sheep farming in the area.
[2] Evident from author's field work. The fields lay sometimes on Kimmeridge clay, sometimes on the limestone, but usually on both. They thus occupied the shelf of higher land which was 100 to 200 ft. above the level of the Vale clayland. Few open fields extended beyond the 'cliff' line into the carr land. Such land was, however, cultivated in the mid-Vale region near the River Rye, for example, between Ryton and Great Habton the ridge and furrow of the open field is very evident.
[3] B. Waites, 'Aspects of Medieval Arable Farming in the Vale of York', in *Ryedale Historian* No. 2, April 1966, pp. 5-11.

of prosperity so far evolved? Allertonshire and Pickering Lythe have the highest assessments per acre. East Langbarugh, Whitbystrand and Birdforth have the lowest, and Ryedale with West Langbarugh are intermediate. The pattern presented by Fig. 5.1 does, then, reproduce the regional distribution of prosperity previously established. That is to say, the lowland Vales of York, Pickering and Teesmouth are emphasised as very prosperous areas while the coastal region in particular, together with the area included in Birdforth wapentake are relatively inferior.

3. *Comparison of the Valor of 1292 and the Fifteenth of 1301*
Is this analysis of 1292 substantiated by later sources? The Fifteenth Subsidy (1301) can be used to answer this question.[1] Its value is enhanced because the basis and incidence of the assessment was different from the Valor of 1292 – and yet not so different as to invalidate a comparison. The unit of assessment was the vill or grange, not the parish; the Fifteenth was taken on moveables, which consisted mainly of animals and cereals.[2] Thus it was more closely related to agricultural realities than the 1292 Valor. Both documents were close to each other in time; relative agricultural prosperity could scarcely have changed materially in nine years.

Briefly, it may be said that the similarity between the distribution of agricultural wealth in 1292 and 1301 was great. The Vale of York, Pickering and Cleveland were still the wealthiest regions. In particular the line of villages along the northern margin of the Vale of Pickering and in the western half of the Vale were high in agricultural prosperity – as their corresponding parishes were shown to be in 1292. Similarly the villages on the edge of the Teesmouth alluvium, southwest of Kirkleatham were particularly emphasised. But the subsidy of 1301 showed more clearly how the monasteries had extended the areas of agricultural prosperity to include parts of the moorland (e.g., Upper Eskdale). The Valor of 1292, assessed on a parish basis, had not been able to indicate such finer points as this.

THE REASSESSMENT OF 1318[3]
1. *Purpose*
'Set quid in istis partibus accense Scottorum furore hiis diebus vobis enarrare nescimus, nisi quod quicquid coram ipsis inveniunt in pulverem et cinerem convertunt, (non) parcendo statui, sexui vel etati ... '

So wrote Archbishop Newark in 1298.[4] The ravages of the Scots were to increase in range and intensity during the next half century. The Archbishops' Registers are full of the injuries suffered by the diocese before and after the great defeats at Myton and Byland. The effect on religious houses was as severe as on towns and villages and the subsidies

---

[1] A fuller discussion of the 1301 Lay Subsidy, especially its value in the geography of settlement is given in, B. Waites, 'The Monastic Grange as a Factor in the Settlement of North-East Yorkshire', *Yorkshire Archaeological Journal*, Pt. 160, 1962, pp. 627-656.

[2] A good idea of what moveables were taxed is given in the lay subsidy of 1297 which relates mainly to the West Riding. This states taxable goods in full. They were almost entirely agricultural, e.g., sheep, cattle and cereals. *Yorkshire Lay Subsidy* (1297) ed. W. Brown, Yorkshire Archaeological Society Record Series, xvi (1894).

[3] Published by the Record Commission alongside the Pope Nicholas Taxation.

[4] In a letter to Master John de Langton. *Register of Henry of Newark, Lord Archbishop of York* (1296-1299), Surtees Society, Vol. 128, pp.316-317.

levied by both King and Archbishop were an added burden. In 1310, for example, Guisborough Priory provided 70 animals and 100 quarters of corn to aid the King, and Rievaulx 70 animals and 30 quarters of corn.[1] But actual material damage was more disastrous.

> 'Abbathia de Fontibus in qua jacuit magna pars exercitus Scotorum, adeo spoliata et depraedata existit, grangiae et loca exteriora destructa et combusta ac depraedata in tantum, quod omnia bona ad dictum monasterium spectantia non sufficiunt his diebus ad sustentationem professorum ejusdem.'[2]

The state of Rievaulx and Byland, which had a large-scale battle fought almost within their precincts, can well be imagined. Several houses had to be evacuated and sent to safer places such as Bridlington Priory.[3] After his defeat at Myton, together with the loss of his plate, Archbishop Melton himself was compelled to beg aid from his diocese.[4]

The Vale of York was a severely affected area. By 1322, for instance, 128 villages had been destroyed by the Scots, and even as far south as the East Riding 12 villages had suffered.[5] It was little wonder that such wholesale devastation called for a reassessment of benefices, 'that have been destroyed by the Scots, and to cause those that have not been newly taxed for this reason to be newly taxed according to their fine value so that a tenth of the clergy may be levied according to such taxation.'[6] The reassessment took place in 1318. An examination of it shows how agricultural wealth had been affected between 1292–1318. It is very necessary to have this picture because it was to remain characteristic for at least the first three decades of the fourteenth century.

2. *Comparison of the 1292 Valor and 1318 Reassessment*

A glance at Appendix I is enough to show that some violent changes in value occurred. The most remarkable were in the Vale of York. Rudby was reduced from 1600s to 900s; Thirsk from 733s to 240s; Northallerton from 1467s to 533s; Kirby Wiske from 1200s to 667s, all places in the direct line of advance of the Scots. The western half of the Vale of Pickering and the Teesmouth region had both been severely hit. Values in the eastern half of the Vale, however, with a few exceptions, remained unchanged. This was no doubt due to a pact made between certain men of Pickering and the Scottish King, whereby all the Vale east of the River Seven was to be spared invasion for a sum of money.[7] Along the Coastal Plateau,

---

[1] *Calendar of Patent Rolls* (1310), p. 299. In some instances the aid demanded was greater. Jervaulx supplied 110 sheep and 50 qrts. of corn; Fountains 100 wethers, 30 oxen and cows and 80 qrts. of corn; Bridlington 100 wethers and 60 qrts. of corn. On the other hand Byland supplied only 20 animals and no cereals, Malton 60 wethers and only 10 qrts. of wheat.
[2] *Letters from Northern Registers*, ed. J. Raine, Rolls Series, Vol. 61 (1873), p. 282.
[3] E.g., Malton Priory and Rosedale Abbey, *ibid.*, pp. 318-323.
[4] *Ibid.*, p. 295.
[5] P.R.O. E 359/14, Collection of 1322 North Riding.
[6] King's Writ authorising the enquiry is in J. Raine, *op. cit.*, pp. 279-282.
[7] John Topclife, Rector of Seamer, William Wyvern and John Wickham, with others of Pickering, with the assent of the whole community on Tuesday, 13 Oct. 1322, purchased from Robert Bruce for 300 marks, the immunity of the Vale of Pickering from the River Seven on the west, to the sea on the east. Hostages were given as surety that the money would be paid and though 'all the men and all the townships, manors, hamlets, lands and tenements of the said Vale within the bounds aforesaid were preserved from all damage and injury whatsoever' no money had been paid so that the hostages were still prisoners in Scotland in 1325. *Honour and Forest of Pickering*, ed. R. B. Turton in 4 vols., North Riding Record Society, New Series, London, 1894-96, vol. 1, pp. 3-4.

and in the Moorland the difference in value was comparatively small. (From the data available the Wolds also appear less severely hit.) These regions had been off the main line of Scottish advance and the decline in values might have been due to other various but more normal hazards.

The fall in values per acre between 1292 and 1318 is seen to be great. Allertonshire, 1.47d per acre in 1292, was only 0.66d per acre in 1318; Pickering Lythe, 1.13d per acre in 1292, was 0.5d per acre in 1318. It will be evident that it was just those areas which in 1292 had been to the forefront of the agricultural wealth of the northeast, which suffered most. Did this affect the picture of relative prosperity as seen in 1292? In fact although the assessments per acre of 1318 were all much lower than they had been in 1292 almost the same relationship between the wapentakes had been preserved. In 1318, as in 1292, Allertonshire and Pickering Lythe were the most prosperous while the wapentakes along the coast, plus Birdforth, were once again the poorest. While suffering great reductions in the Valors of their benefices, Allertonshire and Pickering Lythe yet remained predominant. This may become clearer if the assessments per acre for each wapentake are set down side by side for the years 1292 and 1318 in the order of importance.

It is clear that the distribution of agricultural prosperity in 1292 and 1318 followed a pattern of development. At both times Allertonshire was the most prosperous wapentake: Pickering Lythe, Ryedale and West Langbarugh came next, and Whitbystrand, Birdforth and East Langbarugh were far behind. This relative importance had been observable in Domesday times; it was to be the theme of succeeding centuries too.

1292	pence per acre	1318	pence per acre
Allertonshire	1.47	Allertonshire	0.66
Pickering Lythe	1.13	Pickering Lythe	0.50
Ryedale	0.84	West Langbarugh	0.41
West Langbarugh	0.74	Ryedale	0.38
Whitbystrand	0.48	East Langbarugh	0.28
Birdforth	0.48	Whitbystrand	0.27
East Langbarugh	0.47	Birdforth	0.17

THE NONARUM INQUISITIONES (1342)

1. Purpose

In 1342 Parliament granted a Ninth of the corn, wool and lambs of the kingdom to aid Edward III in his French and Scottish wars. This tax was levied on laity and religious by parishes. Parishioners from each parish declared on oath the true value of the ninth of corn, wool, and lambs for the past year. The Ninth was, in fact, equal to a tenth since the tithe of the parish had been taken before the Ninth was collected, and thus was excluded from assessment. For this reason the Valor of 1292 was consulted by the Commissioners and was included alongside the Ninth Inquisition for reference purposes. The Commissioners were to levy more if the Ninth exceeded the 1292 assessment and less if it fell below it. In every parish in the northeast the Ninth naturally fell below the Papal Valor since clerical incomes included much more than the tithe on corn, wool, and lambs. The parishioners explained the difference between the old and new assessments by referring to the revenues from glebe land, tithe of hay, small tithes in general, land uncultivated and so on. The parish of Easington, for example, was assessed at £20 for Pope Nicholas' Tax (1292) but the Ninth of corn, wool and lambs was only £6 15s 10d. This was £13 4s 2d less. The discrepancy was explained as follows by the parishioners on oath: a great part of the parish was uncultivated which, if it had been cultivated, would have been worth £4 to the Rectory; the church was situated in the moor where the parishioners live mainly by sheep from which the rector used to receive a tithe worth £6 1 3s 4d per year (2 sacks wool) and 60 lambs, now he scarcely receives 12 stone of wool and 10 lambs; the tithe of hay was worth 10s a year, altar dues, oblations, mortuary fees and other small tithes were worth 5 marks a year.[1] Other parishes had similar explanations. Kirby Wiske for instance, explained that the rector's income from wool and lambs had decreased, and besides 'due carucate terre fuerunt destructe per enundacionem aque de Swale ...'[2]

The Nonarum Inquisitiones is an extremely valuable and direct indicator of agricultural prosperity. Previous assessments discussed contain non-agricultural elements which partly obscure a complete picture of agricultural prosperity. A study of the Ninth validates their usefulness, however, because it confirms their results. The usefulness of the Ninth is not restricted to this. Because the composition of the tithes and the extent of uncultivated land is given it becomes possible to see in detail what were the particular farming activities of a parish and how much of that parish was out of cultivation (and also the monetary loss this produced). Besides, the monastic share in the agriculture of a parish can be seen, because they too contributed to the Ninth. The relative wealth and importance of towns and markets can be evaluated because burgesses were compelled to contribute one-fifteenth of their goods to the subsidy. For the present the Inquisition will be used solely to assess the distribution of agricultural prosperity in 1341.

Several difficulties have to be overcome in using this document. The Inquisition is not as full and as informative for Yorkshire as for some other parts of England. In Sussex, for example, the Ninth was separated into its component parts - corn, wool and lambs, but in Yorkshire only the total Ninth was given. Wool and lamb tithes were sometimes quoted separately, sometimes together; sometimes they were given in sacks, sometimes in money value. More serious were the errors and omissions which the Record Commission volume of the Nonarum Inquisitiones contained. At Lastingham, for example, it did not mention that 160 lambs were part of the tithe. Similarly reference to two sacks of wool valued at five marks, for Kirkdale, is omitted.[3] The important word, arable, is frequently in the manuscript but not in the Record Commission version. The latter, too, often mentions a tithe as being from wool, when actually it was from wool and lambs. As for the monastic Ninth, the Record Commission version gives only the total contributed but the

---

[1] *Nonarum Inquisitiones*, p. 231.
[2] *Ibid*, p. 234.
[3] P.R.O, E. 179/211/19, m. 107, Subsidy Rolls.

manuscripts give many details. Nothing is said, for example, about the Abbot of Rievaulx's nine carucates in Helmsley, five uncultivated and four 'in agricultura' from which the Ninth of corn was worth two marks and the ninth of wool and lambs 23s 4d[1] Therefore, the manuscript of the Nonarum Inquisitiones, as well as associated documents have been used together with the printed version.[2] Appendix II contains extracts from the Inquisition (arranged in regions) to illustrate the type of information it gives. Fig. 5.1 has been drawn to show the Ninth in terms of pence per acre for each wapentake.

2. *The Nonarum Inquisitiones and Agricultural Prosperity in 1341*

The distribution of agricultural wealth throughout the northeast in 1341 is clearly reflected in the information given by the Inquisition. The features common to the distributions of 1292 and 1318 are once more emphasised.

The relative importance of the various wapentakes is shown by the following table:—

Wapentake	pence per acre
Allertonshire	0.98
West Langbarugh	0.52
Ryedale	0.43
Pickering Lythe	0.38
Birdforth	0.38
East Langbarugh	0.26
Whitbystrand	0.16

The Coastal Plateau was again the least prosperous region in terms of corn, wool and lambs. Birdforth, however, appears rather more wealthy than it seemed to be in 1292 and 1318 when it was among the most lowly-assessed wapentakes. The Vale of York and Cleveland stands out much more clearly than in 1292 and 1318, although then it was very prominent. As earlier, the richest parishes in terms of agricultural production were those in the Central Vale. Rudby (1200s), Northallerton (1000s), Kirby Wiske (733s), Birkby (400s) and Thirsk (400s) were among the richest in the entire northeast at this time. Evidently they had made a partial recovery from the Scottish devastations which had caused such a decline in 1318.

The area included in Ryedale and Pickering Lythe wapentakes contained a great deal of moorland, as well as the lowland of the Vale of Pickering. Sheep farming was the main source of income in the large strip parishes included in the wapentakes. Some individual parishes made very large contributions to the Ninth. Pickering, for example, contributed 1333s, more than all the Moorland parishes put together and almost as much as the total

---

[1] *Ibid*, m. 20.
[2] The relevant mss. used were:—
   P.R.O. E 179/211/16-18, Sales and Valuations of the Ninth.
   P.R.O. E 179/211/19, Inquisition for the Ninth.
   P.R.O. E 179/211/37, Fraud in Collection of the Ninth.
   There are no figures for the East Riding in either the published or manuscript sources.

Ninth for the Coastal Plateau region (see Appendix II). This obviously reflected the great advantages of the parish – with its fertile soils flanked to the north by wide moorland sheep walk and to the south by rich water meadows. Easy movement for men and animals along the periphery of the Vale emphasised these fundamental advantages. Again, the stimulus of monastic agriculture must be mentioned.[1] The figures in Appendix II by themselves are enough to show how great this was in these strip parishes. Thus at Pickering the monastic contribution was 227s (coming mainly from the granges of Rievaulx in the Marishes). In Helmsley parish, too, the monastic share in the Ninth was as much as 90s.

A continuity of regional development in terms of agricultural production is evident between 1292 and 1342. The broad framework of agricultural prosperity was well established.[2] All the assessments examined indicate that there was a distinctive theme in the distribution of this prosperity. The Vales of York, Cleveland and Pickering maintained a leadership over the Coastal Plateau and Moorlands in terms of prosperity. Despite the varying economic and political fortunes of the northeast this remained the persistent theme. Was this preserved or destroyed during subsequent centuries?

The Valor Ecclesiasticus and Agricultural Prosperity in 1535.
When Henry VIII decided to acquire the Papal First Fruits and Tenths for himself the first requisite was to find out their true value. Thus a completely new assessment was made of all benefices. This was the Valor Ecclesiasticus of 1535. Since this document is outside the period of the present study it will be used briefly and specifically. The dangers and values of the Valor have been noted by A. Savine.[3] For the purpose of the historian interested in agriculture its scope can be great. For example, because it gives the value of benefices, a good idea of agricultural prosperity can be gained, and because it describes tithes due, some idea of the type of husbandry in the parish is possible. Information about the compostition and value of tithes is unfortunately not given for every parish so that in such cases the total income is the only information. Use of the tithes will be made later when arable and pastoral farming are discussed. For the present, attention will be directed to the total income for each benefice to see what bearing it has on the distribution of agricultural prosperity.

Without introducing too much tedious detail, certain general conclusions can be stated about the significance of the Valor. The distribution of agricultural prosperity in 16th century North-East Yorkshire seemed to be very similar to that of the 13th and 14th centuries. The pattern which was evident then had been preserved, despite the many years which intervened and the varying influences at work. The richest parishes were still to be found in the Teesmouth region and Vale of York. Most of them were the same as previously – Rudby (2800/-), Thirsk (700/-), Coxwold (884/-), Kirkleatham (1134/-). As

---

[1] B. Waites, *Moorland and Valeland Farming in North-East Yorkshire: the monastic contribution in the thirteenth and fourteenth centuries*, Borthwick Institute of Historical Research, York, 1967.
[2] The national pattern is given in E. J. Buckatzsch, 'The Geographical Distribution of Wealth in England, 1086-1843', *Ec.H.R.*, 2nd Ser., iii (1950) pp.180-202. Also R. S. Schofield, "The Geographical Distribution of Wealth in England, 1334-1649,' *Ec.H.R.*, 2nd Ser., xviii (1965), pp.483-510.
[3] *English Monasteries on the Eve of the Dissolution. (1909)* Book I, Ch. II.

the tithe figures show arable farming was the predominant occupation of the Vale of York. In some cases the value of the corn and hay tithe was extremely high. This was particularly evident in Kilvington, Northallerton, Thirsk, Kirby Wiske and North Ottrington which were situated in the centre of the Vale near to the River Wiske and the fertile alluvial/gravel soils there. The continuing influence of these soils was a remarkable factor in the development of the region. Just as significant as the influence of the limestones and light gravels which fringed the Vale of Pickering had been in that region's development. The importance of easy communications and accessible markets for produce was an additional advantage of the parishes in the Vale of York. Both Thirsk and Northallerton had been the principal market towns of the region for many centuries, dealing not only in cereals and cattle, but also in wool.[1] Situated, too, on the Great North Road, their importance in a wider sense had been emphasised. In fact, the vulnerability of their position in time of war was shown by the severe damage both Thirsk and Northallerton suffered from the invading Scots, entering England by this route.

While the parishes of the Coastal Plateau region had become relatively more important in terms of agricultural production than they had been, those of Pickering Vale and the Pickering Vale/Moors region had apparently declined. How far this decline was due to an incompleteness in the Record Commission Edition of the Valor it is not possible to say. For some parishes only a summary total of the Valor is given for the Vicarage. It seems likely that in some of these cases the value of the Rectory should be added to give a full assessment. Unfortunately it is not possible to obtain this information as the manuscript too is incomplete in this respect. Beyond minimising the importance of the two regions, however, the possible deficiency is not so very detrimental.

Conclusion

The broad framework of agricultural prosperity during the Middle Ages has been established. All the assessments examined indicate that there was a distinctive theme in the distribution of this prosperity throughout the centuries. The Vales of York, Cleveland and Pickering were always ahead of the Coastal Plateau and Moorlands in terms of prosperity.

It remains to examine, in the following chapters, the details that made up this particular distribution of prosperity. What was the farming activity practised in the region? Was arable production more important than pastoralism? Is there any indication that regional specialisation occurred? What did the monasteries contribute to all this?

---

[1] Thirsk was mentioned in Pegolotti's list.

APPENDIX I

The Valor of Pope Nicholas (1292) and the Reassessment of 1318.
(arranged regionally)

COASTAL PLATEAU				PICKERING VALE/MOORS				PICKERING VALE			
Benefice		*1292*	*1318*	Benefice		*1292*	*1318*	Benefice		*1292*	*1318*
Loftus	...	267	160	Seamer	...	1067	533	Stonegrave	...	667	293
Easington	...	400	240	Hutton Bushel	...	507	507	Oswaldkirk	...	267	120
Hinderwell	...	333	333	Brompton	...	1067	1067	Gilling	...	320	160
Whitby	...	667	400	Wykeham	...	200	200	Nunnington	...	93	80
Lythe	...	667	267	Thornton	...	367	200	Hovingham	...	800	200
Sneton	...	133	67	Middleton	...	1067	453	Slingsby	...	267	133
Fyling	...	320	160	Pickering	...	7467		Appleton	...	1033	400
Skelton	...	347	147	Kirby Moorside	...	533	133	Barton	...	400	160
Scalby	...	480	480	Helmsley	...	1200	400	Malton	...	427	427
108, 485 acres	...	3614	2254	Kirkdale	...	467	200	Normanby	...	267	100
Pence per acre	...	0.39	0.25	172,630 acres	...	13942	3693	Kirby Misperton	...	733	333
				Pence per acre	...	0.97	0.31	Edston	...	133	80
								Sinnington	...	160	80
								Salton	...	1067	400
				YORK VALE				Ampleforth	...	800	800
MOORLANDS				Benefice		*1292*	*1318*	Filey	...	400	400
Benefice		*1292*	*1318*	Ayton	...	400	200	Scarborough	...	907	800
Danby	...	267	160	Rudby	...	1600	900	61,290 acres	...	8741	4966
Hawnby	...	267	80	Welbury	...	200	100	Pence per acre	...	1.71	0.97
Scawton	...	100	—	Crathorne	...	213	100				
Lastingham	...	600	300	S. Ottrington	...	213	80	YORK VALE/MOORS			
Levisham	...	100	80	N. Ottrington	...	333	200	Benefice		*1292*	*1318*
Hackness	...	667	320	Thirsk	...	733	240	Kildale	...	106	67
70,717 acres	...	2001	940	Kilvington	...	333	133	Cowesby	...	100	60
Pence per acre	...	0.34	0.16	North Allerton	...	1467	533	Osmotherley	...	560	240
				Sigston	...	400	200	Kirkby Knowle	...	333	160
				Rounton	...	200	80	Kirby	...	467	240
				Birkby	...	467	100	Ingleby	...	240	147
TEESMOUTH				Kirby Wiske	...	1200	667	Stokesley	...	1067	467
Benefice		*1292*	*1318*	Coxwold	...	1067	300	Whorlton	...	133	80
Kirkleatham	...	1600	1067	Stainton	...	520	320	Leake	...	1067	533
Marske	...	333	173	Marton	...	173	107	Arncliffe	...	213	133
Ormesby	...	333	200	Levington	...	400	267	Felixkirk	...	200	80
Middlesbrough	...	100	100	Thornton le Street		267	133	Guisborough	...	240	120
25,262 acres	...	2366	1540	145,518 acres	...	10186	4660	90,973 acres	...	4726	2327
Pence per acre	...	1.12	0.73	Pence per acre	...	0.84	0.38	Pence per acre	...	0.62	0.31

APPENDIX II
EXTRACTS FROM THE INQUISITION FOR THE NINTH (1341).
(included to show the type of information given)

PARISH	NINTH Total	Monastic Share	TITHES Wool Lambs	Hay	Uncultivated Land	Ninth Value (If cultivated)
COASTAL PLATEAU						
Loftus	120		93(10)		3 parts	53
Easington	136		ii(xiist) lx(x)	10	great part	80
Hinderwell	200		67(20)	40	6 parts	30
Whitby	203		iii(i) C(xxx)		half arable	120
Lythe	247				3 parts arable	107
Sneton	60		40(10)		2 parts	33
Fyling	113		160(53)		3 parts	40
Skelton	258		100		4 parts arable	40
Scalby	360	40	106(40)	30		40
Total	1697	40				503
Pence per acre	0.19					
PICKERING VALE/ MOOR						
Hutton Bushel	320		i+ lxxx(xxx)		3 carucates	80
Brompton	533	40	200(80)	244*	10 carucates	133
Wykeham	135	40		30•	2 carucates	20
Thornton	160		i(vst)	80	3 carucates	30
Middleton	533	40	267(67)	267*	3 carucates	40
Pickering	1333	227				
Kirby Moorside	409	10				
Helmsley	603	90	v(i+) CC(xl)	40	13 carucates	93
Kirkdale	283	17	133(33) C(xxvi)	27	5 carucates	50
Seamer	672					
Total	4979	464				446
Pence per acre	0.35					
MOORLAND						
Danby	200		133(–)		3 parts	(not given)
Hawnby	215	82	i(xst) xx(iii)	40	2 carucates	20
Scawton	53			10	2 carucates	20
Lastingham	453		160(67)		15 carucates	67
Levisham	48			13	2 carucates	20
Hackness	215		400(80)		half arable	120
Total	1184					247
Pence per acre	0.20					

Sources: P.R.O. E. 179/211/19 and *Nonarum Inquisitiones*, Record Commission, 1807.
The values of the Ninth are given to the nearest shilling and then the pence per acre figure is worked out for each region.
The Roman numerals in the Wool tithe column refer to actual numbers, i.e. in the case of wool – sacks; in the case of lambs – the specific number comprising the tithe.
Figures unbracketed refer to what the Rector 'used to receive'; bracketed figures refer to what he receives 'this year'.
* hay tithe and 'dos ecclesie' included together.

6 ARABLE FARMING

THE MOORLANDS

'The Moorlands' comprised very varied land-forms. The major contrast was between the High and Low Moors. The former were more than 1,000 feet high and composed very largely of infertile sandstones which had in most places developed a podsolised surface capable of sustaining only heather. The Low Moors, however, were more fertile. The so-called Tabular Hills, for instance, were mostly well below 1,000 feet and composed mainly of Corallian limestones (this was the dip slope region north of the Vale of Pickering). A narrow clay vale separated the High and Low Moors along much of their length. This vale stretched in a discontinuous belt from Ryedale eastwards to the complex valley system of Hackness. On its northern side the High Moorlands rose gradually as a heather-clad mass; to the south an abrupt scarp face frowned over the small vale. This marked the edge of the Low Moors, but it belied their real nature, for once the scarp had been ascended and its belt of woodland passed, there was a gradual slope of mainly fertile soils falling gently southwards to the Vale of Pickering. The distinction between High and Low Moors had been real in medieval times: in 1351, for example, the Abbot of Whitby had granted pasture 'in les hautes mores'[1] and the accounts of the Duchy of Lancaster contain several references to 'agistamento averiorum in alta mora' during the fourteenth century.[2]

Besides the broad distinction between High and Low Moor, the dales must be considered. They were especially significant because they were the only areas of cultivation within the High Moors during medieval times.[3] Their soils were either Lias clays or, in Eskdale, boulder clays and gravels. Although by no means ideally suitable for arable cultivation they were farmed because there was nowhere else to farm. At Domesday the dales had been largely woodland and, except for Eskdale, most had been devoid of village settlement.[4] The extent of cultivated land in the eleventh and early twelfth centuries consequently must have been very small. Even the entry of monastic settlers to the areas did little to extend arable cultivation, for the monks were interested mainly in the value of the dales for pasture or iron working. Thus Guisborough Priory, despite its varied interests in Eskdale, ranging from the iron workings of Glaisdale to the cattle farm of Dephill Bridge, had no substantial arable holding there. What arable land there was existed to supply the requirements of the animal-keepers or smelters and was very subsidiary to these concerns.

This was typical of most of the monastic settlements in the dales. Rievaulx, instance, was granted extensive pasture rights in Farndale and Bransdale but no mention is made of

---

[1] *W.C.* no. 475 (Grant to the Burgesses of Whitby).
[2] N.R.R.S. (New Series) vol. 4, p.200 (Ministers' Accounts and Duchy Coucher Book).
[3] I include the interior vale of Oxford clay in the category of the dales.
[4] Robert de Stutville had granted to Keldholme Priory the bark of trees in the forest of Bransdale (1154-66), *E.Y.C.* vol. 9, p.92. Roger de Mowbray granted to Rievaulx two woodlands in Farndale, at Middlehead and Dowthwaite (before 1155), *ibid.* Timber was to be taken from Spaunton Forest to repair Kirby Misperton Mill (1140-55), *ibid.* vol. I, p.476. There are many such indications that forest in the dales was extensive in the twelfth century and later. Details of Danby Forest in 1272 in *Inq.* vol. I, p.139.

arable land and, so far as it is known, no abbey granges were ever established in these places.[1] In Westerdale too, where the monks had a lodge to superintend their animal farming, only about two bovates of land was attached.

The dales remained largely woodland even until as late as the sixteenth century, although complaints about the destruction of the woods, especially by smelters, became more and more frequent during Elizabeth's reign.[2] The extent of woodland had had a great deal of influence on the type of arable holding and farming in the dales from Domesday times. Thirteenth century evidence shows that this contributed to two major trends in dale agriculture: fragmentary or dispersed holdings and early enclosures.

The villages were, of course, centres of cultivation. In 1272 Danby in Eskdale had at least 100 bovates of land being worked by villeins and freemen; at Westerdale 60 tenants farmed 53 bovates.[3] However, land was being worked in many places outside the fields of the villages. Many freemen were working land within Danby Forest, each having mainly about 20 acres or less. For example, Rodger de Middleheved held 19 acres of land and 4 acres of meadow for 12s. 4d. The total land worked by the tenants of Peter de Brus in 1272 in the forest was 149 acres. The value per acre was moreover as good and sometimes better than that of Danby or Lealholm fields.[4] At Aislaby, a long list of closes in the hands of tenants at will showed that a fragmentation of holding occurred there; Johanridding, Rughclose, le Westclose, Terricroft, Arnouzhill, Blapit, Synfield, Laximancroft, le Couclose and le Park.[5] In Farndale in 1276, 545 acres were 'per bovatum terre non tenentes set secundum majus et minus'[6] – They were held in separate plots in various places. Some tenants held waste places also in separate localities. At nearby Douthwaite (apparently not a village but just an area worked by scattered holdings) certain men held plots of land variously distributed in the moor. The great amount of assarting which took place in some of the dales during the thirteenth and fourteenth centuries contributed to scattered arable holdings. This was particularly so in Rosedale. The Coucher Book of the Duchy of Lancaster shows that assarting was frequent at Cropton, Tranmire and Hartoft in the early fourteenth century, for example. Much of the land must have been marginal in character and, if left unenclosed, liable to revert to moorland again. Most of the assarts were small – about 9 acres usually – and sown with oats as their first crop. Sometimes greater amounts of land were assarted – almost 500 acres at Goathland and Allantofts, for instance.[7]

---

[1] The monastic unit of 'exploitation' in such areas was probably the 'cote' or sheep-house, dependent on a more distant grange but allowing the shepherds shelter for a night or so. Skiplam Grange might have been the headquarters for Farndale and Bransdale sheep farming as it was conveniently situated for them.

[2] The abundance of wood was, incidentally, a principal reason for the iron-working in the dales (plus ore, of course): B. Waites, 'Medieval Iron Working in Northeast Yorkshire'; *Geography, vol.* xlix (January 1964), pp.33-43.

[3] *Inq.* vol. I, p.139 *et seq.* See also the Extent for Westerdale, 133S; P.R.O. C.I35/44/6: also Ministers' Account, *c.* 1318, P.R.O. S.C.6/835/2.

[4] *Inq.* vol. I, p.139 Et *seq.*

[5] *C.I.P.M.* vol. 12, p.219.

[6] *Inq.* vol. I, p.167 *et seq.*

[7] Duchy of Lancaster, Coucher Book, P.R.O. Exchequer Q.R. Misc. Books, vol. 8. Extracts printed in *N.R.R.S.* (New Series) vols. 2 and 4.

No indication was given that there was any normal field-system in some of the dales. Farndale and Bransdale, for example, within the manor of Kirby Moorside, had a total population of more than 150 in 1282, yet no reference to a village community was made.[1] Instead, the usual description was 'in a certain dale called Farndale' or some such equivalent, when the tenants were being referred to; never 'in the village of'. This, too, suggests that settlement and arable farming in the dales was scattered, and not nucleated.

In fact, just as assarting implied enclosures, so the preponderance of meadow land implied the same thing in the dales.[2] Once a man had cleared an area of woodland it was logical for him to enclose it to keep out prowling animals and the renewed spread of surrounding wood. This had evidently been generally true of the dales, because references to enclosed plots, whether for pasture or arable, were very many in the thirteenth century. Those at Aislaby have been mentioned, but they occurred at Danby, too e.g. 'quoddam clausam vocat Le Heved', Horsehouse close, 20 acres of meadow.[3] The extent of such lands must have been great; in the forest near Lealholm, for example, Peter de Brus had 114 acres of demesne meadow, much of it in separate places, in 1272, and at Danby considerable amounts of meadow occurred in clearings within the forest, for example 80 acres in Selythwaite, 40 acres in Yarlethwaite, 60 acres in Sourbylaunde, 120 acres in Westmanhouthwaite ('thwaite'=clearing).[4] Many of the freemen in the forest of Danby had, in fact, assarted land for arable and meadow: William Harkel held nine acres of land and eight acres of meadow for 12s. 2d.; Lyolph del Dale held four acres meadow and one waste place of a certain bercary for 8s. 6d. in 1272.[5] Such small, scattered holdings, usually enclosed from the forest, seem to have been typical of the dales. Cultivated land took, then, two forms; it was concentrated in village fields, where villages existed, but mainly it was scattered in various places within the extensive woodlands of the dales. This latter was typical of an area in the process of becoming settled and cultivated.[6]

The Low Moors – the most important area of arable cultivation in the entire moorland – were a different proposition. There settlement, in the form of villages and monastic granges was much more profuse than it was in the dales. There was a series of villages perched on the scarp top of the Corallian; Gillamoor, Spaunton, Cropton, Cawthorn, Newton, Lockton; and more villages were located further south, on the dip slope: Carlton, Pockley, Fadmoor, Appleton le Moor, Kingthorpe. These were all, of course, the principal areas of lay cultivation; but the presence of large numbers of monastic granges had extended this area. Rievaulx Abbey, in particular, had several granges in the region (for example, Griff, Stilton, Newlathes, Skiplam and Sproxton) but other houses had granges at Murton, Old Byland, Snileswath, Appleton, Spaunton and Kingthorpe. The granges

---

[1] *Inq.* vol. I, p.249.
[2] 'The more pasture predominates, the less the common field arable is able to resist the tendency to enclosure.' G. Slater, *The English Peasantry and the Enclosure of the Common Fields* (London, 1907).
[3] P.R.O. C.135/44/6.
[4] *ibid.* also *Inq. vol.* I, p.139 *et seq.*
[5] *Inq. vol. I,* p.139 *et seq.*
[6] Note that enclosure was also an early feature of the central Vale of Pickering, especially the Marishes. Both the Marishes and the moorland dales were mainly pastoral, in the process of settlement, largely woodland or marshland – both in fact were very marginal areas.

situated in this area were the largest and relatively the most prosperous of all monastic granges in the North-east. This can be assessed from the contributions to the 1301 Subsidy. The acreage can be estimated from various sources: at Griff, for example, the monks had 4 carucates given to them in their foundation grant.[1] Presumably all this was arable land; at least, in 1341, there were 4 carucates 'in agricultura' here.[2] The Dissolution Accounts give more details; the total holding was just over 490 acres, of which 206 acres were arable and 284 pasture.[3] This is a high amount of arable, considering that the trend of sixteenth-century farming had been towards pasture.

At Stilton the extent of arable was greater; 5 carucates, that is about 600 acres.[4] However at Newlathes the arable and pasture totalled just over half that, namely 374 acres.[5] It is evident that these granges were very large arable farms, especially early in their history.[6] Details about the other granges are unfortunately not forthcoming. The form of the description given by the Dissolution Accounts provides some interesting suggestions about the grange lands of Griff and Newlathes, which could throw light on two obscure questions: whether the monks had a distinctive field system on their granges and whether their lands were more completely enclosed than those of laymen.

A full answer is too much to hope for, but a few clues can be found. The first is straightforward: at both granges almost all the land, whether it was arable or pasture, appeared to be enclosed in 1538. The enclosures varied very much in size: Fogg Close was a pasture close of only 10 acres at Griff; Fatte Close was also for pasture but its area was 24 acres; Stoke Ing was 40 acres. Certain land was described as 'field'; for instance at Griff the following occurred:[7]

1 field or flat land (arable)	northside of lathgarth	30 acres
1 ,, ,, ,,	Mortenpo	6 acres
1 ,, ,, ?	Coote Flat	6 acres
1 ,, ,, ?	Abbot Hagg	60 acres
1 field of arable land	Jodicefield	60 acres
1 field called	Tlysteleyfield	40 acres

The acreage of the areas described as 'fields' is 130. By a strange coincidence the acreage of the 'fields' of Newlathes grange was also 130:

1 pasture called	Lyngery	Field	30 acres
2 ,, ,,	Thistleley	Field	40 ,,
1 ,, ,,	South	Field	40 ,,
1 close ,,	Coneygarth	Field	20 ,,

---

[1] *R.C.* p.16.
[2] P.R.O. E.179/211/19, m.20.
[3] *R.C.* pp.312-13
[4] *ibid.* p.16.
[5] *ibid.* pp.313-14.
[6] For example, there were at least fifteen plough beasts working at Griff Grange about the middle of the thirteenth century which were pastured in Sproxton, a few miles away. *R.C.* p.293.
[7] From Dissolution Accounts, *R.C.* p.312 *et seq.*

Could it be that there were remnants of the earlier system of tillage adopted by the monks on their granges? The individual acreages for each field was as follows:

    at Newlathes they were 30. 40. 40. 20
    at Griff   they were 30. 60. 40. (omitting the dubious areas).

There is a great similarity between them. Could it be that the monks divided their holding into fields on a similar basis to the village fields? This fragmentary evidence seems to suggest this as a possibility. The monks could not have been following a previously established field pattern at Newlathes because it had never been the site of any previous settlement. Griff had been mentioned at Domesday as waste and it is unlikely that any field system remained as a basis there.[1]

This evidence by itself is inconclusive, especially because it is so late, although it is surprising how accurately the sixteenth century accounts portrayed the size of the grange land in earlier times. This was proved by comparing earlier sources; might it not be as accurate for the amounts enclosed and the system of tillage adopted? It is worthwhile remembering that monastic lands remained remarkably stable after the middle of the thirteenth century. The suggestion that the largest monastic granges devoted to arable farming were organised on a three-field system, similar to that of village economy, requires a great deal of examination. Little or nothing is known about how the monks organised their grange land in areas which had never been settled. Much regional and detailed work may provide an answer which is impossible to deduce from scanty sources available in the North-east.

Although little detailed information is available to give a full picture of arable farming in the moors, certain conclusions are possible. Arable cultivation was not extensive. It was confined to the dip slopes of the Low Moors and the dales within the moorland. In the former, the arable farm or grange developed to a great size and lay farming was very important: in the latter, monastic arable farming was at a minimum and lay farming was characteristic of a recently settled forested area. That is to say it was generally scattered in small plots within the woodland areas and enclosure was common. The village farming area was more important in Eskdale than in the southern dales because, in the latter, the separate homestead seems to have been the substitute for the village community.

THE COASTAL PLATEAU[2]

This region appeared one of low agricultural prosperity in 1341. The reasons for this are not far to seek; in fact the Inquisition taken in 1342 supplies some of them. Loftus and Easington parishes were largely moorland where 'the parishioners lived for the most part by sheep' which they kept.[3] The land which was cultivated was marginal and liable to revert to waste. This seems to be the main explanation for the great amount of land out of cultivation in 1341. A great part of the cultivated land in Easington parish lay untilled;

---

[1] Dissolution evidence elsewhere leads to similar conclusions: at Kekmarsh Grange, for instance, all the land appeared to be enclosed and there was also a 'great field called East Field' though no indication was ever given that Kekmarsh was a village at any time after 1069. Here is evidence again of a field system on what appeared to be always monastic property, cf. information from Abbey leases: R.C. p.349 *et seq.*
[2] The small area of coast plain in Scalby parish is not included in this section.
[3] *N.I.* p.231.

three parts of Loftus, three parts of Lythe, four parts of Skelton, half the arable of Whitby parish – and so the list goes on, describing land out of cultivation, which had at one time been worked. The total value of this land if it had been cultivated would have been £226 7.0.[1] This was a substantial loss. The explanation appears to be the marginal character of arable farming in the area, as the Inquisition itself suggested.[2] What other causes could there be? The effect of the plagues of the mid-fourteenth century had not yet been felt along the coast. For instance, John de Fauconberg had 24 bovates of poor moorland in demesne at Skelton which was worth £4 16. 0. 'before the mortality of men in these parts this year'.[3] The date is significant; 1350, later than the Inquisition of 1342. Even so, the effect of the plague when it did arrive does not seem to have been great in this remote area. Its incidence, too, was least in the highland districts, as A. H. Thompson has shown from a study of benefices in the diocese of York between 1348 and 1369.[4]

The effect of Scottish raids could be a more plausible explanation of land uncultivated in 1341. The Scots certainly reached the area; John de Eune, for example, had a vaccary or cattle farm worth 30s. a year in peacetime but in 1326 worth nothing 'because of the destructions of the Scots'.[5] Whitby Abbey had complained in 1316 that their 'corn and victuals ... have been destroyed as well by the frequent inroads of the Scots as by accidents so that the Abbot and Convent have had to seek sustenance elsewhere'.[6] Later, in 1323, the monks received a mandate to appropriate the church of Seamer, worth 80 marks, because 'they suffer from the barrenness of the soil, and the incursions of the Scots'.[7] By 1328 some of the Abbey's benefices had been destroyed by the Scots and the Archbishop appointed 'some trustworthy men' to survey the damage.[8] The reassessments of benefices throughout the whole of the area in 1318 resulted in great differences from the 1292 *Valor* of Pope Nicholas IV.[9] The value of the church of Easington fell from £20 in 1292 to £12 in 1318; Lythe church and chapels were reduced from £33 6.8. to £13 6.8; Skelton from £17 6.8. to £7 6.8. However the coastal district, despite all this, did not appear to be among the hardest hit parts of the North-east. It was out of the main line of advance of the Scots, which was through the Vale of York. The damage might have come from irregular visits of raiding parties. Since no land was described as uncultivated because of the Scots devastations by the parishioners on oath in 1342, it seems likely that by this time the effect was small. The parishioners would have been ready enough to forward it as a reason for their lower assessment, if they could.

The arable land of the Coastal Plateau seems to have been, like that of the moorland region, very marginal. Besides the evidence of 1341, several Inquisitions and Extents

---

[1] ibid. p.231 *et seq.*
[2] A. R. H. Baker, 'Evidence in the *Nonarum Inquisitiones* of Contracting Arable Lands in England during the early Fourteenth Century', *Economic History Review*, Second Series, vol. XIX, no. 3, (December 1966). Good discussion of 'half-wanted lands'.
[3] *C.I.P.M.* vol. 9, p 177
[4] 'The Pestilences of the Fourteenth Century in the Diocese of York', *A.J.* vol. 71, pp.97-154.
[5] *G.C.* vol I, pp.103-4.
[6] *C.P.R.* (1316) p.389.
[7] *Calendar of Papal Letters* vol. 2 (1305-42).
[8] *C.C.R.* (1328) p.280
[9] The reliability of the 1292 and 1318 Assessments is discussed by R. Graham, *English Ecclesiastical Studies*, (London, 1929) pp.271-301.

indicate the same thing. In 1279, for instance, Peter de Malo Lacu had one third of his arable land in Lythe uncultivated, one quarter uncultivated at Cucket Nook, and more than one fifth uncultivated at Goldsborough.[1] This was rather odd in a period when demesne farming was increasing. No reason was given for the land being uncultivated but it seems quite obvious that some would have been fallow and the rest had been allowed to revert to moorland because of its poorness. The land at Cucket Nook, for instance, was on the very edge of the clay soils of the plateau and verged on the moorland. It was, besides, at a height of 650 feet; very high for cultivation in such an exposed district.

Nearly every village in the area, too, had a great deal of assarted land attached to it. At Skiningrove there were 'tofts and crofts with assarts' and three assarts in Playgreve worth 2s. 1d.; at Girrick (around 700 feet high) there were two assarts worth 12s. and 14s.; at Skelton, Moorsholm and Stanghow the number of assarts was even greater.[2] Obviously such land would be in and out of cultivation very frequently: it could not always be relied upon for cultivation. The marginal character of arable farming was emphasised by the high level of most of the settlements and the cultivation.[3] Of course 600-700 feet may not seem very high, but it is the limit for successful arable production. There are very few areas cultivated at that height in England today, despite the fact that the present-day farmer can use many advantages denied to his predecessors, such as seed specially selected and adaptable to varying climatic conditions.

It is all the more surprising, then, to notice that much of the arable land of the Coastal Plateau was above 500 feet in the thirteenth century. Peter de Brus had 382 acres of arable at Brotton, for example, in 1272, and at Skelton he had 567 acres in arable demesne.[4] Peter de Malo Lacu had 160 acres arable at Cucket Nook in 1279, and at Goldsborough 307 acres arable in demesne[5] Besides, although some villages e.g. Mickleby, Barnby, were located in valleys, a line of settlements followed the boundary between the clay plateau and the moorland at a height of about 600 feet or more. These were all, of course, areas of arable cultivation though the amount varied at each. At Moorsholm and Stanghow it was about 37 bovates, for example.[6] In fact, the coastal area was well settled despite its bleakness and none-too-fertile boulder clay soils (which were often very wooded, especially in the coastal denes, which cut deeply into the plateau in several places). This was mainly because of the variety of occupations which were possible in the area. Sheep could be kept, fishing engaged in, and some arable farming, too; one occupation could make up for the deficiencies of the other. Fishing thus became important in the coastal villages. Peter de Brus had a fishery worth 4s. at Skiningrove in 1272, and at Sandsend the sea fishery was worth 13s. 4d. a year.[7] Villages further inland, too, such as Moorsholm, also had a hand in the fishing. This was typical of an area in which so much of the arable was marginal, localised and unreliable.

---

[1] *Inq.* vol. I, p.191 *et seq.* Reference to uncultivated demesne land is a rarity in the Extents examined for other places in the North-east in the last quarter of the thirteenth century
[2] *Inq.* vol. I, p.139 *et. seq.*
[3] Several villages were located on the gravel which was interspersed with the boulder clay in certain places.
[4] *Inq.* vol. I, p.139 *et. seq.*
[5] *ibid.* p.191 *et. seq.*
[6] *ibid.* p.139 *et. seq.*
[7] *ibid.* p.139 and p.191 *et. seq.*

The suggestion so far has been that arable farming was very localised in this area during the middle ages. The emphasis seemed to be more on sheep farming, sometimes associated with fishing. The *Valor Ecclesiasticus* (1535) seems to support this. The following list shows the percentage corn, hay and livestock (i.e. wool, lamb and calf tithes) tithes were of the total agricultural tithe.

Benefice	% of Total Agricultural Tithe[1]	
	Corn-hay tithe	Wool-lamb-calf tithe
Lythe	54	46
Loftus	69	31
Hinderwell	60	40
Sneton	44	56
Easington	63	37

Corn and hay tithes were generally rather low, with the exception of Loftus. At Sneton, in fact, the animal tithe exceeded the corn tithe. It was almost as much in Lythe parish and well over half as much in Easington and Hinderwell. These figures show a remarkable contrast to the figures for the Vale of York. There, the tithes from arable production were very high and those from livestock correspondingly low.[2] A study of the value in 1535 gives the impression that pastoral farming was as significant as arable in some parishes, although in a few it was of greater overall importance. This supports the impression derived from earlier evidence: the importance of pastoralism had been evident from the tithe values quoted by the Inquisition of 1342. Clearly the area of arable farming was restricted. Besides, the lack of any reference to the Coastal Plateau as a source of corn for the King's Wars between 1298 and 1360 appears to substantiate the idea that arable cultivation was not as important in this region as it has been shown to be elsewhere (for example, in the Wolds).[3] It is possible that in an area like the Coastal Plateau, where arable farming was often marginal in character, there would have been very little surplus for marketing.

It remains to be seen whether the monastic farmers in this region followed the same trend away from arable farming. Whitby Abbey, it will be recalled, had a great deal of property in the region. In 1301 it had at least seven granges here:

Grange	Fifteenth contributed to 1301 subsidy[4]
Eskdale	6s. 11d.
Stakesby	41s. 8d.
Whitby Lathes	11s. 5d.
Lairpool	11s.
Fyling	13s. 9d.
Hawsker	10s. 2d.
Normanby	14s.

---

[1] The total Valor only is given for other parishes in the region (i.e. Whitby, Fyling and Skelton) so no tithe percentages can be worked out for them.
[2] For example, Kirby Wiske: 96% corn-hay tithe; 4% wool-lamb-calf tithe. For a full discussion of this see B. Waites, 'Aspects of Medieval Arable Farming in the Vale of York', *Ryedale Historian*, no.2 (April 1966) pp.5-11.
[3] There was one reference to 100 quarters of oats going from Lythe to Whitby in 1298.
[4] *Y.A.S.R.S.*, vol. 21.

As the table shows, the contributions were, with the exception of Stakesby, low: low, that is, in comparison with the other granges of the North-east which were mainly devoted to arable farming (e.g. the 'limestone' granges of Rievaulx). This implies that the granges of Whitby were less prosperous in terms of agricultural production.

In fact, arable farming was more important on the Whitby granges than this suggests. As late as 1366, for instance, when there is evidence of much leasing of monastic property over most of England, the monks of Whitby still held three of their granges in their own hands.[1] Stakesby had four ploughs working there; Whitbylathes, three; Fyling, two. Besides, the monks were working land at Lathgarth (called a grange in 1394) and Middlewood: there were two ploughs at each of these places. Except at Stakesby, and perhaps Whitbylathes, it is unlikely that arable farming was of great importance at this time. The abbey at any rate needed to spend over £250 on the purchase and carriage of corn in 1366, so that their own production seems to have been well below their requirements.[2]

The collection of corn-tithes supplemented the personal efforts of the monks at several of their granges. An interesting document, which gives details of the corn at some of the abbey granges in 1394, can throw some light on the importance of arable farming there.[3] At the abbey grange, for example, there were 13 quarters of corn and 79 quarters of malt, barley and oats in store; at Stakesby there were 58 quarters of corn (62% of which was oats); at Lathgarth 122 quarters of corn (of which 74% was oats); at Whitbylathes 120 quarters of corn (of which 66% was oats). This corn was derived from the grange land and from tithes and so gives some idea of the significance and character of arable farming in the area. The granges nearest to the abbey seemed to be most important as arable farms, and oats, as might be expected in a coastal region of high land, was the predominant crop.[4] However, wheat was sown; 17 acres at Stakesby, 30 acres at Lathgarth, and 30 acres at Whitbylathes were sown in 1394. It was here that most ploughs were at work and the arable farming of the monks most pronounced. Although the monastic grange in the Coastal Plateau region did not appear so important as an arable farm compared to the granges in other regions, its importance in a district where arable farming was not emphasised strongly should not be forgotten. At least the Whitby granges showed that arable farming achieved a certain standard despite the monks' constant complaint of the barrenness of their land. If information were available for the period before 1301 it might well show that such farming was more intensified because then the abbey was at the apogee of its development.

The canons of Guisborough Priory had not much interest in the greater part of the region, except for a few places. Apparently they had only one grange in the region, at Brotton, although the extent of lands owned by them at Ugthorpe and Loftus suggests that granges might have been established there. The prior owned a great deal of arable land at Skelton; at least 28 bovates at Loftus, as well as 300 acres of moor; and at least 5 bovates,

---

[1] *C.B.M.*, vol. III, pp.63-8.
[2] *ibid.*
[3] *Officio Instauri Monasterii, C.A.W.* vol. 1, pp.318-20.
[4] Throughout the history of all the monasteries the granges nearest the mother house were always the most important and usually the last to be leased (if leased at all).

128 acres of land in Moorsholm.[1] He held more scattered lands elsewhere in the region, but those at Skelton, Loftus, Moorsholm and Ugthorpe were the most extensive. It was in these places that the canons cultivated land. There is no evidence to show the scale or character of their exploitation, except at Ugthorpe. Here, an interesting series of cartulary documents indicate that arable farming was important in and around Ugthorpe.[2]

The canons had acquired land in the vill during the twelfth century. In 1161, for example, William de Hamby had demised two carucates to the canons: a few years later they had two bovates from William de Argentum for a yearly payment of 2s. Land acquisitions continued into the thirteenth century; sometimes they were purchased.[3] It is in the middle of the thirteenth century that more detail can be found. In 1254 Guisborough Priory, with Handale Priory, a small nunnery nearby, partitioned the waste of the manor of Ugthorpe between them. Guisborough obtained most of this and the purpose was for cultivation; enclosures were made and Guisborough even set up its own windmill to grind the produce. Later the canons obtained all the waste and in 1262 also obtained a lease of Handale's land in the valley of Ugthorpe. Seven years later another lease was secured for 'quadam summa pecuniae quam praefati Prior et Conv. praedictis Sanctimonialibus prae manibus dederunt'. This expanded the already extensive possessions of the canons in Ugthorpe to include much of the land in nearby Percybiggin. Finally, in 1280, the canons acquired all the rights in the manor of Ugthorpe from Peter de Malo Lacu. Thus in little more than twenty years the canons had vastly extended their lands in the area.

What is the significance of this in the arable farming of the Coastal Plateau? Once again, the theme of high level cultivation is illustrated. The canons' land was mostly above 600 feet. It is interesting to see not only intensive arable farming here, but actual increases in the cultivated area by reclamation of waste land on a fairly extensive scale.[4] This might have been carried out by the canons at Loftus, too, where they owned such a large portion of the moor. This was important in a region which, generally speaking, was not the scene of the large monastic arable granges, and in which pastoralism was dominant.

The Coastal Plateau, was then, generally unsuited to cultivation on a large scale. It was an area of varied economies, but sheep farming was dominant, Much of the arable land was confined to particular areas, and because most of these were at a high level, sometimes near the moorland edge, much of the arable was marginal in character. Land values were frequently less than in other regions. Monastic activity seemed to reflect the lay picture, with however a few notable exceptions. These exceptions were at Ugthorpe, Loftus, Stakesby, Whitbylathes and Lathgarth, where Guisborough Priory and Whitby Abbey held and worked large arable farms. But apart from these, the value of granges in

---

[1] *G.C.* The Priory had at least 15 messuages, 19 tofts, 28 bovates and 30 acres of land in North Loftus in 1362 *(C.C.R.* p.367), but it had additional lands in Loftus, apparently reckoned separately. The Dissolution Accounts show that the Priory had a total of 45 bovates, 10 messuages and 4 cottages.
[2] *G.C.* nos. 668, 668a, 668b, 943, 944, 945, 946, 947b, 988, 989.
[3] Robert de Ugthorpe sold certain land to the canons; G.C. no. 985.
[4] The Dissolution Accounts (P.R.O. S.C.6/Hen.8/4636) show that by 1540 most of the Priory land in Ugthorpe was enclosed; evidence of earlier enclosures into the moor itself was clear – e.g. 'le intak on the moor called Leith Hill ... one close called le moore close'.

the coastal region, in so far as this can be estimated from the Subsidy of 1301, was generally much less than that of granges in other regions (such as on the Corallian dip slope). This, it is suggested, was a reflection of the minor role played by arable farming in the region.

THE VALE OF PICKERING

As a region the Vale stood high in agricultural prosperity. Together with the Vale of York it was the richest in the whole of the medieval North-east. At first sight this appears paradoxical: the greater part was marsh, mere, forest or ill-drained land. Lacustrine clays intermingled with patches of sandy alluvium and these were further diversified, especially in the eastern half of the Vale, by areas of heavy, boggy, infertile peaty soils utilised, if at all, only for the turves they provided. The remarkable flatness of the Vale floor was an impediment to natural drainage in the area. The River Derwent had been unnaturally diverted from its old, direct course to the sea by glacial interference. Instead of flowing a few miles to join the sea near Scarborough it ran all the way along the Vale to Malton through the Kirkham Gorge and joined the Ouse in the vicinity of Selby, thence flowing to the sea via the Humber estuary[1].

Though this diversion had occurred in the distant past, its influence on subsequent settlement and land use in the Vale was profound. Thus, the Derwent assumed a doleful and uncertain course, to be joined by many moorland streams, which added to the difficulties, already great, of drainage.

North of the Vale too, were moorlands, unsuited, except in certain places, for arable cultivation. Even the fertile limestone of the Low Moors appears to have been partly covered by woodland. How did it come about then, that the Vale of Pickering could be so predominant in terms of agricultural prosperity?

First, it should be explained that sheep farming was a large element in this prosperity. Parishes on the north and south margins of the Vale were strip parishes and thus included either wold pasture or moorland pasture. Arable cultivation, equally important, occurred mainly along the margins of the Vale. The significance of the marginal settlements has been mentioned. The line of villages which surrounds the central Vale was continuous. Their sites were particularly favourable to arable farming: on the southern margin the area of fertile gravels extending from Stonegrave via Hovingham to Malton and thence along the foot of the Wold scarp varied in width from half a mile to two miles. It was raised above the level of the marshy Vale, so that it was a well drained platform at a height of about 100 feet. On the northern margin similar conditions prevailed: there were large patches of gravel soils at Seamer and Pickering, though no continuous platform as on the south. Instead, the settlements were situated at the foot of the limestone dip slope, which in places was diversified by Kimmeridge clay. Both margins, then, were outlined by a series of settlements all the more significant because they followed the junction between contrasting areas.

---

[1] Kendal, *Q.J.G.S.* vol. 58.

Field investigations as well as documentary evidence have shown, that the village open fields lay upon the peripheral areas described and that the three-field system was typical.[1] This was usual in a highly arable area though it provided an interesting contrast with field systems on the nearby Wolds. Here, in the few instances where information was available, a two-field system seemed to prevail.[2] The high value of the peripheral Vale was emphasised in 1301 and 1342, but as late as 1535 it was evident that this was the main area of corn production. More detailed information about arable farming in these areas is given by a list of the possessions of Thomas de Westhorpe of Brompton.[3] This man was an important wool-grower and dealer in the district during the fourteenth century. He also participated quite strongly in the farming activities of the northern Vale at Brompton, Snainton, Sawden and Ebberston. His emphasis was on sheep and cattle farming and in both he achieved a prominence equal to some of the monasteries in this area. For instance, his total stock of sheep was more than 2,700 in 1366 and he had at least 468 cattle on all his lands in the same year. His arable holdings were also extensive and provided a pointer to the basis of cultivation in the Brompton area in 1366.

Thomas had 183 acres of land sown with crops in Brompton, Snainton and Sawden and 55$^1/_2$ acres in Ebberston. Barley and wheat were sown in more than three-quarters of his Brompton lands, and at Ebberston they were equally predominant. The total value of the sown land was high; £46 10. 0. at Brompton and £17 10. 0. at Ebberston. Together this amounted to £64, about one-eighth of his entire possessions which were valued at £512 16. 7. The value of wheat and barley was great. In fact, out of the total value of £64 for sown land, these cereals together comprised £54 14. 0. Although the emphasis in cultivation was strongly in favour of wheat and barley, it was not exclusively so. Rye, oats, beans and peas were also grown. No mention is made of ploughs used or expenses entailed, but the importance of arable farming is evident from this single example. An examination of monastic evidence serves to emphasise the importance of the margins of the Vale in arable cultivation.[4]

The Inquisition for the Ninth of 1342 showed that the monastic share in the prosperity of the Vale settlements was large. At Pickering, one-sixth of the tax came from monastic corn, wool and lambs in the parish, at Helmsley one-seventh and at Appleton le Street, one fifth, but almost every parish could show similar figures. In fact, a large number of granges were located on the rich soils of the north or south margins of the Vale. It was here that some of the largest, most highly organised and successful arable holdings in the North-east were situated. The Malton Priory granges, for example, in the middle of the thirteenth century, show this clearly.[5]

---

[1] e.g. at Scampston, *C.I.P.M.* (1335-36) p.476.
[2] e.g. at Burton Fleming, *B.C.* pp.66-8.
[3] P.R.O. L.T.R. Memoranda Rolls, E.368/139 (1366-67)
See B. Waites, 'A Yorkshire Farmer in the Memoranda Rolls', *Y.A.J.* vol. 42 (1965) pp-445-8
Also *idem.* 'The Memoranda Rolls as a Source of Medieval History',
The Amateur Historian, vol. 5 (Summer 1963) pp.242-6.
[4] A great deal of lay demesne arable was farmed in this area too. There were, for instance, 380 acres arable on the Stutville manor of Kirby Misperton in 1276; Roger de Mowbray had 245 acres arable on his Hovingham manor in 1298; Robert de Everingham had 166 acres arable in Sherburn manor in 1287; Matthew de Loveyn had 117 acres arable on Fryton manor in 1302. *Inq.* vols. 1, 2, 3 and 4.
[5] See Graham, *English Ecclesiastical Studies,* pp.247-70

Wintringham, Swinton, Sutton and Rillington were all situated on the fertile gravels of the southern Vale. The amount of arable land being worked at each was great, much greater than that of the pastoral granges of the central Vale and the moors. In 1254, for instance, Wintringham had 46 bovates, Swinton 26$^{1}/_{2}$, Sutton 16 and Rillington 22. However, in effect the arable land being worked was often greater than these figures suggest, because the Priory owned lands near the granges, and worked in unison with grange land. Rillington grange, for example, appeared to work 14 bovates in Thorpe, a village only half a mile away. The grange at Swinton probably worked the 12 bovates at Amotherby and 34 bovates at Broughton which the Priory owned.[1] Both these places were soon to develop into granges themselves; in fact, by 1301 Amotherby and Broughton were among the richest of all the Priory granges. By 1257, however, they were still not granges.

The greater part, then, of the arable land worked by the canons was on the gravel bench of the southern Vale. It was in this area that Prior William had, between 1234 and 1256, acquired the greatest amount of land. At Swinton and Amotherby he had accumulated 16 bovates and at Rillington and Thorpe 24 bovates It is known that the Prior spent great sums on buying land at this time.[2] He was, it seems, especially anxious to expand the possessions of his house, and in particular the arable lands, situated along the southern edge of the Vale of Pickering where the soils were so fertile.

All the available statistics emphasise that the granges of this area were, and continued to be long after the middle of the thirteenth century, very important arable farms.[3] It quickly becomes evident that the granges situated along the gravel soils were well developed arable farms. The total number of ploughs in use on these granges was 29; that is, roughly three-quarters of the total ploughs owned by the Priory on all its granges. Individually, it will be seen that granges such as Wintringham (with 11 ploughs), Swinton (7), Rillington (4) and Sutton (4) had the highest number of ploughs working in 1244. They, too, had more workers employed than granges situated elsewhere. The expenses for hired labour at Wintringham, for instance, were 176s. 10d. for the year – more than ten times similar expenses on Ryton grange in the central Vale.

Arable cultivation occurred also on the fertile soils of the northern periphery of the Vale. Fig. 6.1 shows that in 1254 Malton Priory had a good deal of arable at Ebberston, Aislaby and certain other places. Some time between 1223 and 1234 this Priory established a grange at Ebberston, which had three ploughs working by 1244 and which, by 1301, had become the most valuable of all the Priory granges. At Allerston, the Templars had at least 16 bovates in 1246; much of this land, at least 114 acres, was sown with wheat in 1307. Nearby, the gravel soils of Seamer provided admirable conditions for corn cultivation. The Whitby Cartulary shows that the abbey had 274 quarters of corn at Seamer and Cayton which had derived from the tithes due to the

---

[1] An Inquisition (1255-56) showed that Malton Priory had 32 bovates 'tene de proprio' and 2 bovates 'de firma' in Broughton. William Luvel appeared to have the rest, namely 30 bovates. B. M. Cotton MS. Claudius D.XI, fol. 76.
[2] Graham, *op. cit.* pp.247-70
[3] Dissolution Accounts show that even in the sixteenth century many granges remained large arable farms, e.g. Griff grange had about 206 acres arable and 284 pasture; *R.C.* pp.312-13.

monks in the parish in 1394.[1] Lay farming it follows must have been largely occupied with arable production in this area; growing wheat, barley, oats, rye and peas, with particular emphasis on wheat, barley and rye.

The significance of the fertile soil belts fringing the Vale of Pickering could be illustrated almost *ad infinitum*. Several examples have been given, however, which show that in medieval times the most important areas of arable cultivation were on the margins of the Vale. This applied to monastic and lay farmers alike. As usual the clearest evidence comes from the monastic archives. To the monasteries in the area, the fertility of the peripheral zones was a fundamental factor of their economy, and in particular of their arable production. However, the abundance of monastic evidence should not hide the importance of lay arable farming here. Villages and fields were many along the Vale margins; sometimes the area between villages was almost a continuous cultivated stretch. The fields of Wilton, Allerston and Ebberston were so close to each other, for example, that an almost continuous belt of arable land extended for three miles between them. Besides, as the example of Thomas de Westhorpe showed, the lay farmer, too, could sometimes operate on a large scale.

The central areas of the Vale provided very different conditions, however. Where reclamation of marshland had occurred (as in Pickering Waste, undertaken by Rievaulx) cultivation became possible, though the heavy damp clays typical of the central parts were not always suitable. Consequently such cultivation as there was became localised, and pastoral farming seems to have been the chief occupation. The details of arable farming are few but they are none the less significant: the Templars, for example, had part of their land at Foulbridge sown with wheat in 1307. They had a granary there which contained 124 quarters of corn, so presumably cultivation occurred directly alongside the River Derwent at Foulbridge.[2] The value of the site was increased because it was one of the few bridging points of the river in the area.[3] The largest arable holdings in the central Vale appear to have been the two granges of Rievaulx Abbey situated in Pickering Marshes – Loftmarsh and Kekmarsh granges. Extensions of the farming area within the marshes had been going on since the middle of the twelfth century. By 1206 cultivation at Kekmarsh seems to have become quite extensive, for the monks owed a considerable amount in tithes to the Dean of York in that year.[4] Later, in 1220, the monks came to an agreement with the Dean that a composition fee of 66s. 8d. a year would be paid in lieu of tithes on Kekmarsh and Loftmarsh.[5] Again this high figure suggests that farming had become very extensive in the former waste of Pickering. Expansion continued: in 1240 Abbot Adam promised to pay

---

[1] *Officio Instauri Monasterii* (1394), W.C. pp.318-20.
   The Abbey accounts (1394-97) add some interesting details. Between November and May 1394-95, 87 quarters of corn, almost all barley, were sold from the tithes of Seamer. This fetched £16.0.0. Barley sold from the tithe between November and June 1396-97 fetched £22.6.10.
[2] P.R.O. Ancient Extents: possessions of the Knights Templars (1307), E.142/13/10. Nearby, also by the River Derwent, cultivation occurred at Yedingham. There was a three-field system here and lay farming was apparently extensive; *M.A.* vol.4, p.273 *et. sq.*
[3] Other bridging points in the Vale were Yedingham, and Friars Bridge over the Costa Beck, linking Malton and Pickering by road.
[4] *R.C.* p.255
[5] *ibid.* pp.255-6.

tithes to Pickering church on the lands he would acquire within the marsh,[1] and even in 1335 the Abbot of Rievaulx was still claiming his right to build houses and sheepfolds and bring land into cultivation.[2] By 1274 the grange of Kekmarsh had 300 acres of arable and 300 acres of pasture;[3] and by 1308 seven carucates were being cultivated by Rievaulx in Thornton Marshes alone.[4] Moreover, the high contributions these granges made to the Subsidy of 1301 was comparable with that of the largest arable granges of Rievaulx Abbey situated on the limestone soils of the dip slope (e.g. Griff, Newlathes).

Granges elsewhere in the central Vale do not appear to have been such large arable holdings. This seems to be reflected in the relative contributions, in 1301, from monastic granges in the Vale of Pickering. It will be recalled that the Subsidy was levied on moveables, principally animals and crops. It thus gives a good and almost direct impression of relative agricultural prosperity of the granges in the lowland Vale and on the more fertile peripheries:

Grange Contributions to the Fifteenth (1301)*

Central Vale Marshland Granges		Peripheral Vale Gravel/Limestone Granges	
Loftmarsh	25s. 1d.	Griff	61s. 4d.
Kekmarsh	38s. 8d.	Newlathes	46s. 4d.
Lund	15s. 6d.	Welburn	35s. 3d.
Newhouse	16s.	Broughton	32s. 8d.
South Marton	22s. 2d.	Swinton	27s. 10d.
Edston	5s. 10d.	Ebberston	37s. 5d.
Ryton	7s. 1d.	W. Newton	24s. 6d.
Selleybrig	7¼d.	Aislaby	(10s. 8d.?)
Kirby Misperton	6s. 8d.	Amotherby	14s. 4d.
Rook Barugh	8s. 8d.	Skiplam and Skiplam Cote	21s. 5d.
Normanby	12s. 9d.	Wombleton	18s. 4d.
		Kingthorpe	17s. 5d.
		Sinnington	10s. 2d.

Loftmarsh and Kekmarsh were the highest contributors among the marshland granges. This no doubt reflected the greater emphasis on arable farming, as the high contributions of the peripheral granges did.[5] However, whereas the peripheral granges, with very few exceptions, showed consistently high assessments, the marshland granges had much lower ones. The contrast between the groups emphasised the attraction of the fertile

---

[1] *ibid.* p.201.
[2] *N.R.R.S.* (New Series), vol. 3, p.90.
[3] *Rotuli Hundredorun*, vol. 1, p.107. Certain granges of Rievaulx had been despoiled by the Burgesses of Scarborough in 1274 and lost 78 quarters of corn. The granges concerned were probably those in the eastern marshes; *ibid.* p.131.
[4] *Register of Archbishop Greenfield*, vol. 5. p. 239. (Surtees Society, vol. 153). In 1278-79 there was a dispute over 2 messuages and 40 bovates of arable land in Thornton Marshes which Rievaulx possessed. William de Wyvill claimed them; *R.C.* pp.402-3. The area of arable production was obviously increasing very much in the Vale during the thirteenth century.
[5] The contribution of Griff grange (about 490 acres) and Broughton grange (34 bovates), both peripheral, reflected their importance as arable farms.
* Compiled from 1301 subsidy printed in *Y.A.S.R.S.* vol. 21.

gravel/limestone soils of the periphery for the monastic farmer. In fact, arable farming on the marshland granges, excluding Loftmarsh, Kekmarsh and possibly South Marton, never was great, though it certainly existed. Though the monks of Rievaulx owned 3 carucates of land at Lund grange in 1308 they had only two ploughs at work there in 1341.[1] The grange might have been more important as a sheep farm. Cultivation by the Abbey was still going on as late as the sixteenth century. Robert Gamble of Kirby Misperton, aged 78, gave testimony in a tithe cause in 1572, 'that he did knowe the Abbey [of] Rivox xxtie yeres before it was suppressed and Did then knowe the grange or lounde house articulate and the groundes belonging the same ... and haith sene the servantes of the saide abbates of Ryvox kepe and fede the cattell of the saide abbates and convent in the said groundes perteyning ... and likewyse Did till the groundes of the said lounde house to thuse of the said Abbates and convent of this examinates certyne sighte and knowledge'.[2]

The marshland granges of Malton Priory, too, did not show a marked emphasis towards arable farming. At Ryton, for example, the Priory had only 2 bovates of arable land in 1254, with one plough to work it. Almost fifty years later, in 1308, the Priory had only increased the arable land appurtenant to the grange to 4 bovates. At Kirby Misperton grange the extent of arable was the same in 1254 and in 1308 – 16 bovates; but despite the larger amount of arable at Kirby only two ploughs tilled it between 1244 and 1257. Similarly at Edston grange, where the amount of arable was about the same, only two ploughs were at work in the mid-thirteenth century.[3] On this evidence alone it would be legitimate to conclude that the purpose of most of these granges in the marshland was not to be arable farms, but cattle or sheep stations.

Whatever arable farming there had been in the Vale east of Pickering Beck was mainly the work of the monasteries. West of Pickering Beck, however, areas of lay cultivation became more important. This was largely because of the topographical differences between the two halves of the Vale. In the east, the marshland had only one village in it – Yedingham, on the main road across the Vale; this was largely monopolised by Yedingham Abbey. Both vill and abbey owed almost everything to the fact that the Derwent was bridged and ferried at that point. Most of the eastern marshlands, in which Yedingham (otherwise called Little Mareis) was situated, were waterlogged carr-land, at the best; more usually they were complete marsh or lake. As late as 1447 it was found necessary to retain Flixton Hospital 'for divers lieges of the King passing at night ... in winter, unless they be entertained there, would be in danger of water, marshes and swamps'.[4] Leland too, found a great mere to the south-west of Seamer where there is none today.[5] The condition of this part of the Vale in earlier times was worse. Thus lay settlement had found little to attract it there and any exploitation of the area was made

---

[1] P.R.O. E.178/211/19 m.109.
[2] Borthwick Institute, York: R.VII.G.1628. It was very significant that although the grange was worked by the monks for so long, leasing never appears to have occurred. This was not so on all the Abbey granges.
[3] *Reg. Greenfield*, vol.5, pp.224-5
[4] *C.P.R.* (1447) p.69.
[5] *The Itinerary of John Leland*, ed. L. T. Smith (London, 1907) vol. I, p-5

from the peripheral villages.[1] The western Vale had held more promise for the early settlers, however. 'Islands' of clay stood out above the general level of the marsh or carr-land; about 100 feet above it. These provided a nucleus for settlement on a dry site free from flooding, which could be ploughed. Almost all the villages in this area were to be found on such sites, e.g. Edston, Marton, Thornton Riseborough, Normanby, Salton, Great Barugh, Little Barugh, Kirby Misperton, North Holme and South Holme. Here, too, were the arable fields of the villages.[2] The area of lay cultivation in the western Vale was thus strictly localised.

Some cultivation occurred close to the River Rye. A small group of villages stood above the alluvial flats of the river on a higher terrace of warp and lacustrine clay, at about 80 feet. Their fields stretched from Brawby to Great and Little Habton and thence to Ryton Grange and Manor House, giving an almost continuous belt of cultivated land above the river alluvium for four miles.[3]

Apart, then, from cultivation of the 'islands' and certain terrace land, the western Vale was mainly marsh or meadow – valuable for hay, turves and pasture only. No evidence has been found to show that lay cultivation extended beyond the localities mentioned, despite the stimulus that monastic efforts at reclamation (mainly from 'island' sites) might have been expected to give. In conclusion, the Vale of Pickering was, in effect, divided in two from the point of view of arable farming. The peripheral areas were extremely fertile, actively exploited by both monasteries and laymen and highly productive. Arable holdings were generally very large in size, when they were outside the open fields. The central Vale contrasted very strongly with this; cultivation was severely limited to certain areas. In the eastern Vale it was almost exclusively in the hands of the monasteries: in the west the lay farmer took a greater share. The indications were, however, that with a few exceptions the whole of the central Vale was more an area of pastoral than arable farming.

THE YORKSHIRE WOLDS

The emphasis on arable farming in the Wolds was stronger than might have been expected during medieval times. At the present day, the immense stretches of cultivation over most of the area were made possible largely by the eighteenth century improvements of Sir Christopher Sykes. Arable farming on any considerable scale might, therefore, be considered a comparatively modern phenomenon. Thus, it might reasonably be suspected, as William Marshall suggested, that before these eighteenth century improvements the Wolds were largely, 'applied to sheep-walks; much of it being over-run with furze and heath'.[4] Certainly conditions did not appear favourable: the Wolds were almost treeless and this meant that at a height of around 800 ft. there was little shelter for animals or

---

[1] Domesday Book shows that a few settlements had existed in the marshes before 1069. It is not possible to say whether these were villages or isolated homesteads. They (e.g. Loftmarsh, Theokonarais and Chigogesmere) were listed as waste in 1086.
[2] Attempts to extent the arable area in the western Vale often failed when they were made on carr-land, e.g. there were 57 acres of poor land south of Sinnington as well as 19 acres nearby 'debil et morosi' unable to be cultivated or let. Thus such land was generally left as meadow; *P.R.O.* C.135/44/6.
[3] Evidence from Field-work.
[4] Marshall, W., *The Rural Economy of Yorkshire* (1788) ii, p.244.

crops, except in the deeply incised dry valleys. The soil, too, on the High Wolds was only a few inches in depth so that ploughing turned over much of the underlying chalk stone.[1] Medieval complaint was that 'a great part of the land lies in deep valleys and is worth nothing for sowing on account of its dryness and weakness'.[2] The deeper, more fertile boulder clay soils were limited to the lower dip slopes of the Wolds. The deficiency of water was a further deterrent: the valleys, though numerous, were streamless and the low water table meant that springs were limited to a few valley sides or to the scarp face.[3] Such conditions, which have been overcome today by planting, rotation, new crops and mechanisation, in medieval times contributed to a localisation of farming.

The limited number of places where water could be obtained had encouraged a nucleation of settlement. This was reinforced by the fact that the dry valleys were the most favourable areas for farming in the Wolds. Here shelter was adequate and soils often deeper and more fertile.[4] This was especially so in the Great Wold Valley and its associated valleys, which stretched from east to west across the centre of the Wolds. Here, the only stream in the whole of the northern Wolds, the Gypsey Race, flowed intermittently, through a deep loam soil.[5] The villages of the Northern Wolds were confined entirely to this valley system (e.g., Helperthorpe, Weaverthorpe, Butterwick, Foxholes, Wold Newton, Burton Fleming, Argam, Bartindale, Grindale, Fordon). Such inhibiting factors combined with the static organisation of medieval agriculture did not, however, prevent a significant development of arable cultivation by monastic and lay farmers. In fact, the monasteries, by the introduction of the grange system to the Wolds, were beginning a type of farming settlement best equipped for the exploitation of the area. The great extent of cultivation today is only possible because the working unit is the dispersed farmstead.

Malton Priory established two granges on the Northern Wolds, Mowthorpe and Linton. The former was one of the earliest of the Priory granges (established 1169-78): the latter was formed sometime after 1257. By the middle of the thirteenth century the amount of arable land being worked by the Priory on the Wolds was considerable. This has been indicated in Fig. 6.1, which was constructed from the details of lands given in the Norwich Taxation of the Priory in 1254.[6] There were 24 bovates at Linton, and nearby land was being worked at Duggleby (2 bovates) and Thoraldby (32 bovates) from the grange of Mowthorpe. Land was being worked outside as well as inside the village fields.

---

[1] 'In many areas a depth of only 4 ins. is found above the solid chalk, and unless care is taken in ploughing, the chalk is brought to the surface. All over the area chalk pebbles are to be found in abundance ... 'S. E. J. Best, *East Yorkshire: A Study in Agricultural Geography* (1930), p. 23.
[2] C.I. Post Mortem, vol. x, pp. 78-79, Northgivendale (1354).
[3] The building of dew ponds and sinking of wells helped to alleviate the problem. The water table is liable to fluctuate a great deal. For instance, a well sunk into the chalk near Hull some time ago (c. 1925) to augment the town's water supply caused the water table of the nearby Wolds to fall so much that farmers on the high land to the west and north-west had to deepen their wells.
[4] The fertility of the chalky gravel soils in the valleys varied from place to place, being more fertile where glacial material was present. Marshall found the dry valleys near Thixendale to consist of a gravel 30 ft. thick, finely comminuted and covered with a very thin coat of soil, incapable of holding tillage and requiring constant manuring. *Agricultural Survey of the East Riding* (1812).
[5] '... juxta quem famosae illae aquae, quas vulgo Gipse vocant, numerosa scaturigine e terra prosiliunt, non quidem jugiter, sed annis interpositis, et, facto torrente non modico, per loca humiliora in mare labuntur;' William of Newburgh, *Historia Rerum Anglicarum,* Rolls Series 82, (1884), p. 85.
[6] B.M. Cotton MS. Claudius D xi, f. 279 *et seq.*

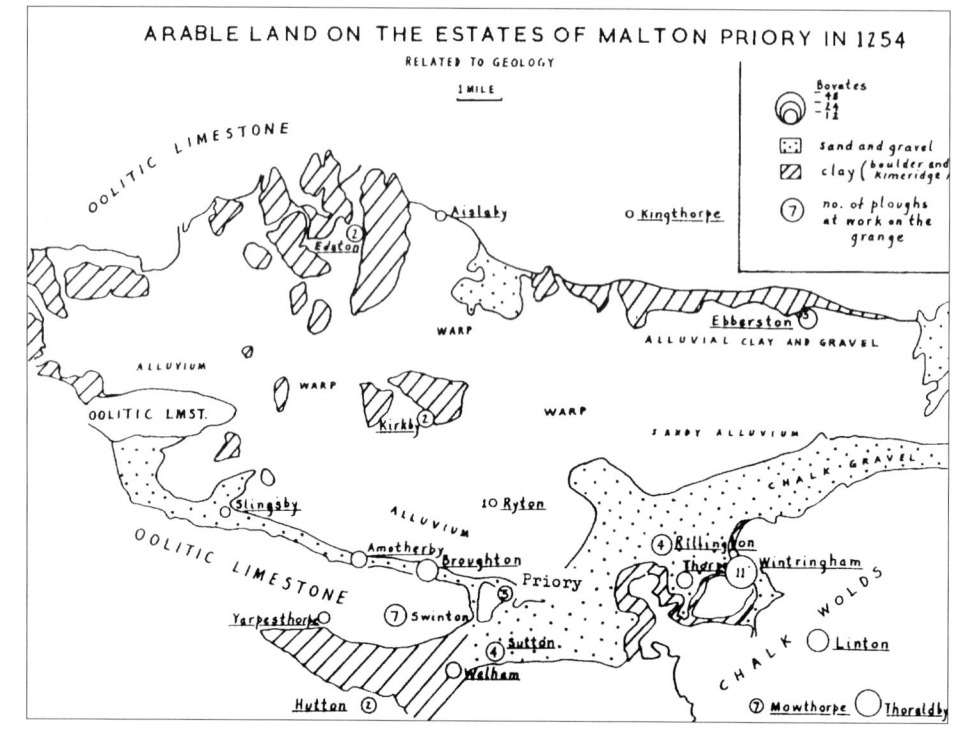

Figure 6.1 *Arable Land on the Estates of Malton Priory in 1254*

At Mowthorpe grange, for example, 8 bovates were held in the vill but the Canons were also working arable in nearby valleys – Bugdale, Keldale and Cawthorp – outside the village fields. Enclosures were made in Bugdale for cultivation. These facts were important for two reasons: they showed that the monastic cultivation was entirely within the valleys but that the Canons were extending the areas of cultivation beyond the normal limits. That is, they were reclaiming land. It will be shown later how the Canons of Bridlington Priory were doing the same at Burton Fleming.

The importance of the Malton granges as arable farms in the thirteenth century can be assessed from the detailed accounts given in the Chartulary, which cover the period 1244-1257.[1] At Mowthorpe, for example, seven ploughs were working. Only Wintringham with eleven, and Swinton with eight had more, and they were situated on the much more fertile gravel bench at the foot of the Wold scarp. The contrast with the more pastoral granges of the Priory was a sharp one; at Ryton and Kirby Misperton in the central Vale only one and two ploughs respectively were at work. At Dinsdale grange, on the moors near Lockton and Levisham, only one plough was mentioned. The numbers of workmen hired by the granges bears out this contrast. In 1244 at Mowthorpe grange a total of 36 men were

---

[1] *Ibid.* ff. 273-74.

employed during the year; the number on the pastoral granges was much less. At Dinsdale, for example, only 12 men were hired during the same year. Total expenses for hired labour at Mowthorpe in 1244 were 70s. Between 1244 - 57 the average annual cost of workers was about 67s. Expenses never fell lower than 64s 10d (in 1252), and rose to 79s 2d in 1256. Again only the granges at Wintringham and Swinton exceeded this outlay for workers. Labour expenses on the central Vale granges were only about one third of those at Mowthorpe. At Dinsdale, for instance, they totalled 19s 10d, and were as low as 15s on Ryton grange.

Looking at the general running expenses of the Malton granges, Mowthorpe again was among the highest. The period 1250-52 appeared to produce the highest expenditure (£12 13s 11d; £10 10s 6d; £15 8s 5d respectively) and the lowest was in 1256 (£5 9s 4d).

Wintringham and Swinton showed greater annual expenditure, generally about £20, but the remaining eight Priory granges were much less. Those of the central Vale, for instance, had about half the expenditure of Mowthorpe. The expenses of arable granges would naturally be higher than pastoral granges because of the additional labour, equipment and seed required.

All the figures quoted, then, suggest that the Wold granges of Malton Priory were important arable farms. The Priory certainly needed to develop this sphere of its activity since the large purchases of corn made during 1244-57 suggested that its own production was inadequate for its needs.[1]

A more detailed picture of arable farming on the Wolds is possible from two grange accounts for Bridlington Priory, which have survived in the possession of the Diocesan Registry, York.[2] Such accounts rarely survive and, in fact, these appear to be unique so far as the north-eastern monasteries are concerned. The accounts relate to Burton Fleming and Speeton in the middle of the fourteenth century. The Priory had been granted both vills early in its history, and had at least 13 carucates of land at Burton Fleming and 3 carucates at Speeton.[3] The opportunity for the development of large arable farms was great in both places because of the extensive land owned, the Priory's position as lord of the vill, and, at least in Burton Fleming, the availability of a labour supply from the villeins.

The Canons' land lay either in cultures within the open fields or outside, on the Wolds. At Burton Fleming in 1299 they had, for example, seven cultures in East Field and ten in West Field.[4] The culture varied in size from place to place, but at nearby Brompton it ranged from 14 to 21 acres.[5] On this basis the Canons would have had about 350 acres lying in the fields of Burton Fleming. All this was being cultivated in 1299. But they were

---

[1] Largest amounts purchased in 1245,1252-54; lowest 1246-50. Just over 700 qts. wheat were purchased each year 1246, 49, 50, but by 1251 this had increased to 850 qts.; in 1252, 880 qts.; 1253, 1069 qts., 1254, 880 qts. Purchases of rye and barley were high but generally much less than wheat (usually around 600 qts./year). Considerable quantities of malt were purchased. The only indication of home production was given in 1247 when there appeared to be 100 qts. of corn from the demesne (de dominico) at Wintringham, 80 qts. at Rillington and 50 qts. at Mowthorpe. B.M. Cotton MS. Claudius D xi, f. 282.
[2] York Diocesan Registry R. H. 60 (Burton Fleming); R.VII H.2096 (Speeton). There is a third account which is rather short. It appears to relate to the Manor of Filey for the year 1329-30, but the name of the place is obscured.
[3] *Chartulary of Bridlington Priory* (1915), Ed. W. T. Lancaster, q.v., especially Confirmation Charter of Edward II (1312).
[4] *Ibid.*, pp.66-68.
[5] *Ibid., p.* 143.

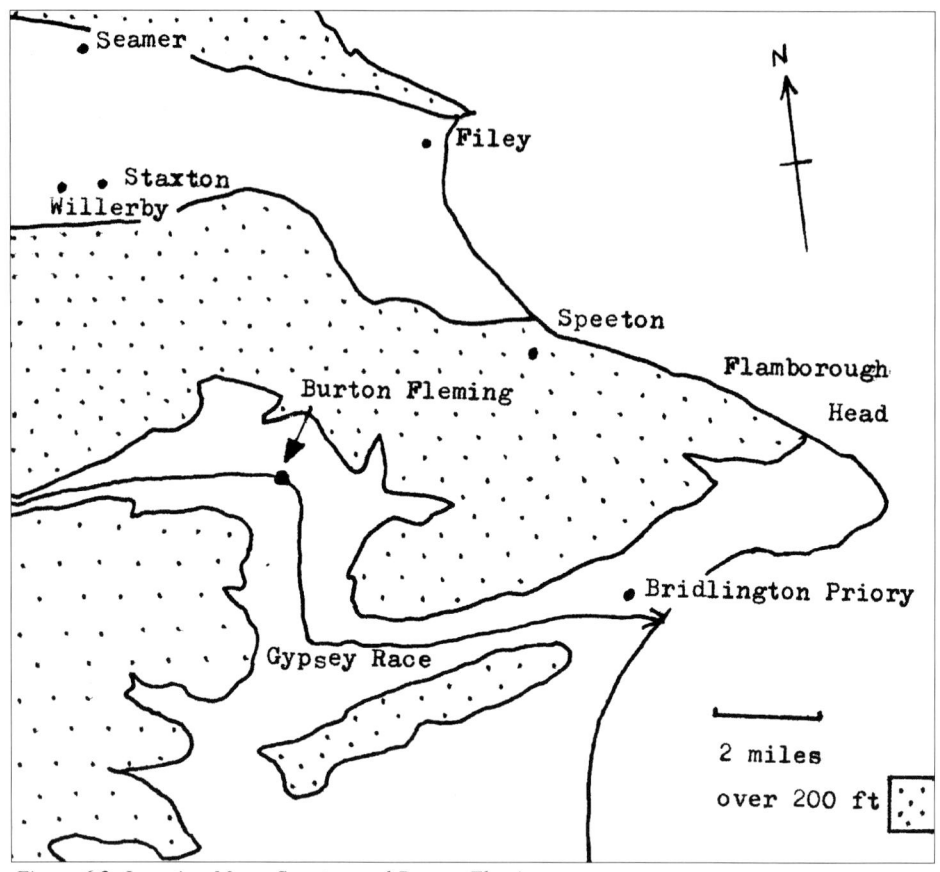

Figure 6.2 Location Map : Speeton and Burton Fleming

also cultivating land outside the fields, '. . . in the territory of Burton Fleming'. They had 160 acres on Staxton Wold, for example.[1] Such land was known as 'ovenam' which seemed to mean land taken out of the common or elsewhere enclosed and cultivated. The word was used in most of the northern chartularies to refer to similar work of reclamation. Its use was not confined to any particular area or landscape and variants such as 'ofnam', 'hovenam' occurred.[2] The Priory had one separate 'ovenam' between the fields of Burton Fleming and those of Argam, a vill just over a mile away. Another 'ovenam' was described as being near the boundary of the West Field, but separate from it. Thus the Canons were expanding the area of open field cultivation which lay on the broad valley floor, and beginning cultivation of more remote valleys and hillsides which had not previously been worked.

---

[1] *Ibid., p.*94.
[2] A.S. of = from, out of, nima = to take, seize; hence ofnam = land taken up from or out of a larger tract hitherto unenclosed. In other words an intake or enclosure.

During the middle of the fourteenth century the productive capacity of the grange at Burton Fleming seemed to be high despite the general economic recession of that time. The effect of the plague in highland areas may not have been as severe as elsewhere, however. Between 1355-56 the cultures alone produced 348 qts. of corn, of which 216 qts. were barley.[1]

A list of autumn works showed the actual acreage sown with certain crops in part of the Priory land:—

12 acres drag	at Wandaill
26 acres oats	at Newtonbergh
6 acres barley	at le bouttes at Hunmandbydikis
10 acres barley	at Thorndaill
8 acres barley	at Croftes
48 acres barley	at Southbergh
12 acres barley	at Ovenam
16 acres barley	at Ovenam and Westdaill

It is evident that barley cultivation was emphasised. Almost 100 acres out of the 136 acres grew that crop. This is interesting because later sources, mainly the Cause Papers in Tithe which relate to the fourteenth, fifteenth and sixteenth centuries, show that barley was the most widely grown crop of lay farmers. The question of possible specialisation in this crop must, however, be deferred for a while. The places mentioned in the list of autumn works appear to be all outside the fields of the vill, and the frequency of 'daill' in the place names shows that cultivation of this type was also mainly in the Wold valleys.

The produce was disposed of in various ways. During the year 1355-56 more than 151 qts. of corn had been sold at Filey, Seamer, Scarborough and Willerby. Nearly the whole of this was barley. The receipts of the sales was £17 10s 10d, much more than the sale of stock which had realised £4 3s 3d. Just over half of the corn produced was kept for seed, but even so the grange needed to buy 4 qts. of wheat in addition. Some corn had gone to servants for work done. Six shepherds received 26 qts. of wheat, and five ploughmen 21 qts. for the year's work. Then, also, the guest house attached to the grange needed its supplies; the account showed that visits were often made by the Prior, Sub-Prior, Cellarer and other Canons.

The number of servants attached to the grange was quite large. The account mentions twelve names, and, it should be remembered, these served mainly in administrative roles, since much of the actual labour was done by villeins or hired workers. Simon Crell was the seedsman or sower, for instance, and received the highest wage of all. Adam Stethird had the custody of the cows and Adam Swinhird was the chief ploughman.

The Canons no doubt met many of the difficulties that face the present-day Wold farmer. The thin soil, for example, contains many chalk-stones which blunt and

---

[1] The following information comes from the grange accounts already mentioned. Compare 'Account Roll of the Manor of Little Kelk 1323-4' Y.A.J. vol. 63, 1991, pp.59-76.

sometimes break the plough, and expenses over equipment can be high.[1] The ploughing expenses at Burton Fleming grange were £1 16s 4d for the year of the account. Several of the items provide interesting reading: as many as 18 ploughsoles were required, and numerous steel accessories, as well as ploughstaves, 'arvspindles' and rakeshafts. The ploughsoles were the most expensive item. Though the account does not specify the total number of ploughs at work on the grange land it must have been high in view of the large areas cultivated. Some idea of the number can be inferred from the expenses just mentioned, and at least six ploughmen had been employed during the year.

Speeton grange was four miles to the east of Burton Fleming. There the chalk Wolds were flanked by morainic deposits along the coast, which might have made cultivation less important. The details of the arable farming of the grange do not appear too clearly since the account covers only a five week period. The issues of corn were quite naturally small for the period and convey nothing of the farming bias of the grange. A few scattered items are of more significance. In the short period three ploughmen and three shepherds had been employed, and quite a large number of cattle had been received into the stock of the grange.[2] This gives the impression that pastoralism might have been more important than arable farming at the grange but in view of the incomplete evidence this can be no more than a suggestion. The expenses incurred in threshing and mowing were fairly large for such a short period (total 70s 8d). Of course, both arable and pastoral farming were inseparable on most granges, and the Wolds were certainly a very important sheep farming area. The difference between granges was mainly one of emphasis but in certain suitable areas, as at Burton Fleming, the emphasis could be strongly in favour of arable farming.

The manors and granges of Bridlington Priory on the Wolds were certainly among the richest possessed by the Canons. The assessment of the Valor Ecclesiasticus (1535) showed that Burton Fleming was worth 602s, more than double the next most valuable manor (Bessingby 300s); Speeton was worth 240s.[3] This suggests that both holdings continued as important agricultural units long after the middle fourteenth century, retaining a great deal of the predominance they showed then.

Despite certain apparent disadvantages, then, the Wolds were the scene of monastic arable farming often on a considerable scale. But how did this fit in with lay farming in the area? Little detailed information can be obtained about the methods and work of the lay farmer, but it is possible to discover the extent and character of arable production on the Wolds during the thirteenth and fourteenth centuries. This can be done through a series of Exchequer Accounts of corn bought in Yorkshire for the Kings Wars during the period 1298 – c. 1360.[4] These give the amount of corn purchased, the places or persons supplying it, and the routes used to transport it to the ports for shipment, mainly to Scotland. Accounts for every year between 1298-1360 do not exist but the years covered

---

[1] A farmer living at Flixton and working land on the Wold top told me in 1963 that his expenses for ploughing his Wold fields were high; much more than ploughing expenses in fields on the gravel soils of the scarp foot.
[2] From 29 August to 29 September 1349, the cattle received were:–18 beasts, 11 cows, 7 calves, 1 bull, 4 oxen and 65 sows, pigs, young pigs. By the time of the account the cattle had become less in number due to various causes.
[3] Valor Ecclesiasticus, Record Commission (1825), vol. 5, p.120.
[4] P.R.O. Exchequer Q.R. E 101/6/32, 38: E 101/12/8. Exchequer K. R. E101/597/1-19, 26, 27, 31-36.

are enough to give a comprehensive idea of the importance of corn production on the Wolds compared to other nearby regions, such as Holderness.

The corn from North-East Yorkshire was shipped from four main ports – Hull, Yarm, Scarborough and Whitby. Hull was by far the largest exporter, but all, except Whitby, had very extensive hinterlands from which corn was collected. Corn produced on the Wolds was despatched either to Scarborough or Hull. When sent to the former port the journey was entirely by land through the Vale of Pickering. But when Hull was the exporting centre, part of the journey was by land and part by the River Hull. Two important intermediate collecting centres were at Wansford and Beverley, on this river.[1] At both corn was collected from the locality preparatory to despatch by boat to Hull. Wansford, on the upper water of the River Hull, was probably the head of navigation.[2] Here packhorses new in from the Wolds unloaded their corn-panniers or wool sacks on to waiting vessels, which sometimes went direct to Hull and at other times stopped at Beverley.[3]

Wansford was the principal collecting point of Wold corn and the accounts show that the produce it handled was often large in quantity. In 1298, for example, 195 qts. wheat, 93 qts. oats and 93 qts. peas went from Kilham to Wansford and 'thence by water to Hull'.[4] In the same year 136 qts. wheat from Bridlington, Kilham and Rudston was sent the same way. 430 qts. wheat was also despatched from Wansford in 1298 but no places supplying it are mentioned. Such figures which recur during the period covered by the accounts are enough to show that corn production was high in the Wolds. It is information like this which makes the medieval historian wonder about some of the so-called axioms which his fellows have declared, such as the basis of medieval farming being for subsistence, being non-specialist and not organised towards marketing.

Beverley appeared to be the main collection centre for corn from the Southern Wolds and the low lying plain of Holderness. The King had a granary there, and sometimes the corn was milled nearby before being sent to Hull. In 1298, for example, 200 qts. of wheat were carried by boat from Beverley to the Mill of Melsa (owned, it should be noted, by Meaux Abbey.)[5] Holderness and the Vale of Pickering, neighbouring regions to the Wolds, did not appear to supply corn on such a large scale as the Wolds during 1298 – c. 1360. One account

---

[1] The subsequent importance of Beverley as the main collecting centre and market for much of the Riding can be seen illustrated frequently by H. Best in his *Rural Economy in Yorkshire in 1641*, Surtees Society 33 (1857).

[2] The River Hull was being navigated as late as 1641 but it had its dangers. 'They account it from Wanstorth to Hull thirty miles by water; and say that one that is not very skillfull in the way may very well come to leave his boate behind him, there are so many stakes stucken downe, and here and there shallowes; yet they say that from the beginning of May to the latter ende of July, or beginning of August, they can goe in one day and come in another, if they bee stirringe betimes and the winde favour them anythinge.' Henry Best, *op. cit.*, p.112. Compare this with three hundred years earlier; in 1345 for instance, the distance from Wansford to Hull was described as being 30 leagues and the cost of carrying 117 qts. wheat, 17 qts. beans in three boats was 4s a boat.

[3] Water transport to Hull was especially useful in the fourteenth century and earlier because of the lack of good roads to Hull. The roads on the Holderness clay land were especially poor. By 1302 'no roads have yet been made to our new town by which merchants may bring their things and merchandise ... which is well known to turn to our loss and the hurt of the said town ... we assign to you to supervise and make ... roads ... leading to the said town ...' So the King commanded. By 1303 four roads had been or were being made from the town. One 'versus Waldas' via Anlaby and Swanland; two others going northwards to Beverley via Skidby and Woodmansey; the fourth was north-eastwards in the direction of Bilton Bridge. It is interesting to notice that the road pattern then established is the same as that of today. Without doubt the creation of a new town at Hull stimulated the economic development of the East Riding, and a much wider area. Its effect on the subsequent decline of the inland ports such as York, Selby, Beverley, Hedon was a counter-balance to this.

[4] P.R.O. E 101/597/3. One account refers to provisions collected from 'del Wald de Wandesford'.

[5] *loc. cit.*

for 1304 which lists the amounts supplied by villages in the Wold district and Holderness emphasises the distinction which was becoming apparent from previous evidence. The Wold villages contributed much more individually: Birdsall, for example, 21 qts.; Sledmere 15; Kilham 10; Rudston 10; Cowlam 20; Prior of Watton 20. But the Holderness villages had amounts as low as 2, 3 or 4 qts. There were, in fact, only a few villages which supplied anything at all comparable with the Wold villages (Wawne 10 qts.; Hornsea 10 qts.; Burstall 10 qts.)[1] The predominance of corn supplied from the Wapentakes of Buckrose, Dickering and Harthill – all mainly on the Wolds was marked throughout the period. Even earlier, 1298 – 1304, though other places were mentioned, corn was largely bought in the Wolds and often from monasteries. Thus the Abbot of Bardney provided 60 qts. wheat from his grange at Hunmanby; the Abbot of Rouen 30 qts. wheat from Kilham, and the Prior of Bridlington 280 qts. wheat.

This much can be estimated about arable farming on the Wolds: its productive capacity was high; its participants, lay and monastic, were extremely active; its basis was not entirely for subsistence. Lay and monastic farmers alike sold large amounts of the corn they produced. It seemed that, compared to the claybound districts around, the Wolds was the foremost producer of wheat and barley, probably emphasising the latter crop. These conclusions were made from a consideration of the whole of the Wolds, including the fertile dip slope on the south-east. But the same trends seemed applicable to the Northern Wolds, even though the areas of cultivation were more localised and the degree of fertility less, than on the dip slopes.

It would be unsound to conclude from the evidence so far discussed that medieval arable farming in the Wolds consciously specialised in, or concentrated on, the production of barley. Evidence from the Cause Papers in Tithe, which are a wonderful source of agricultural history especially in the sixteenth century, indicates that a variety of crops was grown.[2] As well as wheat, rye, oats and peas, the cultivation of flax and hemp was fairly extensive in the fourteenth century as well as later. But the Cause Papers, especially those referring to the late fifteenth and early sixteenth centuries, convey the impression that the farmers found the Wolds particularly suited to barley.[3] From the abundant references it would be difficult to regard barley as anything but the most widely cultivated cereal on the Wolds. It is tempting to see already in medieval times something of that concentration on sheep-barley agriculture which is typical of the Wolds today.[4] But this presupposes many things. Specialisation in sheep farming certainly existed, but feudal conditions prevented such a complete development in arable production. The monastic farmer perhaps was able

---

[1] E. 101/597/12. Wold villages also supplied largest amounts of malt barley.
[2] The Cause Papers in Tithe are in the Diocesan Registry, York. A selection has been printed by Dr. J. S. Purvis in the Y.A.S. Record Series, vol. 114.
[3] Variety of crops grown illustrated by Cause tithes at Hunmanby in 1347 and 1543; rights to flax and hemp tithes. D. Reg. R.VII, E.254, G.315. Wheat, rye, barley, peas, grown in south field of Weaverthorpe, Reg. Askwith 16/20 (18-20). N.B.: abundance of barley – given to villages as payment for sheaving. Many villages had a tithe of barley rakings, e.g., Middleton on the Wolds R.VII G.111, G.279 Details of Wold Agriculture in the early sixteenth century very well illustrated by R.VII G.379. Tithe of Fleeces at Wharram Percy.
[4] And was typical of the Wolds in 1641, q.v., Henry Best, *op. cit.* Best recognised the suitability of chalk land for barley. 'It is no pointe of good husbandry to sowe barley on lande that is exceedingly fatte, for lande may be too fat for barley viz: such clay land as is newly riven forth, and such barley will come upp very thicke and ranke, and usually full of weedes ... the barley itself sloumice and not pubble ...', pp. 53-54

to go further and, in fact, it may well have been due to his influence that the Wolds began to show, in medieval times, a bias towards the farming which is characteristic of it at the present time.

THE VALE OF YORK AND CLEVELAND

This region was the northerly extension of the great midland plain of England. Besides being geographically related, their historical development had strong affinities, often stronger in some respects than the affinities between the Vale and the highland areas of the North-East. Despite numerous set-backs, ranging from the devastations of the Conqueror to the ravages of the Scots, the Vale had retained its predominance as an intensively settled and widely farmed region. In particular, within the Vale the persistent influence of certain soils, e. g. the alluvial gravel soils of the mid Vale and Teesmouth, was a notable factor in the distribution of agricultural wealth and activity throughout the medieval period. But what were the details within this broad regional pattern? Was arable farming more or less important than pastoral farming?

These questions can best be answered by means of the Valor Ecclesiasticus.[1] For most of the parishes in the Vale of York the Valor gives full details of tithe values. Such details were much less for other regions; occasionally they were entirely absent e.g. in the Vale of Pickering. Since tithe values reflected the agricultural economy of a parish a study of them makes it possible to assess the relative importance of arable and pasture farming in that parish, and because the information is comprehensive, in the region as a whole. This method has, in fact, been used before. Of course, the result of this will be to show the significance of arable farming in the early 16th Century, and although a well-marked continuity is noticed in the agricultural development of the North-East from the 12th to the 16th Centuries, the Valor of 1535 may not necessarily reflect the broad framework of medieval agriculture. The aim here is to examine the Valor and establish the relative importance of arable farming in the Vale in 1535; then to see how far this can be applied to the region during medieval times.

The following table has been derived from the Valor.[2] It shows what percentage corn-hay, wool-lamb-calf tithes were of the total agricultural tithe of the parish. The table has been arranged to show parishes of the mid-vale in the left "benefice" column and parishes with a good deal of moorland in them in the right "benefice" column. The first general impression which the figures convey is the preponderance of the corn-hay tithe. The tithe figures for the Coastal Plateau show a marked contrast. There the corn-tithe and the animal tithe showed a very similar percentage and, in fact, at Sneton the animal tithe was greater than the corn tithe. This, together with other evidence, leads to the conclusion that pastoralism was more important than arable farming in the Coastal Plateau as a whole.

---

[1] *Valor Ecclesiasticus* (Record Comm. London, 1825), vol. V.
[2] Nine parishes have had to be omitted because the total Valor only is given for them. viz. Ingleby, Whorlton, Arncliffe, Guisborough, Ayton, Rudby, Levington, Kirkleatham, and Middlesbrough. The wool tithe only is given for Marton and Stainton, Ormesby and Marske. (For the purposes of this study the areas have been limited by the R. Tees to the north and the R. Wiske to the west.)

	% of Total Agricultural Tithe			% of Total Agricultural Tithe	
benefice	corn-hay tithe	wool-lamb-calf tithe	benefice	corn-hay tithe	wool-lamb-calf tithe
Kirby Wiske	96	4	Felixkirk	87	13
Kilvington	95	5	Kirby Knowle	80	20
Thirsk	90	10	Leake	77	23
Welbury	88	12	Stokesley	75	25
N. Ottrington	87	13	Kirby	67	33
Coxwold	86	14	Kildale	66	34
S. Ottrington	81	19	Cowesby	63	37
Crathorne	78	22	Osmotherley	58	42
Birkby	78	22	Sigston	55	45
West Rounton	75	25			
Thornton Street	74	26			
Northallerton	71	29			

Obviously this was not generally true for the Vale of York. The corn tithe in those parishes near the River Wiske in particular was very great (Kirby Wiske, Kilvington, Thirsk, North and South Ottrington, Kirkby, West Rounton, Northallerton, and Thornton le Street). This was the area which the medieval assessments had shown to be foremost in terms of agricultural prosperity.

Figure 6.3 Lake Gormire and the Vale of York

Undoubtedly, the corn production here was great because of the fertile alluvial gravel soils bordering the Wiske and the market demands of the towns nearby. In parishes such as Kirby Wiske cultivation was often on the flood plain of the river, so near that flooding sometimes put land out of cultivation there. This was also liable to happen in many other parishes since their settlements very frequently followed the river bank (e.g. North and South Ottrington).

A rather interesting feature shown by the tithe figures is that the further eastwards the parishes were the lower was the corn tithe and the higher the animal tithe. This might have been expected since such parishes usually included moorland but it could hardly have been hoped that the table would bring this out so well as it does. The decreasing importance of arable cultivation eastwards can be studied throughout from the River Wiske to the Moorland crestline (Hambleton Hills). In the alluvial gravel flats near the river the corn-hay tithe comprised over 90% of the total tithe at Kirby Wiske, Kilvington and Thirsk; moving east to the Boulder Clay areas the percentage fell slightly but was still around 80% (Welbury, Crathorne). The parishes largely situated on the Boulder Clay platforms at the root of the moorland scarp were of the same order. Coxwold, Felixkirk, and Kirby Knowle, for example, had corn tithes over 80% of the total, Though their boundaries included some moorland it was not as extensive as other parishes partly situated on the Boulder Clay platform but comprising often vast areas of moor.[1] In such parishes the corn tithe fell and the animal tithe rose: pasture farming was becoming more important It was usually the wool-lamb tithe which increased most, showing a corresponding emphasis on sheep-farming. But arable cultivation appeared to be very significant still, in many of these parishes, even if it failed to reach the height of the mid-Vale area. This was noticeable especially in the Cleveland embayment – an area of Boulder Clay and gravel soils which John Tuke found to be " a good deal of deep rich loam ... near the moors, particularly in the neighbourhood of Kildale"[2] Here, Stokesley parish which included much of the embayment as well as Westerdale Moor – detached seven miles away, had 75% of its total tithe, corn. This decrease in arable farming eastwards was partly reflected in the the Inquisition for the Ninth (1342) which showed the amount of uncultivated land in the parish, formerly tilled.[3] Those parishes straggling across the moorland scarp generally had more land out of cultivation than the mid-Vale parishes. This was natural since much of the arable land would be marginal in character. Thus Kirby, Ayton and Ingleby had "a great part of the arable of the Parish" uncultivated in 1341. This meant a loss to Stokesley of 1620/-. At Welbury and Crathorne 48 bovates and three parts of the arable respectively were out of cultivation. These parishes were nearer the mid-Vale and wholly on Boulder Clay soils. In the mid-Vale itself, near the Wiske, land out of cultivation seemed to be less, generally speaking. At Thirsk, for example, no mention was made of such land in 1341. Rounton had two carucates uncultivated, Kilvington 27 bovates, South Ottrington two carucates. Kirby Wiske had been more severely hit by flooding which had put two carucates out of use as well as three more for which no reason was given.

---

[1] And some areas of gravel.
[2] Tuke, *op. cit.*, pp.11-12.
[3] *Nonarum Inquisitiones* (Record Comm., London, 1807).

The value of such evidence is partly discounted because although the Inquisition does not often refer to it, Scots raids had caused land to be put out of cultivation, especially in the mid-Vale, around Northallerton and Thirsk. Whether the Vale had made much of a recovery is hard to say. Certain areas appeared to have been affected in 1341; at Northallerton the parishioners complained that all the parish had suffered destruction and burning from the Scots King and the rebels during the preceding twenty years. Corn production was much less than in old times, they went on to say, and there had been 8500 sheep in the parish "ante destructionem Scotorum " but in 1341 there were only 500.[1] A great deal of land had become out of cultivation in the Vale, only a short time before, due to the Scots. John de Mowbray's manor of Thirsk lay partly waste in 1327; 80 acres were uncultivated due to this.[2] At Cowton, the manor was worth only 1/6 and 60 acres were uncultivated. Further south, Easingwold and Huby had been burnt and devastated by the Scots.[3]

The normal agricultural relationships in the Vale during the 14th Century were upset by such conditions. Later the plagues of the middle 14th Century also had a disruptive effect, especially in the Vale.[4] Just as the devastations of 1069 had left the region prostrate so these later catastrophes interrupted normal agricultural conditions. But the effect of the latter was certainly not so extreme. As the reassessments of 1318 showed, the Vale of York and Cleveland suffered considerable decreases in agricultural prosperity due to Scottish ravages but the region still maintained its predominance in the North-East. This suggests that the relationship of arable to pastoral farming was still of the same order as the Valor of 1535 had shown it to be – that is that arable was far more important. Several documents seem to support this view.

The details of corn purchased for the King in 1300-1 and sent to Yarm for shipment, for example, give the impression that corn production, especially wheat and oats, was widespread throughout the Vale.[5] Although the amounts purchased were generally small the area drawn upon was very wide. This can be seen from the size of the hinterland of Yarm. In particular the Cleveland Plain was emphasised as a principal source for the Royal corn. Northallerton emerged as an important collecting centre for the corn of the southern Vale. Taken by itself this evidence does not necessarily imply that the Vale of York was predominantly an area of arable farming. But collated with other evidence its value becomes apparent. Such evidence can be found in the monastic archives.

The multitude of monastic granges situated in the Vale of York-Cleveland region was enough to show the great value attached to it by the monastic farmer. But it was even more significant that these granges were the largest arable farms and the most valuable that many of the monasteries possessed. This was most clearly illustrated by the granges of Guisborough Priory. The Dissolution Accounts give a good idea of the size of these granges and their value in 1539. The following table[6] lists such details for Guisborough

---

[1] P.R.O. E. 179/211/19 m. 18.
[2] *C. I. Post Mortem* VII pp.52-53.
[3] *ibid.* p.56.
[4] The list of poor villages among which proceeds of felons' goods had been distributed to help them repair losses due to the plague consisted mainly of villages in the Vale of York and Cleveland. There were only a few outside, e. g. Scarborough, Skelton, Loftus, Danby, and Glaisdale, Amotherby, Hovingham and Wombleton. P.R.O.E. 179/211/27.
[5] P.R.O. E. 101/597/5.
[6] Compiled from Dissolution Accts., Lay Subsidy (1301), Valor Ecclesiasticus.

PART THREE : LAND USE

Grange	Grange Land	Total Land	Value of Moveables 1301	Value 1535	Total 1539
Barnaby	347 acres	Same	8. 7. 6	8. 6. 8	21. 12. 8
North Cote	395 acres	Same	6. 6. 3		7. 16. 8
Marton	(not given)	(not given)	22. 5. 0	5. 0. 0	4. 19. 0
Ormesby	12½ bovates	37½ bovates	30. 18. 9	15. 6. 8	16. 18. 4
Yearby	?	405+ acres	64. 3. 9		20. 15. 8
Kirkleatham	?	195 acres		9. 15. 4	8. 10. 11
Coatham	?	3 bovates 262+ acres		20. 14. 0	23. 16. 6
Marske-Redcar	14 bovates	31 bovates 40+ acres	28. 3. 9	20. 13. 10	22. 2. 4
Linthorpe	(not given)	(not given)	8. 15. 0	2. 13. 4	
Thornaby	16 bovates	31+ bovates	11. 6. 3	17. 4. 4	20. 9. 11
Arsum	12 bovates	12+ bovates		4. 0. 0	6. 0. 9

granges in Cleveland. The entire Priory land associated with the granges is also noted as well as the value of the monastic property there at various times.

With the exception of Barnaby and North Cote (mainly pasture) all the land quoted appeared to be arable in 1539. It has been shown elsewhere that the grange sizes in the Dissolution Accounts were usually the same, or almost the same, as the grange sizes earlier.[1] Thus, the Canons cultivated 360 acres at Barnaby in c. 1300; in 1539 the grange was 347 acres, which had turned to pasture. This stability of land ownership enables an estimate to be made of the amount of land attached to each grange and associated with it during the medieval period. The granges in Cleveland were the main centres of the Canon's arable farming. Their other granges and cattle farms in the moorlands and elsewhere were generally much smaller in size and had little or no arable land attached. The table shows that arable on grange land alone was great, but if associated land owned by the Canons in the vill was worked in harmony with it the total arable holding would be greater still. There is reason to believe that this was so.

A Rent Roll (c. 1300) shows the tenants of the Priory at many places and the lands they held.[2] It is possible from this to get an idea of what lands were being cultivated by the Canons and what lands were let out. No tenants were mentioned for Barnaby, North Cote, Yearby, Kirkleatham, Coatham, and Marske so that much or all the land owned there was presumably worked by the Canons. The Roll states, in fact, for Barnaby that they were working 360 acres. At Linthorpe at least 20½ bovates of land was in the hands of tenants, 26 at Thornaby, 15 at Arsum and 9 at Marton.[3] Even so the 1301 subsidy shows that the Priory had moveables at some of these places so presumably land was being worked by

---
[1] B. Waites, "The Monastic Grange as a Factor in the Settlement of N. E. Yorks.", *Yorks. Arch. Journal,* Pt. CLX, 1962
[2] G.C. vol. 2, pp.412-450.
[3] Certain entries in the subsidy were interesting, e. g. "William Werdale for the Grange of Linthorpe; William Rievaulx for Marton and Barnaby". Whether these men were Priory grangers or whether they had been leased the granges is not known.

the Canons. Thus the arable granges of the Canons in Cleveland were large in size, and cultivation was great c. 1300. Leasing of land had begun, speeded no doubt by the disasters which overtook the Priory at the turn of the 13th Century. But the period seemed to be a watershed between wholesale leasing and personal cultivation with the latter retaining much predominance still.

The purpose of this partial diversion has been to show how important the Cleveland plain was in the arable farming of the Canons – here were their largest granges, here the centres of their cultivation. The values quoted by the table emphasise the predominance of the Cleveland granges.

Reference to the granges of the other monasteries in the Vale of York - Cleveland region confirms the importance of arable farming there. This was particularly evident in Byland Abbey granges on the Boulder Clay soils west of the Coxwold gap (Wildon, Boscar, Faldington, Balke) and in the Cleveland embayment.[1] In the latter area Rievaulx cultivated four carucates at their grange of Great Broughton in 1299 each worth 40/- while nearby at Dromonby, the monks of Fountains had an important grange, established about 1180 and still in their hands in 1353.[2] It was also in this area that some of the most agriculturally prosperous parishes were found, notably at Rudby and Stokesley.

The Valor Ecclesiasticus, then, showed that the emphasis of farming in the Vale of York during the 16th Century was decisively towards arable. Earlier sources, mainly monastic, showed that this trend had been active much earlier, and that the farming was predominantly arable at least from the 12th Century. If Domesday Book illustrated normal agricultural conditions in Yorkshire it might well be possible to follow this trend further back in time. But this is denied. Of course, the extent and importance of pastoralism in the Vale and elsewhere must not be underestimated.

---

[1] NB. These granges had large grants of pasture for oxen made to them, e.g. 95 oxen from Wildon and Stocking granges given common pasture in Kilburn (1224, *Y.A.S. Fines* vol. 62, pp.55-56). This suggests that arable farming might have been very important about this time. If used for ploughing the oxen represent 12 teams.
[2] *E.Y.C.* vol. 1, pp.454-5. *Memorials of Fountains Abbey* (Surtees) vol. 3, p.4.

7 PASTORAL FARMING : INTRODUCTION

The Inquisition for the Ninth (1342) gives the first comprehensive picture of sheep farming in the North-East. Including, as it does, the wool and lamb tithe of the parishes, it allows a fair estimate to be made of the relative importance of sheep farming in the area as a whole. The wool tithe of the parish was usually expressed in sacks or money value. Thus at Hawnby the rector used to receive one sack of wool as tithe from the parish; at Whitby three sacks. But at Hackness, the wool tithe was worth 400/- and at Kirby 80/-.[1] These different modes of expression were probably due to the particular whims of the parishioners who gave the information on oath.[2] The wool and lamb tithes were sometimes included together and given as one. At Brompton, for example, the tithe of wool and lambs used to be worth 200/-. But many parishioners gave the wool and lambs separately. In such cases the lamb-tithe was invariably quoted as the number of lambs. Thus in Kirkdale parish the wool tithe was worth 133/4 and the lamb-tithe used to be 100 lambs; in Kirby Wiske the wool tithe used to be worth 300/- and the lamb tithe comprised 100 lambs.[3]

The parishioners made the distinction between the value of the tithes "this year", that is 1341, and the value as "it used to be". For example, the rector of Thornton Dale used to receive one sack of wool worth 80/- but he receives "now hardly five stone". At Easington the rector used to receive each year two sacks as tithe worth 133/4 but "this year he scarcely received twelve stone".[4] In every instance the tithes were said to be more valuable in the years preceeding 1341 than they were in that year. This was to be expected because the parishioners were, after all, trying to account for the discrepancy between the Valor of 1292 and the Ninth of 1342. They could do this by showing that tithes were of less value and therefore that the clerical income had fallen.

How can these figures be used? They are helpful in two ways: first, it is possible to make a rough estimate of the number of sheep in certain parishes; second, it is possible to draw conclusions about the regional importance of sheep farming. The information given in sacks and money can be converted into numbers of sheep. On the basis that there were 200 fleeces in a sack of wool at this time it is evident that the wool tithe represented 200 sheep to each sack.[5] If this is multiplied by ten the total number of sheep in the parish is obtained. Thus the rector of Lastingham used to receive three sacks of wool in tithe; this represents 600 sheep on the basis of 200 fleeces a sack. If the tithe represented 600 sheep the total number of sheep in the parish can be estimated at about 6000. This method gives only a rough estimate but that is very useful in a period remarkable for the scarcity of such information. Here is a short list of estimated numbers of sheep in certain parishes worked out in the way described. In each case the tithe is what the rector "used to receive". –

---

[1] *N.I.* pp.219-243. The Inquisition was taken in 1342 into the corn wool and lambs of the previous year.
[2] It has occurred to me that this different expression may have reflected different ways in which the tithe was rendered. Perhaps it was given in kind where sacks of wool are quoted (mainly in moorland districts) and in money where values only are given (mainly Vale areas). I am not sure how far commutation of tithes had gone by the middle 14th century. Scottish devastations could have been a reason for speeding it up in the Vale of York.
[3] *N.I.* pp.219-243.
[4] *loc. cit.*
[5] This was used by R. A. Pelham as a basis for estimates in his chapter contributed to *The Historical Geography of England Before 1800* Edited by H. C. Darby.

Parish	Wool Tithe (in sacks)	Lamb Tithe (numbers)	Total in Parish Lambs	Sheep
Easington	2	60	600	4000
Whitby	3	100	1000	6000
Hawnby	1	20	200	2000
Kirby Wiske	3	100	1000	6000
Hutton Bushel	1½	80	800	3000
Thornton	1			2000
Lastingham	3	160	1600	6000
Helmsley	5	200	2000	10,000
Kirkdale	2	100	1000	4000

Unfortunately, the wool tithe was expressed in sacks only by the parishioners of the small group of places shown in the table. The rest of the parishes in the North-East, which had a wool tithe, had it expressed in money values. This cannot be so satisfactorily converted into actual numbers of sheep as sacks could mainly because the price of a sack of wool varied from place to place. At Kirby Wiske, in the Vale of York, it was 100/-; at Thornton Dale in the Vale of Pickering it was 80/-; at Lastingham on the moors it was 53/4; and at Whitby it was 66/8.[1] Despite this difficulty sheep population can be estimated from monetary values of tithes in a few parishes. This is so because first, as the prices of wool given by the Inquisition show, the average price of the sack in the north-east of the region seemed to be fairly stable at 66/8.[2] The greater variations in price, especially the increases, were mainly in the Vale areas particularly the Vale of York. Second, it becomes obvious from the examination of tithe values in certain parishes that, in fact, the price of the wool sack was 66/8. Thus at Hinderwell the rector used to receive 66/8 as wool tithe. This was undoubtedly one sack; at Danby the rector received 133/4 – two sacks; at Stokesley the rector received 200/- three sacks.[3] In such cases the figures were clearly multiples of 66/8. In other instances this was not so, and there the sack was a different price and it was not possible to calculate the number of sacks represented by the money value given.

On the basis outlined above tithes expressed in money can be converted to sacks and thence to numbers of sheep. This has been done in the parishes where it is feasible. The following table is a result, and it supplements the table above.

What is the significance of the tables? The Inquisition for the Ninth, as it stands, gives a great deal of information about the regional importance of sheep farming: the tables which have been compiled give a more detailed insight into the composition of this sheep farming. Thus it is apparent from the Inquisition that sheep farming was more widespread

---

[1] *N.I.* pp.219-243.
[2] Sack was stated to be 166/8 at Easington, Whitby, Kirkdale, and appeared to be the same at Hinderwell, Ingleby, Stokesley, Danby, Coxwold, Brompton, Middleton, Hackness.
[3] *N.I.* pp.219-243.

Parish	Wool Tithe in money	Wool Tithe in sacks	Total Sheep in Parish (basis 200 fleeces 1 sack)
Hinderwell	66/8	1	2000
Ingleby	66/8	1	2000
Stokesley	200/–	3	6000
Danby	133/4	2	4000
Coxwold	200/–	3	6000
Brompton	200/–	3	6000
Middleton	266/8	4	8000
Hackness	400/–	6	12000

in the parishes of the Coastal Plateau, the Moorland and the Pickering Vale/Moor regions than in the Vale of York and the central Vale of Pickering. In fact, in the last two Vales there were very few references to any wool and lamb tithes at all. This need not necessarily imply a complete absence of sheep from the majority of parishes in those areas. At Northallerton, although the Record Commission version of the Inquisition omits it, there were 500 sheep in 1341, and the parish had contained about 8500 sheep before the destructions of the Scots.[1] A complete absence of recorded wool tithe need not, then, mean that a parish was entirely destitute of sheep. That would be very unlikely even in the marshy areas of the Vales. But it does indicate, it seems safe to infer, that the number of sheep was low – so low that the profits from the tithe on them was not worth recording separately.

The Coastal Plateau emerges as a very important region of sheep farming. The parishes of Loftus and Easington were described as lying mainly in the moor and pasture where the parishioners lived for the great part by sheep farming.[2] But even if the Inquisition has not made a special allusion to this, the value of the tithes from wool and lambs would have been enough to make it plain. The total value of the wool and lamb tithe in the Coastal Plateau parishes (excepting the large parish of Lythe) was £899/8 – more than the total tithe of parishes in the Vale of York or the York Vale/Moor region. Using the population figures for sheep established by the above tables, it appears that Hinderwell had about 2000 sheep, Easington 4600 sheep and lambs, and Whitby 7000 sheep and lambs. It is evident that in an area so largely infertile in soils, and unpropitious in aspect and elevation for arable farming, sheep husbandry occupied a prominent place in the economy.

In fact, this was a persistent trend: the tithe details given in the Valor Ecclesiasticus show that even in the early 16th century pastoralism, and in particular sheep farming, was highly important. The Valor adds some information too: it quotes the tithe on calves, which gives some indication of the extent of cattle farming in the area. The tithe was

---

[1] P.R.O. E. 179/211/18.
[2] *N.I.* p.219.

comparable in value to that of the York Vale/Moor parishes. On average, the Coastal Plateau calf tithe was greater than that of the Vale of York.[1]

Those parishes in the Moorland were, as might be expected, also important in sheep farming. Danby had about 4000 sheep, Hawnby 2000, Lastingham 6000, and Hackness 12.000 in the middle of the 14th century. All these parishes included valleys within their boundaries, for instance Danby included much of Eskdale, and Hackness the Upper Derwent valley. This made it possible for the sheep farmers to exploit the surrounding high moor tops as Pasture land in summer but to keep to the sheltered valleys and valley sides for the colder weather. Hardy as the highland sheep were the presence of such valleys was a great advantage.

But the region par excellence of the sheep farmer was in the strip parishes extending northwards from the River Derwent into the moors. Their size was large and about three quarters of their area was moorland. The size of the flocks appears to have been invariably high: there were about 3800 sheep and lambs in Hutton Bushel, 12,000 in Helmsley, 5000 in Kirkdale, 8000 sheep in Middleton, 6000 in Brompton, 2000 in Thornton giving a total of 36,800 sheep and lambs (and this excludes several parishes). It was in this region that the great monastic and lay sheep farmers concentrated their flocks. The Duchy of Lancaster, whose Honour of Pickering covered much of the area had well over a thousand sheep on its estate during much of the 14th century. As will be seen later this was a carefully organised business. Then there were other individual laymen, like Thomas de Westhorpe, who had very large flocks. Not least were the monastic farmers: the small nunnery of Rosedale has as many as 2000 sheep in Middleton parish in 1308,[2] while the larger houses had often more considerable numbers. Rievaulx and Kirkham between them had wool and lambs worth 480/- in Helmsley parish at the time of the Ninth Inquisition.[3] Besides, it was this area stretching from Ryedale to the coast, that large numbers of monastic granges were situated, either in the valleys which cut through the Corallian dip slope or on the slope itself. Associated with them were large areas of pasture such as that owned by Rievaulx in Farndale, Bransdale and Bilsdale.

The highland areas of sheep farming just described were in sharp contrast with the Vales of York and Pickering. Parishes situated entirely within the clayland basins of the Vales were, so far as the Inquisition shows, much less concerned with sheep farming. This is not surprising: the effect of foot rot and liver fluke on sheep mortality is well known in such places where drainage may be poor and areas of standing water considerable.[4] It is known that flooding was frequent in both Vales; even in 1794 Tuke could describe the Vale of Pickering as "very low and wet in consequence of the river being very crooked,

---

[1] Note Tuke's comment in 1794: "In the eastern Moorlands and the coast a great number of very good cattle are bred; they are not quite so large as those near the Tees but are clean and fine, and very free feeders ... The good qualities of the cattle stock of this district seem to be more owing to the soil, climate or accident, or all of them united than to breeders, whose spirit for improvements is very feeble indeed". *op. cit.* p.63. In medieval times Eskdale had many vaccaries for cattle in it nb. Guisborough Priory's cattle farming in the Ugthorpe district etc. also Whitby Abbey's vaccaries in the Hackness Harwood area.
[2] *Reg. Greenfield V.* p.239.
[3] P.R.O. E. 179/211/20.
[4] There is an interesting discussion of Liver Fluke in C. Fox *The Personality of Britain*. Three years ago a Folkton farmer told me that he kept his sheep away from the peaty alluvial areas near the Derwent and Hertford drain because of the danger of foot rot. In fact, the majority of sheep in the villages thereabouts were on the gravel soils at the Wold foot.

much choaked, insufficient for the floods ... by which means about 11,000 acres of land ... are greatly injured, or rendered totally useless".[1] Much earlier, in 1366, Thomas de Westhorpe had 60 acres of meadow "of no value because each year it was flooded by the water of the Derwent".[2] But this was a common occurrence throughout the Vale: the Abbot of Byland had built up the banks of the Derwent as levees at Rillington to protect his pasture land, but several men from nearby villages broke the banks and the Abbot's pasture was flooded causing great loss (1342).[3] At Scagglethorpe, too, meadowland was described as of no value in 1323 because it was inundated by the Derwent.[4] It was hardly likely that sheep farming could be widespread in such places, and when it did occur it would be, generally speaking, seasonal.

A few parishes were exceptional however. Northallerton, a very large parish, had 500 sheep in it in 1341 and previously 8500 sheep before Scottish devastations reduced the flocks. The size of the parish largely accounts for this and, though the River Wiske ran through it, areas of well-drained gravels covered part of the parish providing sites for villages and for sheep farming, at a slightly higher level than the surrounding areas of river alluvium. Kirby Wiske had about 7000 sheep and lambs at the same time. Here, the Inquisition itself states that a great deal of land had been flooded by the River Swale.[5] This is not surprising because the parish lay for the most part between two rivers – the Swale and Wiske – and must have been frequently visited by floods from either one or both. The particular interest shown in the parish by Fountains Abbey might have been the reason for the increased importance of sheep farming. The abbey had a grange there before 1181 and had pasture for at least 300 sheep in the vill.[6] The grange was well situated in relation to the Pennine dales, especially Wensleydale, and it seems likely that transhumance between the areas took place. Kirby Wiske was no more than 16 miles from the dales, and it is known that the abbey moved its flocks even greater distances to highland pastures, elsewhere. Perhaps the same policy was adopted at Kirby Wiske as at Fountains Abbey itself where it was the custom to send "some twentie score horses, beastes and shepe from Fountains Abbey to Forngill ... [18 miles distant ...] and in the rest of Fountains Fell which lay open to it they depastured till Michaelmas or thereabouts and then drove them back again to Fountains Abbey." The sheep were clipped about Midsummers Day in the hills, "and the woll whollie caried away to the Abby" ... But the ground was, "...fitt onely for somering and not wyntering...".[7]

With a few exceptions, then, the parishes of the Vales of York and Pickering did not appear to be important areas of sheep farming. The Valor Ecclesiasticus emphasises this by the generally low value of the wool tithe compared to the corn tithe. This question was discussed in Chapter 6. The wool, lamb and calf tithes together, in fact, were at best only

---

[1] Tuke *op. cit.* pp.15-16.
[2] P.R.O. Exchequer L. T. R. Memoranda Rolls 139m.24.
[3] Y.A.S. *Monastic Notes* 1, p.31.
[4] *Cal.I. P.M.* Vol. 6, p.305.
[5] *N.I.* p.234.
[6] By 1456-57 Kirby grange and its associated land had been let out for £8-12-10 a year. *Memorials of Fountains Abbey* (Surtees) Vol. 3. p.4. Worth £12-17-10 at the Valor (1535).
[7] York: D. Reg. R. VII G 3260 Printed in *Select Tithe Causes* (YAS) pp.155-168.

about one quarter of the total agricultural tithe. Usually they were much less. At Kirby Wiske they were only 4%, at Kilvington 5% and at Thirsk 10%.

But in those parishes on the eastern fringe of the Vale of York sheep farming increased in importance. This was especially noticeable in the parishes of Kirby, Ingleby Greenhow, Stokesley and Leake. All these included stretches of moorland within their boundaries. Stokesley had, in fact, an extremely large area of high moorland called Westerdale Moor forming a detached part of the parish where flocks from the Cleveland lowland, went for summer pasture. Ingleby and Stokesley appear to have had a sheep population of about 8,000 at the time of the Inquisition for the Ninth. The rector of Kirby used to receive 80/- wool and lamb tithe, which was not particularly high compared to similar tithes in the Coastal Plateau and Moorland regions. The Valor Ecclesiasticus shows the importance of pastoralism in the York Vale/Moor region better than the Inquisition. Thus in most of the parishes the 16th century wool, lamb, and calf tithes together comprised over one third of the total agricultural tithe. In Sigston, Osmotherley, Cowesby, Kildale and Kirby the animal tithe was well over half the corn-hay tithe. Sheep and cattle farming was obviously not the be all and end all of this region's economy. In fact arable farming was, overall, very important – naturally so, since besides moorland, the parishes contained extensive stretches of fertile clay and gravel land. But it is interesting to see the increasing importance of pastoralism as the moorlands were approached.

The theme of the preceding paragraphs has been, basically, the contrast between highland and lowland areas in respect of sheep farming. The Ninth of 1342 directed attention to those regions of the North-East which were predominant as sheep farming areas – the Coastal Plateau, the Pickering Vale/Moor region, the Moorland region, and to a lesser degree the York Vale/Moor parishes. The Valor Ecclesiasticus reaffirmed the importance of these regions, not only as sheep farming areas but often as areas of cattle farming. The Ninth had no information about the Wolds, and so far this region has not been mentioned. Monastic evidence in particular, shows the Wolds to have been a very important area of sheep farming and this is discussed below. Does the Valor Ecclesiasticus support this?

It is quite clear from the Valor that most of the parishes in the Northern Wolds had a wool and lamb tithe. Sometimes this was fairly large, as at Weaverthorpe (120/-) but usually it was the order of 50/- to 80/-. Undoubtedly some of the figures quoted in the Valor are incomplete: in certain parishes the income of the vicarage alone is given and the rectory income omitted. Nor, in many cases are the missing details supplied under the religious houses which often had appropriated the rectory and its profits. Thus only part of the tithe details of the parishes are there, in the Valor. Luckily, the wool tithes may well be full in most instances; it is the corn tithes which are often most effected. This is because the monastery owning the appropriation of a benefice usually took the corn tithe for itself but left the small tithes, including wool, for the vicar. Thus, the wool tithe may be correct, at worst it gives a minimum picture. That picture is enough to show that sheep farming was widespread on the Wolds, and that it increased in importance in those strip parishes extending over the Wold scarp. At Settrington, for example, the tithe reached the high value of 183/- and at Folkton it was 120/-. As in the moorland areas, it was the strip parishes, which once again emerged as principal wool producers.

PART THREE : LAND USE

The regional pattern of pastoral activities has been established. It can now be said that one area was more important than another in terms of sheep farming. But what were the details within this broad regional pattern? These can be illustrated best by examining the pastoral farming on the estates of the Duchy of Lancaster at Pickering and the lands of Thomas de Westhorpe. This will give a good idea of lay farming: a consideration of monastic estates will provide a useful comparison.

PASTORAL FARMING ON THE DUCHY OF LANCASTER'S PICKERING ESTATE IN THE 14th AND 15th CENTURIES

On 30 June 1267 Edmund Crouchback knelt before his father, King Henry III, to accept the charter which made him Earl of Lancaster. He rose as the possessor of lands in almost every corner of England, from Lancashire to Huntingdon and the Welsh Marches. This grant marked the beginning of the Lancastrian interest in Yorkshire, for it included the Honour and Forest of Pickering, together with the manor of Scalby.[1]

The Honour extended over a wide and diverse area: from the River Derwent in the south almost to Eskdale 16 miles to the north, and from the River Seven in the west to the coast 20 miles to the east (Fig. 7.1). It included moorland over 1000 feet in height, which gradually declined southwards to be replaced by the fertile dip slopes of Corallian limestone – the site of a series of prosperous villages of which Pickering was the chief. Further southwards still the meadowland and carrland of the Derwent valley stood out in contrast.[2]

This diversity makes the Duchy estate peculiarly suitable for study, because an insight into both demesne and tenant farms is possible. Thus, besides being able to examine Duchy sheep farming, the historian can see the economy of the whole area covered by the Honour. Since the Honour was so large a part of the North-East of England, it is evident that any conclusions reached about the economy within it will be very significant for the region as a whole.

A discontinuous series of Ministers' accounts give a very good picture of Duchy farming in the Honour during the fourteenth century. These are the Reeve's accounts for 1313-14 and 1322, and Keeper's accounts for 1325-27. After a lapse of fifty years Reeve's and Bailiff's accounts occur again in 1377-78. From 1438 the series continues unbroken throughout the fifteenth century. Receiver's and Auditor's accounts are available for this latter period but are generally less useful than the detailed Reeve's accounts. In addition to these the Coucher Book of the Duchy provides much background material. The contents of the book are varied including such items as forest offences, charter grants, and claims for certain privileges – all these falling under the general heading of Pleas of the Forest.[3]

---

[1] See R. Somerville, *History of the Duchy of Lancaster I*, 1265-1603 (1953).
[2] The boundaries of the Forest of Pickering are delineated in document No. 399 of the *Whitby Chartulary* (Surtees Society, Vols. 69 (1879) and 72 (1881)).
[3] The accounts for 1313-14, 1322, and 1325-27 are printed in R. B. Turton (ed.), *The Honour and Forest of Pickering*, North Riding Record Series, new series Vols. 2 and 4 (1895, 1897). The account for 1377 and subsequent accounts are in the Public Record Office, D.L. 29/490/7934-7956. Receiver's accounts are Bundle 500 and Auditor's accounts are Bundle 728. The Duchy Coucher Book has been largely printed in North Riding Record Series, new series 2-4 (cited below as *N.R.R.S.*).

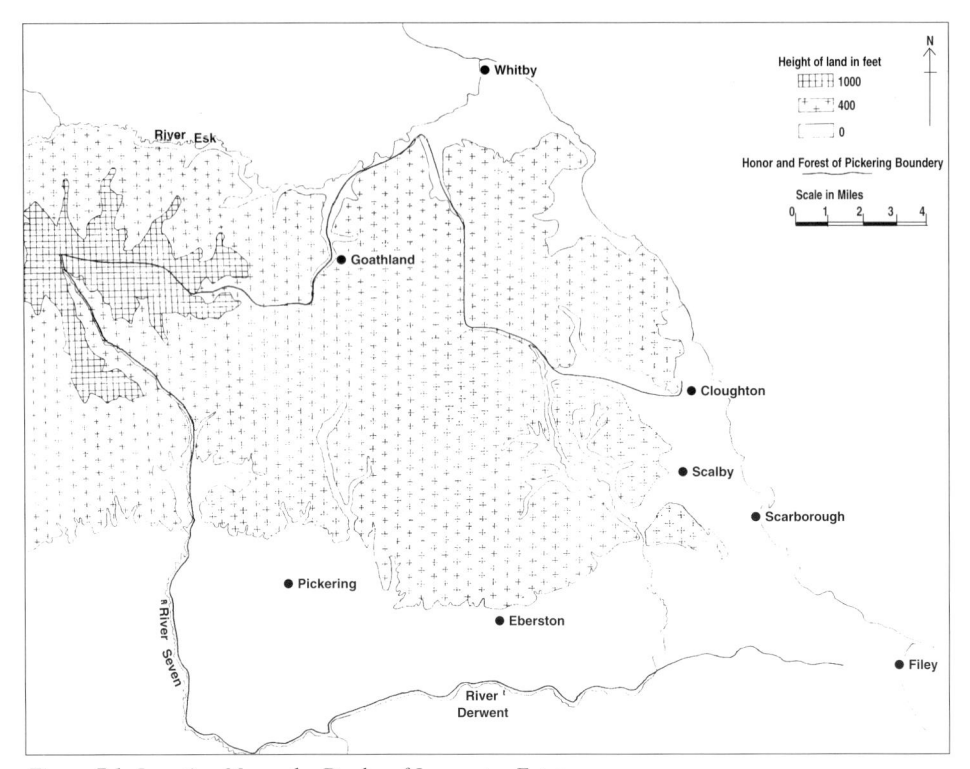

Figure 7.1 Location Map : the Duchy of Lancaster Estate

How far sheep farming had developed on the Duchy estate prior to the fourteenth century remains a mystery. By the date of the first account in 1313, however, it is clear that a well organised system of sheep farming was in operation. This was to be expected since all the Duchy possessions seemed to be carefully administered by a hierarchy of local and regional officials who 'imparted a *unity* of control that was further exercised by the council'.[1] The Dukes of Lancaster, too, seem to have played a much more active part in running their estates than was as at one time supposed.[2]

Sheep farming took the predominant place in the economy of the Honour. While the demesne lands of the Duchy were let to farm early in the fourteenth century, and remained so, sheep farming was retained in Duchy hands until as late as 1434 when the pastures were leased and flocks disposed of.[3] This retention of sheep farming stresses the suitability of the area for this activity. Nowhere else on any of the Duchy estates had sheep

---

[1] Somerville, *op. cit.*, p.89.
[2] *Ibid*
[3] E. Power, *The Wool Trade in English Medieval History* (1941), p. 38. 194 acres of land and 66 acres of meadow were leased in 1313. It remained leased out (P.R.O. D.L. 29/490/7934, account for 1377-8). A great deal of high moorland waste was let out during the fourteenth century. There was still cultivation undertaken by the Duchy itself on some of the Lancaster estates: e.g. 'Letting of demesne lands and direct cultivation were also going on simultaneously in the Northamptonshire manors' and at Gimingham, Norfolk, during the last decade of the fourteenth century (Somerville, *op. cit.* p.95).

farming remained the direct activity of the Earl of Lancaster. The stock-keeper of the Derbyshire Peak sheep farm who had more than 5000 sheep under his control at the beginning of the fourteenth century had only vaccaries in his charge at the end; no mention of sheep was made on any but the Pickering estate.[1] The Northamptonshire sheep farms which were extensive in the second decade of the century had passed into the hands of tenants by the end.[2] The persistence of demesne farming in the Pickering estate in a period characterised by leasing elsewhere becomes more significant when it is recollected that monastic farmers, too, in this region, clung more tenaciously to their lands and flocks than did their counterparts in other parts of England.[3]

Though the Pickering flocks were organised on a centralised system, very similar to those of the Peak district with a stock-keeper (sometimes also the Bailiff) responsible for buying and selling sheep, superintending their pasture and collecting wool, the scale of farming appears to have been smaller. The following table shows the sheep on the Pickering estate at various times: –

Date	Wethers	Ewes	Hoggetts	Lambs	Wool	Wool Sold	Total Sheep
Sept. 1313–Sept. 1314	473	86	53	49	fleece 625	571 pounds 3 sacks 3 1/2 st.	661
Mar.–Nov. 1322	1407	124	56	61	1619	4 1/2 st. locket	1648
Sept. 1325–Sept. 1326	1194	98	39*	55	1340	8 sacks 12 st.	1386
Sept. 1326–Sept. 1327	1119	118	31*	79	1284	7 1/2 sacks 28 st. 4 1/2 st. locket.	1347
Sept.–Dec. 1327	1115	116	31*	74			1336

(* hoggetts and gimmers).

The numbers in the table are the residue in stock after sales and deaths.

The most noticeable feature is that by 1322 the number of sheep was almost three times as great as in 1313. Subsequently from 1325-27 the total number remained very constant. Wethers predominated, being about ten times as many as ewes. Sales and purchases did not assume large proportions so far as the accounts show. In fact deaths from murrain, sheep pox or other causes were about the same as sales in the short period being dealt with. The following table enumerates them:–

---

[1] Power, *op. cit.*, pp.28,38.
[2] Somerville, *op. cit.* p.95.
[3] B. Waites, *Moorland and Valeland Farming in North-East Yorkshire: the monastic contribution in the thirteenth and fourteenth centuries,* Borthwick Papers No. 32 (York 1967).

Sheep and Lambs	1313-14	1322 (34 weeks only)	1325-26	1326-27	Total
Sales	128	74	52	73	327
Deaths	67	73	126	69	335
Lamb tithe	7	8	7	10	32
TOTAL	202	155	185	152	

The Duchy authorities concentrated on the production of wool. They sold all the wool produced and obtained high prices for the best quality. The classification of their wool into clean, refuse and lockets suggests a fairly high degree of experience in dealing with wool merchants. Such a division facilitated business dealings. Prices paid for clean wool ranged from 120*s*. to 140*s*. a sack in the early fourteenth century; refuse wool was 75*s*. *to 80s.* a sack and lockets about 25*s*. a sack. These were very good compared to surrounding areas: in the Vale of York, for instance, during the late thirteenth and early fourteenth centuries the sack was about 100*s*., while along the coastal region the sack was fetching 66*s*. *8d.* in 1341. Even in the Vale of Pickering itself, within a few miles of the Duchy boundaries, the value of the sack appears to have been much less. At Kirkdale it was 66*s*. *8d.* and at Thornton 80*s*. Although it would not be wise to draw over strong conclusions from such variable data it seems likely that the superior organisation of the Duchy resulted in higher prices for wool sold. Incidentally, the monasteries, even more highly organised for sheep farming, received larger prices still.

But sheep had many uses; that was the essence of their value. The accounts show that besides serving the principal function of wool producers, they supplied skins and pelts which were a profitable source of income to the Duchy. There are indications, too, that the milk of the ewes was the nucleus of a small dairying industry, additionally important because, so far as the evidence shows, no cattle were kept on the estate. The milk of ewes appears several times as an item in the accounts and though it was let out in 1322, in subsequent years it was retained for use on the estate-sheep, as Round stresses were 'expected to supply not only mutton and wool, but above all, milk.[1] The production of cheese from sheep's milk was a recognised Essex Industry'. Cheese was made from ewes milk at Pickering and sold.[2] But the supply of milk from sheep was below the demand for it, and collection from over a wide area had to be made. Thus the Reeve acknowledges the expenses of 'a woman collecting milk throughout the country', and of 'a man seeking milk throughout the country for the lambs'.

The organisation which seemed implicit in the well developed wool industry and perhaps in the dairying concerns of the Duchy is, in fact, proven by the accounts. The stockmaster was in general supervision of the sheep farming and was particularly

---

[1] *Victoria County History, Essex*, I (1903), p.360.
[2] Compare this with dairying on the Whitby Abbey estates in the late fourteenth century, e.g. for milk sales, purchase of rennet for coagulating milk, and wages of women for doing the work.

responsible for reporting to his superiors on the state of the flocks and re-stocking.[1] Sheep were often brought great distances for this purpose. In 1313, for instance, 84 wethers had been purchased at Ripon Fair and driven 40 miles to Pickering.[2] It is likely that the best breeds were to be bought at Ripon which lay so near to the rich Pennine pasture lands. Such long distance conveyance of animals for breeding purposes was not uncommon on the larger estates of the North-East. Whitby Abbey for instance had bought cattle at Barnard Castle in 1301 and driven them almost 60 miles to the Abbey by way of Eskdale.[3]

The stockmaster went to Rothwell, near Pontefract, to make his report and along with the Steward's clerk, the Reeve and his clerk, to render account. The whole journey there and back together with the business discussions took four days.[4] Though the stockmaster probably reported on the Pickering stud-farm as well as about the sheep he was not responsible for its running. In fact during the early fourteenth century the management of the pastoral farming on the Pickering estate devolved into the hands of several distinct officials. The stud-farm at Blansby Park – a large tract of woodland and pasture for deer and horses ringed by walls, fences and hedges, north of Pickering – was in charge of a Park Keeper and a Keeper of the Mares.[5] Similarly much of the demesne pasture and meadow was under the aegis of separate officials. There was, for instance, a Keeper of the demesne meadows and of Dalby Dale (a main sheep pasture of the estate), and a Warrener (sometimes also described as Forester) of Castle Ings – an area of rich meadowland in Marishes near the River Derwent, over 100 acres and the source of hay for the stud.[6] How independent these officials were of the stockmaster is not known, and the character of their relationship to him is obscure, but it is possible that they were more directly responsible to the Steward or Bailiff of the Honour, especially in the late fourteenth and fifteenth centuries when leasing of demesne meadows deprived them of many of their old tasks.[7]

The stockmaster was always an official of the Duchy until the flocks were disposed of in the fifteenth century. The accounts of the late fourteenth and early fifteenth centuries contain frequent references to him and though details of sheep under his control are few, expenses entailed in shearing and management recur.[8] The stockmaster appeared to have flocks of his own; Roger Midelwood had at least 1000 sheep, for example, in 1438 – noted, incidentally, for his long and good service as Bailiff and Stockmaster.[9] This combination of offices is interesting: there is no indication of it in the early fourteenth century.[10] This suggests that perhaps the duties of the Stockmaster became less as sheep

---

[1] The stockmaster's wage was 6s. 8d, more than the Reeve's (4s. 7d.) but far less than the Bailiff's (£10). There appear to have been two stock-keepers in the early fourteenth century, possibly under the stockmaster.
[2] *N.R.R.S.*, n.s. 2 (1895), p.22.
[3] Yorkshire Archaeological Society Record Series, 81 (1931), *Monastic Notes* II, p.51.
[4] *N.R.R.S., ibid*, p.23.
[5] In 1490 there was an official here known as Master of the Game as well as the Park Keeper, *N.R.R.S.*, n.s. I, p.124.
[6] William Stuttes, Keeper of Castle Ings and the Derwent and Marshal of the Forest on the south had an annual wage of 45s. 7^1/$_2$d. *N.R.R.S.*, n.s. 4, p.228.
[7] Thus the agistment of Dalby Dale was let out in 1377-78.
[8] E.g. P.R.O. D.L. 29/490/7935/728/11988
[9] P.R.O. D.L. 29/490/7935
[10] In 1313-14 the Bailiff was also the Receiver, but the Stockmaster's office was distinct, *N.R.R.S.*, n.s. 2, p.25.

farming declined on the estate and that he was able to occupy two posts and work them comfortably whereas earlier either one had been a very full-time occupation in itself.

Four shepherds were required to manage the flocks of over 1000 sheep. Temporary labour was employed in particularly busy times, especially for shearing – 'the great moment of the sheep farmer's year'. Then such phrases as '10 men assisting the shepherd and watching the sheep on the High Moors' recur frequently. Sometimes lads were hired to watch the lambs. The whole fascinating sequence opens itself out: the washing and shearing which took place on the High Moor; the amazing variety of materials needed such as ointment, grease and sulphur; the employment of tiles for branding – the next job after shearing; then the collection of the wool and carrying it down to the wool house at Pickering to be sorted and rolled, 'in piles in preparation for the arrival of the merchants', who came from as far afield as Hull, Beverley and York. The shepherds received 4s. 6d. each for their yearly work, almost as much as the Stock-Keepers, who had 6s. 8d. a year as wage. In addition they received an allowance of rye – about 4 quarters each.

But what of the pasture lands – the basis of this activity and wealth? Two main areas were utilised as sheep pasture: the valleys which cut through the gentle dip slope north and east of Pickering, and the High Moors.[1] There is no evidence from the accounts to show that sheep were pastured in the Vale of Pickering, although hay for sheep and horses was cut from the carrland meadows owned by the Duchy in the Vale. The agistment of Dalby Dale and adjoining dales was worth £3 to the Duchy in the early fourteenth century. The former dale seems to have been one of the chief pasture grounds – at any-rate it was important enough to have a special Keeper of its own whose job was 'to preserve the game, and woods and meadows for the sheep. He received 13s. 7½d. in corn for performing this during twenty-six weeks in the year, from January to August. This time limit suggests that the sheep pastured in Dalby Dale only during part of the year. In fact, seasonal movement of sheep on a fairly large scale between the High Moors and Pickering was usual. Summer agistment on the High Moor areas north of Pickering is often mentioned in the accounts When colder weather began the flocks moved south into folds at Pickering and winter fodder was stored in readiness. This was mainly hay from the Pickering marshes or ingland and from Dalby Dale and its tributary valleys: 47 acres were mown at Dalby Dale for the sheep at a cost of 19s. 7d.; 'it is so dear because it lies in a remote spot three miles from the village and in a valley within a wood'. But the hay seemed to be preferred to that of the marshes (which was mainly used for the horses of the stud-farm and was better quality). Each sheep, so the account runs, 'costs ³/4d. in hay' (1325-26).

But the moorland sheep was and is a hardy animal. Even in the coldest conditions it can remain out. 'The Moreland breed of sheep', Marshall noted, 'has always been very different from that of the Vale, and has not perhaps varied during a succession of centuries. It is peculiarly adapted to the extreme bleakness of the climature, and the extreme coarseness of the herbage. They lived upon the open heaths all the year round. Their food

---

[1] The Duchy received dues from agistment of cattle and sheep in Scalby Hay, Allantofts, Langdale, Fulwood Moor and Cloughton, Hayburn, Horcum Pasture and High Moor. This gives a good indication where the main areas of pasture were to be found. Some agistments were let to farm in the early fourteenth century, but not those of Dalby, High Moor and Blansby (the main areas of Duchy pasture).

heath rushes, and a few coarsest grasses; a pasture on which perhaps every other breed of sheep of this Kingdom would starve'.[1] Duchy sheep, folded and sheltered for a few months of the year, perhaps when snow was on the ground, were sent out again in January after having been fed on hay and ling, which could be cut for winter fodder. Ling, in fact, was an abundant and cheap means of sustenance, used also in the eighteenth century – '. . . The common and most profitable food for these sheep is ling . . . There are flocks that from year to year have no other food than what they can pick up from heaths and wastes . . . When during winter there is too much snow on the ground for the flocks to go out into the fields . . . they give them cut ling within doors which had been previously stored up for them the preceding autumn'.[2] The references to ling and bracken being cut on behalf of the Duchy are many in the early fourteenth century.

The pasture of the High Moor was important both to the Duchy and to residents in the Honour. The Duchy accounts show that by the early fourteenth century settlement of the High Moors had advanced quickly, particularly in the Goathland – Allantofts area – moorland well over 900 feet high.[3] Enclosure was the corollary to this settlement. 160 acres had been enclosed for tillage in the wood of Allantofts, for instance in 1282, and when Roger Bigod complained that this had deprived him of the herbage of the area the Duchy's answer was 'that the tenants make inclosures this is true, for only thus can they derive any profit'.[4] In fact, it seemed to be part of the Duchy policy to enclose their demesne and let it out to would-be tenants.[5] Undoubtedly a great deal of enclosure and settlement of these high regions had been stimulated by the seasonal agistment of sheep there.[6] Folds were built and woods cleared for the purpose: the same thing was going on in Scalby Hay as on the higher areas. Approvements for pasture and meadows were made in Chanyte (Goathland), a vaccary was erected in Wheeldalerigg, 408 acres, 7 pieces of waste, etc. enclosed in Allantofts, and licences to reside on the High Moor were granted.

During the early fourteenth century, the valley pastures, mainly Dalby Dale seemed to be largely used by the Duchy flocks. The High Moor pastures were not so restricted and the animals of all the inhabitants of the Honour used them. There were certain periods for agistment of sheep and cattle however, and if animals were found pasturing at other times they were seized. The Duchy Coucher Book has full records of such cattle 'taken in the Forest' during 1334-35.[7] By examining the lists given it becomes possible to see how important cattle and sheep farming was to smallholders living within the Duchy estate. For as Professor Power said, 'it must never be forgotten that thousands of peasant farmers all over England were keeping sheep ... I have a suspicion that even in the heyday of demesne farming peasant sheep flocks exceeded those of demesne, even though the more scientific farming of the latter may have produced the better wool'.[8]

---

[1] W. Marshall, *The Rural Economy of Yorkshire* (1788), Vol. 2, pp. 221-22.
[2] *Communications to the Board of Agriculture (1797)*, Vol. I, pp. 266-67.
[3] But the decay of rents frequently mentioned in this area illustrate its marginal character, e.g *N.R.R.S.*, n.s. 4, p.206. In 1326 land in Goathland and elsewhere on the High Moor could not be let because of 'the poverty of the country' *(ibid., p.*248).
[4] *N.R.R.S.,* n.s. 2, p.41.
[5] *Ibid,* pp.43-44. For example Lord Edmund's bailiffs let 160 acres of the wood of Allantofts.
[6] See A. R. H. Baker and R. A. Butlin, *Studies of Field Systems in the British Isles* (Cambridge 1973), chapter 4.
[7] *N.R.R.S.,* n.s. 3, pp.47-64
[8] Power, *op. cit.* p.29.

The Duchy records of cattle taken in the forest, limited as they are, nevertheless give support to this idea. During 1334-35 more than 800 sheep had been unagisted in fence months at the following places – Ebberston, Allantofts, Dalby demesne, Fulwood moor, Langdale moor, Scalby Hay and – a comprehensive term – 'in the earl's demesne'. The details of owners are interesting; invariably they were various including monastic as well as lay farmers. Thus the Preceptor of Foulbridge had 40 wethers in Dalby demesne; Alan de Bilaclif, 100 sheep in Scalby; Ralph Gegge 20 sheep; Ralph Prest of Suffield 50 sheep; Richard Russell 50 sheep; the tenants of Richard de Skelton almost 300 sheep, Henry de Bougheland 60 sheep in Scalby Hay, the township of Cawthorn more than 100 sheep, and so on. Most of the men mentioned (except the Preceptor) were small farmers. Yet they each had fairly large numbers of sheep unagisted, and, presumably their flocks were more numerous than this. The combined flocks of all such men must, it seems, have far exceeded those of the Duchy itself.

The details of animals taken included sheep, pigs, horses, and cattle. The preponderance of sheep over any other animal is a remarkable feature however, and in itself demonstrates the universal importance of sheep farming within the Honour. The number of pigs taken was fairly considerable, especially in certain places. At Seamer, for example 50 had been taken, at Langdale 36 and many in Scalby Hay (particularly those of the Prior of Bridlington). The numbers of cattle are low, possibly because, unlike sheep, they were not allowed to wander unattended. It is interesting to remember however that little reference to cattle farming, or indeed any cattle at all, was found on the Duchy demesne. In fact, the area covered by the Honour of Pickering was not cattle country. It was in the larger moorland dales and near the coast that cattle became more important, for instance in Eskdale, Farndale, and Westerdale. The Honour did not include such large dales; its boundaries encompassed only part of Rosedale, for example, and almost the whole of the valley system around Hackness (an important centre of the Whitby Abbey cattle farming) was excluded.

The Duchy had however one other important pastoral activity besides sheep farming: its specialised stud-farm. The stud-farm was located in an area of about 2 square miles north of Pickering, called Blansby Park.[1] This was a well defined territory since it was surrounded on three sides by deep valleys. Newtondale formed its eastern and southern boundary and a small valley called Haugh Dale marked its western edge. The land within the park sloped gradually from about 500 feet in the north to 250 feet in the south. The park was enclosed by stone walls, fencing and thorn hedges, which served to keep the horses and deer inside. There were about '1300 deer by estimation' in the park which had hay, ivy and holly cut to sustain them 'in time of snow and ice'. Repairs to the enclosure were frequently necessary: 320 perches of fencing had to be restored in 1325 because it had been 'thrown down by a great flood'. Part of the stone wall had to be repaired too, and this took a man two days breaking and digging stone in the quarry to complete the wall because the stones in the quarry were partly rotten.

---

[1] Evidence used in this section is also from Duchy accounts, *N.R.R.S.* n.s. 4, pp.195-270. Cf. also A. A. Dent, 'King's Horses at Pickering', *The Dalesman,* 33 (1971), pp.290-92.

The care taken over such details illustrates the careful organisation with which the whole stud was superintended. Thorn trees and rushes were stubbed up from inside the park so that the horses would have good pasture, and agistment of cattle or sheep was forbidden except when the mares were not there.

The stud-farm was not large: details of its composition are only available for 1322 and for 1325-27. The accounts for 1313-14 contain no direct reference to the stud, but Blansby Park and expenses connected with it are mentioned several times. Then, as later, there was a Park-Keeper. What eventually became of the stud is also obscure. It was perhaps disbanded in the period for which there is no record, 1327-77, for in the subsequent accounts consulted there appears to be no reference to it. The following table summarises the details known about its composition in the early part of the century.

Date	Stallions	Mares	3 year olds	2 year olds	Yearlings	Foals
Mar.–Nov. 1322		21		5		6
Sept. 1325–Sept. 1326	2	17	6	7	4	10
Sept. 1326-Sept. 1327	2	18	9	8	13	
Sept. 1327-Dec. 1327		18	8	10	13	

Stallions generally remained only temporarily on the farm before going elsewhere. It was usual, in fact, for the Master of the King's Horse to send them from the royal stud farm in Knaresborough Forest to Blansby Park for breeding purposes. Thus two black stallions, Morel of Merton and Morel of Tutbury, were sent by Adam de Hoddesdon under the king's writ of privy seal to cover the mares in the park from 22 April to 24 May, 1325; Deliveries of colts and fillies were made fairly regularly to Adam de Hoddesdon, the king's Master of the Horse, 'for the king's use'. In 1326 six colts were despatched to London and it took six grooms 22 days to get there. The journey was made in fine weather from June into July and when London was reached it was eight days before the colts were delivered to the king.

The stud was supervised by the Keeper of the Mares who no doubt worked in liaison with the Park Keeper. The latter received a yearly wage of 6s. 8d. – as much as the stockmaster – he had a very responsible position. In addition he received an allowance of corn worth 15s. 10 1/4d. a year. There were several buildings in the park, the chief one being the stud house. There was a hay barn in which winter fodder for the horses was stored. A later survey of the Duchy Lordship in 1608 mentions two lodges in the park, an upper and lower in which two keepers resided. By 1608 the walls surrounding had decayed in many places and there were said to be only 100 deer in the park. There were at least 300 cattle pastured there at this time each year. Besides the buildings referred to, shelters were made in various parts of the park for the deer in the fourteenth century.

Large amounts of provender were bought for the stud. Hay was carefully selected. Of the three main sources – the valleys, the marshlands and around Pickering itself – the second was the best. Hay from nearby Pickering was described as 'hard and rushy' and consequently was cheap. But prices varied according to several interesting factors, which small and incidental as they are bring medieval farming to life. Thus hay cut in Blansby Park itself was dear 'because it lay in the shade within the covert'; in 1322 the high price was due to the need to re-spread and remake 'on account of the rainy weather'. Another year, the hay was poor quality because of the dry summer. Sometimes, the price was more because the distances the hay was brought were long, at Dalby, for example it lay 'in a remote spot'. The best quality hay appears to have been brought from the Marishes district south of Pickering. The Duchy owned over 100 acres of meadowland at Castle Ings near the junction of the Rye and Derwent rivers. Though this was about 9 miles from the Park, it, together with the Rievaulx grange of Kekmarsh nearby, supplied most of the fodder for the stud. The importance of Castle Ings can be judged from the special officer who had custody over it whose wage was as high as 45s. 7^{1}/$_{2}d$. a year. It was the practice to burn the old grass in the Ings about February to encourage the growth of new and luscious herbage – 'et in veteri herba comburenda in pratis de Edithmerske ut nova herba possit ibidem crescere post festum Purificationis beate Marie VIII d.' This was a common practice in the moorlands where burning of heather stimulated the growth of succulent shoots for sheep to graze on. The right of burning heather was, incidentally, vigorously demanded by the Abbot of Rievaulx in the Helmsley district.[1]

The Pickering estate of the Duchy furnishes an example of the lands of a great magnate whose wealth in that area was based on sheep farming. The de Fortibus estate had been developed in the marshes of Holderness not far away as another large sheep rearing region, but different conditions there resulted in different organisation and emphasis. Besides, the de Fortibus sheep farm was most flourishing in the boom period of the thirteenth century. There is no evidence to show whether the Duchy, too, participated in those years of high farming. Available evidence for the fourteenth and fifteenth centuries shows that even in what was a period of decline in wool growing elsewhere, at Pickering a strong specialisation in sheep farming persisted.

There was a certain distinctiveness about the Pickering estate which derived partly from its careful organisation, specialisation and its long history. The intricate hierarchy of officials conducting the estate's business was so contrived that management of regional estates and of the Duchy as a whole dovetailed perfectly. This was an organisation scarcely inferior in scope and efficiency to that of the monasteries, the other great sheep farmers in the area. Like the monastic farmer, the Duchy estate showed adaptation to geographical conditions, a vast influence and a stability in a period of decline rarely found elsewhere in England. It is little wonder that the political power of the Dukes of Lancaster became so strong when their economic position was so firmly established.

---

[1] Rievaulx Chartulary, Surtees Society Vol. 83 (1889), p.3: 'Dicit ergo quod contra eundem finem comburi facit brueriam in pastura infra praedictos boscos ad magnum detrimentum praedictae pasturae'.

A YORKSHIRE FARMER IN THE MEMORANDA ROLLS

One important class of records has proved to be a rich source of history, springing pleasant surprises from time to time with reasonably consistency – the *Memoranda Rolls*. They hold many secrets, some of which have been discovered but most lie unsuspected and unknown. It has been ably shown that they can be of immense use in tracing out the intricacies of the medieval wool trade, among many other things. Professor Power was among the first to build up a wonderful story of this trade mainly through a diligent use of the Cely and Stonor Papers together with the *Memoranda Rolls*.[1] Occasionally, we may be fortunate enough to find within the *Rolls* details of individuals. When we do we must treasure them; they are priceless. So much of our notion of medieval economic life is created by a study of the great monastic farmers, the mighty lay lords or the omnipresent wool merchants that we lose sight of the matrix into which they were fixed. We forget the peasant farmers, the craftsmen and the smaller wool dealers. And yet, they probably contributed most to the complete picture. 'If we know less about them', wrote Professor Power of the peasant farmers, 'it is simply because, unlike the manors, they have left behind them very little documentary evidence.'[2]

But within the dusty confines of the Public Record Office upon a Lord Treasurer's Remembrancers *Memorandum Roll* for 1366-67 there can be found such documentary evidence of a Yorkshire farmer called Thomas de Westhorpe.[3]

In 1366 Thomas was declared an outlaw: his lands were forfeit and an inquisition made into his possessions. The details of this are given in the *Memorandum Roll*. Because they are unusually full they give an important indication of the type of farming practiced by a smaller land-holder in the North-East of Yorkshire in the fourteenth century.

The reasons for Thomas's outlawry are obscure. It was said to be the result of a suit with William Haldane in Buckinghamshire and heard in King's Bench as a plea of trespass, but Thomas appears to have died only a few months after the Inquisition. He certainly had been a man of influence within the Vale of Pickering, which lies to the south-west of Scarborough. He held lands in several villages, notably in Brompton, Snainton, Sawden and Ebberston, all near to each other, along the northern margin of the Vale. Besides being a farmer he was a wool dealer of some importance. The two occupations were connected for he kept large flocks of sheep throughout his lands. Thomas had many contacts with local wool growers, and appeared to be a collector and middleman, despatching the wool he purchased to the great merchants of York and Beverley. He was found to have a treasure box,[4] for instance, containing not only £200 but also details of many debts owed to him by men such as William Playte of Scalby, Robert de Malton, William de Appleton and Thomas Thurnes of Ebberston, all men whom

---

[1] See especially, *The Wool Trade in English Medieval History*, (London, 1941).
[2] *Ibid.*, p.29.
[3] *L.T.R. Mem. Roll E* 368/139 *m*.24
[4] Richard de Westhorpe, a relative of Thomas, was accused of seizing the box and its contents which contained 'divers obligations which the said Thomas holds of divers men' (*m*.34).

the *Assize Rolls* show to have been wool buyers in the district during the middle fourteenth century.[1] These men appear to have been the lower stratum of merchants and producers from whom Thomas de Westhorpe obtained the wool he subsequently sold to the merchants of Beverley and York. The *Memorandum Roll* refers to his connections with such merchants: Thomas de Beverley was said to have bought half a sack of wool from Thomas de Westhorpe; John de Giseburn and John de Stoke were said to be indebted to the extent of one hundred marks.[2] Again, the contemporary *Assize Rolls* show that these were prominent wool merchants of York with a widespread sphere of activity.

The farming of Thomas reflected his activity as a wool merchant and middleman. Pastoral farming was, for example, his main concern, and in particular sheep farming was emphasised. His total possessions were valued at £512-16-7. One third of these issues derived from sheep and lambs owned by him. He had a total of 2,723 sheep and 152 lambs on all his lands in 1366. Twice as many, that is, as the Duchy of Lancaster on its Honour of Pickering in the early years of the century. Even some of the great monasteries had fewer at this time; Whitby Abbey having only 1,307 sheep and Meaux Abbey 1,471 in 1366.[3]

The value of cattle on his lands was only slightly less than that of sheep. Both were well suited to the land he farmed; the former flourished on the alluvial carrlands of the Vale while the latter found ample sustenance on the High and Low Moors nearby. Thomas had 135 pigs at Brompton, 53 oxen at Brompton and Ebberston cotes, 253 cows, calves and young oxen with 28 horses, and foals in the same places. He had, thus, a total of 469 animals other than sheep on his lands. His arable farming was small, in comparison: only one eighth of the issues noted at the Inquisition came from sown land. In fact, the amount of land sown with wheat, barley, oats, rye, peas and beans was larger than its value would suggest. 238 acres, for instance, was the total amount of land sown with crops by Thomas in 1366, a much larger amount than most farmers cultivated in the district. But, on the evidence given by the Inquisition it is clear, without doubt, that pastoral farming was the predominant interest of Thomas de Westhorpe.

Thomas can hardly by regarded as a typical farmer of the fourteenth century. His dual role of merchant and producer made him unusual. Moreover, the scale of his activities was much greater than might at first have been thought possible for an individual who was not a great lord. His activities as a farmer illustrate several general themes in the medieval development of the North-East. His specialisation in sheep farming was paralleled by the Duchy of Lancaster, the monasteries and even, it appears, by peasant farmers. The area was particularly suited to sheep farming which, in turn, was conducive to the development of large estates. Thomas de Westhorpe was at least a typical product of the North-East: from the twelfth century the agrarian scene had been characterised by the landowner who farmed large estates and devoted himself principally to sheep farming, conducted on a

---

[1] See, *Yorkshire Sessions of the Peace* (1361-64), Edited by B. H. Putnam for the Yorkshire Archaeological Society Record Series, Volume 100 (1939).

[2] *Membranes* 28, 34 – details of other debtors on *m*.9, 25, 33.

[3] *Chapters of the English Black Monks* (1215-1540), Edited by W. A. Pantin. Volume III, pp.63-68 (Camden Series, Vol. 54, 1937). Also, *Chronica de Melsa* (Rolls Series No. 43, Ed. E. A. Bond) III. p152.

very large scale, carefully organised and adapted to physical and economic conditions. The monastic farmers were the outstanding example of this but it should not be forgotten that modest laymen such as Thomas also illustrated this very important theme. Thanks to a small insertion in the *Memoranda Rolls* we can achieve a better sense of historical perspective and at the same time acquire many interesting details of an individual's farming activities.

EXTRACTS FROM AN INQUISITION INTO THE POSSESSIONS OF THOMAS DE WESTHORPE OF BROMPTON, OUTLAW, HELD AT SHERBURN IN HERTFORDLITHE (1366)

HE HAS GOODS AND CHATTELS TO THE VALUE OF £473-0-4 OF WHICH THE FOLLOWING INQUISITION TAKES NOTE:—

In Brompton, Snainton and Sawden:

		£	s.	d.
64	acres of land sown with wheat value/acre 6/-	19	4	0
6	acres of land sown with rye at 6/- per acre	1	16	0
80	acres of land sown with barley at 5/- per acre	20	0	0
14	acres of land sown with beans and peas at 3/4 per acre	2	6	8
19	acres of land sown with oats at 3/4 per acre	3	3	4

At Ebberston cotes:

		£	s.	d.
27	acres of land sown with wheat at 6/8 per acre	9	0	0
16½	acres of land sown with barley at 5/- per acre	6	10	0
11	acres of land sown with peas at 3/4 per acre	1	16	8
1	acre of land sown with oats at 3/4 per acre		3	4

In Brompton:

		£	s.	d.
37	oxen value 13/4 each	24	13	4

At Ebberstoncotes:

		£	s.	d.
16	oxen value 13/4 each	10	13	4

At Brompton (Langedon) and Ebberstoncotes:

		£	s.	d.
152	cows and beasts value 10/- each	76	0	0
55	year old oxen at 4/6 each	12	7	6
46	calves at 2/- each	4	12	0
12	cart horses at 6/8 each	4	0	0
8	foals at 5/- each	2	0	0
6	(stagges) at 3/4 each	1	0	0
1	horse 'pro sella suo' at 20/-; another horse at 6/8	1	6	8

And he has in the vills and places aforesaid:

		£	s.	d.
1350	sheep at 1/6 each	120	15	0
1350	hog sheep 'les drapes' at 11d. each	73	15	10
144	lambs at 9½d. each	5	14	0

At Hutton Wood in the custody of John del Hay:

		£	s.	d.
23	sheep at 20d. each	1	18	4
8	lambs at 9½d. each		6	4

At Brompton:

80	pigs at 3/- each	12	0	0
38	small pigs at 2/- each	3	16	0
17	young pigs at 6d. each		8	6
15	acres meadow at 1/6 per acre…	1	2	6
60	acres meadow 'of no value because of flooding by the river Derwent'			
1	close of 2 acres meadow at 1/6 per acre		3	0
1/2	acre close, meadow, at 1/- …		1	0
	From rents of free tenements each year	1	11	0
	In Ebberston also free rents/year	1	1	0

The sums of money given in the *Roll* do not always add up correctly but no attempt has been made to correct them here. A further inquiry values Thomas's goods at £512-16-7 the difference coming mainly from 16 sacks 10 stone of wool valued at £73-14-7, previously entered as 11 sacks valued at £40-6-8.

Many more details are given in the *Roll* relating to Thomas's varied possessions, including personal ones, debts owed to him, transactions with wool merchants, etc.

Source: P.R.O., *L.T.R. Memorandum Roll E368/139m.* 24.

PASTORAL FARMING ON THE MONASTIC ESTATES

From the earliest days of their foundation the monasteries had owned large flocks of sheep. By the middle of the twelfth century, for instance, Rievaulx had already acquired most of her pasture lands, many of them extending over large areas. Initial advantages such as these were amplified by privileges to particular houses or to orders. Pope Honorius III, in 1221, had commanded the rectors of parishes in which the Cistercians pastured their sheep not to exact the customary tenth of wool, milk or lambs from them, for example. Besides, sheep were not to be distrained in case of debt: Meaux Abbey had a charter of protection from King John forbidding 'on pain of forfeiture, your making any distress upon their sheep, so long as they may be destrained in any other way'. It is hardly surprising that the monasteries quickly developed their sheep farming when such privileges existed (and these were but some of many, which included the freedom from tolls, forest regard and so on).[1]

The cartularies of the North-eastern monasteries vary a great deal in the amount and character of information about sheep farming. The Rievaulx Cartulary is very good, but the Whitby and Guisborough Cartularies are poor, and contain, in fact, little reference to the sheep farming which undoubtedly existed. Of course, cartularies cannot be expected to give details of organisation for they are collections of charters dealing with acquisition of property or rights. We must look elsewhere for details of how the farming was worked and, in fact, such details are scarce. What can be gained from the cartularies, which is very valuable indeed, is a record of most of the pasture land given to a particular monastery. Grants of pasture were mainly of two kinds; either in the common pasture of a village (usually the number of animals to be pastured was specified – this was the 'stint') or in a

---

[1] "The main source of income of the canons of Malton, their wool, was untaxed, for in accordance with their charters they were exempt from all customs at the ports or elsewhere.' Graham, *English Ecclesiastical Studies* p.63.

MONASTIC SHEEP PASTURE
mid 12th. to early 13th. century

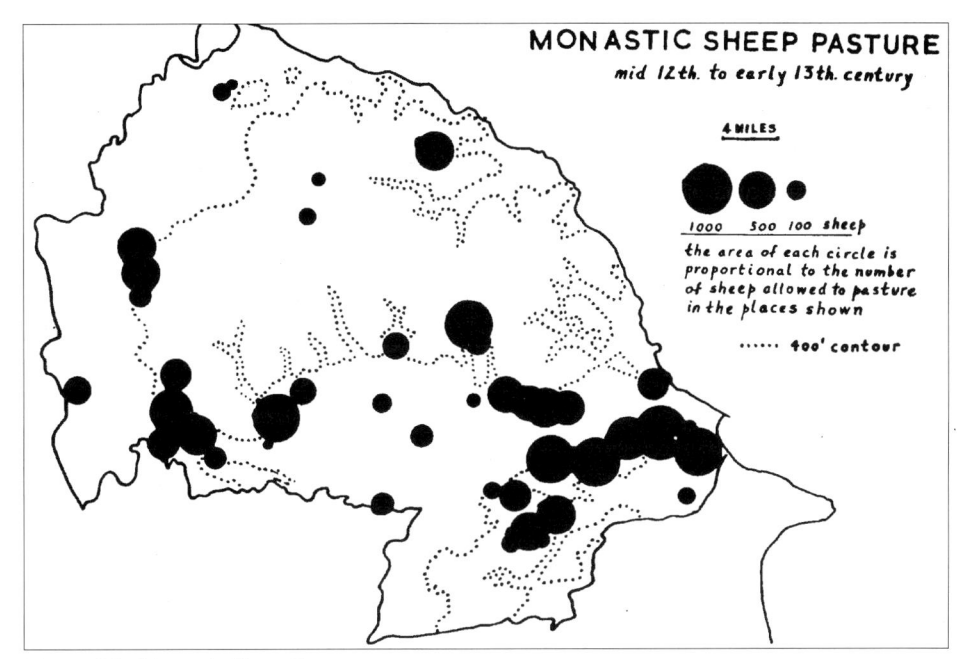

Figure 7.2 Monastic Sheep Pasture

very large area of moorland, marsh or waste. In the latter, although boundaries were specified, no limit was placed on the number of animals to be pastured there. If the former type of grants can be gathered together and plotted on a map a good picture of the main areas of monastic sheep pasture can be obtained.

Figure 7.2 represents an attempt to do this. All cartulary references to sheep pasture grants to monasteries in the North-east have been inserted. In addition, other scattered references from such varied sources as Inquisitions have been used. Twelfth and thirteenth century grants only have been plotted. In fact, most grants received by the monasteries were in the late twelfth or early thirteenth centuries, and are thus close together in time. The picture presented is deficient in several ways and unless these are explained it could be misleading. The Cartularies of Whitby and Guisborough do not give very much information about sheep pasture owned and the map cannot reproduce what is not given. Yet other sources show that both houses had flocks of at least several thousand sheep each; it can only be assumed that the Cartularies omit to mention these. Consequently the map is emptier than it should be. The coastal area suffers most in this respect. The map must be examined with this in mind: it is, perhaps, a minimum picture of monastic sheep pasture in the North-east. As such, it has the value of indicating the areas utilised by the monastic sheep farmers.

Another difficulty concerns the actual number of sheep pastured and the number allowed by a grant. Henry de Willerby might have granted Rievaulx pasture sufficient for 300 sheep in the village of Willerby, but did the Abbey actually feed 300 sheep there? All the evidence seems to support the idea that the monasteries did utilise the grants to the full. As late as 1299, for example, Bridlington Priory did in fact pasture 500 sheep, driven from Burton Fleming and Flotmanby, in the field of Hunmanby, where they had been granted pasture for 500 in the twelfth century.[1] In fact, the probability was that a monastery would be more likely to pasture a greater rather than a lesser number. Meaux Abbey, for instance, was involved in a lawsuit for pasturing more than the allowed number of sheep in Octon, and such cases occurred frequently.[2] Certainly, in the twelfth and thirteenth centuries it seems safe to infer that pasture grants were fully utilized.

Bearing in mind these reservations, what is the value of the map? Three main areas stand out as concentrations of pasture grants: the chalk Wolds, the limestone slopes north of the Vale of Pickering, and the North York Moors (especially their western margin). The Vales of York and Pickering are almost devoid of pasture grants; this is not because of lack of information, since it is only in the Cleveland Plain and along the coast that the picture is affected by this, the conclusion is that the highland, in particular its margin and the dales within, was the main area of monastic sheep pasture.

The conclusions drawn from this map are supported by a study of the distribution of monastic granges (4.1). Monastic sheep farming was administered from granges and cotes located in geographically suitable places among the possessions of a particular monastery.[3] The map showing monastic granges in the North-east shows concentrations in the Wolds and Moors (especially the margins). The granges in these areas were concerned mainly with sheep farming. Other groups, located in the lowlands, generally dealt with other tasks. Both the size and staff of granges varied considerably according to the order involved. Generally, however, they were run by lay brothers, and the Granger made regular visits to the mother abbey with daily reports about the stock.[4]

Guisborough Priory had most of its sheep granges and cotes in Eskdale, the great east-west valley of the moors. These were within easy reach of watermeadow, dale pasture and moorland grazing. Whitby Abbey concentrated its sheep farming activities along the south-east margin of the moors in Hackness Dale, and Rievaulx made Bilsdale its most important area, Here there were five granges and many associated cotes assiduously exploiting a quite small region.

The size of monastic flocks cannot usually be accurately estimated: in a few cases the numbers are stated. At Whitby, for example, there were 4,000 sheep on the estates in 1356. Ten years later the number had fallen to 1,307 due partly to mismanagement, partly to disease.[5] By 1393 the number had increased to 2,709. These numbers were quite high for the late fourteenth century when the heyday of monastic sheep farming had passed. Even the small Houses appear to have possessed large flocks. Rosedale Priory had more than 2,000 sheep in 1308. Earlier, monastic flocks had been much larger; in fact, the

---

[1] *B.C.* p.73.
[2] *Chronica de Melsa*, ed. E. A. Bond, vol. 1 (Rolls Series no. 43) p.430.
[3] The *Oxford English Dictionary* defines grange' as 'an outlying farmhouse with barns etc. belonging to a religious establishment or a feudal lord, where crops and tithes in kind were stored'; 'cote' is described as 'a slight building for sheltering small animals, e.g. sheep, or for storage'. Monastic granges were rather more important units and more active farms than this definition implies.
[4] Further details of the character and distribution of granges can be found in Waites, *Y.A.J.* vol. 40, pp.627-56.
[5] C.B.M. vol. III, pp.68 and 286.

numerous contracts made with the Italian merchants at the turn of the thirteenth and fourteenth centuries usually included large amounts of wool, which could only be supplied by monasteries with large flocks of sheep.

Towards the end of the thirteenth century Pegolotti made a list of monastic wool suppliers.[1] The following list gives the sacks of wool supplied by monasteries in North-east Yorkshire. An attempt has been made to give a rough estimate of the flocks from which the wool was taken on the basis of 200 fleeces to the sack.

Monastery	Sacks	Possible Flocks[2]
Rievaulx	60	12,000
Bridlington	50	10,000
Malton	45	9,000
Byland	35	7,000
Whitby	30	6,000
Kirkham	30	6,000
St. Mary's, York	30	6,000
Guisborough	20	4,000
Newburgh	13	2,600
Keldholm	12	2.400
Arden, Rosedale	10	2,000
Wykeham	4	800

Some support for these figures can be obtained from various sources. The Whitby Abbey flocks totalled 4,000 sheep in 1356; the above reckoning estimates 6,000 for about fifty years earlier, when flocks might be expected to have been larger. Rosedale Priory was said to have 2,000 sheep in 1308; the estimate tallies with this figure. If the pasture grants for Rievaulx are added together (this can only be done where the number to be pastured is specified) a total of nearly 8,000 sheep is obtained. This is below the estimate of 12,000 on the list but the discrepancy can be explained by the fact that Rievaulx owned a great deal of moorland pasture upon which there was no limit to the number of sheep pastured. The total pasture grants in the Malton Cartulary were for just over 6,000 sheep, again below the estimate of 9,000 on the list. A similar explanation could be put forward to account for this discrepancy. Besides, the monasteries were collectors of wool: the supply mentioned on Pegolotti's list may not all have been 'de proprio stauro et pastura'. Meaux Abbey, for example, agreed to provide wool from Holderness 'towards Bridlington and towards Kirkham as far as York'.[3] Malton made such a large profit from wool sales that it seemed 'utterly impossible for the canons to have obtained the whole of the wool from their own flocks. The conclusion is that they organised an immense trade in Yorkshire, and collected wool with great success'.[4]

---

[1] Printed in W. Cunningham, *The Growth of English Industry and Commerce*, 5th ed. (Cambridge, 1910) pp.628-41.
[2] See F. M. Powicke, *The Thirteenth Century*, 1216-1307 (Oxford, 1953) pp.637-8 for details of Pegolotti and many other useful references.
[3] P.R.O. L.T.R. Memoranda Roll, E.368/53/14.
[4] Graham, *English Ecclesiastical Studies*, p.264: the canons made £5,224 9. 3. from sale of wool between 1244 and 1257. The best year was 1251 when the gross profits were £460 16. 8.: the worst was 1255 with profits of £243 19. 8.

The list, must, then, be used with reserve, but it seems to give a fairly good estimate of monastic flocks in the late thirteenth century. It has further drawbacks which should be noted. It is not clear, for example, whether the number of sacks quoted is the total yield of the house or the amount likely to be purchased by one firm. Meaux is said to yield 25 sacks but it engaged to supply 30 sacks in 1280, 36 sacks in 1281, and 42 in 1282 to the Society of Circulorum of Florence alone. A Memoranda Roll for 1294-5, showing wool due from monasteries to Italian merchants and collected for the king's use, indicates that several houses on Pegolotti's list were capable of yielding a larger number of sacks than is stated there.[1] Malton supplied 56 sacks and Kirkham 57 sacks, but they were said to yield only 45 and 30 sacks by Pegolotti.

House	Sacks	Due to
Drax	11	Frescobaldorum Alborum
Malton	56.14 stone	,, ,,
Salley	16.5 stone	,, ,,
Selby	8.4 stone	,, ,,
Jervaulx	All wool for the present year	,, ,,
Byland	29	,, ,,
Marrick	All wool for the present year	
Bolton in Craven	30	Circulorum alborum
Newburgh	8	,, ,,
Marton	10	,, ,,
Ellerton	8	,, ,,
Brother Wm. de Beland	10	,, ,,
Bridlington	3	,, ,,
Rievaulx	54	Circulorum Nigrorum
Watton	42	,, ,,
Kirkham	55	,, ,,
Bridlington	3	,, ,,
Arden in Blakhomer	10.16 st.	Frescobaldorum Nigrorum
Kirkham	2	,, ,,

Despite all such drawbacks certain conclusions are evident. The North-east was an area in which monastic sheep farming reached a predominant position over every other sphere of monastic activity. The size of the flocks was very large, especially on the Cistercian estates (notably at Rievaulx). There were not less than 50,000–60,000 sheep belonging to the monasteries in the area in the thirteenth century. Rievaulx, Bridlington and Malton appeared to be foremost as sheep farmers: representatives, it should be noted of three different orders. Byland, and the Benedictine houses of Whitby and St. Mary's, York, were less important. Even so, Whitby, for instance, had a well-developed sheep farm compared to most houses of their order in the country. Guisborough appears the least important of the larger monasteries; whether this impression comes from lack of detailed evidence is hard to say. In the background, behind the contribution of the greater monasteries, smaller priories and nunneries played a significant part in the area's sheep farming activities.

---

[1] *Wool Collected from the Italians in Yorks etc. for the King's Works.* (long list follows of wool due to the merchants and collected on behalf of the King. It is mainly monastic. Extracts only given). PRO. KR Mem.Roll No 68 m. 64.

The organisation of farming showed similarities between the various houses involved. Rievaulx and Guisborough, for example, used granges, cotes and vaccaries as their main instruments.[1] The cote and vaccary seem to have been similar, although the former was more typically for sheep and the latter for cattle. But little discrimination appears to be made between them. Thus the canons of Guisborough had 2 bulls, 40 cows, 90 beasts, 52 sheep and 1 horse at Dephill Bridge in Upper Eskdale in 1308.[2] Marrick Priory had a similar mixture of animals in its vaccary in Marrick. The Nuns had 80 cows, 500 sheep, with horses, mares and swine without number there.[3] The vaccary was an integral part of the animal economy; they were "more than mere stretches of pasture land, and were permanently established cattle farms in which stock were regularly reared and bred."[4]

Guisborough had the majority of its vaccaries and cotes in Eskdale, within easy reach of the water meadows, dale pasture, and moorland grazing. (e.g. Sledale, Waywath, Lengrive, North Cote, New Cote, Hullersbusk, Dephill, Scale Foot).[5] These were in upper Eskdale, above Danby; lower down the dale at Glaisdale the Prior had 4 vaccaries in 1228, each said to be worth 5 marks a year.[6] The prior had obtained permission to enclose land for pasture there and he had Keepers of the cattle to superintend his farming. The dale was the site of several lay vaccaries as well: Arnald de Percy had two in Lonsdale and Waywath, near to those of Guisborough, and John de Eure had a vaccary worth 30/- a year near the mouth of Eskdale.[7]

But the concentration of vaccaries and cotes in the dales of the North York Moors was a common feature in medieval times. Whitby Abbey had several in the Hackness area, notably at Harwood, Kesebeck and Hackness itself.[8] In fact, the Abbey accounts show that it was in this area of deeply dissected valleys that the pastoral activities of the monastery were concentrated. There are indications that horse farming was important both at Hackness and along the coast near Hayburn. Bridlington Priory and Whitby Abbey were both active in this respect. The former had a vaccary at Hayburn which each third year they were allowed to move if they wished, to more suitable places.[9] An agreement (1231) between the two monasteries provided that the Canons should have common pasture for 50 cows from their vaccary to the bounds of Kesebeck and Helwath.[10] The Canons were further allowed to have 20 unbroken mares in the same pasture. This suggests that the Priory managed a stud of mares allowed to lead a wild life, their young being taken up after the age of three years. The Whitby Chartulary contains an interesting affirmation of this in the Consuetudines Cotariorum de Hackness.[11] It was the duty of the cottars to help to catch (ill aqueari) the brood mares and their young making folds for

---

[1] Oxford English Dictionary definitions: cote – "slight building for sheltering small animals as sheep, pigs, fowls or for storage": vaccary – "a place where cows are kept and pastured".
[2] G.C. Vol. 1. pp.269-73.
[3] E.Y.C. Vol. 5. p.79.
[4] G. H. Tupling, *Economic History of Rossendale* p.18.
[5] Y.A.S. Vol. 21, p.45. gives list in Lay Subsidy (1301).
[6] *Fines* Y.A.S. p.119.
[7] G.C. Vol. 1. pp.103-104, 272 n.
[8] See Accounts and Memorials of foundation in Chartulary.
[9] B.C. p.270.
[10] *ibid.* p.271.
[11] W.C. p.366.

them, and driving and securing the animals – "ibit ad stod". This, of course, referred to the Whitby estates only; it seems clear that both houses were working stud farms in the neighbourhood however.[1] It is interesting to recall Tuke's comments when he visited the district five hundred years later, "The dales of the eastern Moorlands and the coast rear many horses which are rather of a small breed than those before described (i.e. Cleveland and Ryedale), but are a hardy, useful race, though generally too low for the coach".[2]

Bilsdale was the great centre for cotes belonging to Rievaulx Abbey. There were at least five there, working in close collaboration with the granges situated in various parts of the valley.[3] The significance of the cote as the main exploiter of distant moorland pastures was great. The Cistercian statutes provided that herds or flocks should not "go to pasture in the day at a greater distance than will allow of their nightly returning to the monasteries own lands and bounds …"[4] But often pasture land was far from a grange: thus, the Farndale pastures were several miles from Skiplam grange. In such circumstances a cote or small lodge for animals and shepherds on the spot solved the difficulty which the Statutes provided. It appears likely that such centres which the abbey had in Bilsdale worked the pasture not only of the dale itself but of the surrounding moors (e.g. the cotes of Elmirecote, William beckcote Colthouse, Stirkhouse, Sproxton cote). A similar system is evident elsewhere on the abbey estates. The granges of Skiplam and Welburn had associated with them Lund cote and Sunley cote, while in the Pickering marshes a large number of subsidiary centres seem to have developed from the granges established there.[5] Thus besides the four main granges of Kekmarsh, Loftmarsh, Newstead and Lund there were Ewe cote, Cowhouse, Dereholme, Newhouse, Westead, Selleybridge, and Bellyfax all preoccupied with reclaiming and exploiting the marshes in more detail than was possible by the granges alone. So it was that a system well adapted to sheep farming could have more varied uses. This serves as a reminder that it was largely the infinite capacity of the monks adapting themselves to various conditions both of physical and economic environment which ensured their success as farmers and merchants.

It has been shown that so far as the Duchy of Lancaster and lay farmers were concerned transhumance between the High Moors and the surrounding lowlands was a cardinal element of their sheep farming. Sheep farming organised on an inter-manorial basis occurred on many of the important monastic estates in England, notably at Fountains Abbey and Christ Church, Canterbury.[6] In such places movement of flocks over great distances was not uncommon. Unfortunately, in the North-East, the area par excellence of the sheep farmer where such organisation might justifiably be expected to be most clearly developed, evidence of it is scarce. Little can be seen of the transhumance of sheep which

---

[1] These should be compared with Rievaulx's stud farming at Middleton in Teesdale. Bernard de Bailiol had granted the monks "Communam pasturam 60 matribus equabus cum nutrimento suo per totam forestam meam de Thesedale … Concedo etiam eis omnia asiamenta in praedicta foresta mea; scil. materiam ad faldas faciendas ad equas illaqueandas, et logias ad opus pastoram". Similar lodges were built in Westerdale q.v. R.C. pp.157-159.
[2] *op. cit.*, p.66.
[3] Y.A.S. Vol. 21. p.56.
[4] Institutioner Capituli generalis II 59 in *Nomast. Cist.* (1892) 225.
[5] This is evident in the Dissolution Accounts R.C. pp.312-334.
[6] After Henry Eastry's reorganisation of 1288 sheep from manors as far off as Surrey and Essex were sent to Canterbury. Smith *op. cit.* p.148.

must undoubtedly have taken place. Since the estates and pasture lands of the North-Eastern monasteries were generally grouped closely together in the area movement over great distances would be unlikely. Guisborough Priory for example, probably moved some of their animals from the moor top into Eskdale as winter approached, others would go down to the Cleveland Plain to the Priory granges there. The Rent Roll of c1280 shows, in fact, that a special office existed for custody of the sheep on these granges.[1] The sheep of Bridlington Priory oscillated between the Wolds and the surrounding lowland. Thus sheep movement from Flotmanby and the marshlands of the Vale of Pickering at Ganton and Willerby to the Wolds, particularly at Hunmanby was usual. The Canons placed a high value on their lowland pasture. In Willerby, for instance, they owned all the pasture of the vill. To safeguard this they obtained pledges that no other religious should be introduced into the area "whereby the pasture of the Canons may be curtailed". No man was to cut turf in the marshes, no beasts were to be in the pasture without the canons sanction. They even secured a pledge from Henry de Willerby that he would "not plough any land except what was ploughed in his father's time nor will he allow anyone else to plough so whom he is reasonably able to restrain" so that their pasture may remain whole. The Canons had control over exchange and sale of lands in Willerby. Richard de Willerby, for example, was to give them half of any land he should acquire and if he wished to give or sell any land or rent he should do so to no one save the house of Bridlington and he put himself in their advice on all matters. Henry de Willerby made a similar pledge.[2]

Short distance seasonal migration of sheep then, appeared likely, especially between the Central Vale of Pickering and its surrounding limestone slopes. Rievaulx owned much meadow-land in the Vale itself at Harome, Muscoates, North and South Holme, the Marshes and elsewhere. In nearly every instance grant of free passage to and fro for sheep was allowed. Thus they had free way through the moor of Holme for leading and bringing back their livestock.[3] Probably the only large scale movement of animals over great distances took place between Rievaulx Abbey and its furthermost estates 40 miles west in Wensleydale and 44 miles north-west in Teesdale. Both were extremely important as animal farms, the latter emphasising horse breeding at Middleton in Teesdale Forest. The total value of moveables owned by Rievaulx in Wensleydale and Swaledale at East Bolton, Bellerby, Vaccary of Muker, Oxenhope, Waylle, Appletreekeld and Birkdale in 1301 was £102-3-9 and most of this came from the stock there.[4] Some contact between these areas and the Abbey across the Vale of York must have been usual, although there is little evidence to prove it. However, one interesting grant "de libero transitu et pacifico chimino habendo praedictis monachis et conversis suis, hominibus et servientibus eorundem, per forestam ipsius Com. de Richmund"[5] suggests that movement of flocks through the great forest of Richmond, lying to the east of the Pennines, and into the Vale of York beyond might have occurred. If it did the abbey granges in the Vale (Angram,

---

[1] G.C. Vol. 2. pp.412-450.
[2] B.C. pp.100-108.
[3] R.C. p.209.
[4] Lay Subsidy (1301) *YAS* vol.21.
[5] R.C. p.305.

Morton, Broughton, Crosby and Hesketh) would play an important part since they lay between the Abbey itself and the distant lands in the Pennines.

The object of this chapter has been to evaluate the regional importance of pastoral farming within the North-East and then, by selecting examples of lay and monastic farming to fill out the picture in more detail – to sense something of the work and organisation behind the broad pattern. A great deal has been said about sheep farming; the reason is that it was the dominant feature not only of the pastoralism but of the entire economy of the area in medieval times. How far the North-East was already a sheep farming area before the advent of the New Orders is hard to say. If Whitby Abbey was similar to other Benedictine abbeys elsewhere in England it is probable that it had considerable numbers of sheep on its estates before the Augustinian Canons arrived at Guisborough and before the Cistercians came to Rievaulx. Professor Power pointed out, for instance, that some Benedictine abbeys had considerable flocks; Ely had 13,400 at the time of the Domesday survey.[1] This implies a large scale and well-developed organisation. R.A.L. Smith allowed for this possibility when he wrote "attention has been largely concentrated on the Cistercians, and no considerable literature has yet arisen on the subject of Benedictine sheep-farming. This is probably because the Benedictines undertook sheep farming on a less spectacular scale than the Cistercians and as a pursuit ancillary to their main occupation of arable farming."[2]

Unfortunately, it was only too evident from Chapter 2 that Domesday Book gives no help in the solution of this problem. In fact, any attempt to penetrate into pre-monastic times to discover the extent of sheep farming can only be based upon surmise. To judge from the intensity of Anglo-Saxon and Scandinavian settlement in the Wolds and the Vale of Pickering it would appear probable that some peasant sheep farming occurred, but on a small scale.[3] It would, indeed, be exceptional if it did not. The rapid adherence of the Cistercians to this type of farming activity suggests that they might have found something which could be developed and built upon; besides, it is not inconceivable that the earliest converts, many of them important landowners, conveyed their flocks along with their other goods to the monastery where they were to serve as monks or lay-bretheren. The Byland Chronicle tells, for example, how great men rushed to join the community, bringing with them their "temporal goods".[4] Moreover, the peculiar rules of the Cistercian order were likely to help any tradition of sheep farming to persist and develop. The lay-bretheren, for example, would be men who knew the countryside; who had already been farmers of some sort. They might well have been the means by which traditional sheep farming practices were transmitted to, and absorbed by, the monasteries.

On the other hand, it is well to remember that the Mother houses of Citeaux and Clairvaux were situated in similar hilly, limestone country where sheep farming had developed before Rievaulx itself was founded. Several of the founders of the Abbey came from Citeaux and had close contact with it. This contact remained firm; indeed the

---

[1] *op. cit.*, p.33.
[2] *op. cit.*, p148.
[3] Maps of settlement in F. Elgee *op. cit.*
[4] *Mon. Angl.* V p.350 et seq. When Ailred became a monk at Rievaulx, "He divided all his goods, he abandoned every thing that he had". Walter Daniel *op. cit.*, p.15.

regulations of the Order commanded such closeness.[1] In circumstances like these it is probable that some preconceived plan of supporting the community by sheep did exist.[2]

The truth may lie somewhere between the two: what can hardly be denied is that the real stimulus to sheep farming in the area came from the monasteries. Whatever importance it had before the 12th century was increased many times afterwards. In fact, the great devastation of 1069 probably effectively stiffled any sheep farming of consequence had it existed, so that when the monks and canons came to the North-East about fifty years later they found as little development of sheep farming as they found of arable cultivation.

Figure 7.3 Rievaulx Abbey 1956

---

[1] In addition there was a great deal of personal contact between Ailred and St. Bernard by letters and visits. W. Daniel *op. cit.* Introduction by the editor, F.M. Powicke, p.lvii.
[2] Necessary, at least for vestments: "...certain monks had come to England from across the sea, wonderful men ... white monks by name and white also in vesture. For their name arose from the fact that, as the angels might be, they were clothed in undyed wool spun and woven from the pure fleece of the sheep". *ibid.* p.10.

8 MEDIEVAL INDUSTRIES : IRONWORKING

There is little evidence to show the scale or character of industrial activities before the twelfth century in this area. In fact, the first real notice of iron and salt working occurs in the records of the many monastic houses located there. Domesday Book, which gives useful details for other areas, for example, the Lincolnshire salt pans,[1] gives little or no indication about industries in northeast Yorkshire. It would be unwise, however, to suggest that the monasteries introduced iron or salt working into the district.

Earlier peoples had certainly some experience of mining and trading in minerals. Jet was mined and worked as early as Neolithic times and became quite fashionable during the middle Bronze Age, so much so that an important and widespread trade developed which persisted at least into Viking times. Where iron outcropped on the surface, as it did in several places along the coast and in the dales, it could be recovered and used without the necessity of mining. The mineral was certainly accessible: whether the inclination and ability to use it were there too remains doubtful. To judge from the general sparsity of settlement in the moorlands before 1086, and especially in the dales where the major iron outcrops were found, it is likely that only sporadic and localized exploitation of minerals occurred.[2]

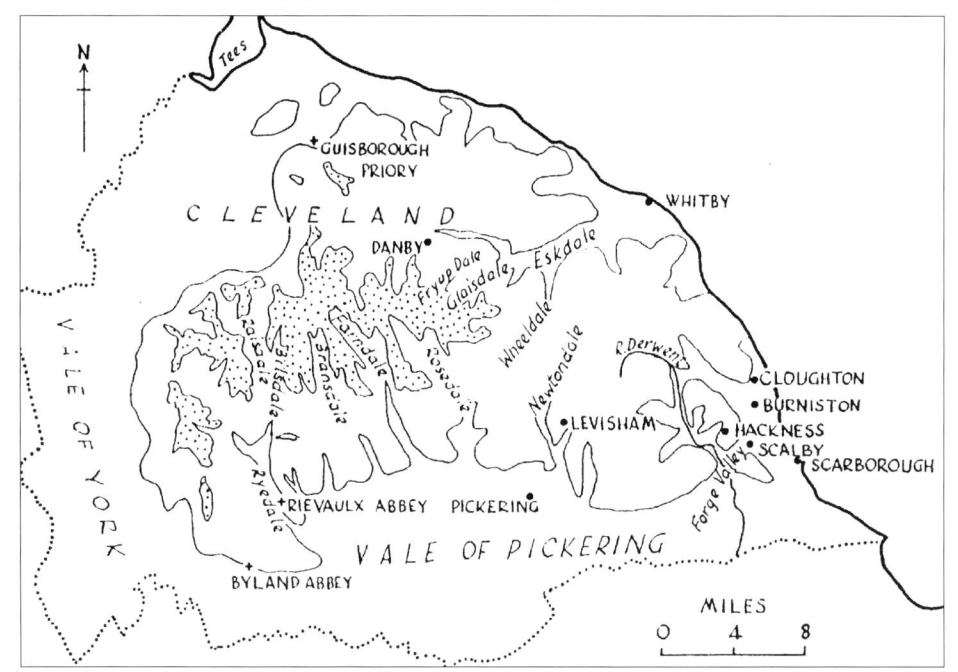

Figure 8.1 Location Map. Contours at 400 feet and 1000 feet shown. Land over 1000 feet is stippled.

---

[1] See H. C. Darby, *The Domesday Geography of Eastern England*, Cambridge, 1952, pp.69-70.
[2] Little has been uncovered so far relating to the Iron Age in this district. See J. G. Rutter, *The Archaeology of Scarborough and District*, Scarborough, 1956.

Fortunately, because the ironstone is found only in certain areas,[1] possible locations of iron workings during medieval times can be described fairly precisely and greater clarity can be given to contemporary, documentary evidence. Two types of area were sites of iron working, the moorland dales and the coast. The dales cut down deeply into the barren Estuarine Sandstone moorland revealing the iron-bearing Lias, Dogger and Eller Beck formations and making outcrops easily accessible. They were also areas of dense woodland which could be used for charcoal – Danby Forest, for instance, occupied a large part of Upper Eskdale; Rosedale Forest was extensive, and most of the other moorland valleys were heavily wooded – and the proximity of running water may have been an advantage, although this is uncertain. Most of the sites of medieval workings do occur very close to streams, for example in Glaisdale, Rosedale and Fryup Dale. The valleys were often relatively easy of access and sometimes carried important routeways, such as Eskdale which linked the coast with the Vale of York.

An impression of the distribution of medieval forges and iron works can be gathered from Fig. 8.2 which shows these features in relation to the ironstone outcrops. Doubtless other sites existed of which relevant records have been lost or remain untraced.[2] Although the map is probably an incomplete picture of iron workings in the district, it is clear that the iron industry was widely scattered throughout the moorlands, and that Eskdale and its tributary valleys were the leading areas. There both lay and monastic efforts were intensive, the main concentrations being in upper Eskdale and along the valley sides to the south. A great lord and landowner, Peter de Brus, had smithies in Glaisdale during the early thirteenth century, and it was he, in fact, who gave the canons of Guisborough Priory the extensive rights in Glaisdale and nearby areas which were the foundation of their important iron industry of Eskdale. He granted them, "the entire smithy of Glaisdale with all things to the same belonging: to wit, that it may be lawful for them to seek and take iron ore whenever they are able to find it within the said bounds, without hindrance."[3] Within these bounds the canons had a monopoly of iron mining. Thus Peter provided that neither he nor his heirs should ever "set up any other smithy or allow others to so do, or take minerals within the said bounds". In addition, the canons were to have "free way into and out of the pasture and wood of Glasedale … and three lodges on Glasedale Moor for the use of their shepherds, carpenters and charcoal-burners … each lodge 20 feet long and 12 feet wide…".

By 1228 the canons had developed the area not only for its ironstone but also for its value as a pasture. They had several smithies, each said to be worth ten marks a year, as well as four vaccaries each worth five marks a year. It seems that the canons were employing animals from the vaccary for haulage of ironstone, and perhaps also of wood to be used as charcoal for smelting. This prosperous state of affairs was not to last, for Peter de Brus's son adopted an antagonistic attitude to the canons which resulted in

---

[1] See V. Wilson, *British Regional Geology : East Yorkshire and Lincolnshire*, London, 1948.
[2] Records used in compiling Fig. 8.2 were Inquisitions Post Mortem; *The Duchy of Lancaster Coucher Book* and other Duchy Records; the Pipe Rolls; *The White Vellum Book of Scarborough*; monastic chartularies; Ministers' Accounts.
[3] *The Chartulary of Guisborough Priory* (ed. W. Brown), Surtees Society, vol. 89, Durham, 1984, pp.190-8. See also, *Feet of Fines for the County of York, 1218-1272* (ed. J. Parker), *Yorkshire Archaeological Society Record Series*, vol. 62, 1921, pp.51-3, 119-21; vol. 67, 1925, pp.21-2.

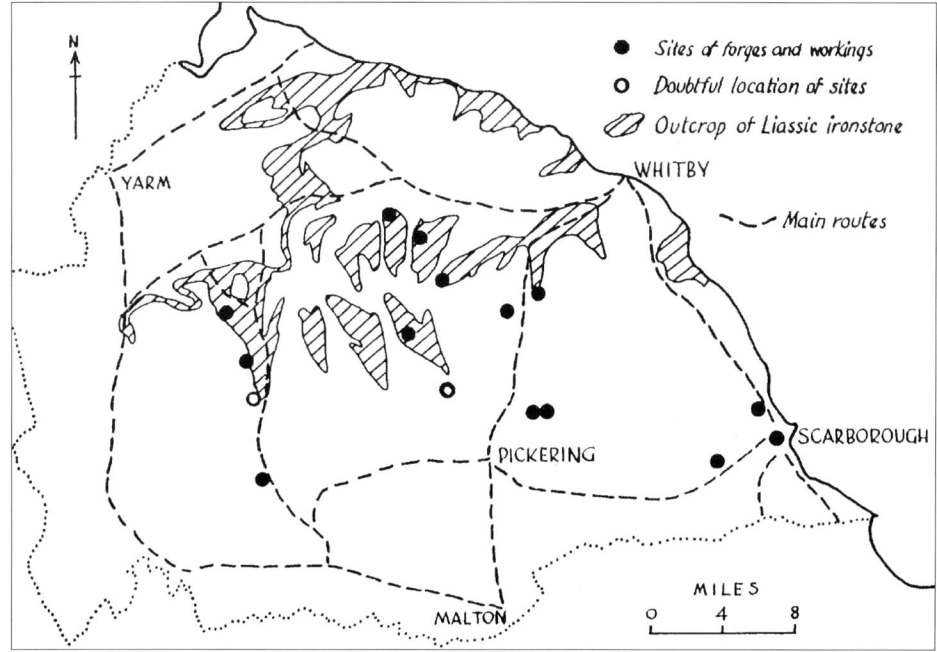

Figure 8.2 Forges and Iron Working

damage to their property and long-drawn-out litigation between the two, recorded in the Feet of Fines.[1]

Peter de Brus II had acknowledged his father's grants to the canons in 1223 but only a few years later, in 1227, he destroyed their "houses" and caused damage to the vaccaries and smithies amounting to twenty pounds.[2] After the resultant court case Peter undertook to "do all in his power that all free men ... allow the Prior to re-erect his vaccaries, hedges, smithies as they were before". In his turn the Prior was ready to "forgive Peter the loss due to the destruction of his houses" providing that Peter "shall get charters made to the Prior from the free men aforesaid". This reference to "free men" may be the clue to the cause of the trouble. In the original grant to the canons an important reservation had been made by Peter de Brus – "it shall be lawful for the ... men of Danby in crossing by the said places ... to unyoke and pasture their oxen if they wish".[3] It seems probable that either these men or others dwelling in Danby Forest had demanded more pasture than was due to them, or that the canons had denied them the right to pasture and so provoked them to destroy the buildings of the Priory in and around Glaisdale.

Whatever the reason, the remedy was long delayed, for in 1229-30 Peter acted contrary

---

[1] Peter de Brus had smithies of his own in Danby Forest but the most valuable of them was worth only three-quarters the value of the canons' smithies. *Yorkshire Inquisitions* (ed. W. Brown), *Yorks. Arch. Soc. Record Series*, vol. 12, 1892, p.139.
[2] J. Parker, *op. cit.*, vol. 62, pp.120-1.
[3] *The Chartulary of Guisborough Priory, op. cit.*, vol. 89, pp.190-1.

to the decision of the court. The Prior complained that Peter "hinders him from making lodges for the use of his carpenters, shepherds and lay brethren of Gisburn in Glaisdale wood: and from making fires there to cook the victuals for the said carpenters and making charcoal for their use, although it is stated in the chirograph that the Prior, his successors and canons may at their pleasure cut and carry from that wood ...".[1] The settlement of this dispute is not known, but Peter at any rate admitted the rights of the canons in 1234 – for the time being.

This insight into the day-to-day happenings on the Guisborough iron workings in Glaisdale is instructive. The persistence of litigation implies that the canons attached great value to their workings which appeared to be developed on a large scale and were possibly very profitable for them. There are indications, however, that their activities as iron miners extended to many other parts of Eskdale. They had property widely scattered in other parts of the valley (8.3). The Priory had an extensive grant on Danby Moor, for example, at the head of Fryup Dale, and on the north side of the river Esk at Waytlandside and Stanigateside. In these areas, as well as in upper Eskdale, it is probable that they worked iron ore, which lay close at hand. Although there is no documentary evidence to prove this, as there is in the case of Glaisdale, the idea is supported by field investigations and the identification of medieval slag heaps which are numerous in many sections of the dale.[2]

The coincidence between Priory lands and some slag heaps is striking and certainly lends weight to the idea of a widespread monastic iron industry in Eskdale. The map, of course, cannot be conclusive by itself, but combined with the knowledge that the Priory had very important workings in one part of the dale it seems likely that they also mined ore on their other properties in the neighbourhood.

But laymen also took a very important share in the industry in Eskdale, and especially in the Danby area. Many of the slag heaps noted in Fig. 8.3 would be, no doubt, remnants of this lay industry. Already by the eleventh century settlers were moving into Eskdale and Danby was soon to become one of the largest villages in northeast Yorkshire. By 1301 it had more than fifty people assessed to the subsidy at £6 4s. 3d.[3] A record of Peter de Brus's lands in 1272 shows that there were five small forges worth ten shillings and two other forges in the Danby Forest worth four pounds, which seems to indicate that various types of forges were at work in the area.[4] The forest in Eskdale was described as being three leagues long and three leagues wide in Domesday Book. "Danbeium nemus" was a recognizable district even in Leland's time and later Danby on the Forest became the name of the parish. Lay iron working must have achieved some prominence in the fifteenth century, sufficient to have an office of *Archiferrarius* of Danby Forest, in addition to having a Chief Forester.[5] This suggests a definite organization of the industry

---

[1] J. Parker, *op. cit.*, vol. 67, pp.21-2

[2] Medieval slag heaps in Eskdale are listed by J. C. Atkinson in "Existing traces of medieval iron working in Cleveland", *Yorks. Arch. Journal*, vol. 8, 1884, pp.30-48.

[3] *Yorkshire Lay Subsidy, 1301* (ed W. Brown), *Yorks. Arch. Soc. Record Series*, vol. 21, 1897. Whitby had 96 people assessed in 1301 and Scarborough had 99 assessed in 1327.

[4] "Extent of Peter de Brus's lands (1272)", (ed. W. Brown), *Yorkshire Inquisitions, op. cit.*, vol. 12, p.139.

[5] *Calendar of Patent Rolls (1467-1477)*, London, 1900, p.206. In consequence of the minority of Richard Nevile, heir of George Nevile, Lord Latimer, Edward IV granted the office of Archiferrarius of Danby Forest to Richard Cracestre.

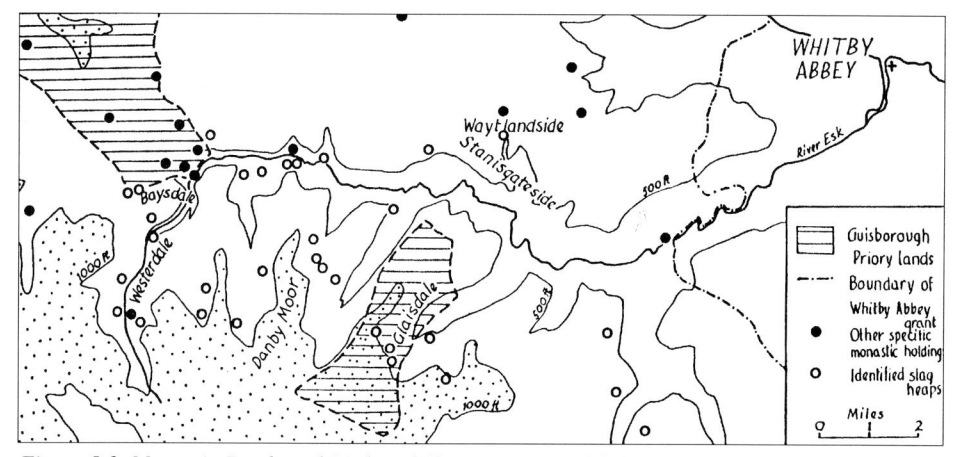

Figure 8.3 Monastic Lands and Medieval Slag Heaps in Eskdale. Land over 1000 feet is stippled.

probably under the de Brus family at first and later under the Latimers. Its details remain a mystery, but it was obvious that some control of tree-felling would be a necessity. Such control proved to be ineffectual in conserving timber for much of the woodland had disappeared by the end of the sixteenth century, for which the smelters were chiefly responsible.[1]

The activity in Eskdale of the Cistercian monks of Rievaulx Abbey appears to have been much more limited than that of the canons of Guisborough, no doubt because they had fewer lands there; but it is possible that some mining occurred in Westerdale where the monks of the Abbey had a lodge with pasture rights as early as the twelfth century, although no mention of a mineral grant is made in the charters. It was in Ryedale, Bilsdale and Raisdale, nearer to the Abbey, that the monks worked iron. Their interest in the industry appears to have begun much earlier than that of the canons. Already, by the middle of the twelfth century they were mining for ironstone on a large scale in the West Riding in the vicinity of Wakefield.[2] The organization of their industry here comes out much more clearly than it does in the North Riding.

As in the Guisborough Priory workings in Glaisdale, the attempt to obtain and maintain a monopoly was a principal concern of the monks. In Halton, Shipley, Heaton and several other places in the West Riding, they received a guarantee from the grantor, Adam fitz Peter, that no one else should be allowed to mine, or work, ironstone within the specified areas. Besides, they obtained right of way into and out of their workings, as well as a supply of charcoal. It is significant that many of the iron working sites were on assart land; thus Adam fitz Peter granted the monks as assart called Hogathwait in Stainborough

---

[1] Public Record Office. Special Commissions (Duchy of Lancaster), Nos. 286 and 287. Certificates as to enclosure of waste lands within the forest and as to encroachment, spoil, etc. (1579). Also Special Comm. Exch. E178/2705. Deposition as to felling timber for iron smelting in Danby Forest (1588).

[2] *The Chartulary of Rievaulx Abbey* (ed. J. C. Atkinson), Surtees Society, vol. 83, Durham, 1889, pp.56-60. An excellent series of grants almost all by Adam fitz Peter.

township, to which he added 15 acres in Blakeker for the erection of a bloomery for making iron and forging therefrom the implements necessary for their monastic house. As in the case of the Guisborough workings in Glaisdale, the monks sited their forges or bloomeries invariably near to a river – "they shall have all their forges next to the river which is called the Dove …".[1] What the connexion between rivers and forges was is hard to say, but it does seem likely that the rivers might have been the source of power for the industry – an early example of industrial location.

Rapid expansion of industry was typical of the Cistercian enterprise in most activities which they undertook. By 1171 their workings had developed so much that they began to find themselves competing with Byland Abbey which also had granges working ironstone nearby. As the result of an agreement drawn up between the houses in 1171 a large area of productive seams was divided between them.[2]

The brethren of Rievaulx were to exploit the Shitlington and Flockton area while the monks of Byland had similar rights in Emsley, Denby, Birstall, Homehill and Bretton. It was such large-scale enterprise as this that left any laymen competitors far behind, for they could hardly hope to develop similar powers of organisation and control.

Rievaulx's iron working further north, nearer to the Abbey, is not so clearly seen. The monks appear to have had workings at Stainton, in Bilsdale, a village which has subsequently disappeared, and it seems probable that they diverted the nearby river Rye, perhaps to transport some of the ore to the Abbey precincts. Whether this diversion can be associated with the alterations made to the river further downstream (the so-called "canals") is hard to determine. Stone used in the construction of the abbey buildings seems to have been transported by river or waterway in the twelfth century, and it is possible ironstone came the same way from Stainton and Raisdale.[3] The Ministers' Accounts for Rievaulx mention "a forge called Iron Smythes" in Bilsdale in 1540, "with one licence to dig ore", formerly belonging to the Abbey.[4] The account goes on to say "lambert Semer holdeth at will of the Lord the Iron Smythes adjoining unto the site of the late monastery", which seems to imply that some smelting might have been done very close to the actual precincts.

It seems likely that the monks established some kind of iron working near Rievaulx which became a basis for later developments. Otherwise it would be difficult to explain the rapid development of iron mining under the Earl of Rutland when he took over the Abbey after the Dissolution. He had many important iron workings nearby, and Rievaulx became for a time a great mining and smelting area. "Sir William Bellasis is anxious to sell you his woods", wrote Lancelot Turner to the Countess of Rutland in 1588, "which adjoin Rievaulx, they would be commodious for your ironworks."[5] The trade between

---

[1] Their workings at Emsley were also near the river. See *The Chartulary of Rievaulx Abbey*, p.58. The same document granted the monks the right to make a mill on the river and divert the water into the mill pond.
[2] *Ibid*, pp.176-80.
[3] H. Rye, "Rievaulx Abbey; its canals and building stone". *The Archaeological Journal*, vol. 57, 1900. J. Weatherill, "The building stone of Rievaulx Abbey", *Yorks. Arch. Journal*, vol. 38, 1954, pp.333-54.
[4] Public Record Office E315/401 and *The Chartulary of Rievaulx Abbey*, pp.311-2, 315.
[5] *Historical MSS. Commission*, Rutland MSS. No. 24, vol. 1, London, 1888, pp.138, 261. "Rievaulx weight" was a standard in the iron industry of the sixteenth and seventeenth centuries. Further details of ironworks, output, etc., in H. R. Schubert, *History of the British Iron and Steel Industry c. 450 B.C.–A.D. 1775*, London, 1957, pp.295, 401.

Rievaulx and other distant places, such as Sussex, was great during the sixteenth and seventeenth centuries.[1] It seems unlikely that the Earl of Rutland discovered mineral resources which the monks overlooked, and probable that he took over what had earlier been a flourishing iron industry in Ryedale, under the monks or their tenants.

Elsewhere in Ryedale Rievaulx Abbey had secured the right to make charcoal in several places. Everard de Ros had allowed them "that place in Rycal wood for their charcoal and charcoal burners" in the thirteenth century, and in 1251 they obtained the right to "make charcoal from the woods in various places …".[2] This indicates a good deal of industrial activity throughout the length of the valley. The fact that it was also an important routeway, as was Eskdale, emphasized its value to the iron miners. Lay interest in the area was evident: in 1260, for example, Simon de Ver granted Rievaulx Abbey more land to increase their already great possessions in Raisdale but significantly reserved for himself the minerals to be found there.[3]

Iron mining elsewhere in northeast Yorkshire seems to have been very largely in the hands of the laymen. There were smelting places and charcoal works in Wheeldale and Newtondale in 1313; in the same year R. Short, smith, was given licence to reside there by the Duchy of Lancaster.[4] In Levisham Wood, near Newtondale, smelting works had long been established. The earliest mention appears to be in 1210 when the Sheriff of York received two shillings rent for it.[5] In 1214 the rent was six shillings and a default of waste is mentioned.[6] Roger Bigod bought the ironworks here in 1256 and obtained mineral rights throughout his bailiwick, paying two shillings rent to the Duke of Lancaster.[7] There was still a forge here in 1651 and the rent remained two shillings.[8]

The Newtondale and Levisham district seems to have been an important centre of iron working, once again not far from the Pickering–Goathland route over the moors. Bigod obtained protection for his demesne woods there in 1282 but John de Levisham who employed men to make charcoal in Levisham woods nevertheless sold it for fuel.[9] No wonder that when Norden came to survey the area in 1619 he complained that the woods had been carried away in Newtondale. "There is little timber left in the sayde foreste", he wrote, "and that it hath bene taken and felled long since. And that which is lefte in Pickering Woodes, is ill preserved but powled and cut by the haulfe Boale."[10]

In Rosedale, a few miles to the west, there was a Cistercian nunnery. Iron working was carried on in the valley by laymen but there is little indication of working by the monasteries here. Robert de Stuteville granted the Vale of Rosedale to the nunnery

---

[1] In 1605 many materials to be used in the Rievaulx forges were sent from Sussex, e.g., anvils, hammers, etc., Rutland MSS., *op. cit.*, vol. 4, p.494-.
[2] *The Chartulary of Rievaulx Abbey*, pp.3-6, The woods were Helmsley, Pockley and Plocwood.
[3] *Ibid.* p.226.
[4] Duchy Accounts in *The Honour and Forest of Pickering, North Riding Record Series* (ed. R. B. Turnton), 4 vols., New Series, vol. 2., London, 1894-6, p.19.
[5] Printed Pipe Roll No. 56, *Publications of the Pipe Roll Society*, vol. 26, New Series, London, 1951, p.151.
[6] Public Record Office, Pipe Roll No. 60.
[7] Duchy Coucher Book, *The Honour and Forest of Pickering, op. cit.*, vol. 2, pp.44-5.
[8] Commonwealth Survey, *ibid.*, vol.1, p.103
[9] "…injuring the Lord and annoying the deer" (1334), *ibid.*, vol. 3, p.1. His right to make charcoal and lead wood to his furnace was upheld, however.
[10] *Ibid.*, vol. 1, pp.28-9.

Figure 8.4 Rosedale

together with his meadow of Bagthwaite. The Royal confirmation of this gift is dated 1209. An Inspeximus and Confirmation of 1327-8 repeats the grant but significantly excepts a forge in Bagthwaite, suggesting that lay iron working was being carried on at this time.[1]

About the same period, in 1339, an interesting indenture between the Abbot of St. Mary's, York, and John, son of Richard the Chief Smithman, was made which referred to the iron working in Rosedale.[2] The Abbot owned extensive lands hereabouts, mainly between the rivers Dove and Seven. He had granges at Spaunton and Appleton, only a few miles from Rosedale. Although there is no indication that St. Mary's engaged in mining, it appears that the monks were aware that their land contained ore for the Abbot granted John liberty to occupy a chosen plot of land within the Abbot's forest of Rosedale, with freedom to search for, burn and make his profit out of the iron ore within the bounds of the grant. John was further allowed to take fuel for smelting the ore from the Abbot's wood at the assignment of his foresters and he might keep seven horses within the Abbot's common pasture. In his turn, John promised that he would deliver sixteen stone of iron each week to the Abbot's servant at Spaunton, every Sunday, from the time when he should begin to work the ore into iron until the following Christmas. But if it should happen that John should find any ore before Christmas then he was to render eighteen stone each week. John must have been resident in the area and already working iron nearby for it would be difficult otherwise to explain the short respite he was allowed before payments in iron were to begin. The Indenture was executed on 18th August, 1339, and weekly payments of sixteen stone had to begin only eleven days later, too soon surely

---

[1] *Early Yorkshire Charters* (ed. C. T. Clay), *Yorks. Arch. Soc. Record Series*, vol. 9, Wakefield, 1952, p.126.
[2] Extract from a register of St. Mary's, York, in *The Honour and Forest of Pickering, op. cit.*, vol. 4, pp.194 f.

for someone from outside to come into the district, find, smelt and despatch ore. It is more likely that he supplied ore from existing works.

Iron working occurred on and near the coast, as well as inland in the heart of the moorlands. A seaside location had distinct advantages, however. Ore outcropped along sections of the coast in the cliffs, and where boulder clay had not slumped over the iron seams access was quite easy. North of Scarborough the boulder clay is limited in extent, but its heavy soils favoured tree growth and wood for charcoal was plentiful. Scalby Forest was the largest area of woodland in the area, although there was a discontinuous cover of woodland as far as Burniston and Cloughton, a few miles to the north. An additional incentive may have been the coal which washed up on the sands. This was certainly used by the salt-panners further north, round Teesmouth, but its use in the iron working here can so far only be surmised, not proved.

The iron works at Levisham, Newtondale and Wheeldale may have owed their growth partly to the demands for iron goods by Pickering and the Dukes of Lancaster in residence there; the coastal workings were, on the other hand, favourably situated in relation to the port of Scarborough.[1] However, it is unlikely that the coastal iron industry was anything more than locally important since the workings were too scattered to suggest otherwise, but at least the production was of sufficient size to satisfy normal local demands. For instance, the sale of ironstone from the cliffs near Scalby in 1314 and 1322 fetched a total of twenty-six shillings and eightpence.[2] According to Thorold Rogers the average price of iron ore was six to seven shillings for twenty-five pieces at this time,[3] twenty-five pieces then comprised a hundredweight. The total given here for the two years may, then, represent just over four hundredweights of ore. This of course, was an isolated figure in the Duchy of Lancaster Accounts and makes no mention of other people engaged in extraction and sale of ore.

Certainly there were others working ore nearby for the Duchy received a rent of ninepence in 1322 for two forges in Newby and Scalby. At Hackness, too, mining and smelting occurred although the scale of the industry is uncertain. Several facts were very suggestive: the size of Hackness, for instance, was much greater than most of the other coastal villages; only in Scarborough and Whitby had larger populations. The subsidy of 1301 shows fifty-five contributors for Hackness and many personal names given to indicate that the village was an important trade centre.[4] Further, the accounts of Bridlington Priory's grange at Burton Fleming on the Wolds, ten miles to the south, show that iron was purchased from Hackness: in 1355-6 thirty pieces were bought there for fifteen shillings. The accounts show the prominent part iron goods took in the total expenditure of the grange.[5]

---

[1] Iron goods were evidently shipped from Whitby, the natural outlet of Eskdale; e.g., the bailiffs were allowed to charge 1d. toll on every cart or horseload of iron passing over the bridge into the town in 1351 (Grant of pontage, P.R.O. Patent Roll (1351) part 3 m. 19). There is little evidence to show the part played by Whitby Abbey in iron working, but see *Victoria County History, Yorkshire*, vol. 1, p.41 and vol. 2, pp.338-55.
[2] Duchy Accounts, *op. cit.*, vol. 2, p.20; vol. 4, p.201. "Sale of ironstone on the sea shore at Fullwood."
[3] T. Rogers, *A History of Agriculture and Prices in England*, vol. 1, Oxford, 1866, p.480.
[4] E.g.,. Fullor, Turnover, Tixtore, Cissore, Fabro, Gynnour. See Gustav Fransson, *Middle English Surnames of Occupation 1100-1350*, Lund, 1935.
[5] Document R. H. 60 in the York Diocesan Registry.

Iron working at Hackness may well have been associated with Henry de Percy's works in Seamer Woods, a few miles south. He claimed it his right to have forges and the minerals in the woods (1339), which would be situated in Forge Valley where the river Derwent flows rapidly through an overflow channel.[1] This situation was, like all the coastal workings, much more accessible than those in Eskdale, though in the latter the very active interest of the monasteries was a factor which made accessibility a less important consideration.

THE SALT INDUSTRY

Salt is an essential part of the diet of people and animals. Since the dawn of time there has been trade in salt, and reminders like Saltersgate and Salt Way can still be found in the landscape. Animals are known to have travelled hundreds of miles to find a salt lick. Roman soldiers were paid salarium or salt money, from which the modern word salary derives.

In early times salt was obtained mainly from the evaporation of sea water, a method known as salt panning. Domesday Book shows that this method was used particularly along the southern and eastern coasts of England. One leading area in medieval times was Teesmouth. Here the low lying flats, regularly flooded by the tides, were especially suitable.

On the north of Teesmouth, Cowpen, Greatham and Hart were the villages associated with the industry. Frequent reference to them and the salt they produced are given in the Account Rolls of Durham Abbey. In 1375-76 for instance, the Bursar records, "20 quarters of salt bought this year from the tenants of Cowpen at 3/4 a quarter – 66/8d. Even as late as 1438 the Cellerar's Account acknowledges £7-3-4, "from 16 tenants in Cowpen for all the salt-pans … 35 quarters and 6 bushels of salt at 4/- a quarter."[2]

On the south bank of the estuary salt making was equally, if not more important. The main centre was an area known as Coatham Marshes, a very low level place bordering the river. Into it ran numerous becks which were partly responsible for its being marshland. Here, and along the coast between Marske and Redcar were the main salt-working areas. (4.6)

The industry was a mainstay in the economy of the region. The emphasis on salt-making was marked because elsewhere the coast was too rocky to allow a similar industry to develop. Consequently Teesmouth became a specialised area of salt production. No evidence has been found to indicate whether the salt had a wide market but it seems likely that the herring fishermen who were frequent visitors to Coatham and Whitby would be the main buyers.[3] Most of the monasteries supplied their own needs from the salt-pans they owned themselves.

---

[1] *Calendar of Patent Rolls (1338-1340)*, London, 1898, p.246.
[2] *Durham Halmote Rolls* (Surtees 82)
Durham Account Rolls (Surtees 99-103)
[3] In 1580 the inhabitants of Cowpen petitioned Mr Thomas Wylson, Secretary of State and dean of Durham, against the sale of salt at Yarm by the Scots, who paid no duty for unloading. *V.C.H. Durham*, Vol. II, p.294.

Little is known about the medieval methods of panning salt, but it was probably the same as that used in the North-East during the 16th century. Then the procedure was as follows: the rising tide flooding parts of the low land was directed into small vaults probably resembling the old bell-pits of the Yorkshire coalfield. The salt water was boiled and reboiled several times by means of a fire under the vaults. The fuel used on the fire was often the coal washed up by the tide but this would have to be well dried first. The fires were kept going by the use of bellows. Sometimes the sea water had to be boiled eight or more times before salt was deposited. It is uncertain whether any attempt was made to purify the salt when it had been obtained. A letter describing the antiquities of the district and written perhaps by one of the Cholmeley family in the reign of Elizabeth contains a reference to this method: "and as the tyde comes in, yt bringeth a small wash sea-coal which is imployed to the making of salte, and the Fuell of the poore fisher Townes adjoining: the oylie sulphurousness beinge mixed with the salte of the sea as yt floweth, and consequently hard to take fyre, or to keepe in longe without quenchinge. They have a means by making small vaults to passe under the hearthes, into which by fore-setting the wynde with a board, they force yt to enter, and soe to serve insteede of a payre of bellowes, which they call in a proper worde of Art, a Blowecole."[1]

It was to be expected that the monasteries would be interested in such a valuable commodity as salt. Teesmouth became one of those areas in which both monastic and lay activity overlapped and intermingled in a very pronounced fashion, comparable to the Vale of Pickering and the Cleveland Plain. For example, Rievaulx, Guisborough, Byland, Newburgh and Fountains had lands and/or salt pits in close proximity to each other at Redcar, Marske, Coatham and Normanby. William de Kilton had granted Byland (1190-1206) a toft and croft with buildings, salt house and yards, with 5 acres of "terre lucrabilis" in Coatham. Fountains and Rievaulx came to an agreement that the former should have the right to acquire salt-pans in Normanby (1170-88).[2] Both had fishing rights in the Tees here, and it may be assumed that salt was important for salting fish apart from its other uses. Rievaulx rapidly acquired grants here which were obviously connected with the salt industry – one culture in Saltcoteflath, and land in Saltcotehills, for example.

But increasing pressure from Guisborough Priory, by the late 12th and 13th centuries expanding very rapidly in this area, together with Rievaulx's desire to acquire arable land and pasture near to their abbey, induced the monks to place their grange at Normanby in the custody of the Canons for a payment of 2/- per year.[3] (1192-99). This was another increase in the already great influence that the Canons held in this small triangular area. They had a group of their richest granges concentrated within a few miles of each other – Coatham, Marske, Brotton and Yearby. Of course, a great deal of the importance of these granges derived from their farming activities. But it is not unreasonable to suppose that their growth was influenced, perhaps quite largely, by their interest and participation in the nearby salt industry.

---

[1] B. M. Cotton MS. Julius, F. VI, 185 fo.455; also *V.C.H. Durham* Vol. II, pp.293-294 for salt working further north near South Shields.
[2] R.C. pp.175-176.
[3] "quod ego, Emadlus Abbas, et Conventus de Rievalle, concessimus et commisimus Domino Roaldo Priori et succ. ejus, et Conventui de Gyseburne, custodiam omnium terrarum quas habuimus in territoris de Normanby" G.C. Vol. II, p.3.

The Canons themselves owned and utilised at least eight salt works by the early 13th century, mainly concentrated in Coatham, but also in Redcar. Their efforts were never haphazard or ill-directed. In Markse and Redcar, for instance, they acquired lands fringing the sea, and where possible, furnaces already built.[1] They secured rights of way to and from their works and wherever possible consolidated their scattered lands into one manageable whole. Besides, they amplified their own salt production by securing rents in kind from tenants who were also engaged in salt panning, instead of money rents. They were unceasing in obtaining confirmations of their salt-pits and lands.[2]

Besides the monasteries and ordinary small tenants, the greater magnates had a share in the industry. It was Peter de Brus's right to take one skep of salt from every salt pan in Coatham Marsh each year.[3] And active participation is implied in an assignment of dower to Isabel de Fauconberg at Coatham in 1366 when manorial salt pits are mentioned.[4] Altogether, it seems quite probable that the salt industry was a decisive factor in Coatham's development as a port in the 13th century. The industry went hand in hand with the fishing always a principal activity along this coast and down the River Tees.

As late as 1580 the inhabitants of Coatham petitioned the Secretary of State and the Dean of Durham against the sale of salt at Yarm by the Scots, who paid no duty for unloading it there.

Looking back to medieval times, and the salt pans of Teesmouth, it seems that this was the beginning of the area's specialisation in the chemical industry. Today, if you stand on the Cleveland Hills and overlook Teesmouth, you will see the massive concentration of ICI and associated industries reaching as far as the eye can see, even to the brink of the sea.

It is fascinating to contemplate that this immense pile stands, at least in part, on the site of the old salt pans. Not far away to the south, the recent interest in potash around Whitby also follows the old tradition of salt and alum, started centuries ago.

OTHER INDUSTRIES

Iron mining and salt panning were by far the most important industrial activities in the medieval North-East. Quarrying for building stone from the Corallian limestone was undertaken, especially north of Pickering.[5] Bridlington Priory quarried and carted stone for its buildings from as far away as Filey, which shows the high opinion they had for this particular kind of limestone.[6] Whitby Abbey was more fortunate and had its quarries very near to the Conventual buildings. A short distance away was the Aislaby sandstone which

---

[1] "... 21 acres of land in the fields of Redcar, next to the 10 acres I previously gave them, lying together, also a furnace (furno) standing between the same and the sea." Grant by Ivo de Redcar (c1218) G.C. Vol. II, p.235.
[2] Hugh, son of Ralph Deblel de Lyum gives three salt works to the Canons in Coatham marshes, lying to the east of the mill they had there (windmill for power?) and confirmed all the other salt works they had there "of the fee of my ancestors". G.C. Vol. II, pp.115-116.
[3] *Inquisitions* Y.A.S., Vol. I, p.139.
[4] *V.C.H. Yorkshire: North Riding*. Vol. II, p.399.
[5] q.v. Duchy Accounts *N.R.R.S.* passim, for castle repairs, etc. "The tenants of Pickering and Newton are accustomed to digg stones in the common quarries for the repairs of their howses." Commonwealth Survey (1651) *N.R.R.S.* Vol. I, p.93.
[6] Ralph de Nevill granted stone in the quarry of Filey for the building of the monastery and offices to the Priory between 1194 and 1230. *E.Y.C.* Vol. II, p.466. The Priory was situated on chalk which is unsuitable for large scale buildings. Consequently they had to look elsewhere.

is of excellent quality.[1] The theory has been put forward that the building stone for Rievaulx Abbey came via the "canals" which the monks constructed at a very early stage of their establishment in Ryedale.[2] This is quite plausible since charter evidence shows that the "canals" were in existence by the 1140's, and that later extensions were made to them on several occasions during the following seventy years.[3] Besides, the various building stones used in the Abbey have been identified as probably coming from certain quarries which lie conveniently near to the courses of the "Canals". Whether this is merely coincidence, is uncertain even knowing the course of the "canals", the date of their construction and their capacity for floating stone-laden barges, the actual use is unproven, and may always remain so.

Tanning, was perhaps, the most important of the lesser industries. The reasons may have been the excess of skins and the abundance of bark. Since the North-East was such an important sheep-run a constant supply of pelts was available. Besides, its wildness allowed many wolves to roam there. These were trapped and their skins used by the tanners. Rievaulx had the right to set traps to catch wolves on Westerdale Moor, and the Whitby Abbey Accounts mention the cost for tewing 14 wolf pelts. The export of pelts from Whitby and Scarborough certainly occupied a large part of their trade. In a grant of pontage to Whitby in 1351 Edward III, among other things, allowed it to be levied on sheep-skins, lamb, kid, hare, rabbit, fox and cat skins at the rate of 3d/100 weight.[4] Frequent references to bark sold are made in Whitby Abbey and Duchy of Lancaster Accounts of the late 14th century. There was a tannery at Rievaulx Abbey, too, although the size of the pits remaining today does not suggest that it served others except the Convent itself.[5] At Whitby there was certainly some importance attached to tanning. Gregory Conyers, Bailiff of Whitby owned at least one "barkehouse" in the town which he valued at not less than 100 marks.[6] The commonness of Tanner as a surname in the town suggests that others may have been similarly occupied. The activities of the Burgesses was never strictly limited; they had many occupations, some being merchants as well as farmers.

Conclusion

The exploitation of iron and salt by monks and laymen emphasised the process of colonisation in the North-East. The monastic interest in sheep farming had already ensured that much of the hitherto uninhabited moorland should be used. But it had not necessitated permanent settlement, except in a few areas such as Westerdale and Commondale. The working of iron did, on the other hand, require permanent settlement and so both monks and laymen were attracted to what would otherwise have been an uninhabited area. Since smelting involved tree-felling, it followed that a great deal of

---

[1] This sandstone was used for London Bridge, the Admiralty Pier, Dover, and the facing of the old Houses of Parliament.
[2] H. Rye and J. Weatherill *op. cit.*
[3] R.C. pp.180-181, 43-44.
[4] P.R.O. Patent Roll (1351) Part 3 m. 19.
[5] "The tan-pits still filled with oak-bark, which have been discovered at Rievaulx Abbey, are evidently on a scale only sufficient for carrying on the tanning industry for the convent itself and not for sale." H. E. Wroot, "Yorkshire Abbeys and the Wool Trade" in Thoresby Society (1930).
[6] *Testamenta Eboracensia* Vol VI, p.110 (Surtees 106).

clearance occurred, which was the forerunner of more extended settlement. This is most striking in Eskdale. Here the number of villages at the time of Domesday was small (Westerdale, Danby, Lealholme, Egton) and confined to the lower floor of the valley. As a result of the monastic iron working at Glaisdale, Danby, Westerdale and Commondale, the line of settlement extended and colonisation of the higher land to the south of Eskdale took place (mainly 13th century). It was significant that the monastic smelters should also become cattle farmers in the same areas. This provided even greater incentive to make permanent settlements.

Expansion into the moorlands found its parallel in exactly opposite locations – the tidal flats of Teesmouth. For here, the ordinary interest of both monks and laymen in salt-making had induced them to engage in some reclamation work. This again would have been a negative area for settlement had it not been for the attraction of the salt industry.

Such a movement towards these areas affected the relative value of the sub-regions within the North-East. The enlivened interest in the Teesmouth area served to reassert the importance of the Cleveland Plain, of which it was part. The resources of the Cleveland Plain, however, hitherto entirely agricultural, became more diversified. On the contrary, the interest in iron mining had given the Moorlands more importance than they had had as a region. Previously, the distribution of wealth and population in the North-East was strictly confined to three main areas:– the Vale of Pickering, the Cleveland Plain and the Vale of York, and while the predominance of these lowland regions remained a persistent theme in the development of the area as a whole from Domesday times through the 14th century and beyond, the utilisation of ironstone in the moorlands had done more, perhaps, than any other single factor to render them more attractive, both to lay and monastic settlers.

PART FOUR : THE ECONOMIC LANDSCAPE

'Every inhabited area has its particular economy and every economy is equated to a particular kind of economic landscape shaped fundamentally by the character of the operating units and the aims of production'

Leo Waibell

9 Medieval Ports and Trade

10 Medieval Fairs and Markets

11 Monasteries and the Wool Trade

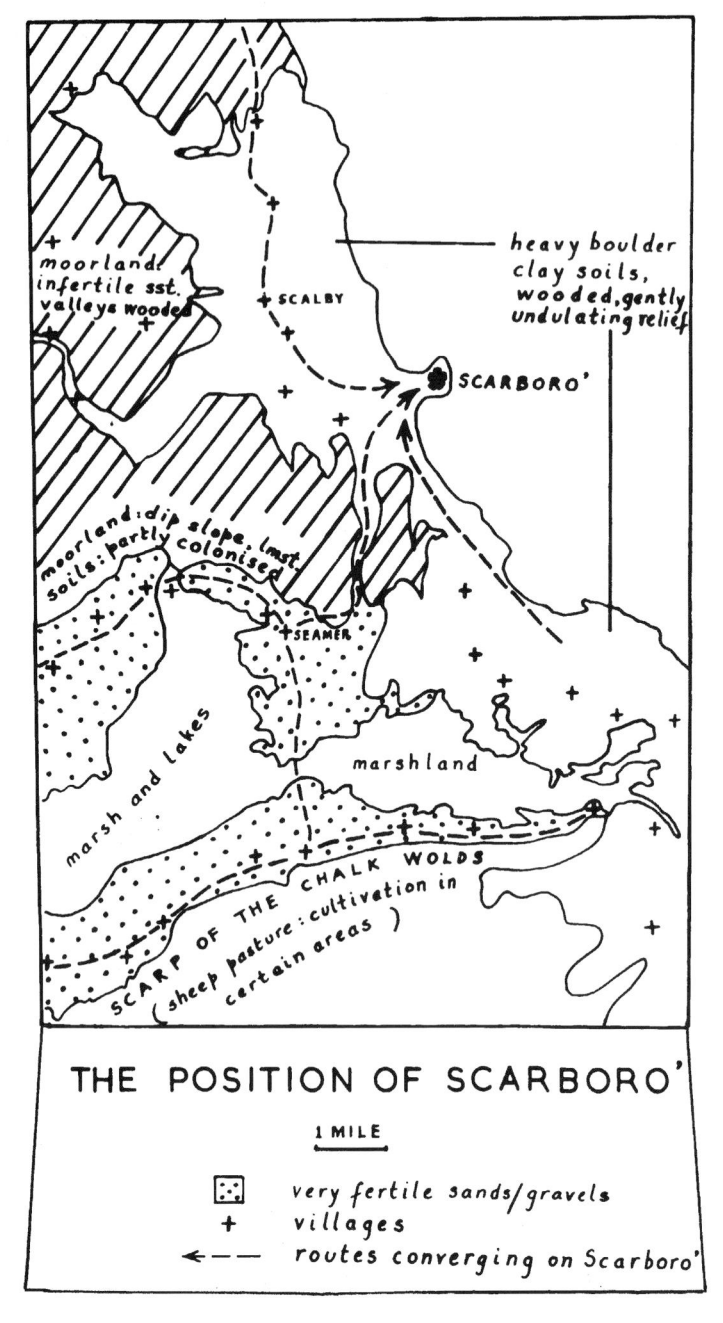

Figure 9.1 The Position of Scarborough

9 THE MEDIEVAL PORTS AND TRADE

The sea played a conspicuous part in the development of the North-East, especially in the earlier centuries. The coast had been a convenient landfall for the predatory Saxons and Scandinavians. The latter, especially, during the 8th and 9th centuries ravaged villages and monasteries alike, establishing a reign of uncertainty and violence along the coast.[1] When their inclinations led them to more sedentary pursuits and settlement replaced marauding it was the North-East coast which again figured prominently.[2] The traditional connections with Scandinavia remained. A great deal of trade between England and Scandinavia before the Conquest took place along this coast.[3] Even in the 14th century Norwegian fishermen and merchants still occupied a high place in the greatly expanded trade of this coast.[4]

But, besides the nearness of the North-East coast to the Continent – historically and physically – certain other factors emphasised the importance of the sea as a regular and usual means of communication. The inhospitable moorland which extends inland from the coast, rising ever higher towards the Cleveland Hills, acted as a great barrier to land travel in medieval times. Of course, "barrier" must be used with caution because very often the pack-animals of the medieval traveller were capable of penetrating localities which today might be inaccessible to the motor-car. The influence of physical factors is, in fact, very much determined by the technical environment of the particular period. Even so, there are several indications that land travel was difficult in the area. In 1323 the monks of Whitby complained of the "barrenness of the soil", the incursions of the Scots, and the inaccessibility of the Abbey;[5] as late as 1453 in petitioning for the appropriation of Hutton Buschel church they renewed their complaints: ...the said monastery is situated by the sea-coast and frequently exposed on all sides to hostile attacks and also because of the long and dangerous routes the place is difficult of access for men and draught animals by land; expenses are great and continuous. Repairs to the church nave of the said monastery, pending now and in the future, are manifestly and notoriously needed and for the reason they piously and deservedly stand in need of help...[6]

Great laymen, too, might have found the same difficulties. Sir Richard Cholmeley, for example, apparently used his ships in the administration of his more inaccessible estates along the coast.[7] Overall, the sea was the main artery in the trading activities of the North-

---

[1] e.g. the destruction of St Hilda's monastery at Streoneshal (Whitby).
[2] Place-names are a valuable indication of this ... "the Riding underwent in the ninth and tenth centuries a Scandinavian settlement of exceptional thoroughness, which has left innumerable traces in the local nomenclature of the present day." A. H. Smith, *Place Names of the North Riding of Yorkshire*. (1928) Introduction.
[3] Norwegian settlement was heavy in Cleveland and along the coast in Whitbystrand Wapentake. The Danish settlement was concentrated mainly in the Vale of Pickering. Many place-names contain later elements which indicate continued connections with the Scandinavian countries at least to 1000 A.D. The pretensions of Harold Hardrada and Tostig as late as 1066 demonstrate the strong connections still existing even then.
[4] See Customs Accounts P.R.O. E 122/57/1. Especially Norwegians at Hull and Ravenser in accounts for similar period. The trade was not one-sided: even in 1415 the Bailiffs of Whitby were instructed that, "no fishing for one year is allowed to the island parts of the realms of Norway and Denmark, especially Islande". *C.C.R.* (1415) p.297.
[5] Mandate to appropriate church of Seamer. *Reg. Papal Letters* II, (1305-42).
[6] Yorks: D.Reg. Register of Archbishop William Booth fo. 224.
[7] A suggestion by Gaskin in *The Old Seaport of Whitby* (1909) p.238.

East. But the coast itself was rocky and dangerous. Harbours were few, and far between: from the Humber to the Tees the only ports were Scarborough and Whitby. The scarcity of safe anchorages served to emphasise the value of these places as ports of call in rough weather, as well as the only outlet for a considerable area inland – mainly the eastern half of the Vale of Pickering and the Coastal Plateau.

The effect of the wars between England and Scotland during the late 13th and 14th centuries had been two-fold. While the monasteries complained about the Scottish devastations[1] and lay landowners also reported much of their land uncultivated because of similar incursions,[2] the merchants were reaping a profit and the ports were growing. Calamitous to one section, the Scotch wars were beneficial to another. Whereas many inland fairs and markets suffered losses in trade and profits, especially in the Vale of York, the ports developed as commercial centres. For many of the King's supplies were bought in the North-East and transported by local merchants to Berwick or Newcastle.[3]

It was in this coastal trade that Roger le Carter, whose successors were later to rise to prominence in Scarborough, began to accumulate his wealth. In 1298, for instance, he transported 458 quarters of wheat and 112 quarters of oats to Newcastle on one journey. At the same time, Robert de Barton, John de Selby, John le Heer, and many others took part in the trade.[4] Besides such direct advantages to local merchants, the importance and value of the trade attracted merchants from elsewhere, who brought increased traffic to the ports. The Newcastle to London coastal trade, which flourished especially in the 14th century and later, was an equally effective stimulus to the development of the North-East coast. London merchants are mentioned in the Customs Accounts of both Whitby and Scarborough, and in the latter at least one London merchant, Thomas Castell, owned land in the town.

The 14th century coal trade took a predominant place in the coastal trade from Scarborough and Newcastle southwards to London. The Whitby Abbey accounts for 1394-95 mention cauldrons of coals arriving from "a ship of Shields", "one ship from Newcastle", "William Rede of Sunderland", and so on.[5] Sometimes it appeared that ships from other east coast ports had a share in the trade. Thus, the accounts mention "a ship of Lyn" and "a hoic of Norfolk" importing coals to the Abbey at Whitby.[6] Even merchants from inland towns, such as Thorne in the West Riding, participated in 1321, for example, a ship of Gravelines in Flanders attacked Walter Rayny of Thorne between Fyling Wick and Scarborough. In his ship were eighty cauldrons of sea-coal of the price of 20 marks, 42 stone of cheese and other goods, which were seized.[7] This trade, then, was especially instrumental in adding to the importance of the North-East ports.

But the area had a trade of its own. The ports did not only derive their importance from the coasting trade. Two main avenues of trade were evident. The first was the River Tees

---

[1] C.C.R. (1328) p.280 *Reg. Papal Letters* Vol II (1305-42).
[2] At Settrington, for example, P.R.O. C. 134/82. See also Cal. of Inquisitions.
[3] For corn bought in Yorkshire in 1298 see P.R.O. E 101/6/32 and also FIGS. 9.4, 11.3.
[4] P.R.O. E 101/6/38 and 12/8. Corn expenses (1304) and details of carriage.
[5] W.C. Vol. II, pp.612-613.
[6] *loc. cit.*
[7] C.I. *Misc.* (1321). p.137.

and the second the Vale of Pickering, both allowed inland contacts to be easily made by turning the flanks of the moorland which stretched between them. The Tees enabled the Cleveland Plain to have trade relations with a wide area: "there ought to be, and has been from time beyond memory, common passage of ships and boats and a common fishery for all from Thormotby to the sea ... "[1] Yarm, seventeen miles up the river was the chief port of the region, and as Fig. 9.4 shows it had an hinterland in the 14th century which included the Pennine foothills and the Vale of York, far south of Northallerton. Earlier still, in 1205, Yarm had been the most prominent port in the North-East despite its inland situation.[2] The Fifteenth on merchants' goods taken in that year gives a good idea of the relative status of the ports. Yarm contributed £42-17-10; Scarborough £22-0-4^{1}/$_{2}$d; Coatham 11-11d; and Whitby 4-0d.[3]

Yarm's predominance was not to last. The inland position was a disadvantage and during the late 13th and 14th centuries, ports such as Coatham, which were nearer to the sea, began to overtake Yarm. Thus in 1341, when the goods of the burgesses of Yarm were valued so that a fifteenth could be taken from them, they totalled only £60-10-0d. But at Scarborough the burgesses' goods were valued at £246-0-0 and those of Whitby at £150-5-0.[4] It was obvious that the latter ports had made tremendous strides forward whilst Yarm had declined. By 1341 Yarm seems to have become more important an an inland market than as a port.[5] Its splendid site always assured it of some importance as an economic centre, however. The roads from Catterick and Thirsk united east of Yarm and then crossed the Tees at the only bridging point between Cleveland and Durham. Yarm commanded this crossing point.

Even at the height of their prosperity, however, none of the North-East ports entered the same category as Hull and Newcastle. In 1205 these great ports had contributed £344-14-4^{1}/$_{2}$ and £158-5-11 respectively to the subsidy, far larger sums than Yarm or Scarborough.[6] And, although the influence and importance of Whitby and Scarborough rose sharply in the 14th century it was always far below that of Newcastle and Hull.

Scarborough had distinct advantages over Coatham and Whitby. It was a convenient collecting centre for the products of the Vale of Pickering, especially for the villages along the northern fringe of the Vale. FIG. 9.4 illustrates a hinterland of Scarborough in 1298. It has been drawn from information about purchases of corn in the district for the Scotch war, and transported from the port.[7] Of course, the map tells only part of the story of Scarborough's hinterland and must be used with reserve. Even so, it has many features of interest which illustrate the port's growing importance. Corn was carried there from as far away as Kilham and Eastburn, over 25 miles to the south. Even Settrington at the western

---

[1] *C.P.R.* (1358) p.157.
[2] Yarm shipped lead from the Richmondshire mines in 1182 Pipe R. 28 Hen.II (Pipe Roll Soc.) The principal exports seem to have been corn and agricultural products in later centuries. *(C.P.R.* 1338-40 pp.198.201). This is to be expected from a port whose hinterland was the Vale of York.
[3] Document given in N.S.B. Gras, *Early English Customs Systems*, pp.221-222.
[4] *N.I.* pp.243-245.
[5] The value of its burgesses' goods was, for example, comparable to several large market towns of the North-East, e.g. Northallerton £46-0-0; Malton £33-0-0.
[6] Gras *op. cit.* pp.221-222.
[7] P.R.O. E 101/6/38.

extremity of the Wolds delivered corn to Scarborough by pack horse and carts.[1] This was rather remarkable considering the influence of Beverley, Hull and York merchants in the area. The Assize Rolls (1361-64) show that at least in the wool trade the sphere of influence of Beverley merchants extended into the Vale and was strong in the Wolds.[2] The York and Hull wool merchants had an even greater purchasing area, which embraced the whole of the western Vale of Pickering (11.2). Wool was, in fact, transported from the Vale over the Wolds near Malton and thence to the headwaters of the River Hull at Wansford and so by the navigable water to Beverley and Hull.[3] But the indications seem to be from the corn purchases of 1298 that the predominance of Beverley, York and Hull merchants was limited to the wool trade and that in general trade Scarborough merchants held their own over quite a large area including the Vale of Pickering and the Wolds.

Certain physical factors emphasised Scarborough's importance in the area, and provide some explanation why its hinterland should be so large. It was situated at the eastern end of the Vale of Pickering. Though the centre of the Vale was occupied by the swampy ground fringing the Derwent River, the northern and southern peripheries were very fertile and highly settled regions. An examination of the Lay Subsidy (1301) indicates that in population and wealth this area far exceeded any other in North-East Yorkshire (4.5).

Although so rich and productive, the Vale was somewhat isolated. York was more than twenty miles away and Hull was nearly thirty miles. Though merchants would be willing to trade for wool in the area it was unlikely that they would be drawn there for other less valuable commodities, such as corn. Adam Pund of Hull, John de Gisborne of York, Hugh de Mitton of York, and William Chamberlayn of Beverley – all great wool merchants – were frequently seen in the district.[4] No word however is heard of merchants from the same towns trading to the same extent in other commodities.

It was Scarborough which handled such goods (and later took over some of the wool exports). It was eminently well situated for the task. Fig. 9.1 shows how the routeways converged upon the town. The line of villages to the north of the Vale were connected by a road which ran eastwards to Scarborough. Two ways from the south, linked the town and Wolds district.[5] Both were the only easy ways across the marsh and lakes of the eastern Vale. One followed close along the coast and the other along the drier gravel areas between Seamer and Staxton. North of the town, an area of fertile Boulder Clay flanked the barren sandstone of the moorlands. Here another series of villages had been sited (Cloughton, Burniston, Scalby, Newby) which found their natural centre at Scarborough only a few miles to the south.

With such fundamental advantages Scarborough increased in importance over the other ports in the area. It had a wooden pier at latest by 1225, and a more permanent quay by

---

[1] *ibid.* "from the Rector of Settrington 80 quarters of oats carried to Scarborough through twelve leucas at a cost of 16/8".
[2] Thus "William Tirwhit of Beverley bought from John of Foxholes 2 sacks, each sack 30 stone and each stone 12 pounds, in 1361; and of John Stut of Weaverthorpe and of Thomas of Nawton 1 sack Y.A.S. Assize Rolls (1361-65) in *Sessions of the Peace*. Vol 100, p.16.
[3] P.R.O. E 372/183/47. Pipe Roll for 1338 but this is dealt with more fully in Chapter II.
[4] Wool merchants on a national scale: they had been summoned to Edward III's council of merchants. Y.A.S. *Sessions of the Peace*. Vol. 100, p.xliv.
[5] The Bridlington Priory grange at Burton Fleming on the Wolds sold much of its corn in Scarborough. York: D. Reg. R.H. 60.

1252.[1] Coatham had no harbour; the sand was its dockland.[2] Though well placed to engage in the trade entering the Tees, its position was very exposed and the roadstead it provided negligible. Even so the salt industry and the nearness to the heavily settled Cleveland Plain encouraged its growth. Whitby was situated in Eskmouth and allowed more shelter for ships, in addition it was the largest and focal town of the Coastal Plateau, which was moderately settled. The Esk Valley, too was the only easy route across the Moorlands to the Vale of York beyond.[3] Though Whitby Abbey, which was Lord of the town and port, attracted, and itself produced much business, Whitby did not really flourish as a port until the 14th century.[4] Its hinterland was restricted. The Sheriffs' Accounts show that when Edward I purchased his corn in this area the cartage was never considerable. Lythe, for instance, which supplied 100 qt. oats in 1298 was only four miles from Whitby.[5]

The Burgesses of Scarborough held of the King. This and the presence of the King's castle in the town encouraged its growth. Used as an administrative and transmitting centre during the Scottish wars, its trade increased. The Pipe Rolls clearly indicate that the castle depended on the town and port for its provisions, which also stimulated trade there.[6]

The Confirmation charter to Scarborough (1253) indicated the extent of the port's importance.[7] Three of its clauses were particularly significant for the port's development. The first allowed all merchandise to be freely brought into the borough whether it came by sea or land, and depart freely without impediment. The second allowed the Burgesses to hold a fair every year from 15th August to Michaelmas – an exceptionally long period of forty-five days. This was much longer than most towns, where eight days was more usual.[8] Even the two great East Coast ports of Hull and Ravenserod only had fairs of thirty days' duration. Such a great event attracted many merchants, among whom the Flemings were most numerous.[9] The third clause allowed the Burgesses the right to carry packs along the sea coast free from payment, and provided that neither the King nor anyone else was to make or suffer to be made any harbour or quay between Scarborough and Ravenserod (on Spurn Point, at the Humber estuary).

This last concession was very instrumental in Scarborough's growth at the expense of other ports. By the middle of the 14th century the Burgesses were attempting to extend their monopoly of traffic along the coast. They obtained a Letter Patent providing that no boats or ships should be loaded between "Raclif and Flaynburgh."[10] Though this monopoly was frequently broken, it did go a long way to retard port development south of Scarborough, especially at Bridlington.[11] Attempts to centralise the coastal trade had been

---

[1] *C.P.R.* (1225) pp.2.5.8. etc.
[2] G.C. Vol II, p.120. The Canons' ships were free from toll at "the port of Teyse and at the sand (sabulum) of Coatham".
[3] Y.A.S. *Monastic Notes* II. Vol. 81, p.51.
[4] Gaskin *op. cit.*
[5] P.R.O. E 101/6/38.
[6] e.g. in 1212 the cost of provisions bought for a few months was £173-3-4: 600 sides of bacon, 60 beasts carcases, 14 ton wine, 10 lasts of herring, 40 "ascis" of salt, 1000 "esperducis ferri" 20 marks worth of corn and 10 librates of hay. Pipe R. 14 John. (Pipe R. Soc. No. 58).
[7] *C.Ch. R.* I. p.147.
[8] See Ballard and Tait, *British Borough Charters (1216-1307).* (1923) pp.303-305.
[9] Hinderwell, *History of Scarborough.* (1798).
[10] Documents contained in the White Vellum Book of Scarborough Corporation No. 10A.
[11] There is little evidence to show that the Priory did anything to stimulate a port at Bridlington. In fact, the Canons exported some of their wool from Filey in the late 13th century. (*Rot.H.* Vol. I, p.115).

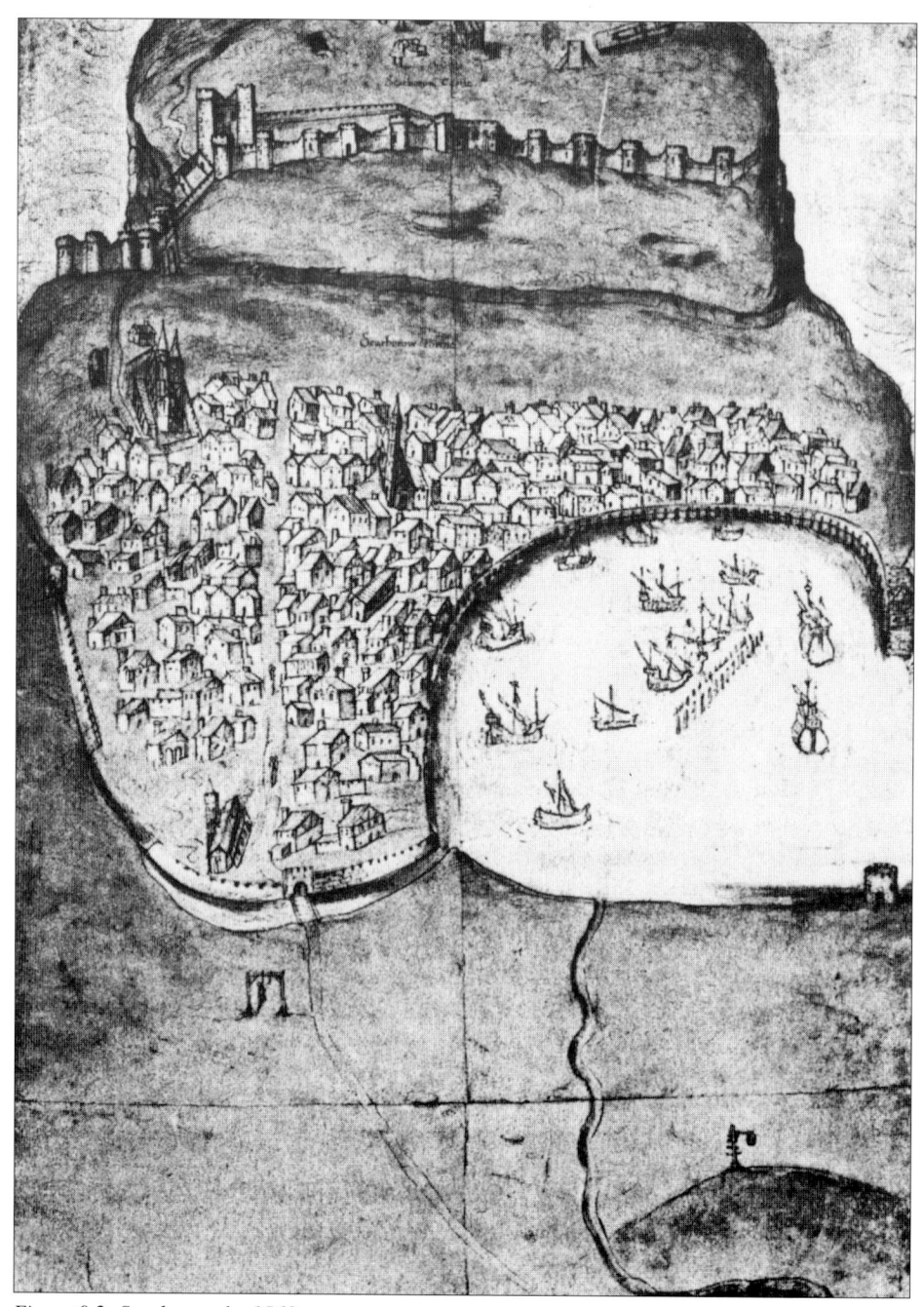

Figure 9.2 Scarborough c1560

made during the first quarter of the 14th century. In 1320 a cocket seal was made for the port and Collectors of Wool customs appointed. Sometime later a petition for a Trone to be appointed at Scarborough for weighing wool and customing it, was made – "as the great sheep pasture of Blakey Moor is far from Kingston-on-Hull and the wool is being shipped to Flanders from small coast towns without being customed, to the loss of the King."[1]

But, not content with such powers over coastal traffic the Burgesses tried to monopolise inland trade too. In 1256 they complained that the markets of Filey, Sherburn and Brompton were a nuisance to their borough and market and successfully pleaded for the abolition of them.[2] This attempt was part of what seems to have been a persistent tradition. For even in the 16th century they accused the Seamer market of being responsible for the town's decay – "The navigation, pere, and whole force of Her Majesty's said towne dothe utterlie decay by reason of the said market, notwithstandinge that the same is the best harbour for passengers upon the sea as also a great help unto the cuntrie thereabouts, if the said market were suppressed."[3]

Something of the differential development of the ports of the North-East has been detailed so far, and the factors influencing this have been mentioned. But the extent and character of foreign trade and the relative importance of coastal trade have yet to be dealt with. Fortunately a series of Customs Accounts for the North-East ports which are particularly full for the early 14th century allow a fairly accurate assessment of these questions.[4] The series is incomplete, and almost entirely refers to imports, but its value is great. This was the period in which Whitby increased its influence as a port. It was also the period of Scarborough's prosperity, allowing a glimpse into what was destined to be replaced after the middle of the century by a declining and decaying trade.[5]

Figure 9.3 makes an attempt to plot the origin of merchants trading to Scarborough and Whitby in the early 14th century. Of the foreign merchants the Flemings are by far the most numerous. In 1307-8, (Sept.-July), for example, three quarters of the merchants paying customs on imports to Scarborough were from Flanders. Of these almost one third came from Iser. Bruges, Blankenberg, Ostend, Sluys, St Marikirke and Lapscure were also represented. The remaining merchants were largely French, from Dieppe, Dunkirk or Calais. The following year shows the same pattern. Again Flemish merchants predominate but French merchants have increased and Norwegian, Danish, Stralsund and Hamburg merchants appear. This is not extraordinary. An Inquisition (1294) into alien ships at Scarborough showed that out of twelve ships landed there, six were from Stavoren in Zeeland, one from Kampen in Frisia and another from Ludingekerk in Frisia, one from Riga and three from Stralsund.[6] Subsequent customs accounts from the first

---

[1] A. Rowntree, *History of Scarborough* (1931) p.168.
[2] *C.P.R.* (1256) p.477.
[3] J. T. Cartwright, *Chapters of Yorkshire History* (1872) pp.267-270. There was a later dispute (1584) between Scarborough and Seamer over their boundaries. *N.R.R.S.* Vol. I, p.229.
[4] The following, among many others examined for Whitby, Scarborough, Hull and Ravenser, proved useful: P.R.O. E. 122 55/16; 55/23; 56/3; 56/7; 56/10; 56/14; 57/1; 134/2; 135/3.
[5] Three main factors influenced the port's development in the late 14th century: war, town riots and oligarchic administration of a particularly odious kind. This brought about a decline.
[6] P.R.O. E 163 Q.R. Exchequer Misc. 2/1. See also "Shipping and Trade in Newcastle upon Tyne 1294-96" J. Conway Davies in *Archaeologia Aeliana* Vol. 31, 4th Series (1953), pp.175-204.

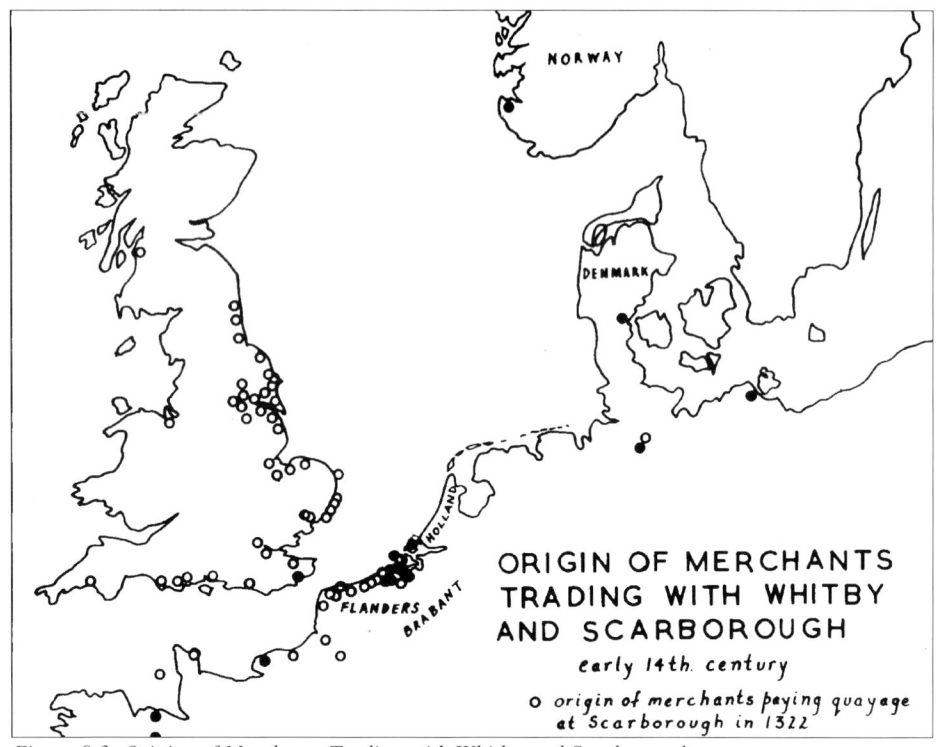

Figure 9.3 Origins of Merchants Trading with Whitby and Scarborough

quarter of the 14th century convey the same impression: Flemish and Brabantine merchants being the most numerous and German merchants rather scarce at Scarborough and rare at Whitby. The Quayage taken at Scarborough in 1322 gives a full record of all ships berthed at the quay for a year.[1] Again, of the foreign merchants, those from the Scheldt, Blankenberg, Westcapel, Flushing, Ostend and Waben predominate. Tydeman Wolfaghen is the only Hamburg merchant named.

At Ravenser and Hull, however, the Eastland, Hansa and Norwegian merchants occupy a much more dominant position in trade at this period, and their organisation is clearly seen. At Ravenser in 1307, for example, Herman Hemeler has five other merchants listed beneath his name with a share in the trade being conducted. The trade of the smaller ports of Scarborough and Whitby seems to have been much less influenced by the great companies of merchants, either of London or the Hanse. The individual merchant, trading singly, or sometimes in association with a few of his townsmen is generally the rule. Usually, too, the ship owners are also the merchants. Whereas at Ravenser, for example, one Lubeck ship had goods belonging to merchants from Lubeck, Münster, Gotland and Cologne (1294). At Scarborough and Whitby this is rare. The only major exception

---

[1] P.R.O. E. 122/134/3.

noticed concerned exports from Scarborough (1310-12). Here a Calais ship carried the goods of a Renne merchant, a Dieppe ship carried goods of a Campe merchant, and Amiens, Abbeville merchants used other ships for their exports. But even so the practice was not well marked: only 6 out of 16 ships leaving the port were organised in such a way.

The incidence of foreign merchants on the North-East Coast was variable as might have been expected. The largest numbers came in the summer months – mainly during August and the first week in September. After this period a distinct fall off of traffic of all types but especially foreign, is evident. At Scarborough in 1321, for instance, from mid-February to mid-May the trade was almost entirely local. With only a few exceptions (Flemings from Schelde and Waban or a Frenchman from Calais) the ships paying the quayage were from English ports, such as Whitby, Newcastle, Hartlepool, Saltfleet, Lynn, Winterton and Beverley.

Towards the end of May, but especially in July, the numbers of foreign traders increased, until they reached a maximum during August. By far the largest number of ships berthed in these weeks and the profits from quayage for one week were three times as great as for a typical week in the winter and spring months.[1] Such an unbalanced trade was not evident at the larger ports. Why was it so conspicuous in this area? Two main reasons may explain this.

The size of the market for foreign goods was not large and the variety of products offered for export was limited. Cereals seem to have been the largest article of export from Scarborough and this could hardly attract merchants from afar in large numbers at all times of the year. It is likely that certain of the goods listed under exports from 1310-12 were not actually from Scarborough but had been shipped perhaps at Newcastle and charged customs on berthing at Scarborough quay. Coal, for example, was an improbable export for this part of the coast. Undoubtedly wool export had occupied a conspicuous part of the trade of the North-East ports, even from early times, but this trade appears intermittent.[2] The establishment of a staple at Newcastle and the extensive range of York and Hull wool buyers did not encourage it. Besides, much more of the wool trade was overland. The attempts to make Scarborough into a major wool exporting centre during the 1320s was belated and unsuccessful. The great period of the wool entrepreneur was fading; the drastic effects of European war were soon to produce complete changes in the pattern of the wool trade. Besides, other movements, such as the emergence of an English cloth trade and the development of a home market for wool, had already begun to make themselves felt.[3]

All this will explain the possible absence of foreign merchants, but it does not account for their presence in large numbers during the late summer months. A clue to the explanation can be found there, however. For, if the attraction of the North-East was limited, the sea in its immediate vicinity was not so. One of the greatest herring fisheries

---

[1] P.R.O. E. 122/134/3.
[2] e.g. Hacun de Scardeburg sent wool to Flanders in 1199. Other Scarborough merchants were also mentioned in the published Pipe Rolls about this time. See also *Hundred Rolls* Vol. I, pp.115, 121 for participation of Scarborough merchants in the 13th century wool trade. The Assize Rolls (1361-65) indicate the growth of a body of wool buyers and dealers in the town and district.
[3] See E. Power, *op. cit.* for the "awakening" of English merchants and the development of the home market.

in England was located there. Merchants came from Flanders, Norway, Germany, France and Scotland to buy herring at Scarborough and Whitby. Others fished off the coast and then put into the ports to salt and barrel them. Some bought up large amounts of herring either in the ports or before the fishermen landed, such engrossing often caused the inhabitants grave losses, "qui per exercitium allecis maxime vivunt, et statum suum mediorcrem hactenus supportarunt."[1]

Whitby specialised in the herring trade more than Scarborough. In 1307 during a period of only three months, 237 lasts of herring and at least 244 "wagas" of salt entered the port. Few other commodities challenged this. Only Herman Calneshond and William Engleys both from Stralsund brought in a more varied cargo which included bords, "pannos de Wadmale, tymbre de Greywerke", and coal. From 4 July to 26 Sept. 1304 all the entries on the Custom Account for Whitby are, without exception, for herring, when £40-13-4 was the total value. Again, for the same period in 1315 herring was the exclusive cargo. Merchants from "Lumbardy", St Mariekirk, Dunkirk, Ostend, Brule, Blankenberg, Dieppe, Calais were engaged in this trade.

The emphasis was upon September and August which were the months when the herring shoals appeared off the coast. This was a principal reason for the greatest numbers of aliens arriving at this time. The Customs Accounts for Scarborough (35-36 Edward I 29 Sept.-7 July) illustrate the transition from general trade to herring and salt in the latter part of the year.[2] In December and January Hugtred fitz Arnald, William Folour and William fitz Boyd, all of Sluys import very varied cargoes which consist of Spanish iron, wax, cloth, bords, Guernsey apples and oil. Hardly any merchants are named as importers from February to April. In May numbers increase and salt is the principal cargo. 126 "wagas" of salt are listed for the month introduced by a very representative selection of merchants. In June rice, canvas and butter are among the imports in which salt again predominates. In July herring imports increase until they reach a high maximum in August. In this period the numbers of merchants vastly increase and their ports of origin vary more considerably than before.

Incidental reference has been made to the typical cargoes which the 14th century brought into the North-east ports. They were predominantly Baltic goods, such as pitch, wax, timber, bords, oil and cordwain, but besides there were many other commodities often brought from afar, mainly by middlemen. Laurence de Hamburg, for example, brought rice, and William Folour of Sluys brought Spanish iron. Foreign ships also played an important part in the English coastal trade at this time. Such trade occupied a great share in the economy of the North-East ports. It was mainly this local trade which maintained the ports during the Winter and Spring months. Although there were merchants from Chester and Wales engaged in trade with Scarborough and Whitby, the greatest proportion of English merchants come from the East and South-east coast. FIG. 9.3 shows that three areas were predominant; the East Anglian coast, especially around the Orewell estuary; the north and east coasts of Kent; and the Humber-Ouse district. The

---

[1] W.C. Vol. II, pp.672-673. *C.C.R.* (1394) p.386.
[2] P.R.O. E. 122/55/23 Petty Custom on Imports.

latter is most surprising since Pontefract, Snaith, Bawtry and York are so far inland. But river navigation was an extremely important means of transport in medieval times. Traffic along rivers was often long distance: lead was regularly sent from Nidderdale to York and thence to Hull entirely by water, for instance, and the Abbot of St. Mary's, York, had his ships plying to and fro between Boston and the Abbey, by river.[1]

Of the East Anglian ports, ships from Ipswich, Winterton, Orford, Spalding, Wisbech, Blakeney and Lynn occur most frequently. Sandgate is most regularly represented among the Kentish ports. A great deal of traffic between the small coastal towns of the North-East occurred. The Quayage accounts at Scarborough (1321) show that Whitby, Filey, Flamborough and Hornsea ships put into the port with regularity. Newcastle and Hartlepool ships were frequent visitors, but ships from Hull and Boston were never mentioned in the series of Accounts examined.

Scarborough and Whitby, then, were active ports on a coast which was busy with foreign and home traffic. The early 14th century shows them participating strongly in this trade. Scarborough was by far the more important of the two, although the development of specialisation in herring fishing had given a stimulus to Whitby. Neither, however, can be compared to the large and intricately organised ports such as Hull. Within their own area, nevertheless, they provided a useful and much used avenue for trade – important where land contacts were difficult and large towns distant. Had their growth been stimulated by the monasteries?

Certainly Whitby Abbey held a dominating and unique position in the town. It owned both the town and the port. The Royal Charters which the abbey obtained from time to time particularly emphasise "…portum maris".[2] Nor were its powers limited here. It was the Abbey, not the townsfolk, that the right to hold a fair was granted. The market was the Abbot's; the houses were the Abbot's, and no property could be sold or exchanged without his sanction.[3] The townsfolk did suit at his court and he superintended a Merchants' Court which was held daily. But his rights over fishing and trade were even more impressive. He had a tithe from ships in the vill, which in six months (1396-97) produced £21-18-5 from 13 ships; he could levy plankage on alien vessels landing at the port, and an entry in the Accounts for "tolnetis et costumis vill de Whitby" suggests that his rights were even more extensive.[4] Indeed, they were forcefully observed. As late as 1378 Nicholas Penok, a Whitby merchant, complained that the Abbot and his men assaulted him and abstracted 3 qts salt and sundry nets valued at £10 from his ship. The Abbot's reply is interesting as a general statement: he said that, "…the town of Whitby was an ancient borough and port in which many burgesses dwelt; that the Abbot was lord of the town, and that in the town was an ancient custom that if any stranger brought victuals to the town, that is corn, barley, beans, peas, malt, salt, coals or other victuals, either by land or water, for sale, one

---

1   P.R.O. E. 372/207 m. 46 and Bawtry to London m.51.
2   W.C. Vol. I pp.147-149. "Et prohibeo, super forisfacturam regiam ne ullus aliquis hominum aliquo modo se intromittat de terris eorum; nec de hominibus suis ubicunque fuerint; … nec de aquis eorum in Portu de Wyteby…"
3   *ibid.* p.212. "Si quis autem terram suam vendere voluerit, primitus hos Abbati ostendere debet, et ei terram, si eam emere voluerit, vendendam offere, pro rationabili pretio…"
4   Abbey Accounts in W.C. Vol. II pp.553-625; also financial statement and inquisition in 1366. (*C.B.M.* Camden Soc. Vol. 54, pp.63-67).

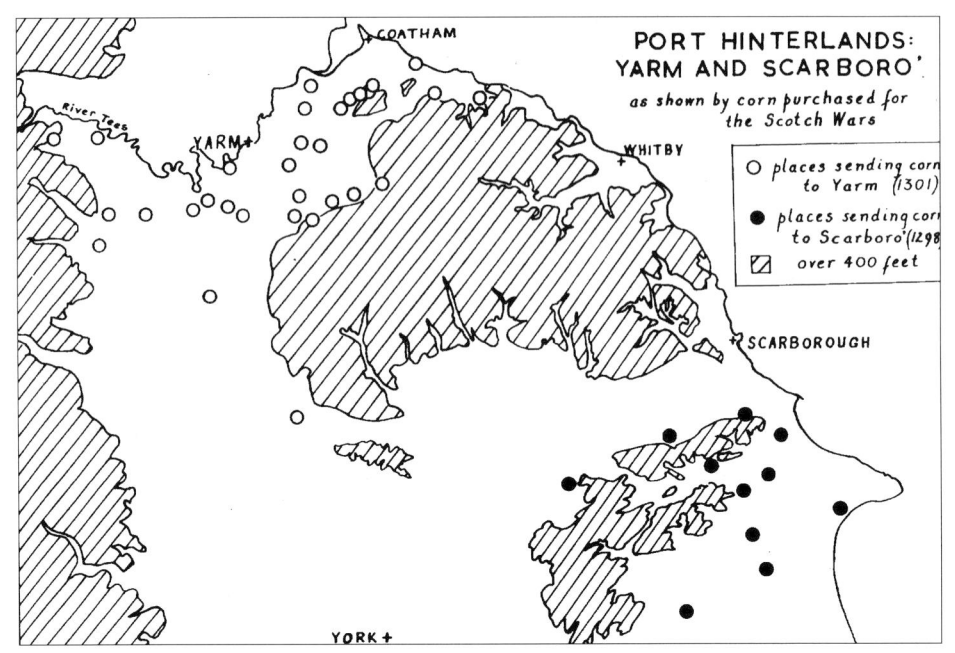

Figure 9.4 Port Hinterlands : Yarm and Scarborough

of the burgesses might buy those victuals for the use of the lord and the burgesses, so that every burgess as well as the lord might have as much as his condition required..."[1] The Abbot, it appears, had taken an excessive share.

His interest in the town's fishing industry was equally dominating. Even in 1211 the income from the fishery had reached £17-13-4.[2] By 1394-95 sales of fish (derived from tithes) were three-quarters of the total sales during six months. This was supplemented by dues from net-drying which fetched £2-13-4 in the same period.[3] Although, then, it is plain that the Abbey depended to an exceptional extent on the trade of the port, the question of its direct participation in it is harder to determine. Did the abbey have its own ships, for example? The Prior of Guisborough certainly had in the 13th century, supplying the Priory through the nearby port of Coatham.[4] He had at least seven boats there before 1240. Peter de Brus, Lord of Coatham, had granted that, "ships carrying things of the Prior and his successors to the port of Coatham – whether they be the Prior's own ships or hirelings, hired by the Prior – shall be quit of all levy of toll and demand for moorage (pro situ navis): if the said ships carry other things, they shall not be quit of levy or toll, due and customary for such things are other than for the use of the Prior's household brought over for use and not for sale." Neither the Prior's tenants in the vill, nor aliens on

---

[1]. Y.A.S. *Monastic Notes*. I Vol. 17, p.234. (De Banco 1378).
[2]. Pipe R. 14 John (Pipe R. Soc. Vol. 30 New Series).
[3]. W.C. Vol. II. pp.553-625.
[4]. G.C. Vol. I, p.119. also Y.A.S. *Fines* Vol. 67, p.129-130.

his land were to be charged toll. Such concessions presuppose a very important interest in the area's trade on the part of the Priory. Coatham's growth may well have been stimulated by this.

Little evidence can be brought to show that the Abbot of Whitby had similar direct interests. A payment to "the Master of the ships" is recorded in the 14th century accounts but this may not mean very much.[1] Several references, however, suggest that the Abbot might have owned shares in vessels belonging to others. Indeed, the Abbot seems to have been implicated in the piracy which was so much a feature of this coast in the 14th century. Agnes de Vescy, for example, in the late 13th century had accused the Abbot and his men of capturing her goods valued at £75-16-8 by an act of piracy on her vessel coming from Flanders.[2] Much later, the Abbot, together with several well-known burgesses had purchased goods from a French pirate, "perfectly knowing the same ship and goods to be the propre goodes of your said Suppliant."[3] Whitby was certainly as notorious a haven for pirates in medieval times as it was in the 17th and 18th centuries.

The monasteries situated further from the sea, or navigable waterway might be thought, at first sight, to have little influence on the development of ports and coastal trade. Although evidence is scarce it is enough to indicate that, in fact, certain inland monasteries did contribute to port development. Rievaulx and Malton, for instance, although more than twenty-five miles from the coast influenced Scarborough's development in various ways. Both seem to have had some sort of negotiating or trade centre in the port from which they conducted business, perhaps with the Italian or Flemish wool merchants who called there. Malton's house in the town is described as "a grange", in the chartulary.[4] It would be interesting to discover whether the organisation of this town "grange" was similar to that of more usual monastic granges elsewhere. It was the base for the Canon's interests in the fishing industry of the town and no doubt most of the Priory supplies of herring came from Scarborough. Thus, in the 14th century, the Duchy of Lancaster Coucher Book notes that "the Prior of Malton took green hue of thorn and hazels in Allantofts within the demense ... and carried it to Scarborough for kippering his herrings (pro allece suo desiccando)".[5]

As far as Rievaulx was concerned, the port had an added attraction: Citeaux had established a cell in the town which probably was used to strengthen the bonds between Mother and Daughter houses.

The monastic share in the development of the North-East ports appears to have been, then, quite considerable although its detailed application is rather obscured. It remains, now, to examine the fairs and markets of the North-East during medieval times.

---

[1] W.C. Vol. II, p.607. "Magistris navium, ad potum, ex praecepto Abbatis 3/4d".
[2] *Select Cases on the Law Merchant.* Selden Soc. Vol. 46. p.lxxix. "...the men of the Abbot of Whitby ... with force and arms made an assault on the ship ... and took and carried away the cloths and wax and chattels ... being in the same ship, to the priors of Whitby."
[3] *Y.A.J.* Vol. II, pp.246-251. Inventory of goods and tackle abroad.
[4] B.M. Cotton MS. Claudius D XI.
[5] *N.R.R.S.* Vol. III, p.28.

10 MEDIEVAL FAIRS AND MARKETS

The medieval fair "was an institution of political, religious, legal, judicial and above all, commercial importance."[1] It was the scene on intense business activity on both a local and international scale. It was here that the farmer came to buy and sell his corn and cattle; it was here that the Italian merchants came to negotiate for the wool they were to buy.

The North-East was fortunate to have a large number of fairs and markets within it, in the 13th and 14th centuries, as Fig. 10.1 shows.[2] Fairs were granted to Whitby Abbey and Bridlington Priory as early as the 12th century, but the majority of grants for fairs were, as the Calendars of Patent and Charter Rolls show, in the 13th century. Thus, Barton le Street received its grant in 1246, Heslerton and Hovingham in 1252, and Scarborough in 1253.[3] Such grants were usually a recognition of what had long existed, Scarborough for example, had been an important trade centre for many years previous to 1253, and so had many other towns in the area.

Figure 10.1 draws attention to several important features in the distribution of the fairs and markets. Each port, for example, had its own fair. Nearly always the grant was an early one. Thus at Whitby Henry II granted and confirmed "to the aforesaid church in the

Figure 10.1 Medieval Fairs and Markets

---

[1]   K.L. McCutcheon, *Yorkshire Fairs and Markets*. Thoresby Society. (1940). p.3.
[2]   Constructed mainly from grants of fairs and markets in *C.Ch.R.* and *C.P.R.*
[3]   McCutcheon, *op. cit.* p.161.

said vill of Whitby burgage and a fair on the feast of St. Hilda."[1] At Bridlington, a much inferior port, the grant had been made in John's reign. Yarm, Coatham and Scarborough had fairs which were very important mainly because of the sea connections the town had, and the greater variety of trade this brought them. Scarborough fair "Attracted a great gathering of trades from most parts of Western Europe accommodation for them being provided by means of booths and tents pitched in Merchants' Row between Palace Hill and the south-east boundary wall of the town."[2] This busy trade, largely due to the facility of sea travel over land travel, probably was the reason for the unusually long duration of the fair, which lasted forty-five days.

The fairs and markets were, as might be expected, mainly in the lowland towns and villages. It is noticeable, however, that the majority were on the fringes of the highland. Whorlton, Kildale, Great Ayton, Guisborough, Skelton, Lythe and Egton all marked the boundary areas of contrasting economy. The greatest concentration of fairs and markets was the peripheral villages of the Vale of Pickering. This reflected the wealth and economic activity of the region which emerged so clearly from previous chapters. Pickering and Malton were the chief markets of the Vale and were typical of most of the fairs and markets in the region – marking the junction on the one hand a moorland economy; on the other a Valeland economy.

The other lowland fairs were in two groups: in the Cleveland Plain, from Stokesley to Coatham; and in the Vale of York, south of Northallerton. This latter group, which comprised Northallerton, Kilvington, Thirsk, Topcliffe and Coxwold, was in an unrivalled situation in relation to routeways. The Northallerton Gap was the principal north-south road, leading directly to York. The partiality the Scots showed for it is ample proof of this. Paradoxically, the chief reason for the importance of the fairs and markets in the area was also the cause of their distress on numerous occasions. Thus, in 1327 Thirsk manor, including the fairs had been partly wasted by the Scots.[3] At Boroughbridge, the town had been burned and wasted to the impoverishment of the tenants and in consequence the profit of the market and fair had fallen by 73/4.[4]

The fairs of the Vale of York had a great deal in their favour which made such set backs only temporary. They had, for instance, a wide area to draw upon: to the west were the rich dale pastures of the Pennines; to the east the sheep country of the North York Moors, and lying between, the Vale itself, with its emphasis on arable production.

The importance of routeways to fairs and markets was, of course, obvious. It is interesting, however, to see how close a correspondence there often was between them. This is clearest in the Vale of Pickering where the markets all lie along the only roads of any importance, namely the Scarborough-Helmsley, Helmsley-Malton roads. Incidentally, the predominance of Scarborough was due in no small measure to the existence of a road running westwards from the town linking it with a line of market-towns.[5] Scarborough was, consequently, the natural collecting point for inland trade in this district. Similarly,

---

[1] W.C. Vol. I, pp.147-148.
[2] McCutcheon, *op. cit.* p.132.
[3] *C.I.P.M.* VII p.53.
[4] *C.I.M.* II (1307-1349) p.95.
[5] The burgesses were quit of cheminage through the Forest of Pickering in 1256. *N.R.R.S.* IV. p.92.

the dominance of Malton and Pickering as market towns in the Vale was due mainly to the north-south road which connected them across the marshy vale – one of the few crossings in the Vale, in fact. It is significant that the Abbot of Rievaulx had some control over this route: in 1334, for instance, he was said to be responsible for repairing "Friar's Bridge over the Costa, across which people are wont to pass by horseback or on foot from Pickering to Malton. Since it is so badly repaired people have had to make a diversion of about half a mile in the forest, treading down the deers' pasturage in consequence."[1] In fact, all but one of the other crossing points of the Vale seem to have been in the hands of the religious. The Prior of the Hospital of St John had to repair the bridge and road of Pul (near Foulbridge) in 1334, which was a "common highway for carriages, carts, drifts and pack-saddles."[2] Further west the Prioress of Yedingham was responsible for the road and bridge near her abbey but in 1334 it was in good repair.[3]

Both Pickering and Malton were focal points of considerable importance. The former was within easy reach of the villages along the northern margin of the Vale, it was the central town, in fact. Its connections with the moorland, and perhaps with the Whitby area, 18 miles to the north were facilitated by Newtondale and Saltergate (in the 18th century a busy route of pannier-men)[4]. Malton was even better situated. The roads of the southern part of the Vale converged upon the town linking it with all the villages from Stonegrave to Staxton; the wool road over the Wolds to Wansford opened out not only the Wolds themselves but Holderness, otherwise rather inaccessible to the Vale.[5] In addition to all this Malton stood at the entrance to the Kirkham gorge, one of the few easy exits from the Vale of Pickering into the Vale of York – and to York beyond (compare Coxwold's position in the other gap leading from the Vale.)

The markets of Stokesley, Great Ayton, Whorlton and Kildale all in the Cleveland embayment, were conveniently placed in respect of the Eskdale route which led directly through the moors and to Whitby. Egton Fair probably owed its existence to this route too. It is rather surprising, in fact, to find a fair so far up Eskdale at all. Much of its business was probably local; it would be an excellent centre for the farmers of that valley. (The position of Thwing and Kilham in the Great Wold Valley can be compared to Egton and Whitby at the mouth of Eskdale. Both valleys were the most usual and easiest ways of entering the highlands of which they were part.)

If the distribution of monasteries and their granges is compared to the distribution of the fairs and markets it will be seen that the former were well situated in relation to the latter. That is to say, no grange was inaccessible to a fair or market. The granges of Byland, Rievaulx and Guisborough in the Vale of York were very close to many fairs and

---

[1] *ibid*. III. p.2.
[2] *ibid*. p.4.
[3] *ibid*. pp.4-5.
[4] See "An Account of Some Mediaeval Roads Crossing the Moors South and South-West of Whitby" in *The Whitby Literary and Philosophical Society Report* (1922).
[5] Henry Best used this route to take his goods to Malton market in the early 17th century. "It is ill going to Malton with draughts, when the fields adjoining to the high-way are most of them fough; when our draughts wente eyther to Malton or Hiddisley quarry, looke how many wente, and they had each of them victuals putte up for three meales; for they went forth usually on Fryday aboute fower or five of the clock, and wente usually as farre as Duggleby field, and there loosed and tethered theire cattle." *op. cit*. p.102.

markets such as Northallerton, Coxwold, Stokesley and Yarm. The granges in the Vale of Pickering were just as well placed. Even the moorland granges were within fairly easy reach; thus Guisborough Priory's granges in Eskdale had Kildale, Guisborough, Skelton and Egton fairs no more than six miles away: Rievaulx's granges in Bilsdale had Whorlton to the north of the valley and Helmsley to the south. The incentive to use such fairs was clear; besides their importance as trade centres the monasteries often had privileges which gave them an advantage over other merchants and farmers. Henry II, for example, had granted the monks of Byland and their men the privilege of being free from tolls and levies in all cities, boroughs, markets, fairs, bridges and ports throughout England and Normandy, and many other houses (e.g. Malton) had similar grants.[1]

But did the monasteries use local markets and fairs on any scale? Much of their trade was large scale and long-distance. In their wool dealings, for example, it was the international fairs like Boston and St Ives where much of their business was negotiated,[2] and it was large towns like York that drew much of their trading interests. They had, indeed, property in such places which they used to further their trade. Moreover, many of their cattle purchases were made in places far outside the North-East; thus Whitby obtained stock from Barnard Castle in the early 14th century.[3] At first sight it might be expected that such advanced, highly organised trading communities as the monasteries could have little to do with local trade.

The amount of evidence bearing on this is unfortunately, small. It appears, from the Whitby Abbey accounts of the late 14th century that corn was sold at Seamer and Hackness, and in the same places fattened hogs and horses were sold between Nov. 1394 and May 1395.[4] Much earlier in the abbey's history it had been the custom to buy much of its corn "in Waldo vel Pikeringe-lythe" – once again emphasising the Wolds as corn land in the middle ages.[5] Of course, the abbey's status as lord of the vill meant that the fair and market of Whitby town was very much used by the abbey. It was in its own interest to expand the trade of market and fair as much as possible so that its income from tolls, plankage, net drying, fishing-boat tithes and so on, could increase.[6]

Malton Priory, similarly, had a great interest in Malton market and fair. Most of the victuals bought for use in the Priory were obtained in Malton market. The Canons' dependence on it could have drastic consequences; in 1283, for instance, Agnes de Vesey and several of her ministers "assaulted brothers William de Malton and William de Crauncewyk, canons and others, lay brothers of the said house, in the common way near the church of St Leonard, Malton, took, imprisoned, and maltreated them, and on many occasions took their horses, sheep, oxen and other cattle of the plough ... and would not

[1] *V.C.H.* III, p.133.
[2] e.g, Recognisance of the Abbot of Byland to Guidon Chissain and Jacob Amadur, merchants of Florence of £1000 silver for 120 sacks of wool. The same to be paid through 6 years at 250 marks/year in two instalments of 100 marks at St Edwards Fair, London and 150 at St Ives Fair. (1278-79). P.R.O. K.R. Mem. Rolls. No. 52.
[3] Y.A.S. *Monastic Notes* II. p.51.
[4] W.C. Vol. II, pp.553-585.
[5] *ibid.* p.367.
[6] In later years "Whitby as the only market town within twenty-one miles drew to itself the trade of the district. From all the countryside for many miles, and from all the villages, people gathered into Whitby with their produce for sale – with their wants to be supplied." R.T. Gaskin, *The Old Seaport of Whitby* (Whitby 1909) p.224.

let them be replevied, and detained them without food, so that the greater part died of hunger, AND BY PUBLIC PROCLAMATION, IN THE SAID AGNES'S FULL MARKET OF MALTON, PROHIBITED ANY PERSONS FROM SELLING OR TAKING ANY VICTUALS TO THEM AND FROM HAVING ANY COMMUNICATION WITH THEM, and frequently took away by force victuals brought for their use, and from day to day, by various distraints, prevent them from cultivating their lands, carrying their hay or corn, storing it in their barns,"[1]

Such dependence derived in part from the nature of Gilbertine Rules and in part from the distribution of the Priory granges. Malton was the natural collecting point for the produce of the granges. In fact, the relation between Malton Priory and its granges was closer than in any other North-Eastern monastery, due mainly to the convergence of roads on the Priory. In respect of the wool produced by each grange it "was ordered ... to be collected from the various granges and brought together at the abbey without any separation of the wool or of any fleeces or wool fells."[2] This centralisation on Malton was likely to emphasise the importance of the fair and market held there, as well as the trade of the Canons there.

The connection between local fairs and markets and the monasteries was evidently fairly strong. Several more examples can be given to illustrate this. The Bridlington Priory grange of Burton Fleming sold the corn it produced in the nearby markets of Filey, Seamer and Scarborough in 1355-56,[3] and Rievaulx Abbey was purchasing large amounts of corn in Scarborough during the middle 13th century. In 1262, for example, "a certain Gregory, a merchant coming to the port of Scardeburg with 198 qts of wheat in a certain ship" had sold all except 24 qts "to the attorney of the Abbot himself."[4] Besides such definite connections as these, it may be reasonably assumed that the wool collecting activities of most houses, such as Byland, Rievaulx and Malton in the districts around the abbeys (as the documents phrased it, "lane bone collect' circa dom' nostram de Bella Landa"[5]) would bring the monks into direct contact with local farmers in both fair and market. The later development of industries in some market towns, cloth making at Whitby for example;[6] the emergence of a body of wool dealers making purchases throughout the district in the 14th century (see Chapter 11); and the establishment of Royal wool collection centres in towns like Malton, all helped to emphasise and increase the importance of local fairs and markets.

Did the fairs and markets of the North-East develop any specialist functions in catering for their particular districts? Outside the area, especially in many Pennine towns, such specialisation had occurred. Masham was a famous sheep market; Middleham was well known for cattle and swine; Bedale for lead.[7] These markets were a reflection of the areas

---

[1] *C.P.R.* (1281-1292) p.76.
[2] Scripta de Fratribus XI in *M.A.*
[3] York D. Reg. R.H. 60.
[4] Y.A.S. *Assize Rolls* 44. Hen III.
[5] P.R.O. L.T.R. Mem. Roll (1298-99) No. 70. cf Meaux owed 53 sacks of good wool "de collecta de Holderness versus Bridlington et versus Kirkham usque ad Eboracum" L.T.R. M.R. 53.
[6] *C.C.R.* (1304) p.134. "all weavers in places outside York, Thirsk, Scarborough, Malton, Beverley, Kirkby and other Royal demesne boroughs must cease to ply that trade."
[7] *V.C.H. North Riding* I. pp.251,255,323.

in which they were situated, for the Pennine dales were famous for sheep, cattle and minerals in the Middle Ages. By the 17th and 18th centuries, at any rate, the fairs of the North-East were renowned for certain things. *Owen's Book of Fairs*, published in 1769 described "The Commodities which each of the said Fairs is remarkable for furnishing."[1] Thus, Guisborough was noted for horned cattle and linen cloth; Helmsley for horned cattle, sheep, horses and woollen cloth; Malton and Seamer for horses. Marmaduke Rawdon noted in his diary for 1664 as he passed through Northallerton "This happened to be a faire day for oxen, kine, and sheepe, the greatest in England." Later he says of Malton, "thir is kept the greatest horse-fair in England; also it is a greate faire for cattle and other commodities which booth English and Scotch sell thir."[2] It is also obvious from the account of Henry Best, the East Riding Farmer, who wrote in 1641, that markets had their specialist functions. Each fair met the requirements of its own neighbourhood and in doing so developed along particular lines. The farmers were well aware of this, and the conditions influencing the state of the markets: "White wheate is most in request att Malton", wrote Best, "Dodd-read wheate goeth oftentimes well of att Bridlington ... we sende our dodd-read wheate and massledine usually to Malton markette; our barley to Beverley and Pocklington in winter time, and to Malton in Summer."[3]

It is likely that the medieval farmers thought in similar terms and that the markets and fairs showed the same leanings then as they did in the 17th and 18th centuries. Thus, although Whitby dealt in corn, iron and many miscellaneous goods in the 14th century it was clear that the fish market was the most important.[4] Chapter 9 noted the immense quantities of herring entering and leaving the port during late summer, bringing with it an international gathering of merchants. Coatham fair would be largely occupied by merchants trading for salt, since it lay in the midst of a salt working area in which the commodity was almost a currency in itself.[5] The connection between the great herring marts of Whitby and Scarborough and the salt mart of Coatham must have been great. Merchants purchasing salt at the one to use in barrelling at the other.[6] Thirsk, along with York, appeared to be the main wool markets in the area in the 13th century, although the 1361-64 Assize Rolls show that at least at that time wool was purchased in many markets throughout the district, very often illegally.[7] Kilham's importance as a corn market, drawing mainly upon the Wolds, was emphasised by the Royal corn purchases in the North in the 14th century.

What evidence there is, then, suggests that the medieval fairs and markets in the North-East were important centres of economic activity, frequented both by lay and monastic farmers. The distribution of fairs and markets showed many interesting features, the most

---

[1] An extract relating to the Yorkshire fairs is given in McCutcheon, *op. cit.* pp.172-177.
[2] *Life of Marmaduke Rawdon of York* (Camden Soc. 85).
[3] H. Best. *op. cit.* pp.99-100.
[4] A good idea of the miscellaneous goods coming into the town can be obtained from Gaskin, *op. cit.* pp.328-343 who quotes from two Patent Rolls (1307 and 1351).
[5] The Priory of Guisborough stimulated Coatham's trade.
[6] "last year a great number of foreigners etc. being gready of excessive gain, in default of the accustomed catch of herring in foreign parts, repaired to Whitby with vessels, salt and other engines and implements needful for the herring trade, and there forestalled others in buying fresh herring in gross of the fishers, salting part in barrels, drying part ... and taking THE SAME OVER TO FOREIGN PARTS" *C.C.R.* (1392-96) p.386.
[7] Thirsk and York mentioned on Pegolotti's List.

important being, perhaps, that they were accessible to all parts. Often they were exceptionally well placed. Their distribution indicated, in several instances, particular emphasis on the marketing of one or two special commodities which were characteristic of the neighbourhood in which the markets were situated. Thus a traditional association began in medieval times (though fragmentary evidence makes it rather obscure) which persisted into post-medieval times.

# 11 MONASTERIES AND THE WOOL TRADE

More than forty years ago Professor Eileen Power wrote two classic works on the medieval wool trade of England. In the first she confined her attention to the fifteenth century, analysing the development and organisation of the trade through the use of the Cely and Stonor Papers together with the Memoranda Rolls.[1] Her second contribution was on a broader scale attempting to treat the wool trade in its early as well as its later stages. These were the Ford Lectures delivered in 1939 and published posthumously.[2] Both contributions are notable for their clarity. A careful scrutiny of sources was accompanied by an uncommon ability for recreating from them the actual conditions existing. Such conditions provided a very engaging story.

Though these works traced out, for the first time, the main themes running through the medieval wool trade, much remained to be done by later scholars, especially on a regional basis. It is doubtful whether the fifteenth century organisation of the trade, for instance, was typical of earlier centuries. New developments had occurred which were likely to cause differences: the Flemish and Italian merchants who had travelled the countryside and haunted the ports in search of wool during the thirteenth and early fourteenth centuries had been replaced by the English merchant and middleman by the late fourteenth and fifteenth centuries.

Professor Power's preoccupation with the West Country, too, resulted in an unbalanced picture. It was reasonable to expect her to concentrate attention on a particular area and the West Country was suitable because it was a principal wool producing region and because its trade is so well documented. But can it be taken as representative of other areas such as North East Yorkshire? Several facts suggest that it cannot. One of these is the striking absence among preserved documents of a group of powerful English merchants and middlemen comparable to the Celys and Stonors. It would be vain to search north and east Yorkshire for woolmen's brasses in fine churches rebuilt by them in the fashion of the Cotswolds. They are absent from the area despite it being a great wool producing region.

Besides Professor Power's preoccupation with the fifteenth century and the West Country, a closer examination of her work shows that references to the North are scarce and often, when they occur, couched in general terms: '... and we know from the Hundred Rolls of 1275 that both Yorkshire and Lincolnshire were great haunts of wool merchants of all nations.'[3] Who were these merchants? What were their spheres of influence? Did one set predominate over another? What were their routeways? Who were their customers? Which areas supplied the wool? What was the part of local merchants and

---

[1]. 'The Wool Trade in the Fifteenth Century' in *Studies in English Trade in the Fifteenth Century* (Power, E. & Postan, M. M., 1933), pp.39-90.
[2]. *The Wool Trade in English Medieval History* (1941).
[3]. *Ibid.*, p.22.

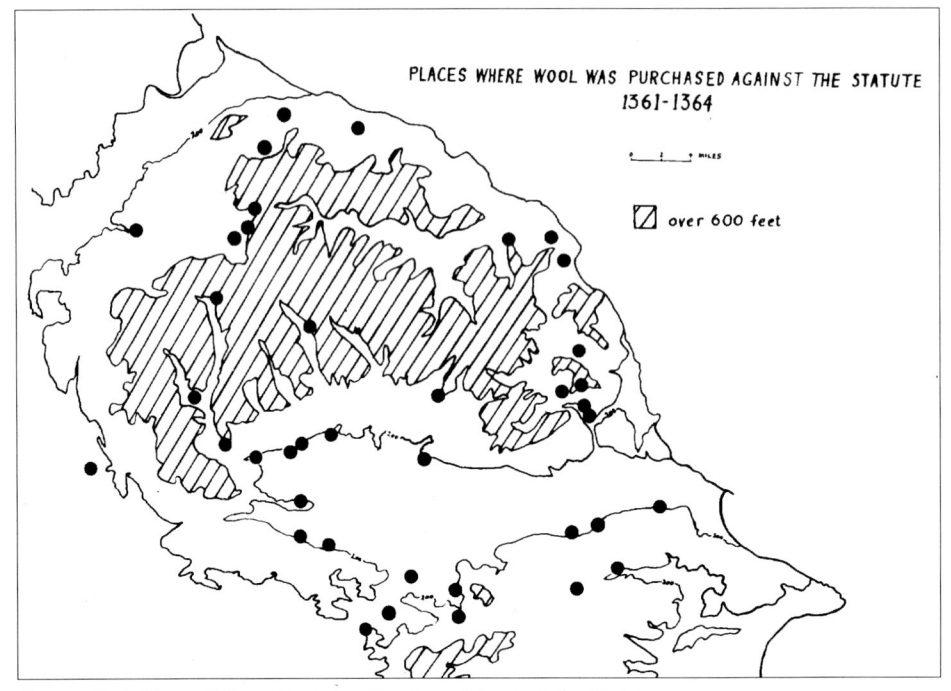

Figure 11.1 Places Where Wool was Purchased Against the Statute

wool dealers? 'The Cistercians were drawn to the Yorkshire dales and moorlands and to the deep valleys of Wales...' hence they became sheep farmers par excellence.[1] But how did they dispose of their wool? What was the relative importance of the monasteries in the wool trade of northeast Yorkshire?

Despite the importance of these questions little has been done in recent years to solve them. Indeed, interest has shifted away from the medieval wool trade as though it was a closed book.[2] This chapter attempts to examine the main issues in relation to north and east Yorkshire.

The Memoranda Rolls, which Professor Power found so useful a source for the fifteenth century, are especially helpful for earlier periods. In particular, the last two decades of the thirteenth century and the middle years of the fourteenth century have been most rewarding for the purposes of this study. The Pipe Rolls and Foreign Accounts have yielded interesting details of collecting centres and carriage of wool, while the Customs Accounts have given some indication of ports and the wool trade. The monastic accounts of Malton Priory and Whitby Abbey have added details of their wool production and disposal which can be usefully compared to the accounts of the Duchy of Lancaster Pickering Estates.[3]

---

[1] *Ibid.*, p.33
[2] Signs of a revival of interest occur in T. H. Lloyd, *The English Wool Trade in the Middle Ages,* Cambridge University Press, 1977.
[3] British Library. Cotton Ms. Claudius D XI (Malton Chartulary), Add. Ms. 4715 (Whitby Chartulary). See also the *Whitby Chartulary*, Surtees Society, Vols. 69 (1879) and 72 (1881). Details of the records of the Duchy of Lancaster can be found in *The Yorkshire Archaeological Journal*, 49, (1977), p.77.

It has been shown elsewhere that sheep farming was considerable in the north east both on lay and monastic estates and the area's wool producing capacity was correspondingly great.[1]

The Duchy of Lancaster Pickering estates were the counterpart of the great de Fortibus estates just over the other side of the Yorkshire Wolds, in Holderness. The former had the Moors as its sheeprun, the latter the marshes of the sea plain. The role of the layman in wool production is constantly in danger of being underestimated. It is always the monasteries, and especially the Cistercians, which spring to mind in connection with sheep and wool. However, the de Fortibus estates had at least 7,000 sheep on them in the late thirteenth century, more than Whitby Abbey and only a few thousand less than Meaux Abbey.[2] Professor Power wisely stressed, too, the possible importance of peasant flocks.[3] Together with those of the lay magnates these must have equalled or exceeded that of the monasteries. This was a development which grew rather than decreased as the fourteenth century passed. Thomas de Westhorpe, for example, owned over 2700 sheep on his lands in the Vale of Pickering in 1366. At the same time Whitby Abbey had only 1307 sheep on its estates.[4] Thomas was, moreover, certainly not a magnate. He seems to have been one of the rising class of local dealer and wool grower, which was so noticeable elsewhere but apparently so rare in the north east.[5] As the monastic share in wool production fell, the lay share seems to have increased. This process was marked after the critical years of the mid-fourteenth century.

It was, however, the monasteries which had stimulated the rapid development of the wool trade in England. In the twelfth and thirteenth centuries it was they who drew the Italian and Flemish merchants so eagerly to the country. The story of how the whole wool of the Cistercians and Premonstratensians for 1193-94 was taken for the King's ransom is well known. But in the North-East little other evidence is available to show the extent of wool production on monastic estates in this early period. The earliest details occur in the Malton Priory accounts for 1244-57.[6]

Profits from wool sales were very large at Malton during this period. £460 16s 8d was taken in 1251. This was the most profitable year in the period 1244-57. The least profitable year (1255) produced £243 19s 8d. Altogether the total from wool sales for the period was £5224 9s 3d. Obviously wool growing was the principal occupation of the monastery, all the more profitable because it was 'an untaxed source of income', for in

---

[1] Waites, B. 'Medieval Assessments and Agricultural Prosperity in North East Yorkshire 1292-1342', *Y.A.J.*, 44, (1972) and *Moorland and Valeland Farming in North East Yorkshire: the monastic contribution in the thirteenth and fourteenth centuries*, St. Anthony's Press, York, 1967. 'Pastoral Farming on the Duchy of Lancaster's Pickering Estate in the Fourteenth and Fifteenth Centuries', *Y.A.J.*, 49, (1977), pp.77-86.

[2] Denholm-Young, N. *Seignorial Administration in England*, Oxford Historical Series, 1937, p.59. Also, *Chronica de Melsa*, ed. E. A. Bond, Rolls Series 43 (3 vols. 1866-68), Vols. II,III. The sheep at Meaux were:

Date	Number	Date	Number	Date	Number
1280	11,000	1310	5,406	1396	2,361
1286	1,320	1356	1,689	1399	2,397

[3] '... if we know less about them it is simply because, unlike the manors they have left behind them very little documentary evidence.' *op. cit.* p.29.

[4] Public Record Office, L.T.R. Memoranda Roll No. 139. m. 24.

[5] Waites, B., 'A Yorkshire Farmer in the Memoranda Rolls', *Y.A.J.* 42 (1965), pp.445-48.

[6] Chartulary: B. M. Cotton, Ms. Claudius D XI fo. 275-276.

accordance with their charters the canons were exempt from all customs at the ports and elsewhere. Such a preponderance of wool suggests that the canons 'organised an immense trade in Yorkshire and collected wool with great success'.[1] This is not easy to substantiate. The prior had large pasture grants on the Wolds and on the Moor Edge (Lockton, Ebberston) which might have accounted for the high wool sales without collection. Certainly no documents so far examined show that any collection of wool was practiced by the canons. Yet there is evidence that Byland, Rievaulx and Meaux acted as collectors. It was a process which had been working at least since William Cade's time despite Chapter injunctions.[2]

It is worthwhile here, to examine the system which did so much to enhance the great wool producing powers of the monasteries. The merchants made a clear distinction between the wool of the monastery and the wool collected by the monastery. For instance, in a Recognisance dated 1288-89 the Abbot of Melsa (Meaux) acknowledged that he would supply eleven sacks of best wool 'de proprio stauro et pastura domus sue ...'[3] Similarly the Abbot of Rievaulx promised 168 sacks to be delivered from 1287-96 being the best wool of their house from their own sheep.[4] On the other hand is the specification of the wool collected. Byland, for example, promised to pay 42 sacks 'de lane bone collect' circa domus nostram de Bella Landa'[5] while a wide area which included Holderness and the Wolds was actually delineated in one acknowledgement of Melsa – 'de collecta de Holderness versus Bridlington et versus Kirkham usque ad Eboracum'.[6] This dual function of the monasteries as producers and dealers was certainly a real one. It seems to have reached its clearest expression in the late thirteenth century when the accruing debts of most monasteries, due to such causes as destruction of stock by the great murrain of the 1280s, necessitated gathering wool from various extraneous sources to implement their own deficiencies in production.

Wool was collected by larger houses from smaller. The Arden nunnery tucked well away in the Hambleton Hills used to send its wool to Byland's woolhouse at Thorpe, 10 miles away, where the agents of the Italian merchants collected it, or where it would be despatched together with Byland's wool to Clifton near York.[7] Malton had a supremely good situation for wool collection. Roads converged upon the town which was located in the only gap southwards from the Vale of Pickering. There was the road from Pickering on the edge of the moors; then running from the east along the foot of the Wolds scarp came an important highway linking a series of prosperous villages (Folkton, Flixton, Sherburn, Rillington, etc.). Its corollary was found approaching from the west along the gravel bench flanking the

---

[1] Graham, R., *English Ecclesiastical Studies*, S.P.C.K., 1929, p. 264.
[2] H. Jenkinson "William Cade, a Financier of the Twelfth Century". *E.H.R.* (April, 1913), pp.209-227.
Some Chapter injunctions:–
1181 Wool of one year may be sold in advance.
1278 Wool may be sold for longer periods but payment must only be for wool of one year.
1279 Wool may be sold for longer terms and a larger sum may be received than they are worth in one year but such a sum must be applied to debts only.
Cistercian Statutes. Ed. J. T. Fowler, *Y.A.J.* Vols 9-11 (1886-92).
[3] P.R.O. E.159/62/15.
[4] P.R.O. E.368/59/19.
[5] P.R.O. E.368/70/58.
[6] P.R.O. E.368/53/14.
[7] *Select Cases on the Law Merchant*, ed. H. Hall, Selden Society, 46 (1930), pp.69-71.

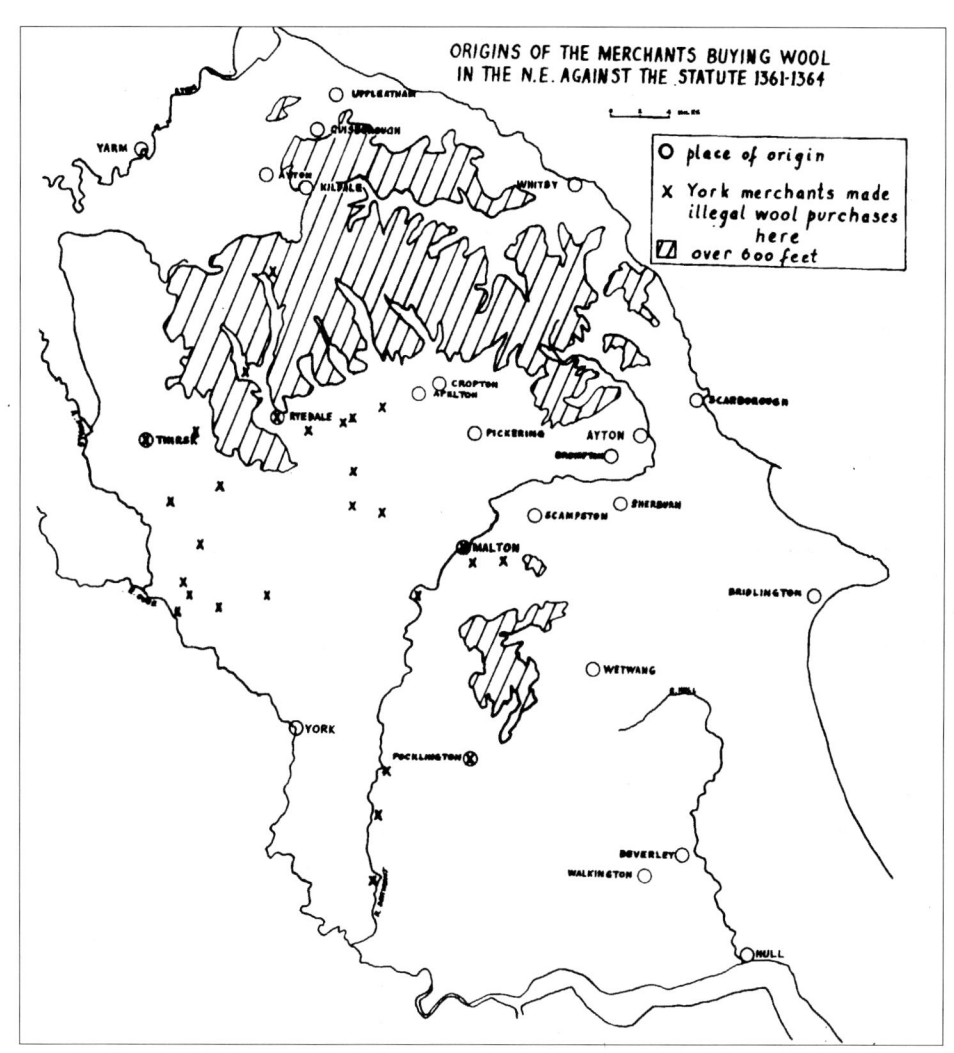

Figure 11.2 Origin of Merchants Buying Wool Against the Statute

Howardian Hills on the north side. This too went though a series of settlements (Hovingham, Fryton, Barton, Appleton, Swinton, etc.). Malton was a focal point just as Thorpe Grange was. The value of this was realised in the mid-fourteenth century when Malton became the seat of the King's wool collector, William Brewhouse.[1] The wool route across the Wolds to Wansford and Hull, and the fact that the Derwent was navigable as far as its confluence with the Ouse, supplemented the extraordinary value of Malton's position.[2]

It was fortunate that Malton Priory was so well situated, for according to the Rules of

---

[1] He had three messuages in New Malton in 1343-44. P.R.O. Pipe Roll 188/15.
[2] Details of Wold route in P.R.O. Pipe Roll 183/47.

the Gilbertines 'the whole of the wool ...' to be collected from the various granges was to be brought together at the priory without any separation of the wool or of any fleeces or wool fells.[1] What was an easy task for the canons was more difficult for the monks. They, it seems established warehouses at what may be termed strategic points in relation to their other lands. These places rather than the abbey became the collecting centres. Thorpe Grange, in the Coxwold-Gilling gap, was the main woolhouse of Byland. Its position was comparable to that of Malton Priory. Situated within the only other easy exit from the Vale of Pickering it was at once within easy reach of the markets at York and Thirsk, and yet near to the Moorland and the western Vale of Pickering. In addition it lay conveniently in relation to the main concentration of the Abbey lands.

Guisborough Priory had its woolhouse within a few miles of the precincts.[2] Thus it was within six miles of the main lowland granges at Yearby, Marske, North Grange, Linthorpe, Ormesby and Barnby and the same distance from the sheep stations in Sleddale, Commondale, Lonsdale and Baysdale. Better still, the port of Yarm was no more than ten miles to the west, while Coatham at the mouth of the Tees was eight miles to the north. How far these ports were used in the wool trade is uncertain. At least in the mid-fourteenth century merchants from Yarm were collecting wool in Cleveland and even Newcastle merchants managed to come so far south.[3] The Prior of Guisborough had his ships using the port of Coatham and he held land both here and in Yarm. In the early thirteenth century Coatham had been much inferior to Yarm in importance but by the middle of the fourteenth century the inland situation of the latter seems to have become a liability and places further down the River Tees such as Thornaby appear to have taken some trade.[4]

It may be well to indicate here the important connection which existed between the monastic houses of the North-East and the main trading centres of the area. Hull and York, were, of course, the chief ports and wool markets of Yorkshire. But Thirsk is named, together with York and Leeds, as a wool market, on Pegolotti's famous list.[5] Beverley was hardly less important than Hull and indeed, the two towns were associated by the navigable River Hull, down which much wool was transported.[6] The influence of these markets was great; they not only received wool from great distances but, at any rate in the middle of the fourteenth century, sent out wool merchants to far off places to negotiate for or collect wool. The Assize Rolls for the years 1361-64 show this influence well since they record purchases of wool against the Statute, which laid down the weight of a sack of wool.[7]

---

[1] Scripta de Fratribus XI in *Monastic Anglicanum*, W. Dugdale, Ed. J. Caley, *et al*., 6 vols., 1817-30.
[2] The Woolhouse paid 8s 5d to the Subsidy of 1301.
[3] e.g. 'The Jury says on oath that John del Chaumber of New Castle bought six sacks of wool from the Prior of Guisborough and other men of Cleveland ... against the statute.' Y.A.S. *Sessions of the Peace* (1361-64), ed. B. H. Putnam, 1939 Vol. 100, p.92.
[4] It seems significant that when the passage of ships down the Tees was confirmed in 1358 it was expressly stated that 'common passage' had existed 'from time beyond memory ... from Thornaby to the sea'. Why not from Yarm to the sea? C.P.R. (1358), p.157. Corn was shipped from Thornaby in the late thirteenth century.
[5] Given in W. Cunningham, *Growth of English Industry and Commerce* (1910) Vol. I, Appendix.
[6] In fact the Poll Tax of 1377 shows that Beverley had almost twice the population.

Beverley	2663 adults over 14 years.
Hull	1567 adults over 14 years.
York	7248 adults over 14 years.

P.R.O. E.369/8c.

[7] Y.A.S. *Sessions of the Peace*, cit. supra.

The York merchants, as expected, were found predominantly in the Vale of York purchasing wool at such places as Aldwark, Tollerton, Raskelf, Huby, Sutton, Flawith and Sessay but more surprising were their activities elsewhere. Thirsk, an important market itself, was within their province; so was Pocklington near the foot of the Wolds. The Vale of Pickering, too, was part of their sphere, apparently a very important part. An interesting entry in a Memoranda Roll for 1368 shows that even the eastern part of the Vale of Pickering was reached by them. This is odd for one would expect that area to be best served by Scarborough merchants or at least by Beverley and Hull merchants. The latter are found there but apparently not exclusively so. The entry mentioned gives details of the possessions of Thomas de Westhorpe of Ebberston at the time of his outlawry. He had been mentioned before and then it was supposed that he was a wool dealer and wool grower of unexampled proportion for this area. The details of his possessions suggest this.[1]

The total value of his goods was given as £512 16s 7d. Besides having more than 2,700 sheep he had 16 sacks of wool in his possession, and, more significantly, obligations from many wool dealers and growers which suggest that he was an important middleman who collected wool from his neighbours and then sold it to the great York merchants such as John de Gisburne of York. Richard de Westhorpe, Thomas's nephew, was accused of taking a box containing divers obligations which men held of Thomas and abstracting £200 which was also in the box. Such an amount would be a necessary lay-by for a dealer accustomed to collect or pay out money regularly. This treasure chest was well named: it disclosed that John de Gisburne, shown by the Assize Rolls to have been a prominent York merchant, owed Thomas 50 marks; several of his associates were also in debt to him. Thomas de Beverley was accused of buying half a sack of black wool from Thomas after he was outlawed. A number of local men who appear on the Assize Roll as wool buyers in the immediate neighbourhood also owed Thomas money. Thomas Thurness of Ebberston and William de Appilton owed £22 4s 3d for instance. William Playte of Scalby owed £20. It is probable that these men comprised part of a lower hierarchy of wool dealers or growers in the district who supplied Thomas de Westhorpe, the middleman, with their wool. Such places as Whitby, Scarborough, Sherburn, Scalby, Malton, Pickering, Cropton, Appleton, Bilsdale, and Ryedale recur regularly in the Assize Rolls. Merchants or dealers from these villages would collect the wool from their own district and it reached the York merchants via Thomas.

The sphere of the Beverley and Hull wool merchants in the middle fourteenth century appears to have been more limited. Adam Pund of Hull and John de Kirkham of Beverley were large scale wool exporters who had been summoned to the King's Council of Merchants. Their influence extended further than the ordinary wool merchant. Adam Pund, for example, was fined for buying wool against the Statute as far off as the western end of the Vale of Pickering and Rydale.[2] Even, so, it would be more typical for the Wolds and Holderness to be the main source for these merchants. Especially since sheep farming appears to have been the major occupation of the Wolds at this time. Adam de Pund

---

[1] P.R.O. L.T.R. Memoranda Roll No. 139 m. 24.
[2] Y.A.S. *Sessions of the Peace*, Vol. 100, pp.14,25,85.

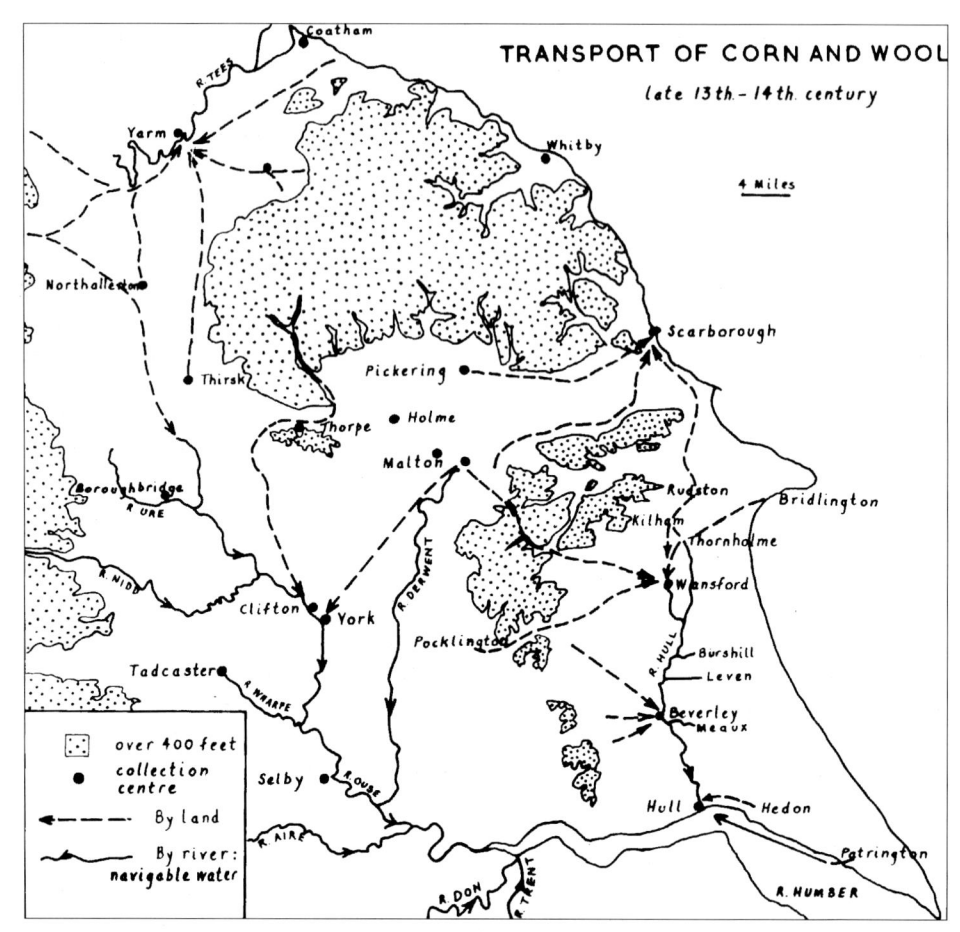

Figure 11.3 Transport of Corn and Wool

bought 20 sacks of wool from Bridlington Priory in 1361, this no doubt derived largely from the manors sited on the Wolds (Burton Fleming, Speeton, Buckton, Sewerby, etc).[1]

Such exporter-merchants as Pund and de Kirkham were paralleled by the equally eminent men trading in the North-East from York. John de Alverton, Hugh Myton (who made the collection of Kirkham Priory wool his special task) and above all, William de Swanland, one of the greatest financiers in England, were among the York wool merchants. And yet while these powerful exporters were to be found doing business in the area, the absence of large scale middlemen (apart from Thomas de Westhorpe) is striking. Men such as Thomas of Scalby, John Cooke of Bridlington and Walter of Scampeston are recorded as wool purchasers on a small scale but whether they are the counterpart of the Midwinters, Forteys and Busshes of the Cotswolds remains doubtful.

---

[1] Grange accounts for Burton Fleming (1355-56) support the idea. York Diocesan Registry, R.H.60.

How does all this affect the monasteries? Besides having a considerable part of their wool purchased by merchants from centres such as York and Beverley in the fourteenth century the monasteries had a long connection with these markets. The merchants mentioned a short while ago were Englishmen who had replaced the great Italian and Flemish wool merchants or earlier centuries. When the Italians had flourished the same markets were just as important. Numerous agreements between monasteries and Italians are recorded in the Memoranda Rolls. They provide a clear picture of the organisation of the wool trade in the North-East.[1]

The Italians sent their agents to inspect the wool at the monastic wool house to see that it was properly packed and weighed 'without cocked and black guard, grey scab, clacked and all vile fleeces'.[2] Sometimes, it appears, they would visit the house and collect direct. For example, the Prioress of Arden said that the Italians used to send 'their attorneys to Arden, within the said priory, who put the said wool in sarplers and packed it and caused it to be packed at the expense of the same merchants … and to be carried to the wool-house of Byland at Thorpe, for delivery to the said merchants …' But usually delivery was made to Clifton, a suburb of York, where the wool was loaded on to the boats and sent down the Ouse to Hull.

The importance of Clifton during the hey-day of the Italians in the twelfth and thirteenth centuries cannot be over-emphasised. It is constantly referred to in the agreements with Byland and Rievaulx. Byland had to deliver 203 sacks here from 1299-1305; Fountains had to supply 130 sacks between 1279-84 to the same place. The Italians found it very conveniently situated for most of the Yorkshire monasteries. One agreement between Rievaulx and the Society of Mosorum in Florence has an important reference to the Abbey's property in York.[3] The abbey was to deliver 18 sacks and 20 stone each year for nine years following 1287 'to the house of the Abbey at York'. This introduces a noteworthy point – that the monasteries of the North-East established negotiating and disposal centres on their lands in the major market towns. It appears quite likely that land was acquired with this specific intention at these places. Rievaulx had, for instance, property in Beverley besides that in York, already referred to. Certain facts suggest that the property in Beverley was used for business purposes. First, the obvious mercantile importance of the town was an attraction. Second, the site of their house was in Flemingate and next to the River Hull, so much a line of traffic in those times.[4] The emphasis on this is marked in Edward III's confirmation (1332) '… de libero ingressu et egrussu per magnam portam lapidae domus Beverlaci in Flamangaria … et de via libera ab eadem donc usque ad aquam quae currit juxta finem fundi ipsius …'[5] Finally, Rievaulx, apparently had some trade connections in the town since in 1342 they acquired another messuage in the town from John le Rede, a merchant.[6]

---

[1] Documents mainly used: L.T.R. Memoranda Rolls 50-61 69, 70, 119, 129. Also K.R. Memoranda Rolls 50-70. These relate to the last quarter of the thirteenth century and to the middle fourteenth century.
[2] 'sine cocto et garda nigra, grisea scabea, clactis et omni vili vellere.'
[3] P.R.O. E.368/59/19. For Rievaulx's property see also *Rievaulx Chartulary,* Surtees Society, Vol. 83 (1889).
[4] The Archbishop of York was at pains to maintain his liberties in the river. P.R.O. Chancery Misc. Bundle 86.
[5] R.C., p.303.
[6] Y.A.S. *Monastic Notes* 1, Vol. 17, p.179.

Whitby Abbey had land in York and just outside at Layerthorpe. Here the connection with trade is a definite one. The abbot sold wool from his lands in York during the period 1356-86, and later is found to be a member of one of the York trade guilds.[1] Such connections, begun at a very early period, continued at least into the fifteenth century so that lands distant from the House which one might expect at first sight to be of little use were in fact of crucial and lasting importance to the economy of the monasteries.

What of the foreign merchants themselves? Rather surprisingly one Society and one particular merchant seem to have dominated the wool trade of the North-East in the late thirteenth and early fourteenth centuries. Rievaulx, in 1280, Byland in 1298 and Arden in 1303 were indebted to the Frescobaldi. However, the debtors of this firm were even more varied and numerous. They included the Archdeacon of York and several laymen such as John Wake.[2] In this period Coppus Coppenni was everywhere. It was he who had the dispute with the Prioress of Arden for non-delivery of wool; it was he to whom Byland owed 203 sacks of wool (1299-1305); it was he to whom Rievaulx was indebted in 1280.[3]

The Merchants of Lucca seem to have concentrated their major efforts in Holderness. The Countess of Albemarle (Isabella de Fortibus) dealt exclusively with the Ricardi of Lucca.[4] The agreements relating to Meaux Abbey in the Memoranda Rolls are mainly records of dealing with the same merchants of Lucca. The Abbot made a contract with them in 1281, for instance, to supply 33 sacks of best wool, and 63 in 1282. He acknowledges a debt of £120 to them in the same year. In 1283 he is found promising 11 sacks of wool and another 11 in 1288.[5] Of course this is not to say that the Societies kept within strict bounds; they did not, but from the evidence examined it appears that they had more dealings with certain areas than with others.

Despite the economic depression which began about 1279 the wool trade made a quick recovery. The Murrain which attacked Lincolnshire in 1276 and the East Riding in 1278 caused Rievaulx to be taken into the King's hand in 1288 being in a state of decay.[6] Earlier, in 1276 the abbey had been taken into custody so that its debts could be paid off.[7] These were often considerable. In 1288 the abbot acknowledged that the abbey owed £1582 to the Society of Mosorum of Florence; the next day he recognised a debt of 250 marks to the Frescobaldi and on the same day £1060 to Society of Bindi de Circulo of Florence.[8] Yet Pegolotti's List of *c.* 1314 shows the capacity of the house to be 70 sacks. This list has drawbacks, which N. Denholm-Young has pointed out.[9] The figures quoted by it may, for instance, only refer to the amount of wool supplied to one Italian firm. If this were so the real capacity of the monasteries would be higher than the figure given.

---

[1] *Chapters of the English Black Monks* 1215-1540, ed. W. A. Pantin Camden Series, Vol. 54, p.279. *The York Mercers and Merchant Adventurers*, 1356-1917, ed. M. Sellers, Surtees Society, Vol. 129, pp.8, 12.
[2] He owed them 50 marks. The Archdeacon and Walter, Bishop of Coventry together owed 1000 marks (to Coppus Coppenni)'. P.R.O. E.368/70/60 date 1298-99.
[3] *R.C.*, p.406; Hall, H. (ed.), *op. cit.,* Selden. Soc., Vol. 46, pp.69-71.
[4] Denholm-Young, *op. cit.*, p.65.
[5] P.R.O. E.368/57/11; E.159/62/15..
[6] C.P.R. (1288), p.294.
[7] C.P.R. (1276), p.152.
[8] P.R.O. E.368/59/19; E.159/62/14.
[9] *op. cit.*, pp.53-54.

Meaux, for example, listed as supplying 25 sacks/year actually contracted to sell 55 in 1281 and 63 in 1282. Even so, the list is a useful guide to the minimum yield of various houses.

An analysis of Pegolotti's List gives a good idea of the importance of this particular area of Yorkshire in the general wool trade of the county. 44 percent of the wool from the Yorkshire monasteries came from the North-Eastern houses, illustrating the emphasis given to sheep farming and wool production in this comparatively small area. The supremacy of the Cistercian houses is closely challenged by the Augustinians and together the houses belonging to these Orders supplied most of the wool from the district. Bridlington Priory, in particular, with its valuable chalkland pasture was very prominent. Malton and Kirkham also had much pastureland on the Wolds, whilst that of Rievaulx, Byland, Whitby and Guisborough was mainly in the moorlands. It is interesting to note that the small nunneries of Keldholme, Arden, Rosedale, Wykeham and Yedingham supplied more than 36 sacks between them.

Rievaulx and Byland obtained the highest prices for their wool – $17^1/_2$ marks/sack best. The unsorted wool of the Augustinian houses fetched four marks or more below this. Lincolnshire wool fetched from 19 to 24 marks/sack at this time (Best wool). So the North-East wool may have been of a poorer quality although accessibility and dealings with different firms of merchants might have produced the disparity.[1] It is certain that cartage of the wool was more considerable than in many other places elsewhere.[2]

There was first the difficulty of getting the wool from the monasteries to the main collecting centres. Houses such as Rosedale and Arden, in the heart of the moorland were badly situated from this point of view. Four main routeways were used in the transport of North-East wool. The first has already been mentioned; it was by way of the Coxwold-Gilling gap, near Byland Abbey, to York or Clifton and thence by river to Hull. This route served the Vale of York, the Pennines and the western Vale of Pickering very well. It is certain that almost all Byland and Newburgh wool went this way. The interest shown by the monasteries in the Ouse navigation is enough to indicate its high value as a routeway. Rievaulx, for instance, claimed its right to have ships in the river and St. Mary's, York, frequently made use of the Ouse and Ure.[3] Lead and many other goods came from as far away as Nidderdale by water to York. Indeed the words of Domesday had lost none of their significance – ' the King had in York three ways by land a fourth by water'. The Ouse was tidal eight miles above the city and though always an important highway when roads were so very bad 'by the middle of the fourteenth century ... the access of York to the sea by the Ouse and Humber had become a factor of greater importance to the welfare of the city than the strength of its military fortifications, or the multiplicity of its monastic buildings'.[4]

---

[1] In the late fifteenth century Yorkshire wool is listed lowest in value in the treatise 'The Noumbre of Weyghtes' and almost lowest in another list dated 1454. See Power and Postan, *English Trade in the 15th Century*, p.49.
[2] Tintern Abbey, for example, was fairly near the River Severn – an important trade highway.
[3] 'Abbot of St. Mary's v Edmund, Earl of Cornwall, for preventing free passage of the Abbot's ships and boats laden with victuals and other necessities for his house, in the waters of Ouse and Ure, which right of free passage the Abbot and his predecessors have had from time immemorial', De Banco (1276) in Y.A.S. *Monastic Notes* I, Vol. 17, p.232-233. For transport of lead from Nidderdale to Hull by water, and from Bawtry to London by water see P.R.O. Pipe Roll 207/46.51.
[4] *York Mercers and Merchant Adventurers*, Surtees Society, Vol. 129, Introduction.

The second route serving the wool traders of the North-East was by way of the Malton gap leading from the Vale of Pickering and thence by the River Derwent to join the Ouse four miles below Selby, and so to Hull. Part of this route ran through the thick forest on the west flank of the Wolds, just as part of the Coxwold-York route ran through the Forest of Galtres. The advantage of transport via the Malton-Kirkham gap was twofold: York was only ten miles away by the old Roman road through Galtres Forest and if the preference was to cut out York the water route along the Derwent could be followed. This river was probably navigable as far as Malton, beyond which it became sluggish, shallow and marshy in the Vale of Pickering. But artificial obstruction often proved a menace. For instance, the Abbot of St. Mary's, York, had a weir in the Derwent which blocked the passage of ships and boats up the river, taking merchandise and goods for the East Riding.[1] The merchants had traded this way 'as of old' but because of the blockage much damage was being done in those parts. The river used to be wide enough between the weirs and channels for ships to pass, and was 24 feet deep between the piles of the weirs and the width between them was 50 feet which was sufficient for all ships to pass. The Abbot was compelled to remove the obstructions. But the complaint was typical and common. The Abbot of Fountains was charged with similar obstructions at Wheldrake on several occasions during the thirteenth and fourteenth centuries.[2]

The third route began at Malton also, and went over the Wolds, probably following the line of the Roman road to Wharram-le-Street, then making for Wetwang. From here wool was taken to Wansford situated near the River Hull, and by the same river to Hull. The Pipe Rolls show this to have been a regular route in the fourteenth century.[3] Its advantages were notable: it served the North-East area better than either route previously mentioned; it was near the wool collecting places in the Vale – Malton, Holme, Swinton and best of all it was half the distance of the other routes, even though it did go over the High Wolds. The wool from the eastern Vale of Pickering and the Bridlington area also utilised part of this route, joining it at Wansford. It should be remembered, too, that the Wolds were a very important source of wool. Document after document stresses this.

The fourth route was completely different from the rest. It was entirely by sea. Despite the three ways mentioned, the eastern half of the region, along the coast, was still badly served by routeways. The monks of Whitby were conscious of their isolation and laymen, too, must have regretted the rough country which stretched so far around them. For the Coastal Plateau, especially in the neighbourhood of Whitby and Lythe was an important source of wool.[4] Some traffic did, of course, occur overland. A great deal of the intercourse between granges and manors had this means only.

The Abbot of Whitby made purchases of corn and cattle from as far afield as the Wolds and Barnard Castle, and in 1367 sold 31 sacks of wool to Henry de Scorby 'including carriage to Malton ... three sacks to be taken every year ...'.[5] Malton was over 40 miles

---

[1] At Cottingwith (1351) Y.A.S. *Monastic Notes* II, Vol. 81, p.66.
[2] *ibid.*, I, Vol. 17, p.68.
[3] Especially valuable Pipe Roll in P.R.O. 183/47.
[4] See Waites, B. *Moorland and Valeland Farming in North East Yorkshire*, p.27.
[5] *Calendar of Inquisitions Miscellaneous* (1367), pp.252-253.

south of Whitby with much difficult moorland between, but it was an important wool market. The main direction of the wool trade of the coastal area, however, even from the twelfth century, seems naturally to have been by sea.

Flemish merchants had been coming to Scarborough in the late twelfth century, and exporting wool from nearby areas. Several entries in the early Pipe Rolls show that certain burgesses were turning their hand to the wool trade.[1] But the greatest development of the trade was in the thirteenth and early fourteenth centuries. The Hundred Rolls have several entries showing that the wool trade to Flanders was important, and that several burgesses of Scarborough had become wool dealers, collecting from an unspecified area 'Dicunt quod Simon Grun', Rog. de Morpathe, Willelmus de Stoketon circa 50 saccos lane collegerunt et vendiderunt, mercantoribus transmarinis ... item dicunt quod Petros Nig.' Henr' de Brumpton, Willelmus de Statest' collegerunt circa 33 saccos lane in alio anno ...'.[2] Italian, Flemish and English merchants were exporting wool from Whitby too, at the same time. Thomas de Karlisle, Camelie de Florence and John Grimbald de Amiens took 85 sacks to places across the sea, while the Abbot of Whitby had been selling his wool for the past two years to the Flemings.[3] By 1348 a woolhouse had been established in Whitby and the wool trade seems to have reached its peak. 60 sacks of wool, for example, were sent by sea to Hull in that year and about the same time the abbot and several local men rendered wool to the King.[4] Scarborough had made an attempt to obtain a cocket for wool export in 1320, complaining that much wool was being shipped all along the coast without being customed. This had, in fact, been happening regularly during the last quarter of the thirteenth century. Peter le Blake, Henry le Karle, Simon Gomer, all merchants of Scarborough sold about 70 sacks of wool at nine marks a sack illegally and 'they sent it to the port of Filey', a few miles south of Scarborough. Peter and Henry are mentioned again as sending 34 sacks and the Prior of Bridlington sold as many as 60 sacks illegally and 'led them to the same port'. At Scalby, too, a few miles north of Scarborough, Simon Gomer, William de Morpathe and Roger de Morpathe had sold 60 sacks of wool 'to alien merchants'.[5] Two things are obvious: shipments of wool from all parts of the coast was usual; and the part played by Scarborough merchants in wool collections and export was great.[6] The same names keep reappearing for this period and it appears that collection of wool from the surrounding district was a profitable occupation. Even so Scarborough maintained a large wool export; in a seven months' period 238 sacks of wool were exported from Scarborough, together with 4076 sheep pelts, mostly by merchants from Dordrecht and Skyddam. The sea, then, provided a substantial and direct route for disposal of wool produced in the coastal areas of the North-East. How far it was the outlet for more inland places is difficult to determine.

The River Tees did allow wool merchants coming by sea a deep penetration inland; in

---

[1] E.g. Pipe Roll 25 Hen. II (Pipe Roll Soc. Vol. 28, p.18).
[2] *Rotuli Hundredorum*, ed W. Illingworth and J. Caley (2 vols. 1812-18), Record Commission, Vol. I, pp.131-132.
[3] *Ibid.*, pp.132,134.
[4] P.R.O. E.372/193/53.
[5] *Rot.H.*, Vol. I, 115, 121, 134.
[6] See Waites, B., 'The Medieval Ports and Trade of North East Yorkshire' in *The Mariner's Mirror*, Vol. 63, No. 2, May 1977, pp.137-149.

the thirteenth century as far as Yarm, 17 miles up the river. This allowed access to the wool of the Cleveland area which was, it appears, in demand especially in the late thirteenth century. The activity of local wool collectors and foreign merchants in this area was great and often well organised on a large scale. Thus William Fleye 'dwelling in Berewyk' (Birdforth wapentake) was said to have collected as much as 1000 sacks of wool and exported them overseas through his agents, receiving 100/- for each sack.[1] Another reference in the Hundred Rolls under Northallerton says that he exported another 80 sacks of wool to foreign parts.[2] There are several similar entries which suggest that wool collection was usual, although perhaps not on the same scale as practised by William Fleye. Thus, Roger de Berewyk was said to have 'carried 16 sacks across the sea'; William Irenpurs of Northallerton 5 sacks.[3] It is likely, but not stated, that such exports went from Yarm. The south part of the Vale of York, however, sent some of its wool via Hull, using the Ouse navigation no doubt for this long journey. Thus Henry de Kirkham was reported to have taken 6 sacks of wool at Thirsk, from John de Kepwick and 'the wool was sold at Hull to Pontio de la More'.[4]

Later, in the middle of the fourteenth century Newcastle merchants began to take an active part in the wool trade of the area. The Assize Rolls contain several examples of illegal wool purchases (1361-64) by them.[5] The merchants of Newcastle were allowed to export wool from this area and Northallerton direct to the Netherlands without staple – an advantage which they frequently abused. Complaints were regular from the Staplers that Newcastle men exported the finer wools, too, from 'Yorkeswold' and further afield.[6] Though the Tees had long been an artery of trade its relative status compared to the other routes cannot have been great, especially in the fourteenth century when Yarm began to decline as a port.

The influence of the wool trade upon the economic development of the North-East was, then, well marked. The character of this influence reaffirms several recurring themes in the region's development so that a study of the wool trade has an extrinsic as well as an intrinsic value. The significance of the Vale of Pickering as the most prosperous, active and well situated part of the North-East is re-emphasised. Besides being near to the sources of wool production in the Moors and Wolds, it was most conveniently positioned for the disposal of that wool both to Italian and to English merchants. The Cleveland and Coastal areas were more negative from this point of view. The coincidence between the Vale and the sites of monastic houses and lands confirmed the importance of the Vale. For the monastic share in the wool trade, though by no means exclusive, was preponderant. It was they more than anyone else who stimulated the activities of wool merchants and wool growers in the area; in doing so they made an unconscious but significant contribution to the development of regionalism and specialisation in the North-East.

---

[1] *Rot.H.*, Vol. I, p.118.
[2] *Ibid.*, p.123.
[3] *Ibid.*, John de Bolmere and his son acknowledged to several Italian merchants in 1286 that they would supply 30 sacks of 'best wool of their own stock and from the vicinity of Thirsk and Ripon by collection'. P.R.O. E.159/60/19.
[4] *Ibid.*, p.122.
[5] They participated in general trade as well: in 1360 John Graper of Newcastle-on-Tyne came into the Tees with 100 qts. of wheat for sale. *C.I. Misc.* (1348-1377), p.146.
[6] Power and Postan, *op. cit.*, p.43.

CONCLUSION

The Contribution of the Monasteries to the Development of the North-East

It is evident from the preceding discussion that the influence of the monasteries on the medieval development of the North-East was not only very great but very widespread. In every sphere of activity considered the monasteries predominated, sometimes they were initiators, as in the settlement of moorland and marshland; sometimes they consolidated and organised what they found, as they did in the arable farming of the Valelands – emphasising in particular the importance of certain soils such as those along the periphery of the Vale of Pickering. Their settlement and agriculture were carefully adapted to the environment in which they found themselves. In fact the capacity of the monastic houses in this respect was largely responsible for their success and influence.

Their contribution has been dealt with in detail in this study. In the broadest terms, it fell into two parts: the contribution made to the development of the "physical" landscape, and the "economic" landscape. The former consisted mainly of clearance of woodland, drainage and utilisation of marshland, and settlement – all elements which can be traced in the make-up of the present-day landscape. The River Rye, for instance, diverted by the monks of Rievaulx in the 12th century, flows to-day along the course they made for it; the canals and ditches which they constructed around their abbey are clearly visible still;[1] Bilsdale, Farndale and Rosedale, once impenetrable woodland were cleared largely by the efforts of the monasteries; their settlement and exploitation of Pickering Marshes laid the basis for subsequent agricultural activities, in what had been a desolate, uninhabited waste in the 11th century.

But it is in the recovery of the landscape after the eleventh century devastations that their contribution is most marked. The North-East, except for a few areas such as the eastern half of the Vale of Pickering had been left a desert in 1069. Even by the end of the century it had not recovered. The monasteries re-settled the once prosperous regions – the Vales of Cleveland, York and Pickering. Here they were consolidating and re-emphasising a pattern which the Domesday Survey shows, however imperfectly, had begun to emerge. The association between these regions of greatest prosperity and concentrations of monastic settlements remained a permanent feature in the medieval history of the North-East. The footing which the monasteries were able to establish after the devastation was the basis for the great influence which they subsequently held.

Though the monasteries were primarily responsible for the recovery of settled areas they did much to extend these. They moved into previously uninhabited districts such as Pickering Marshes and made settlements on the moors or in the dales extending not only the areas of settlement but also the areas of cultivation. The grange was their unique instrument for this; and irrespective of the Order involved it was invariably the unit of

---

[1] See J. Weatherill op. cit. Y.A.J. (1954) Part 151. H. Rye in A.J. (1900) Vol. 57.

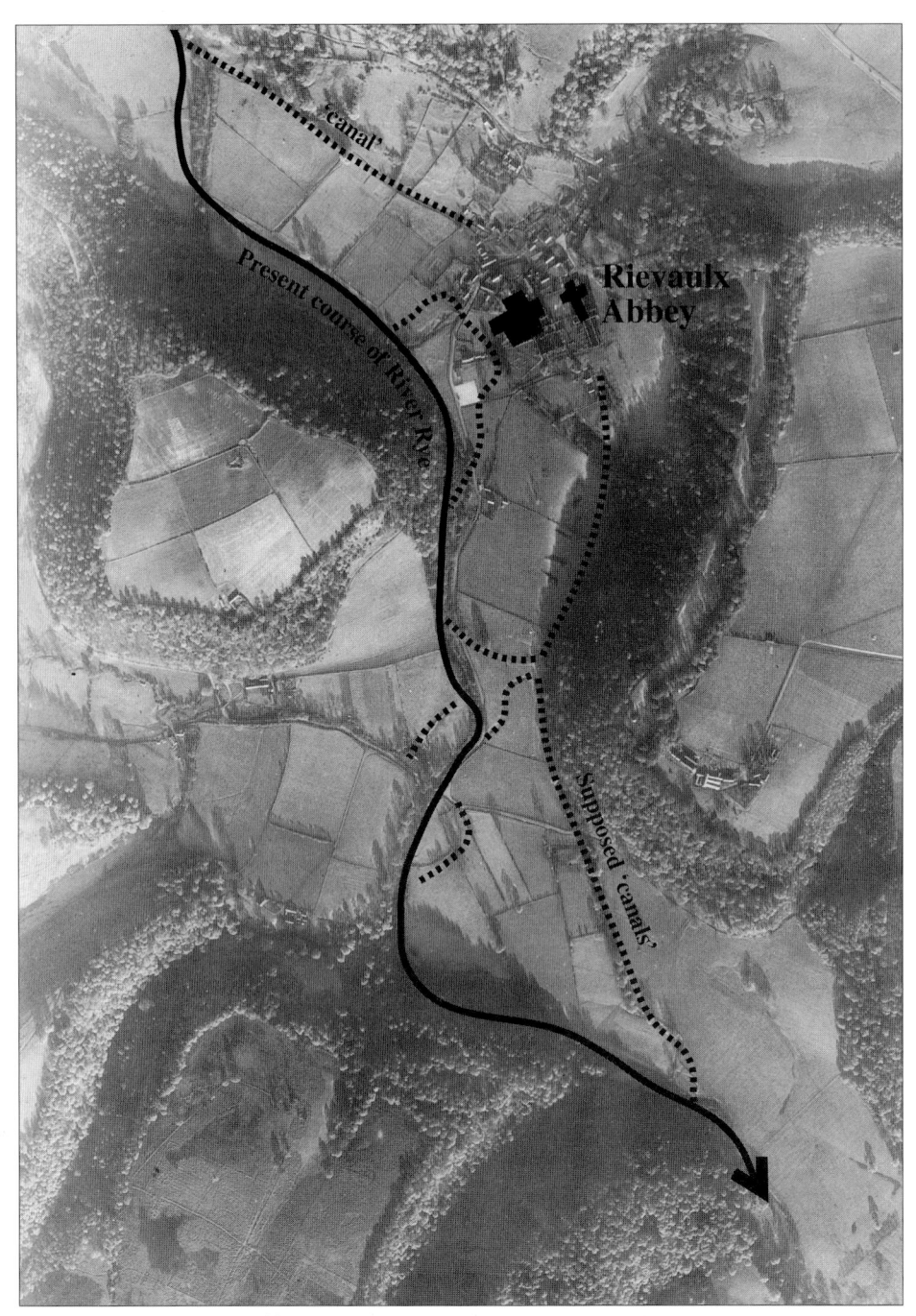

The 'Canals' of Rievaulx Abbey

"exploitation". It was supremely well equipped for the development of a region like the North-East. Some form of dispersed settlement was clearly the best way of doing this and the grange was the first experiment in this type of settlement in the North-East. It was an adaptable instrument of policy and "exploitation": for it could be an administrative, pastoral, arable or industrial unit depending on the area in which it was situated. The success of this type of settlement can be adequately judged by the permanence of its influence. The North-East is still to-day mainly an area of dispersed settlements – many of these farmhouses occupy the exact sites on which the monks built their granges long ago and the farmer still tills the land around, which the monks broke up and ploughed more than seven hundred years before.

By 1301 the North-East had fully developed the trends which became more emphasised in later centuries. The part of laymen in this becomes clearer. Interest in iron mining drew settlers into the dales and clearance quickened in pace, especially in Eskdale. Cattle and sheep farming also led laymen into the moors. Sometimes when sheep farming was organised on a grand scale as on the Duchy of Lancaster estate this process became more emphatic. So, the monasteries and laymen combined to develop the area. But, it should be noted that in industrial activities as well as in agricultural it was the monasteries that led the way – the laymen followed. Guisborough Priory's iron mining in Eskdale and salt working in Teesmouth, for example, were so well and carefully organised that laymen could hardly rise to the same scale in their exploitation. It was natural that the monasteries should be to the forefront of most activities: they were undying corporations with a continuity in policy and administration; they had extensive privileges in markets and ports; they were often exempt tithes, and their property was protected from any kind of violation or intrusion, they had power, organisation and resources which enabled them to acquire monopolistic positions and to act on a large scale. This was particularly evident in their purchase and acquisition of lands. Even large lay landowners like the Duchy of Lancaster were never able to obtain the power and freedom of the monasteries.

The contributions to the "economic" landscape were no less striking: the monasteries had been chiefly responsible for inducing foreign merchants to come into the North-East. Their active part in promoting the wool trade, in particular, encouraged the development of ports, markets and routeways. This, of course, ultimately derived from the major contribution of the monasteries: their specialisation in sheep farming. Here again is an instance of close adaptation. The monks were quick to see the North-East as a splendid area for sheep farming. By doing so they gave the economy of the area a particular bias which persisted through succeeding centuries. Similarly, specialisation in sheep farming and barley cultivation on the Wolds seems to have been encouraged by the monastic farmers in this area. How far the monasteries stimulated laymen to follow similar pursuits is hard to say. Their influence in this direction seems to have been great. Indeed, an outstanding feature of this study is the harmony between monks and laymen in the utilisation of the area.

A more subtle, but permanent contribution of the monasteries follows from their specialisation in certain activities. This was that they encouraged the development of sub-regions within the North-East. Even in 1086 it was evident that the physical divisions of the area were acquiring distinctive characteristics – some were more prosperous than others; some had been more severely wasted; some were more intensively settled; some were more predominantly arable than pastoral. In other words, each was developing its particular ethos. The monasteries encouraged this, without doubt, unconsciously. The concentration of their settlements and their farming activities in the Vales of Cleveland, York and Pickering emphasised the predominance of these regions in the North-East. The trend which was established or re-established after 1086, largely by the monasteries, persisted afterwards and is equally evident today as it was shown to be in 1292, 1318, 1342 and 1535. Though the landscape must inevitably change through the process of time there remain these stable elements in the development of regions which become crystallised.

The monasteries were but an episode in the history of the North-East; a long episode nevertheless, which lasted for more than four hundred years and occurred at a most formative period in the development of the area. No study of the medieval development of the North-East can ignore the influence of the monasteries: it was a factor of decisive significance. Indeed, it is largely through the window which monastic evidence throws open that such development becomes clearly visible.

BIBLIOGRAPHY

I MANUSCRIPT SOURCES

(1) **BRITISH LIBRARY**
Add. MS. 4715 (Whitby Chartulary)
Add. MS. 35285 fo. 168-173 (Missal of Guisborough Priory)
Cotton MS. Claudius D XI (Malton Chartulary)
Cotton MS. Julius D I (Rievaulx Chartulary)
Cotton MS. Julius F VI 185 fo. 455 (A description of salt working in Cleveland. XVI century)
Cotton MS. Nero D III (Chartulary of St Leonards Hospital, York)
Egerton MS. 2823 (Byland Chartulary)
Harl MS. 236 (a chartulary of St Mary's, York)

(2) **PUBLIC RECORD OFFICE**
EXCHEQUER
E 101 King's Remembrancer Accounts
    6/32, 38; 12/8; 597/1-19, 26, 27, 31, 36.   Expenses entailed in purchase and carriage of corn, etc. in Yorkshire for the King. (late 13th and 14th centuries)
E 122 King's Remembrancer Customs Accounts   For Scarborough, Whitby, Ravenser, Hull
    55/16, 23; 56/3, 7, 10, 14; 57/1; 134/2, 3, 4   (early 14th century)
E 142 Ancient Extents
    18/10   Inventory of the possessions of the Knights Templar at Westerdale, Foulbridge, Allerton, Wyddale (1307)
    17   Possessions elsewhere e.g. Hurst, Potterhowe, North Deighton, Wetherby, (used for comparative purposes, same date).
E 159 King's Remembrancer Memoranda Rolls
    Nos 50-70   For details of wool trade (1275-1297)
E 163 Queen's Remembrancer Exchequer Miscellania
    2/1   Arrest of ships and goods at Newcastle, Scarborough and Ravenser (1294-1296)
E 164 Queen's Remembrancer Miscellaneous Books
    Vol 88.   Duchy of Lancaster Coucher Book
E 178 Special Commissions
    2705   Deposition as to felling timber in Danby Forest for smelting iron (1588)
E 179 Subsidy Rolls, etc.
    67/9   New Tax on Benefices (1318)
    211/16-18   Sales and Valuations of the Ninth (1342)
    211/19   Inquisition of the Ninth (1342)
    211/27   Distribution of money from felons' goods among the "villas pauperas" of the North Riding (1357)
    211/37   Fraud in the collection of the Ninth
E 315 Augmentation Office, Miscellaneous Books.
    401   Survey of Guisborough and Rievaulx at the Dissolution
E 359 Enrolled Accounts
    8BC   Poll Tax (1377)
    14/   collection of 1322 for the N.R. Concessions made to villages devastated by the Scots.
E 368 Lord Treasurer's Remembrancer Memoranda Rolls
    No's 50-61, 69, 70, 119, 129, 139.   Details of wool trade: Inquisition into possessions of T. de Westhorpe etc. (late 13th and 14th century).
E 373 Pipe Rolls
    No's 56/19 (1210-11)   Compotus Abbatie de Whitebi (omitted in printed version)
    183 (1337-38); 188 (1342-43);
    193 (1347-48); 207 (1361-62)   [but many more consulted]

CHANCERY
C 47   Miscellania
       Bundle 86 No. 12 Liberties of the Arch. of York in the River Hull
C 66   Patent Rolls
       For 1351 part III m. 19
C 134 Inquisition post mortem Series I (Edward II)
       82 Settrington (extent)
C 135 Inquisition post mortem Series I (Edward III)
       5   Thirsk (1327)
       44 Danby, Glasedale, Leaholm, etc. (1335-36)
       65 Sherburn, Whorlton (1341-42)
       97 Kirby Moorside, Middleton (1349-50)

MINISTERS ACCOUNTS
S.C.6 /835/2   Westerdale (c. 1318)
S.C.6/Hen. VIII/4550   Byland Dissolution Accounts (31-32 Hen. VIII)
S.C.6/Hen. VIII/4618   Malton Dissolution Accounts (32 Hen. VIII)
S.C.6/Hen. VIII/4636   Guisborough Dissolution Accounts (32 Hen. VIII)
S.C.6/Hen. VIII/   Bridlington Dissolution Accounts.

MINISTERS ACCOUNTS
D.L. 29/490/7934-7956   Reeves and Bailiffs Accounts for Pickering etc. (late 14th and 15th centuries)
D.L. 29/500   Receivers Accounts for Pickering etc. (15th century)
D.L. 29/728/11974,   and subsequent membranes relating to Pickering, and the North Parts of
     11978   the Duchy. Auditors Accounts, Valors (late 14th and 15th centuries).

RENTALS AND SURVEYS
S.C. 12/17/28   Valor of the Manor of Kirby Misperton (mid. 16th century)

(3) *DIOCESAN REGISTRY, YORK*
R VII E   Cause Papers XIV   century
R VII F   Cause Papers XV   century
R VII G   Cause Papers XVI   century
R VII H   Cause Papers XVII century
R VII H   2096 Grange account, Speeton (1349)
RH 60 Grange account, Burton Fleming (1355-56)
RH 69 Grange account, Filey (?) (1329-30)
R. Askwith 16/20 Tithe Cause at Weaverthorpe (1544)

II PRINTED SOURCES

(1) *SURTEES SOCIETY* (all published in Durham)
Account Rolls of the Abbey of Durham ed. Canon Fowler XCIX, C, CIII (1898-1901)
Cartularium Prioratus de Gyseburne ed. W. Brown LXXXVI (1889), LXXXIX (1894).
Cartularium Abbathiae de Rievalle ed. J. C. Atkinson LXXXIII (1889)
Cartularium Abbathiae de Whiteby ed. J. C. Atkinson LXIX (1879), LXII (1881).
Halmota Prioratus Dunelmensis (1296-1384) ed. J. Booth LXXXII (1889)
Kirkby's Inquest and the Nomina Villarum for Yorkshire ed. R. H. Skaife XLIX (1867)
Memorials of Fountains Abbey III ed. J. T. Fowler CXXX (1918)
Register of Henry of Newark, Lord Archbishop of York (1296-1299) ed. CXXVIII (1917)
Register of William Greenfield, Lord Archbishop of York (1306-1315), III, V, ed. W. Brown
    & A. H. Thompson, CLI (1936) CLIII (1940)
Testamenta Eboracensia VI ed. J. W. Clay CVI (1902)
The York Mercers and Merchant Adventurers (1356-1917) ed. M. Sellers CXXIX (1918)

(2) *YORKSHIRE ARCHAEOLOGICAL SOCIETY RECORD SERIES.*
Early Yorkshire Charters ed. W. Farrer (3 Vols. Edinburgh 1914-15)
Early Yorkshire Charters ed. C. T. Clay (7 Vols. Wakefield, 1936-55)
Feet of Fines for the County of York (1218-1272) ed. J. Parker LXII (1921), LXVII (1925), LXXXII (1932)
Notes on the Religious and Secular Houses of Yorkshire ed. W. Baildon XVII (1895), LXXXI (1931)
Select Sixteenth Century Causes in Tithe ed. J. S. Purvis CXIV (1949)
Yorkshire Deeds ed. W. Brown, C. T. Clay, M. Hebditch, J. S. Price (10 vols. (1909-1955)
Yorkshire Inquisitions I–IV (Reigns of Hen. III & Ed. I) ed. W. Brown (1892-1906)
Yorkshire Lay Subsidy (1297) ed. W. Brown XVI (1894)
Yorkshire Lay Subsidy (1301) ed. W. Brown XXI (1897)
Yorkshire Monasteries: Suppression Papers ed. J. W. Clay XLVIII (1912)
Yorkshire Sessions of the Peace (1361-64) ed. B. H. Putnam (1939)

(3) *ROLLS SERIES* (published in London)
Chronica de Melsa ed. E. A. Bond 43 (3 vols, 1866-68)
Bracton, H de, *De Legibus Angliae* ed. T. Twiss 70 (Vol III, 1880)
Durham, Symeon of, *Historia Regum* ed. T. Arnold, 75 (2 vols. 1882)
Giraldus Cambrensis ed. J. S. Brewer. 21 (8 vols. 1861-91)
Letters from the Northern Registers ed. J. Raine. 61 (1873)
Malmesbury, William of, *De Gestis Regum Anglorum* ed. W. Stubbs. 90. (2 vols. 1887-89)
Newburgh, William of, *Historia Rerum Anglicarum* ed. R. Howlett. 82 (2 vols. 1884-85)
Registrum Epp. J. Peckham Arch. Cant. ed. C. T. Martin. 77 (3 vols. 1882-86)

(4) *RECORD COMMISSION*
Liber Censualis vocati Domesday Book ed. A. Farley. Vol. I (London 1783)
Nonarum Inquisitiones (London 1807)
Rotuli Hundredorum ed. W. Illingworth and J. Caley (2 vols. 1812-18)
Taxatio Ecclesiastica Angliae et Walliae auctoritate P. Nicholai IV. (London 1802)
Valor Ecclesiasticus Vol. V (London 1825)

(5) *VARIOUS*
Bridlington Chartulary, Abstract of the, ed. W. T. Lancaster (1915)
Calendar of Charter Rolls
Calendar of Close Rolls
Calendar of Inquisitions Miscellaneous (1219-1377)
Calendar of Inquisitions Post Mortem
Calendar of Papal Registers: Papal Letters II (1305-1342)
Calendar of Patent Rolls
Chapters of the Augustinian Canons ed. H. E. Salter (Cant. and York Soc. 29 London 1922)
Chapters of the English Black Monks (1215-1540) ed. W. A. Pantin (Camden Series 3 vols. London 1931-37)
Cistercian Statutes ed. J. T. Fowler (Y.A.J. vols 9–11 1886-91)
Description of Documents Contained in the White Vellum Book of Scarborough Corporation (Scarborough 1914)
Facsimiles of Early Charters from Northamptonshire Collections ed. F. M. Stenton (1930)
Honour and Forest of Pickering ed. R. B. Turton (4 vols. N.R.R.S. new series London 1894-96)
Leland, John, The Itinerary of, ed. L. T. Smith (5 vols. London 1907)
Map, Walter, *De Nugis Curialium* in Cymmrodorion R.S. No. IX (1923)
Monasticon Anglicanum by W. Dugdale ed J. Caley. H. Ellis, B. Bandinel (6 vols. London 1817-30).
Monasticon Eboracense ed. J. Burton (York, 1758)
Publications of the Pipe Roll Society (Various references)
Select Cases on the Law Merchant II (1239-1633) ed. H. Hall 46. (Selden Soc. London 1930)
Vita Ailredi by W. Daniel ed M. Powicke (Nelsons Mediaeval Classics, London, 1950)
Vitalis, Oderic, *Historia Ecclesiastica II* (Soc. de l'histore de France, Paris 1840)

III SECONDARY AUTHORITIES

Addy, S. O.	*Church and Manor: a study in English Economic History* (London, 1913)
Atkinson, J. C.	*History of Cleveland* (1874)
	"Existing traces of Mediaeval Iron Working in Cleveland" *Y.A.J.* VIII (1884)
	Forty Years in a Moorland Parish (London 1891)
	Memorials of Old Whitby (London 1894)
Ballard, A and Tait, J	*British Borough Charters (1216-1307)* (Cambridge 1923)
Best, Henry	*Rural Economy in Yorkshire in 1641, being the farming and account books of Henry Best.* (Surtees Soc. XXXIII Durham 1857)
Best, S. E. J.	*East Yorkshire: a Study in Agricultural Geography* (London 1930)
Bishop, T. A. M.	"Monastic Demesnes and the Statute of Mortmain"
	"Distribution of Manorial Demesne in the Vale of Yorkshire" *E.H.R.* XLIX (1934)
	"Assarting and the Growth of the Open Fields" *Ec.H.R.* VI (1935)
	"Monastic Granges in Yorkshire" *E.H.R.* LI (1936)
Blache, V de la.	*Principles of Human Geography.* (Trans. London 1950)
Bloch, M. L. B.	*The Historians Craft* (Trans. Manchester, 1954)
Cambridge Economic History	Vol. 1 ed. J. H. Clapham and E. Power (Cambridge 1941)
Cartwright, J. J.	*Chapters in the History of Yorkshire* (Wakefield 1872)
Charlton, L.	*The History of Whitby and Whitby Abbey* (York, 1779)
Colvin, H. M.	*The White Canons in England* (Oxford, 1951)
Communications to the Board of Agriculture	(3 vols. London 1797)
Coulton, G. G.	*Five Centuries of Religion* (4 vols. Cambridge 1923-50)
Cunningham, W.	*The Growth of English Industry and Commerce* I (5th ed. Cambridge, 1910)
Darby, H. C.	*Historical Geography of England Before 1800* (Cambridge, 1936)
	The Mediaeval Fenland (Cambridge 1940)
	The Draining of the Fens (2nd ed. Cambridge 1956)
	Domesday Geography of Eastern England (Cambridge 1952)
and Terret, I.	*Domesday Geography of Midland England* (Cambridge 1954)
Davies, J. Conway	"Shipping and Trade in Newcastle upon Tyne (1294-96)" in *Arch, Aeliana* 31. 4 series (1953)
Denholm-Young, N.	*Seignorial Administration in England* (Oxford Historical Series, Oxford 1937)
Dickinson, R. E.	*Germany: a general and regional geography* (London 1953)
Edwards, J. G.	"Edward I's castle-building in Wales" *Proc. British Academy* Vol. 32
Edwards, W.	*The Early History of the North Riding* (London 1924).
Ekwall, E.	*Oxford Dictionary of English Place Names* (3rd ed. Oxford 1947)
	English River Names (Oxford, 1928)
Elgee, F.	*Early Man in North-East Yorkshire* (Gloucester 1930)
Fox, Sir Cyril.	*The Personality of Britain* (4th ed. Cardiff 1952)
Fox-Strangeways, C.	*Water Supply of the East Riding of Yorkshire* (London 1906)
Fransson, G.	*Middle English Surnames of Occupation 1100-1350* (Lund 1935)
Freeman, E. A.	*The Norman Conquest* (Oxford 1867-79)
Gaskin, R. T.	*The Old Seaport of Whitby* (Whitby 1909)
Graham, R.	*English Ecclesiastical Studies* (S.P.C.K. London 1929)
Gras, N. S. B.	*The Evolution of the English Corn Market* (2nd ed. Cambridge, Mass. 1926)
Hinderwell, T.	*History of Scarborough* (1798)
Hoskins, W. G.	*The Making of the English Landscape* (London 1955)
Huizinga, J.	*The Waning of the Middle Ages* (London 1948)
Jeffrey, R. W.	*Thornton le Dale* (Wakefield 1931)
Kendal, P. F.	"A System of Glacier Lakes in the Cleveland Hills" *(Q.J. Geological Soc.* LVIII part 3 1902)
Life of Marmaduke Rawdon of York	(Camden Series 85)
Lunt, W. E.	*The Valuation of Norwich* (Oxford 1926)

Knowles, D.	*The Monastic Order in England* (Cambridge 1940)
	The Religious Orders in England (2 vols. Cambridge 1948, 1955)
and Haddock, R. N.	*Mediaeval Religious Houses of England and Wales* (Cambridge 1953)
and St Joseph, J.K.S.	*Monastic Sites from the Air* (Cambridge 1952)
Marshall, W.	*The Rural Economy of Yorkshire* (2 vols. London 1788)
	Agricultural Survey of the East Riding of Yorkshire (1812)
McCutcheon, K. L.	*Yorkshire Fairs and Markets* (Thoresby Soc. XXXIX Leeds 1949)
Miller, E.	*The Abbey and Bishopric of Ely* (Cambridge 1951)
New Oxford English Dictionary on Historical Principles	(10 vols. Oxford 1888-1928)
Ord, J. W.	*History of Cleveland* (London 1846)
Page, F. M.	*The Estates of Crowland Abbey* (Cambridge 1934)
Postan, M. M.	"The Chronology of Labour Services" in *T.R.H.S.* 4 series XX (1937)
	"Some Economic Evidence of Declining Population in the Later Middle Ages" in *Ec H.R.* 2 series II (1950)
Power, E.	*The Wool Trade in English Mediaeval History* (London 1941)
Power, E. and Postan, M.M.	*Studies in English Trade in the Fifteenth Century* (London 1933)
Purvis, J. S.	*The Archives of the York Diocesan Registry* (St Anthony's Hall publication No 2. London 1952)
Rodgers, J. E. Thorold.	*A History of Agriculture and Prices in England* I. II (Oxford 1866)
Rowntree, A.	*The History of Scarborough* (London 1931)
Rye, H. A.	"Rievaulx Abbey: its Canals and Building Stones" in *A.J.* LVII (1900)
Savine, A.	*The English Monasteries on the Eve of the Dissolution* (Oxford 1909)
Sewell, J. T.	"Some Mediaeval Roads Crossing the Moors" in *The Whitby Lit. and Phil. Soc. Report* for 1922
Slater, G.	*The English Peasantry and the Enclosure of the Common Fields* (London 1907)
Smith, A. H.	*Place Names of the North Riding of Yorkshire* (E.P.N.S. V Cambridge 1928)
	Place Names of the East Riding and York (E.P.N.S. XIV Cambridge, 1937)
Smith, R. A. L.	*Canterbury Cathedral Priory: a study in monastic administration* (Cambridge 1943)
	Collected Papers (London 1947)
Somerville, R.	*History of the Duchy of Lancaster* I 1265-1603 (London 1953)
Stamp, L. D.	*Land Utilisation Survey of Britain: Yorkshire, East Riding* London, 1942)
Stevenson, W. H.	"A Contemporary Description of the Domesday Survey" *E.H.R.* XXII (1907)
Thomson, A. H.	*Bolton Priory* (Thoresby Soc. XXX Leeds 1928)
	"The Pestilences of the Fourteenth Century in the Diocese of York" in *A.J.* LXXI (1914)
Tuke, J.	*General View of the Agriculture of the North Riding of Yorkshire* (London 1794)
Tuplin, G. H.	*Economic History of Rossendale* (Chetham Soc. LXXXVI Aberdeen 1927)
Victoria County Histories:	*Durham* II (1907)
	Essex I (1903)
	Yorkshire: The County of York II (1912), III (1913)
	The North Riding I, II (1914, 1923)
Weatherill, J.	"Rievaulx Abbey: the stone used in its building" *Y.A.J.* part 151 (1954)
Whitwell, R. J.	"The English Monasteries and the Wool Trade" in *Vierteljahrschrift für sozial und Wirtschaftsgeschichte* II, i (1904)
Willard, J. E.	"Taxes upon Movables in the Reign of Edward I" in *E.H.R.* XXVIII, XXIX, XXX (1913-15)
Wilson, V.	*British Regional Geology: East Yorkshire and Lincolnshire* (London 1948)
Wooldridge, S. W.	*Land Utilisation Survey of Britain: Yorkshire, North Riding* (London 1945)
Yates, E. M.	"Mediaeval Assessments in N.W. Sussex" in *Trans. Inst. of British Geographers* (1954)
Young, A.	*A Six Months Tour Through the North of England* (1770)
Young, G.	*History of Whitby* (1817)

IV ADDITIONAL SECONDARY SOURCES

Beresford, M. and Hurst, J. G. — *Deserted Medieval Villages,* Lutterworth Press 1971

Cantor, L. M. (ed) — *The English Medieval Landscape,* Croom Helm 1982

Davis, G. R. C. — *Medieval Chartularies of Great Britain: a short catalogue* (Hoskin, P Amendments & Additions in *Monastic Research Bulletin* 2, 1996, pp.1-12)

Donkin, R. A. — 'The disposal of Cistercian wool in England and Wales in the 12th and 13th centuries', *Citeaux in de Nederlanden,* vol 8, 1957

'The marshland holdings of the English Cistercians before c1350', *ibid* vol 9, 1958

'The Cistercian settlement and the English Royal Forests', *ibid* vol II, 1960

'The Cistercian grange in England in the 12th and 13th centuries with special reference to Yorkshire', *Studia Monastica,* vol 6, fasc I, 1964, pp 95-144

'The English Cistercians and Assarting c1128- c1350', *Analecta sacri ordinis Cisterciensis,* Ann 20, fasc 1-2, 1964

'The Cistercians: Studies in the Geography of Medieval England and Wales, Toronto, 1978.

Edwards, J. F. and Hindle, B.P. — 'The Transportation System of Medieval England & Wales', *Journal of Historical Geography,* vol 17, 1991, pp 123-134

Hodgson, R. I. — 'Medieval colonization in Northern Ryedale, Yorkshire' *Geographical Journal,* vol 135, part I, March 1969, pp.44-54.

Hoskins, W. G. — *The Making of the English Landscape,* Hodder & Stoughton, new ed 1977

Masschaele, James — 'Medieval Markets Reconsidered', *Journal of Historical Geography,* vol 20, 1994, pp.231-271

Platt, Colin — *The Monastic Grange in Medieval England: a reassessment,* London, 1969

Rackham, Oliver — *The History of the Countryside,* Dent, 1980

Thirsk, Joan (ed) — *The Agrarian History of England & Wales,* vol II, 1042-1350, ed H. E. Hallam, CUP 1988 and vol III, 1348-1500 ed Edward Miller, CUP 1991

INDEX

This index is very selective. It was not possible to include the very large number of placenames and personal names. Instead, prominence has been given to those items which illustrate the main themes of the book.

Accounts, Dissolution Ministers'   40n, 58, 89, 95n, 98n, 114, 142, 152
Agricultural Prosperity, & Medieval Assessments   72-85
Archiferrarius, of Danby Forest   150
Arden, nunnery of   29, 140, 186, 191, 192, 193
Assessments,   Valor of Pope Nicholas (1292)   73-77
              Reassessment of 1318   77-79
              The Nonarum Inquisitiones   79-83
Assize Rolls,   134, 166, 181, 188, 196
Atkinson, Canon JC,   1, 16n, 31n, 150n

Bardney, Abbot of   110
Basedale (Baysdale), priory of   29
Bernard St,   27
Beverley, collecting centre   109
Bilsdale,   Rievaulx lands in   39, 43, 46, 61, 63
         Granges   51, 52
         Byland & Rievaulx   63
         Cotes   142
         Ironworking   152
Bishop, TAM   2, 43, 45, 54, 55n, 57
Bridlington, priory of   1, 29, 34, 78, 140, 167n
         Grange accounts   105-108, 155, 166n, 180
         Grant of fair   176-177
         Lands   40
         Quarrying   159
         Sheep pasture   138
         Size of flocks   139
         Transhumance   143
         Vaccary   141
         Wool trade   190, 193
Brus, Peter de   ironworking dispute   148, 150, 151, 158
Brus, Peter de II   92, 149
Byland, abbey of   1, 2, 18, 29, 34, 63, 78, 121, 139, 140, 144, 180
         Collection of wool   186, 191, 193
         Granges   46, 116, 178, 179
         Ironworking   152
         Lands   40
         'redigere in grangiam'   64
         Salt working   157
         Staffing   47

Cambrensis, Giraldus   37n, 47
Canals, of Rievaulx   197-198
Citeaux   1, 175

Clairvaux   1, 144
Cleveland,   Agricultural Prosperity   76, 81, 82, 84, 160
                      Arable farming   111-116
                      Guisborough Priory lands in   35-36, 41, 56
                      Sheep farming   122
                      Whitby Abbey lands in   35, 41
Clifton, collecting centre for wool   191, 193
Conqueror, William the   ix, 19, 25
Corn, shipments of   108-110
Customs Accounts   169-172

Danby,   church   37
                      cultivation in   87, 88
                      Forest   148, 149
                      Sheep   120
Daniel, Walter   47, 144n, 145n
Darby, Professor HC   ix, x, 14n, 22n, 23n, 117n, 147
Derwent, river navigation   53, 96, 99, 194
Domesday   Landscape   13-26
                      Meadowland   22-23
                      Recovery & re-settlement   26
                      Settlement   15-18
                      Survey   2, 13, 72, 102, 147
                      Uninhabited vills   18-20
                      Waste   24-25
                      Woodland   20-22
Durham, abbey of Account Rolls   156-157
Durham, Dean of   158
Durham, Simeon of   13

Ecclesiasticus, the Valor   2, 82-83, 93, 108, 111, 114n, 116, 119, 122
Eskdale,   11th century settlement   16
                      Guisborough Priory lands in   36, 63, 86
                      Ironworking   148, 150, 151, 160
                      Pastoral farming   141
                      Transhumance   143
                      Whitby Abbey lands in   32, 93

Farming, arable   86-116
                      Malton Priory   104
                      Coastal Plateau   90-96
                      Moorlands   86-90
                      Vale of Pickering   96-102
                      Vale of York & Cleveland   111-116
                      Yorkshire Wolds   102-111
Farming, pastoral   117-145
                      on Duchy of Lancaster Estates   123-132
                      on Monastic Estates   136-145
Fisheries, Tees   38
Fortibus, de (Isabella de) estates   132, 185, 192
Foundation grants   30, 53, 54

INDEX

Fountains, abbey of 41, 78, 116, 142, 157, 194
Fox-Strangeways, C 8n

Glaisdale, Guisborough Priory lands in 37, 43, 46, 53, 61, 86
  Ironworking 148, 150, 151, 160
  Vaccaries 141
Grange, the Monastic 45-66
  Common pasture rights 59-60
  Consolidation of lands 55-58
  Definition 45
  Distribution 49-53
  Establishment of 53-61
  In Bilsdale 51-52
  Land attached to 69
  Malton granges 67
  On limestone slopes 50-51
  Ownership of manor 58-59
  Possession of church 55, 68
  Salt industry and 66
  Selection of sites 60-61
Green, JR 5
Grosmont, priory of 29
Guisborough, priory of 1, 2, 28, 30, 31, 36, 63, 86, 137, 181
  Consolidation of lands 56-57, 58
  Granges 46, 53, 54, 68, 69, 94-95, 114-116, 138, 143, 178, 179
  Hired workers 47
  Ironworking 61, 148-150, 199
  Lands 35-37, 41, 94-95
  Prior's ships 174
  Rent Roll 115, 143
  Salt working 157, 158, 199
  Size of flocks 138-139
  Transhumance 143
  Types of settlement 43
  Vaccaries & cotes 141
  Wool collection 188, 193
Gypsey Race, 103

Hackness, Whitby Abbey lands in 33, 46, 47, 117
  grange 48
  smelting 155-156
  Vaccaries & cotes 141
Handale, priory of 29, 95
Harrying of the North (1069), ix, 13-14, 19, 25, 145, 197
Hoskins, WG 72
Hospital, Flixton 101
Houses, Religious 29
Hull, river navigation of 109, 188, 191, 194

Industries, medieval 61, 147-160; Other 158-160
Industry, the salt 156-158; Methods 157

Inquest, Kirkby's (c1284)   61, 65
Inquisitiones,   The Nonarum (1342)   79-83, 91, 97, 113, 117, 118n, 119n, 120, 122
　　　　　　　　Purpose   79-81
　　　　　　　　Agricultural prosperity in 1341   81-82
　　　　　　　　Arranged regionally   85
Ironworking,   147-156, 61, 86
　　　　　　　　Brus, Peter de   148-150
　　　　　　　　Forges & ironworking   148-149
　　　　　　　　In Glaisdale   151-152
　　　　　　　　Laymen   150-151, 153-155
　　　　　　　　Medieval slag heaps   150-151
　　　　　　　　Rievaulx   151-153

Jervaulx, abbey of   140

Keldholme, priory of   29, 86n, 193
Kendall, PF 'A system of glacier lakes in the Cleveland Hills',   7n, 96n
Kirkham, priory of   1, 3, 31n, 140, 190, 193
Knowles, Dom David   1n, 43n

Lancaster, Duchy of
　　　　　　　　Pickering Estate boundaries   123-124
　　　　　　　　Ironworking   155
　　　　　　　　Organisation   126-128
　　　　　　　　Pasture   128-129
　　　　　　　　Sales   126
　　　　　　　　Sheep (1313-27)   125
　　　　　　　　Stud farm   130-132

Lands, Monastic   Conclusions   41-44
　　　　　　　　Distribution   32-44
　　　　　　　　Guisborough Priory lands   35-37
　　　　　　　　Leasing of   42
　　　　　　　　Other monasteries   40-41
　　　　　　　　Rievaulx Abbey lands   37-40
　　　　　　　　Spheres of influence   41-42
　　　　　　　　Whitby Abbey lands   32-35
Leland, John   Itinerary of,   101

Malmesbury, William of   14
Malton, priory of   1, 31n, 78n, 140
　　　　　　　　Consolidation of lands   55-56, 58
　　　　　　　　Distribution of granges   51-53
　　　　　　　　Fairs   179
　　　　　　　　Granges   67, 69, 75, 97-99, 101, 103-105, 179
　　　　　　　　Hired workers   48
　　　　　　　　House in Scarborough   175
　　　　　　　　Lands   40
　　　　　　　　Size of flocks   139
　　　　　　　　Types of settlement   43
　　　　　　　　Wool collection   187-188, 193
　　　　　　　　Wool sales   185

INDEX

Map, Walter 28, 28n, 30n, 64
Markets, Fairs and 176-182
    Distribution of 176
    Monasteries and 179-180
    Routeways 177-179
Marshall, William 6, 7n, 9n, 11n, 102, 103n, 128, 129n
Meaux, Abbey of (Melsa) 64, 109, 134, 138, 139, 140, 186, 192
Merchants, Origin of 169-172
    Flemish 195
    Wool 128, 189
Monastic estates,
    Pastoral farming 136-145
    Organisation 141
    Sheep pasture 137-138
    Size of flocks 138-139
Moorlands, 74, 78, 79, 81
    Agricultural prosperity 82, 83, 84, 85
    Arable farming 86-90
    Breed of sheep 128-129
    Sheep farming 119-120
Moors, North York
    Physical background 8-10
    Pasture 138
    National Park 1
    Vaccaries & cotes 141
Mortmain, statute of (1279) 30
Murrain, the great 31, 192

Newburgh, priory of 1, 29, 31n, 41, 140, 157, 193
Newburgh, William of 103n
Nicholas, the Valor of Pope (1292) 73-77, 91
    Arranged regionally 84
    Comparison to the Fifteenth of 1301 77
    Purpose 73-74
Northallerton, collection centre for corn 114
North-East, a definition 3

Ouse, river, navigation of 187, 191, 193

Pegolotti, list of 83n, 139, 192, 193
Pickering, Vale of
    Agricultural prosperity in 1292 74, 81, 83, 84
    Arable farming 96-102
    Byland in 40, 41
    Domesday meadow 23
    Domesday settlement 17-18
    Domesday waste 25
    Malton Priory lands 40, 41, 51
    Physical background 7-8
    Recovery 19
    Rievaulx lands 39-40, 41, 49
    Sheep farming 118-119, 138, 143

Plateau, Coastal   Agricultural prosperity   74, 81, 83
                   Arable farming   90-96
                   Physical background   10
Ports and Trade,   163-182
                   Coal trade   164
                   Herring fishery   172-173
                   Hinterlands   165, 174
                   Malton Priory   175
                   Origins of merchants   169-172
                   Rievaulx Abbey   175
                   Scarborough   165-169
                   Scottish wars   164
                   Whitby Abbey   173-175
                   Yarm's predominance   165

Quayage Accounts, for Scarborough   173

Ratzel, F   71
Reassessment (1318),   77-79, 91, 114
                   Arranged regionally   84
                   Comparison 1292-1318   78-79
                   Purpose   77-78
Regions, map   8
Rievaulx, abbey of   1, 2, 28, 30, 31, 34, 63, 78, 81, 86, 140, 144, 159, 178, 197
                   Building stone   159
                   Common pasture   59-60
                   Consolidation of lands   58, 59
                   Corn purchases   180
                   Cotes   142
                   Distribution of granges   49-51
                   Granges   46, 53, 69, 75, 82, 88, 94, 99, 100-1, 116, 132, 138, 178, 179
                   House in Scarborough   175
                   Ironworking   151-153
                   Lands   37-40, 41
                   'redigere in grangiam'   64-65
                   Salt working   157, 158
                   Sheep pasture   136
                   Size of flocks   139
                   Staffing   47, 47n
                   Transhumance   143-144
                   Types of settlement   43
                   Wool collection   192
Rosedale, abbey of   29, 78n, 139, 153-154, 193
Rouen, Abbot of   110

Salt making,   66, 156-157
Scarborough,
                   Coal trade   164
                   Coastal trade   164-169
                   Confirmation charter and concessions   167-169
                   Site advantages   165-166
                   Trade   171-173, 195

Settlement,
>> Domesday 15-18
>> Contraction of 64
>> Contribution of the monastic grange 44-66
>> Monastic 28-44
>> Comparison 1086 and 1301 62-63

Stamp, Dudley 1
St Peter's, York 75
St Mary's, York 49, 75, 140, 154, 193, 194
Subsidy, Lay (1301) 61, 62, 96, 114, 143n, 155, 166
Sykes, Sir Christopher 102

Taxation, the Norwich (1254) 57, 103
Tanning, 159
Teesmouth,
>> Agricultural prosperity, 1292 75, 82, 84
>> Monastic granges 46
>> Monastic salt works 157-158
>> Physical background 10-11
>> Salt pans 156-157

Templars, Knights, at Foulbridge 99
Tintern, abbey of 193n
Tithe, Cause Papers in 110
Topographical Names, Marsh 13; Woodland 14
Transhumance, 142-144
Trevelyan, Professor 13
Tuke, J 8n, 10n, 11n, 113, 120n, 121n

Villarum, Nomina 61, 65
Vitalis, Odericus 25

Waibell, Leo 161
Wapentakes, 12
Wansford, collecting centre 109, 194
Westerdale, sheep farming 46, 47, 130
Westhorpe, Thomas de 97, 99, 120, 123, 185, 190
>> Outlawry 133
>> Possessions 97, 134-136, 189

Whitby, abbey of 1, 2, 28, 30, 31, 86, 137, 140, 144, 159, 193
>> Common pasture 59
>> Cattle farms 75, 141
>> Destructions of the Scots 91
>> Granges 46, 47, 53, 54, 68, 76, 93-94, 95
>> Grant of fair 176-177
>> Inaccessibility 163
>> Lands 32-35, 37, 41
>> Land in York 192
>> Purchase of corn 194
>> Size of flocks 138-139, 185
>> Staffing 48
>> Stone quarries 159
>> Trading rights 173-174, 175
>> Wool sales 195

Whitby,
    Herring fishery   172
    Whitby Abbey and the port   173-175
Wolds, Yorkshire
    Arable farming   102-111
    Physical background   6-7
    Sheep farming   122, 138
    Whitby Abbey lands in   34
Wool Trade,
    Monasteries and the wool trade   183-196
    Assize Rolls   184, 187, 196
    Collection   180, 186-188, 195
    Italians   191-192
    Merchants   188-190
    Prices   193
    Transport   190, 193-196
    Wool sales   185
Wykeham, abbey of   29, 34, 35, 193

Yarm, corn shipments   114; as a port   165
Yedingham, abbey of   29, 34, 101, 178, 193
York, Dean of   99
York, Vale of, and Cleveland Plain
    Agricultual prosperity (1292)   76, 84
    Arable farming   111-116
    Destruction by Scots   78, 83
    Physical background   11-12
    Sheep farming   119-121
Young, George   1, 30n